The Little Third Reich on Lake Superior

The Little Third Reich on Lake Superior
A History of Canadian Internment Camp R

Ernest Robert Zimmermann

Michel S. Beaulieu
and David K. Ratz, Editors

THE UNIVERSITY OF ALBERTA PRESS

Published by
THE UNIVERSITY OF ALBERTA PRESS
Ring House 2
Edmonton, Alberta, Canada   T6G 2E1

www.uap.ualberta.ca

LIBRARY AND ARCHIVES CANADA CATALOGUING IN PUBLICATION

Zimmermann, Ernest Robert, 1931-2008, author
   The little Third Reich on Lake Superior : a history of Canadian
internment Camp R / Ernest Robert Zimmermann ; Michel S. Beaulieu
and David K. Ratz, editors.

Includes bibliographical references and index.
Issued in print and electronic formats.
ISBN 978-0-88864-673-6 (paperback).—ISBN 978-1-77212-029-5 (epub).—
ISBN 978-1-77212-030-1 (kindle).—ISBN 978-1-77212-031-8 (pdf)

   1. Camp "R" (Prisoner of war camp). 2. World War, 1939-1945—Prisoners and prisons,
Canadian. 3. Prisoner-of-war camps—Ontario—Red Rock. 4. Prisoners of war—Germany—
History—20th century. 5. Prisoners of war—Canada—History—20th century. 6. World War,
1939-1945—Ontario—Red Rock. 7. Red Rock (Ont.)—History—20th century. I. Beaulieu,
Michel S., editor II. Ratz, David K. (David Karl), 1965-, editor III. Title.

D805.C3Z54 2015   940.54'7271312   C2015-904186-4
                                                 C2015-904187-2

Index available in print and PDF editions.

First edition, first printing, 2015.
Printed and bound in Canada by Houghton
Boston Printers, Saskatoon, Saskatchewan.
Copyediting and proofreading by
Lesley Peterson.
Map by Wendy Johnson.
Indexing by Judy Dunlop.

The University of Alberta Press is committed
to protecting our natural environment.
As part of our efforts, this book is printed
on Enviro Paper: it contains 100% post-
consumer recycled fibres and is acid- and
chlorine-free.

The University of Alberta Press gratefully
acknowledges the support received for
its publishing program from The Canada
Council for the Arts, the Government of
Canada through the Canada Book Fund
(CBF), and the Government of Alberta
through the Alberta Media Fund (AMF).

Canada   Canada Council   Conseil des Arts   Alberta
         for the Arts   du Canada   Government

Contents

Preface

Ernest Robert Zimmermann

THE PURPOSE OF THIS BOOK is to tell the intriguing story of Canada's largest civilian internment camp, at Red Rock in Northwestern Ontario. From its opening on 2 July 1940 to its closing on 26 October 1941, Camp "R," as it was called, housed interned civilian enemy aliens imported from Britain. Telling the story of Camp R involves not only exploring the original circumstances, which brought together the aggregate of 1,150 inmates in the camp, but also examining the multiple facets of incarceration and the conditions of camp life. Telling this story must also necessarily include a discussion of the military operations relating to Camp R: the issues and problems of administration and of guarding this large number of prisoners, as well as these issues' various resolutions. Moreover, the volatile domestic Canadian atmosphere into which this lot of imported foreign internees were injected requires examination.

I first heard about the existence of the Red Rock camp from students, during discussions of the history of the Second World War. The students alleged that in this "prisoner of war camp" erstwhile German submariners and air force pilots had freely mingled with the local citizenry. Intrigued, I began to investigate, and in the course of my readings I encountered Eric Koch's informative book, *Deemed Suspect: A Wartime Blunder*, and discovered his evocative phrase, "the little Third Reich on Lake Superior," with which he described the conditions that prevailed in Camp R.[1] The result of my research is the present book. With Professor Koch's generous permission I adopted his pithy phrase as the title of this book.

The history of Camp R and its inmates is reconstructed on the basis of unpublished and published documentary sources found in Library and Archives Canada in Ottawa, the National Archives of the United Kingdom in Kew, the Swiss Federal Archives in Bern, the Archives of Manitoba in Winnipeg, the Canadian Jewish Congress Archives in Montreal, and the Homefront Archives and Museum in Regina. In addition, I received information from various British and German institutes, which are listed in this volume's bibliography. Memoirs and autobiographies were consulted, and numerous personal interviews with contemporary participants and observers were also conducted. Reports and articles in newspapers, magazines, journals and other secondary sources provided useful information as well.

This subject of this study might not be considered a big theme in the history of Canada's impressive war effort. On the contrary, this book deals only with the incarceration of a small group of civilian internees— and enemy aliens at that—in one single camp. The subject of Canada's treatment of these imported so-called "dangerous enemy aliens" from Britain is discussed extensively in the works of Koch and of Paula J. Draper, to which I refer any reader who may be interested in this study's broader context. Generally speaking, the internment in Canada of these civilian enemies, most of whom were refugees from Nazi Germany, does not represent a praiseworthy achievement but rather a very shameful act. This book deals with human folly, suffering, anguish and cruelty in adversity. And who is to say, after all, that fear and anxiety, despair and humiliation, emotions and hopes, misfortune and ill-treatment, as experienced by individuals and groups, are not in their own way a big theme?

Acknowledgements

MANY PERSONS ASSISTED in the preparation of this study, and I
promised acknowledgement to all of them, whether their contribution
was minor or major; now I wish to keep that commitment.

I thank Ms. S. Spolyarich-Ozbolt, my former student, for bringing
the Camp's existence to my attention. Next, I must thank my friend of
many years, Guenter Siebel of Hamburg, for his support; he acted with
dedication, efficiency and generosity as my unpaid "local secretary"
in Germany for many months, receiving letters and questionnaires on
my behalf from dozens of interviewees (former POWs and internees in
Canada) and answering inquiries and scheduling follow-up interviews
for me during visits to Germany. Also G. Rudi John, Thunder Bay, and
Heinz Blobelt, Hamburg, both former German merchant seamen and
internees, from 1939–1947 and 1940–1947 respectively, allowed me to
share their past internment experiences—though neither was an inmate
of Camp R.

I thank my colleague, Abdul Mamoojee, for valuable corrections of the manuscript.

To Nancy Pazianos, Tracy Muldoon, Joan Seeley and Garth Gavin of the Interlibrary Services Department of the Chancellor Paterson Library, Lakehead University, Thunder Bay, I am deeply indebted, for without their continuous, excellent and dedicated support and experienced advice many books, articles and materials from elsewhere in Canada, the United States, and Germany might never have reached me. I would also like to thank the anonymous members of the Chancellor Paterson Library's Circulation Desk and Technical Services. I owe thanks for their repeatedly and patiently banning the demons from momentarily dysfunctional high-tech microfilm readers and printers. I thank Northern Studies Resource Centre Librarian Trudy Mauracher, who located local records, and Cathy A. Chapin, Department of Geography, Lakehead University, for her valuable advice on local and regional maps.

Robert Henderson of the Homefront Archives and Museum, Regina, granted me generous access to his archives and provided copies of his materials. Paul Marsden, consultant and archivist, provided helpful advice, as did Richie Allen, Reference Archivist, and numerous obliging staff members, all of Library and Archives Canada, Ottawa. Ken Johnson, author and archivist, Ottawa, offered advice and provided references to relevant information.

I obtained copies of important documents and valuable information from these persons: Janine Dunlop of the Manuscript and Archives Department of the University of Cape Town; Franziska Goldschmidt and Miriam Haardt, the Wiener Library Institute of Contemporary History, London; Gitta Grossmann, Institut für Zeitgeschichte, Munich; Janice Rosen, Archives Director, Canadian Jewish Congress, Montreal; Anastasia Rogers, YMCA Canada, Toronto; Garron Wells, University Archivist, and Harold Averell, both of Robarts Library, Archives and Records Management Services, University of Toronto; and Josef Inauen, Chef de service des recherches, Eidgenössische

Militärbibliothek und Historischer Dienst, Bern; M. Christopher Kotecki, Reference Service Assistant, and other staff members of the reading room of the Archives of Manitoba, Winnipeg, helped in processing and providing archival materials; I thank all of them.

Tory Tronrud, Curator, and staff members of the Thunder Bay Historical Museum Society permitted and helped me to access their archival materials relating to regional POW camps. I appreciate also the assistance of staff members of the City of Thunder Bay Public Library system at the Brodie Street and Waverly Park branches.

I thank the members of the Board of the Thunder Bay Military Museum, especially Lieutenant-Colonel Jack J. Young, Curator, and Captain David Ratz, for permission to use their collection and archives. Likewise, I thank the members of the Executive Committee of the Red Rock Historical Society (from 2001 to 2003) for their generous hospitality and sponsorship of two public lectures about Camp R. Marilynn Young, Head Librarian, Public Library of Red Rock, allowed me access to the local archive and its diverse materials. I thank Lloyd Roy, Burton Brown and Frank di Fazio, all of Red Rock, Ontario, who each contributed valuable personal reminiscences.

Karen Zeller, administrator, Centre for Human Settlement, University of British Columbia, Vancouver (UBC), I thank for helping me contact Peter Oberlaender, Professor Emeritus, Centre for Human Settlement, UBC, who clarified certain camp facts. I thank the Rev. Dr. David J. Carter, Medicine Hat, Alberta, for his wise advice; Catherine Walsh, Librarian, Thunder Bay Law Library, for confirming the non-existence of court records; and Jeannie Marcella, Head Librarian, Public Libraries of Terrace Bay, Ontario; Lynn Banks, Librarian, Public Library of Marathon, Ontario, and Carole McLean, Librarian, Public Library of Longlac, Ontario, I thank them for saving me time, money and effort by responding to enquiries in the search for alleged documentary information.

Last though not least I thank John Pedron, William Vinh Doyle, Rebecca Strauss and Laura Nigro, all of whom at various times unlocked for me the mysteries of modern technologies by processing the once simple tasks of ordering a book through interlibrary loan service, or opening up the sluices of the internet, or "formatting" a well-shaped manuscript. Moreover, they were able, seemingly effortlessly, to summon archival documents from Cape Town or Kew by simply reading instructions flashing by on a screen and manipulating a few keys on a board.

None of the above-mentioned persons, however, is responsible for any errors of judgement, interpretation, omission, commission or opinion committed in this study. For all of these, responsibility is mine alone.

Of course to my spouse, Beverley A. Leaman, I owe special and immense gratitude for her continuous and encouraging support and patience, for her participation overseas in mastering the limitations of institutional operation times, for serving as secretary and for subsidising my research expenses from her limited kitchen finances and our savings.

E.R. Zimmermann, PHD
Lakehead University
Thunder Bay, Ontario
August 2007

Supplementary Acknowledgements

AFTER THE UNTIMELY DEATH of Ernest in August 2008, it was not a certainty that this book, which was very important to him, would ever see the light of day. However, thanks to the stellar efforts of the following people, this work has, at last, come to fruition.

My gratitude first goes to Michael Luski who, while at the University of Alberta Press, saw the potential for this book as one that would be of interest to the historical community in Canada and urged Ernest to pursue its publication. Thanks also to Peter Midgley of the University of Alberta Press, without whose championing of the manuscript through the editorial process, and encouragement in its completion, this book would not have been possible. Gratitude is also due to the editorial staff at UAP for their fine work in fine-tuning what must have been a challenging manuscript. Additional thanks are due to Laura Nigro, who assisted Ernest in fact-checking and in formatting the manuscript during the year before his death, and in assembling his last version of the manuscript for submission to UAP, in the weeks after his death.

To my daughter-in-law, Eda Leaman (Ernest's "step-on-daughter-in-law" as he fondly referred to her), a great debt of thanks is owed. Her patience and persistence throughout the completion phase of this work (as well as her encouragement of Ernest during its writing and revision) insured that Ernest's dream of having this book published would be realized. Thanks also to my son, Bruce Leaman, for helping prepare these supplementary acknowledgements.

Finally, my deepest appreciation is due to two of Ernest's former history students, later his friends and excellent historians in their own right, Dr. Michel Beaulieu and Major David Ratz, both of the Department of History, Lakehead University, Thunder Bay. After his death, we discovered that Ernest had asked Michel and David to ensure that if he had been unable to complete this work, they would. True to their word, both Michel and David worked tirelessly, over many years, to help finalize this manuscript. Truly, without their herculean efforts and dedication to both their former mentor and his vision of having this book published, you would not be reading this. Thank you, Michel and David.

> *Beverley A. Leaman*
> Thunder Bay, Ontario
> April 2014

IT HAS BEEN SEVEN YEARS SINCE Dr. Zimmermann, as hundreds of students cannot help but still think of him, unexpectedly passed away. Weeks before meeting for one of our periodic lunches—lunches held at the same restaurant for decades, during which Dr. Zimmermann would regale current and former students on the finer points of historiography and the state of the profession, offset with widespread discussions on contemporary politics and reminiscence of his career—we had no way of knowing this would be our last supper.

Ernest had always lectured his students on the dangers of historians trying to predict the future. However, he nonetheless had an inherent ability to size up individuals or uncannily "predict" things that would transpire. The last time he put down his drink, leaned slightly forward using every ounce of his size and being, looked over his glasses squinting, and lifted his hand to gesture in his signature finger-pointing style (which can only be described as equal parts lovingly jovial and unabashedly adamant), he asked us to finish this project if something should happen to him.

We scoffed, argued that nothing would happen (for we could not contemplate this fixture of our lives and the city never being there), and demurred to this man and mentor whom we respected and loved. In fact it was with pride we realized that he would charge us with this task and that our agreement had dealt with something that clearly had been troubling him. Little did we know it was the last time we would see him.

At his funeral in 2008, Michel spoke about how Ernest was the *Zeitgeist*, the spirit of the age or spirit of the time, collectively of Lakehead University, and particularly the Department of History, for decades. As he was for many, he was for us the defining elemental aspect of our university experience. Not a gathering of former students or historians in the region goes by without some story, anecdote, or Rabelaisian moment. As such, completing this work has been a challenging task, knowing the microscope we are under and wanting to live up to the last assignment Ernest will ever set for his students.

The book you are about to read has been completed in the style and fashion originally intended by ERZ, the acronym used by his family and us in our correspondence. Ernest had a love of history and a love of irony. We are sure he would have enjoyed the similarities between our use of ERZ and ETA, the latter an abbreviation used by Simon

Darcourt, Arthur Cornish, and Maria Cornish to refer to Ernst Theodor Wilhelm Hoffmann as they seek to complete his unfinished opera to be staged at Stratford in Robertson Davies's *The Lyre of Orpheus*.

As anyone who has worked on such a posthumous project can attest, its completion has triggered a bittersweet mixture of feelings, chief among them sadness. In the years since his passing, Ernest's *Geist*—mind, spirit, or definitely in his case ghost—has benevolently haunted us. But unlike the ghost of Davies's Hoffman, trapped in limbo due to the unsatisfactory state of his work, we think we have accomplished his goal. Nonetheless, we know he will still haunt us, because it is, after all, Dr. Zimmermann.

Michel S. Beaulieu and David K. Ratz

Thunder Bay, Ontario

January 2015

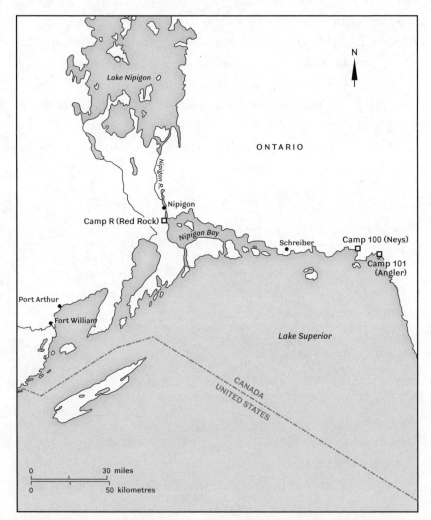

Location of Internment Camps 100 (Neys), 101 (Angler), and Camp R (Red Rock) in the Thunder Bay District.

Introduction

Situating the Red Rock POW Experience

Michel S. Beaulieu, David K. Ratz,
and Ernest Robert Zimmermann

RED ROCK IS A TOWN in Northwestern Ontario, where the mouth of
the Nipigon River spills into Lake Superior. A community of just over
one thousand, Red Rock is best known for its spectacular natural setting and its historic roles in the fur trade and forest industries of North
America. Red Rock's history is thus intrinsically linked to the history of
the development of Canada. Moreover, the history of Red Rock provides
a lens through which to explore the controversial politics of civilian
enemy internment during the Second World War, when over a thousand
British enemies were interned behind the barbed wire of Internment
Camp R: Red Rock, Ontario.

Few Canadians are aware of the myriad of German prisoner of war
camps established by their government throughout the country during
the Second World War, and fewer still are aware of the German prisoner
of war camp established in Red Rock in Northwestern Ontario. As this
book establishes, the story of "Camp R," as it became known, is about
the internment that happened here; however, it is not an account of

nameless prisoners only, but rather an account of the experiences of the aggregate of 1,150 men and boys who found themselves in a remote corner of the world. The experiences of those interned—whether Jews and anti-Nazis, professed Nazis and sympathizers, or captured German merchant seamen—reveal an important aspect of regional history that also fits into the larger history of Canada's handling of prisoners of war and civilian internment operations in wartime.

Prisoner of war camps are typically defined as centres where enemy combatants are detained. Yet in Canada, civilians as well as prisoners of war were detained in internment camps. Martin Auger and John Herd Thompson, in their studies of Canadian internment operations, note that, technically, civilians are held in "concentration camps"; and indeed, during the First World War, sites where civilians were interned were referred to as such. However, the term is not generally applied in historical literature to the facilities set up in Canada (largely due to the association of the term with the camps set up by Nazi Germany). Broadly speaking, the detention of either prisoners of war or civilians in Canada was termed an internment operation, though officials and later scholars often differentiated between the two categories, typically only describing civilians as internees.[1] As noted later in Chapter V, Canadian officials added to the confusion with their own idiosyncratic interpretations of international law, which led to their classifying the enemy aliens transferred from Britain as Prisoners of War Class I and Class II.[2] Although prisoners of war and civilian internees are in many ways different, and although they were subject to different international rules regarding their treatment, in some situations in Canada the two groups were held in the same facilities. It is for these reasons that the two related phenomena are often classed together as one field of study.[3]

The story of Camp R fits into the larger history of Canada's handling of prisoners of war and civilian internees, which dates back to 1914. During the First World War, Canada, like many other countries, took measures to intern civilians of "enemy descent" and later to detain prisoners of war.[4] There was a general assumption that a person owed

Aerial view of Camp R, looking north-northwest. *[Private collection]*

primary allegiance to the land of his or her birth, and this led to the belief that "enemy aliens" could pose a potential threat to the British Empire. An enemy alien was defined as a foreign-born resident of Canada, whose origin was in a country at war with the British Empire or one of the Allied nations, and who was not a Canadian citizen by birth or naturalization. In Canada, the *War Measures Act* (1914) gave the government the power to arrest, detain, exclude and deport those it deemed to be enemy aliens, a power it exercised as initial tolerance of enemy aliens quickly yielded to wartime hysteria and xenophobia. In keeping with British policy, Canada required enemy aliens to register and report regularly. Those deemed a security risk were detained and sent to one of the twenty-four internment camps administered from 1914–1915 by the Department of Militia and Defence and, from

1915–1920, though often still under military guard, by the Department of Justice.[5]

Some 85,000 enemy aliens of German, Austro-Hungarian, Turkish and Bulgarian origin were required to register; of these, 8,579 men were interned. As Desmond Morton has concluded, these men "posed no significant military threat," but it was not easy to convince public opinion of this.[6] Of those sent to internment camps, it was calculated that about one-third of them could be classified as prisoners of war because they were either enemy reservists who, it was thought, had a duty to return to their homeland and rejoin the armed forces or were combatants, mainly sailors, captured elsewhere by the British and transferred to Canada for detention. The others were civilians arrested for various reasons, some of which included failing to register, lying about their citizenship or national origin or, in many cases, simply being unemployed and transient.[7] Ukrainians posed a particular dilemma, since the overwhelming majority of those who had immigrated to Canada had come from Galicia and Bukovina in the eastern portions of the polyglot Austro-Hungarian Empire and were classed as "Austrians." Nativism made it difficult for the majority of Canadians to understand that most of the 5,954 "Austrians" interned were actually Ukrainians who had little loyalty to the Austro-Hungarian Empire.[8] The result was that although it was justified as necessary at the time, the injustice of the internment of Ukrainians has in later generations prompted a campaign for redress.[9]

By 1916–1917, it was determined that most of the civilian internees were not in fact a security risk, and they were released on parole after agreeing to remain loyal, obey the laws of Canada and report to the police periodically. By the end of the war in November 1918, the roughly 2,200 prisoners remaining were mostly prisoners of war. These prisoners did not begin the repatriation process until after the Treaty of Versailles was signed in June 1919; and, due to logistical problems, the last prisoners were not returned until May 1920.[10] Based on these First World War experiences, during the interwar years the Canadian government, like governments in other parts of the British Commonwealth, began planning for future internment operations, should the international political situation once again lead to war. The *War Measures Act* was renewed in 1927, allowing for regulations to govern enemy aliens in periods of war or apprehended war.[11] A government apparatus was put in place in 1936 with the creation of the Canadian Defence Committee, which had enemy aliens as one of many issues under its purview.

Responsibility for enemy aliens was given to a subcommittee in 1938: the Committee on the Treatment of Enemy Aliens on the Outbreak of Hostilities, later renamed the Interdepartmental Committee on the Treatment of Enemy Aliens and Enemy Property. The intent was to be more selective about those interned. With the assistance of the Royal Canadian Mounted Police, enemy aliens considered to be a security risk or involved in subversive activities were identified. This included individuals from Canada's potential future enemies such as Germany, Italy and Japan, as well as Communists.[12]

With growing international tensions, a state of "apprehended war" was declared on 23 August 1939, and on 1 September the *War Measures Act* was invoked, allowing the government to use emergency powers to take steps to protect the country. Subsequently, the *Defence of Canada Regulations* were put in place on 3 September, the same day Britain declared war on Germany. Less than a week later, on 7 September, the Canadian Parliament, after a period of debate, declared war. The regulations allowed for the suspension of civil liberties by detaining any people suspected of behaving in "a manner prejudicial to public safety or the safety to the state," whether they were deemed to be enemy aliens or Canadian "citizens."[13] The result was that, even before war was declared, 16,000 German immigrants who had arrived after 1922 and had not been naturalized were required to register. Of those, roughly 800 were found not to meet the criteria for loyalty and were arrested, mainly for involvement in pro-Nazi activities like the *Deutscher Bund.*[14] With Italy's entry into the war in June 1940 as a German ally, Italian Canadians were also targeted. Through the Italian consuls in Canada during the 1930s, the Fascist government of Italy had garnered a great deal of support for the regime. Certainly among Italian Canadians there was a great deal of pride in their homeland, and many regarded Mussolini as the bringer of stability to his country. The majority were not ideologically attracted to Fascism, but rather drawn to Italian nationalism as a source of self-respect in their new home. This subtlety was lost on government officials, and over 600 suspected of Fascist leanings, including some born in Canada, were interned, even some who had sons serving in the Canadian military.[15] The Ribbentrop-Molotov Pact of 1939 allowed Canadian Communists to be targeted next.

During the First World War and afterward, Bolsheviks and, later, Communists had been the target of state repression.[16] They were viewed as a danger because the Communist Party of Canada (CPC) opposed what it classified as an "imperialist war." After the Communist Party was banned in June 1940, 133 members of the party were eventually interned. Furthermore, unlike the German and Italian fascists, the majority of whom were eventually paroled, many Communists remained behind barbed wire well after the Soviet Union had entered the war on the Allied side and the CPC had changed its official stance in favour of the war effort.[17]

The intent was that, by identifying potential troublemakers in advance, the Canadian government could limit internment operations to those few and not target whole amorphous sections of particular ethnic groups.[18] Yet for Japanese Canadians, the internment experience deviated very controversially from the norm in terms both of the scale of their detention and the injustice of their treatment. Like those of Germany and Italy, Japanese consular officials made an effort to instill a sense of attachment and support for the foreign policy of their country of origin among expatriates in Canada. However, the overwhelming majority of Canadians of Japanese ancestry were either born in Canada or were naturalized citizens. Most subscribed to Canadian democratic values, and there is little evidence that Japanese propaganda had any impact.[19]

Nevertheless, among some Canadians in British Columbia, nativism combined with fear that Japanese Canadians posed a threat, particularly after the attack on Pearl Harbor on 7 December 1941. The process of internment thus began immediately with the confiscation of some 1,300 fishing vessels owned by Japanese Canadians. By mid-December 1941 all Japanese Canadians, regardless of citizenship, were ordered to register. Under the guise of the need to take them into "protective custody," away from reprisals by other Canadians, males between eighteen and forty-five years of age were sent from the coast to inland work camps in January 1942. The rest of the Japanese-Canadian community followed them in February.[20] The whole nature of the internment process was camouflaged as an "evacuation": with the exception of a few thousand individuals, who went to do agricultural work on the prairies, Japanese Canadian families were split up as the women and children were sent to camps in the interior of British Columbia. About 750 men refused to cooperate in the evacuation and were sent to internment camps in Ontario. To compound the injustice, the property of Japanese Canadians was confiscated, including homes, farms, boats and automobiles. The government sold these, and what little money was left, after deductions were made for administrative and other costs, was eventually given to those who had been evacuated.[21]

When the war started Canadian officials only anticipated having to deal with internees detained domestically. However, the nature of Canadian internment operations changed in early 1940 as German armies began overrunning western Europe. At this point in time, Britain had an estimated 75,000 enemy aliens in residence. This number included some Italians, but the majority were refugees from Nazi Germany and elsewhere who were not likely to be a source of risk.[22] In 1939, these people were registered and categorized based on their loyalty and reliability. However, in a climate of xenophobia and war hysteria, the British government ordered all enemy aliens to be interned and began asking Canada to accept prisoners of war, enemy merchant seamen and civilian internees held in Britain. The rationale was that, in the event of a German invasion, the threat of a "fifth column" would be reduced. There would also be less stress on the already stretched food supply, and military personnel would be freed up for other tasks.[23]

After some debate the Canadian government agreed, and the first internees and prisoners of war began arriving by the end of June 1940. From the commencement of Canadian internment operations in September 1939 to October 1944, when the last transfer of prisoners from Britain occurred, Canada would host approximately 35,000 detainees.[24] Canadian authorities were initially unprepared for the influx of prisoners, and the first camps were relatively hastily constructed. Eventually there would be twenty-six main camps, in addition to the dozens of smaller compounds built to hold prisoners employed on farms, in factories and logging. Each camp would be designated to hold a particular type of prisoner such as internees, enemy merchant seamen, officers or other ranks, though combined camps were not uncommon.[25] Camps would occasionally have all of their prisoners transferred to another camp and replaced by a new class of prisoners. For example, Camp 101 at Angler further east along the north shore of Lake Superior initially held prisoners of war of other ranks but in 1942 received Japanese Canadians. Others like Camp R only remained in operation for part of the war.[26]

Auger asserts in his study of the camps in southern Quebec that internment operations could be considered a "home front victory" and that life in the camps "was a positive experience overall."[27] This assertion may, to some degree, apply to Camp R, which functioned much like the other camps in Canada. There were administrative and logistical problems, but these, for the most part, were eventually overcome. Yet however much it may be possible to generalize about the prisoner of war and internee experience in Canada, the quality of leadership and administrative acumen of the commandants varied from camp to camp, from the incompetent and inefficient to the capable and efficient.[28] No two camps functioned identically, which invariably impacted the experience of individual prisoners. Given the multifaceted nature of prisoner-of-war and internment operations in Canada, then, the story of Camp R may be read as a particular variation on Auger's general theme. Here the inmates were exclusively enemy merchant seamen and civilian internees. The camp administration encountered problems with personnel, command and control, as well as with administration and logistics. There was also the need to maintain adequate security and deal with escape attempts. Camp life was fairly orderly, but there were problems associated with anti-Nazi and Jewish refugees who were required to live together with Nazis. Discipline was difficult in a tense atmosphere, which was punctuated by harassment and assaults mainly perpetrated by Nazis against anti-Nazi and Jewish inmates. Officials also had to deal with prisoner complaints and with vexing questions about the correct legal status of the internees.

To date, relatively little has been written about Camp R. Several theses and dissertations on related aspects of the detention of German POWs and internees have mentioned Camp R marginally, but these usually represent the circumstances incorrectly. Eugen Banauch, whose 2007 PHD dissertation examines the literature of German-Jewish refugees in Canada, relies extensively on existing secondary sources for his short discussion of Camp R.[29] One outstanding exception is the older pioneer study by J.J. Kelly, "The Prisoners of War Camps in Canada, 1939–1947." Kelly's analyses are sound and have stood the test of time.[30] The well-known book by David J. Carter, POW, *Behind Canadian Barbed Wire*, which straddles the division between civilian internees and POWs, makes only a fleeting reference to Camp R.[31] *Trop loin de Berlin: des prisonniers allemands au Canada (1939–1946)*, authored by two Québécois journalists, Yves Bernard and Caroline Bergeron, presents a collage of interviews with internees, POWs and their guards as well as excerpts from official documents, interspersed with many photographs and often illegible copies of government documents. However, the only reference to Camp R in this work is incorrect.[32] The popular history by

Pauline Dean, called *Sagas of Superior: The Inland Sea and Its Canadian Shore*, touches on Camp R in a section that also covers POW Camps 100 and 101, both also located on the north shore of Lake Superior.[33] Barbara Chisholm and Andrea Gutsche's work, *Superior: Under the Shadow of the Gods*, which has a brief section on Camp R, offers little that is not already available in the existing secondary sources or better served by examining the archival record directly.[34]

The best Canadian treatise on the entire refugee internment experience in Britain and in Canada, which contains material on Camp R, is *Deemed Suspect: A Wartime Blunder*, by Eric Koch.[35] Although a participant in and, as an internee, a victim of the "wartime blunder" of interning refugees, Koch presents an impartial, comprehensive, compassionate and balanced account of Canada's involvement in this enterprise. Koch's discussion of the deplorable detention of Jewish and anti-Nazi German refugees is supplemented by Paula Jean Draper in her unpublished, but readily available, PHD thesis, "The Accidental Immigrants: Canada and the Interned Refugees."[36] Draper also presents a brief overview of Camp R, along with other internment camps, in "The 'Camp Boys': Interned Refugees from Nazism."[37] While Koch writes dispassionately and with insight about his personal and the collective experiences, Draper presents a very critical account of the Canadian government's actions in addressing the issue of unjustified incarceration and ameliorating its accompanying often unnecessary hardships. Both Koch and Draper justly criticize Canada, but surprisingly avoid any criticism of Great Britain, the original source of so much blundering, suffering and hardship.

Despite all this valuable work, then, there has been as yet no satisfactory, systematic, overarching study of prisoner of war camp and internment operations in Canada.[38] This is perhaps because of the varying nature of these operations and the different experiences of those involved. It can also be argued that, to better understand Canadian prisoner of war and internment operations as a whole, it is necessary to discover the nuances and differences in the histories of individual

A look inside Camp R. *[LAC-e006611162]*

camps. For these reasons, reconstructing the story of Camp R contributes to our better understanding of a significant aspect of Canadian history.

Extensive study of published and unpublished documents in archival holdings provided the bulk of information on Camp R and its inmates. These documents are housed primarily in Canadian federal, provincial, university and private archives. The unpublished sources held by Library and Archives Canada provided most of the information used in this study. However, the Archives of Manitoba, in Winnipeg; the Robarts Library Archives of the University of Toronto, in Toronto; and the Homefront Archives and Museum, in Regina, were also essential to this project. Foreign archives, especially the National Archives of the United Kingdom; the Wiener Library and Institute of Contemporary History, in London; and the University of Cape Town Library Archives, in Cape Town, supplied important materials that complemented the Canadian sources and sometimes assisted in the clarification of claims incorrectly advanced by various authors.

In addition to the documentary and bibliographical resources consulted, numerous interviews were conducted in Germany and Canada with former interned enemy merchant seamen and POWs. These interviews span over twenty years, and were mostly not recorded due to the situation in which they occurred and, often, at the request of those who graciously agreed to share their stories. They have been directly referenced in places but, more often than not, informed the overall narratives and were used as part of composite descriptions for POWs and others associated with the camps. While readers may have hoped for more, and it opens the work up for criticism, such an approach is consistent with the style of the book and with the aim of respecting the wishes of those who shared and whose story is being told.

Other materials consulted were obtained from various Swiss, German and British archives, as well as the Canadian Jewish Congress Archives in Montreal; and the Faculty of Medicine Archives at the University of Manitoba, Winnipeg. The German Military Archives at Freiburg were consulted, but they do not keep documentation concerning merchant seamen. The Bundesarchiv at Bonn was closed to the author for several years as its collection was moving to Berlin. Interestingly, the monumental opus in German on the Second World War POW experience, *Zur Geschichte der deutschen Kriegsgefangenen des zweiten Weltkriege*, includes no reference to Camp R or to any other internment camp housing German merchant seamen.[39] This research was also supplemented by extensive correspondence, all of which provided interesting information that, while unfortunately less about Camp R directly, may prove useful in another more comprehensive study on the inclusive topic of detention of German POWs in Canada during the Second World War.

The structure of this book is relatively straightforward. The twelve chapters that follow this introduction are organized chronologically for the most part; however, occasionally themes are explored at greater length to the detriment of chronology in order to serve coherence. Chapter I presents the scene at the start of the war and during the nine months thereafter as Britain adopted protective measures in attempts to deal with its thousands of alien refugees from Nazi Germany. These measures, unbeknownst at the time to the various participants, did eventually affect the fate of hundreds of future inmates of Camp R. Chapter II discusses the Churchill government's drastic policies of mass internment and overseas deportation which ultimately landed the 1,150 inmates in the Red Rock camp in the summer of 1940. At that time, Allied military defeats created an atmosphere of panic and hysteria, which was greatly enhanced by rumours of a Nazi fifth column that had allegedly caused the Allies' recent setbacks. Fear of an imminent invasion by the victorious German armed forces encouraged the British military and intelligence agencies to conjure up the model of a "dangerous enemy alien" who could be suspected of constituting a military risk. Canada responded to Britain's incessant and pitiful pleas for help and agreed to incarcerate thousands of these allegedly dangerous enemy aliens, along with legitimate POWs.

Chapter III depicts the Canadian political situation into which the deportees were brought, and Chapter IV discusses the acquisition of Camp R as well as the military administration and operation of the camp. Chapters V, VI and VII discuss in detail who the inmates were and the general conditions prevailing in the inmates' enclosure. Numerous aspects of camp life are considered, such as the application of standing orders, recreational and cultural activities, issues arising over the
display of Nazi paraphernalia, the problem of "paid work," and the confusion over the Canadian terminology of "POW, Class I" and "POW, Class II."

In Chapter VIII the Canadian conundrum is examined: Was Canada deceived by Britain about the true nature of the deportees? What, if any, role did anti-Semitism play as Canada addressed the question of what to do with thousands of "unwanted and undesirable" immigrants of Jewish origin, and what part had British Commissioner Paterson in devising appropriate answers? These issues are relevant to the stories of hundreds of inmates in Camp R. Chapter IX provides additional information about camp life, including early escape attempts. Chapter X discusses such dangers as anti-Semitic harassment, bloody rioting and continued escape attempts, while Chapter XI considers both lighter and darker aspects of camp life, such as fraternizing and opportunities for conversation. Wherever appropriate, descriptive portraits of a few notable inmates such as Eugen Spier, camp spokesman Ship Captain Oskar Scharf, Harvard-educated Dr. Ernst "Putzi" Hanfstaengl, Dr. Gustav Lachmann, Nazi Konstantin Baron Pilar von Pilchau and leading camp-Nazi and popular coach and sport-*führer* Edwin Guelcher have been interspersed throughout this narrative. Chapter XII discusses the dissolution of the camp and the final dispersal of the remaining inmates, and the conclusion offers an evaluation of the camp's reputation versus the reality.

Telling the story of Camp R and its inmates raised a multitude of questions, which demanded answers. What exactly prompted Great Britain to commit what Koch refers to as this "wartime blunder"? Did Churchill play any role in it? Did Great Britain practise deception by not informing Canada as to the true nature of the deportees? Why were the interned "aliens," especially those incarcerated in Camp R, deported to Canada? Why and how was Red Rock chosen as a campsite? What part did Camp R play in the overall scheme of Canadian internment operations? What, if any, difficulties occurred in the operation of Camp R? What problems, if any, were encountered with the inmates? Did anti-Semitism influence Canada's attitude towards the Jewish internees in Camp R whom Britain had foisted upon its Dominion ally? Was the camp well run? What was the real situation at Camp R? Did it deserve its bad reputation; how did daily camp life unfold; what were the issues, the struggles and the personalities that dominated life in Camp R? Was fraternization between guards and prisoners a problem? Was escape an issue? Why was Camp R finally closed in October 1941? What, if any, lessons were learned from the operation of the camp? This study will attempt to answer these and other questions, from different perspectives, and to place Camp R in the contemporary British and Canadian context.

At times the author of this book may offer pointed observations and assessments; however, in the composition of this book the general rule of *sine ira et studio* was adhered to as a guideline. Finally, one general, but very important observation must be stated. Whatever conditions existed, life in either British or Canadian wartime internment camps bore absolutely no comparison with Nazi concentration camps. All events retold here, including the story of Camp R and its inmates, are dwarfed in retrospect by the reality of the Nazi German *Konzentrationslager* (KZ) and the criminal brutalities of the Holocaust.

I

From Welcomed Refugees to "Dangerous Enemy Aliens"

ON SUNDAY, 3 SEPTEMBER 1939, Britain entered the Second World War against Nazi Germany, and almost at once the situation of all German nationals living in Britain changed drastically. Confronted with the massive presence of many tens of thousands of German citizens living in the country, the government under Prime Minister Neville Chamberlain declared all German-born residents to be "enemy aliens" regardless of whether they were Jewish anti-Nazi refugees from Nazi Germany, self-professed Nazis, or long-term residents of German origin. Everyone's status was suddenly altered; recent arrivals and long-term residents alike faced internment or expulsion, and the new label suddenly transformed refugees from friends into enemies.[1] When these displaced persons first arrived in England after having escaped the horrendous experiences of Nazi persecution and prosecution, the refugees had felt not only safe but also welcomed. Now the new label of "enemy alien" conveyed the picture not just of a stranger or foreigner, but also of a hostile, inassimilable outsider.

Certainly, the new label was no booster of morale among the refugees, especially among the many who were most eager, anxious and ready to join in the actual fight against Nazism. Refugees felt hurt, insulted and confused. Not surprisingly, many resented and rejected the new label. However, this was only the first step in the long eight-month transformation from welcomed refugee to "dangerous enemy alien."

As war approached, the government first considered a policy of expelling all aliens, thus avoiding a repetition of the mass internment of aliens, which had been a fiasco in the First World War. However, the question of expulsion versus internment was still undecided when war actually started and a new cabinet was appointed by Prime Minister Chamberlain. After reviewing the refugee situation, the new Home Secretary, Sir John Anderson, a man of genuine liberal and humanitarian views, assured Parliament on 4 September that the government would follow "a liberal internment policy," would respect "the freedom of the individual from arbitrary demands by the state" and, furthermore, would attempt "to avoid treating as enemies those who are friendly to the country which has offered them asylum."[2] Later in November, Anderson repeated his assurance that "any wholesale measure of internment would be an inappropriate method of dealing with the alien problem" since imprisonment would be "wasteful" and "wrong" for "enemy refugees" who would be "unlikely to do anything to assist the enemy" but instead would be "anxious to assist the country which has given them asylum."[3] However, Anderson's pronouncements stood in stark contrast to the views of his cabinet colleague, Winston Churchill, whom Chamberlain had retrieved from the political wilderness and elevated to First Lord of the Admiralty. Churchill belligerently demanded the immediate arrest of all German refugees and all German citizens, even those scheduled to be repatriated to their homeland in exchange for British nationals.[4]

After further consideration, the War Cabinet ordered the establishment of a countrywide system of 120 one-man tribunals. Anderson stated in the Commons:

I am asking a number of men with legal experience to assist me....These examiners will sit not only in London but in the provinces, and each of them will examine all cases in the district assigned to him with a view to considering which of these can properly be left at large and which should be interned.[5]

The tribunals were usually staffed by a retired member of the legal profession, perhaps a retired judge, a justice of the peace, or barrister, who was assisted by a secretary seconded from the local police force. The enemy alien supplicant was allowed to present letters of reference and be accompanied by a representative of a local refugee aid agency.

The tribunals were charged with screening all enemy aliens, refugees and residents and sifting out spies, saboteurs and Nazi agents. All aliens were to be divided into three Categories: A, B and C. Those perceived of doubtful loyalty and reliability and suspected of constituting high risks to national security were placed in Category A and were immediately arrested. Those in Category B were deemed of uncertain loyalty but less dangerous and were left at liberty, free to move within five miles from their residence, but faced numerous restrictions on their possessions: no camera, no field glasses, no motor vehicle, no maps, no arms or ammunition. The overwhelming majority of enemy aliens were placed in Category C and retained their liberty, only having to report regularly to the local police. The tribunal chair received confidential information from the local police before each refugee was interviewed in the presence of a local police official and a representative from a local refugee committee. Although memoranda from the Home Office "covered every aspect of the tribunal's work," even "how to judge an alien's loyalty," and the Ministry of Labour, too, sent consultants to provide advice on work permits, nonetheless each tribune expressed his own personal decision in the evaluation of the case before him.[6] This fact produced considerable inconsistency in the verdicts of the tribunals.

Both the verdicts and the procedures of the tribunals caused controversy. Verdicts varied greatly from one tribunal to the next, and some were often ludicrous. Several verdicts displayed extreme ignorance of the existing political realities in Nazi Germany on the part of the presiding tribunes, who exhibited a degree of personal bias akin to racism. For example, a German-Jewish bookseller, fleeing from Nazi persecution, who had been caught by the *Gestapo* in the process of gathering up his savings and valuables to take with him into exile, which under the existing Nazi law was illegal, was admonished by his English tribune: he had acted disgracefully in smuggling valuables out of Germany and "evading the laws of his native country." This refugee was judged Category A and imprisoned. Then there was the pathetic case of a "German poet," who spoke no English, appearing before a tribunal who spoke no German. The resulting linguistic impasse was easily solved by the tribunal with the instant imprisonment of the hapless poet.[7]

Frederic W. Nielsen, a German-born Jew and an internationally well-known anti-Nazi journalist, offered these tragic and comedic examples:

CASE A: Tribune: Are you a Jew?
          Refugee: No.
          Tribune: Why at all then did you leave Germany?
          Refugee: Because I am an anti-Nazi.
          Tribune: Even though you are not a Jew?
          Refugee: Yes.
          Tribune: I don't understand...
          Verdict: Category B.

CASE B: Tribune: Do you hate Germany?
          Refugee: No, only the present regime.

Tribune: Then you desire Germany's victory...

Verdict: [Category A] Imprisonment.

CASE C: Tribune: You were denounced.

Refugee: Denounced? What for?

Tribune: Allegedly you have said, Goebbels is a clever man.

Refugee: Yes, that's what I have said.

Tribune: So you admit it?

Refugee: Naturally. Unfortunately, that's what he is.

Tribune: He is a blockhead...

Verdict: Category B.

These were not isolated cases.[8]

The case of Sebastian Haffner illustrates the prevailing muddle. Haffner, a former Berlin lawyer, was an outspoken, publicly acknowledged, active anti-Nazi journalist. He was placed in Category A in February 1940, then released briefly and re-arrested in May, having just published a successful, internationally acclaimed book, *Germany: Jekyll and Hyde*, which aimed at providing British officials with reliable factual information about Nazi Germany in order to help devise effective anti-Nazi propaganda. However, in his book, Haffner condemned the French practice of mass internment of Jewish and anti-Nazi refugees. Instead of this mistaken policy, Haffner called for the mobilization and utilization of German anti-Nazis in the Allies' fight against the Hitler menace. Generally speaking, tribunals judged German refugees very harshly if they professed loyalty to the vanquished democratic Weimar Republic and expressed hatred of the current Nazi regime; and if they were Jews, they were accused of "typical" Jewish disloyalty to their native homeland. Consequently, most such cases were placed in Category A and arrested. Well-known former Austrian and German trade union leaders and even elected members of the pre-Nazi *Reichstag* were imprisoned, such as Max Braun, former leader of the Social

Democratic Party of the Saarland, who had fled to Britain in 1935 after annexation. Refugees professing left-wing political views suffered the same fate, especially if they confessed to having fought against Fascism in the Spanish Civil War.[9]

Since a detailed discussion of the operation of the tribunal system is not the purpose of this book, these few examples must suffice to depict the circumstances in which German refugees and residents found themselves after 3 September 1939.[10] Not only prominent but even common folks experienced incredible mishandling of their cases as this sample illustrates: A fifty-eight-year-old, Galician-born Jew, nominally still with Austrian citizenship, having lived in England for the past fifty-seven years in an urban ghetto among his own kind, still illiterate in English, who neither knew the need to obtain naturalization nor had the funds, who had fifteen family members serving in the British Army, fighting for King and Empire, Democracy and Liberty, was deemed worthy to be placed in Category A and arrested instantly. Politically motivated denunciations of one political refugee group by another also influenced a tribunal's verdicts.[11] The fact that about one-third of the anti-Nazi and Jewish enemy aliens had already suffered incarceration in either jail or concentration camp in Hitler's Germany did not prevent an English tribunal from placing such a person in Category A and thereby dispatching this refugee once again back to a political prison.

Of course, plenty of tribunal case records reveal a different experience from those presented above. For example, the case of Mark Lynton, once known as Max Otto Ludwig Loewenstein, who had lived in Stuttgart and Berlin and in 1940 was a student at Cambridge, experienced his tribunal meeting as "a decidedly *opera bouffe*" affair.[12] He had obtained a favourable letter of reference from an old friend of his father, who did not know young Lynton personally, but the retired Indian Army Colonel was nonetheless very much impressed by young Lynton's sports acumen, acquired and exhibited at a well-known English public school that functioned as a training centre for potential Indian Army officers. Armed with this reference, Lynton easily earned the coveted status of "friendly alien" from his tribunal. This status, however, did not save him from incarceration in May 1940 and deportation to Canada in June. He returned to England at the end of December 1940. Similarly, sixteen-year-old Henry Kreisel, of Vienna, was awarded the status "refugee from Nazi oppression" at his uneventful tribunal session in October 1939; nevertheless, he was picked up during the mass internment on 16 May 1940 and then shipped to Canada, where he was eventually released.[13] Another example provided by an English companion of an elderly refugee woman, a domestic servant, offered this somewhat self-congratulatory report on the "Alien Tribunal in Croydon" in November 1939:

> [I] was struck by the courtesy of the official and their genuine consideration. From my own considerations, specially in connection with refugees, the treatment by English people of those in distress is something to be proud of...I was asked what I thought of Mrs. W., how long I had known her, whether I thought her a fit person to be granted exemption. Her passport was stamped, and the whole thing was finished in 5 minutes.[14]

The operation of the tribunal system affected in spectacular ways such future inmates of Camp R as Eugen Spier, Dr. Gustav V. Lachmann and Dr. "Putzi" Hanfstaengl. In order to appreciate the tangled circumstances, especially in Spier's case, it seems appropriate first to provide some background information on each of these individuals. These personal accounts vividly illustrate the impact of arbitrary incarceration and the tribunal's categorization process on individuals caught up in the maelstrom of events beyond their personal control.

Eugen Spier, a Jew born in 1891 in southern Germany, had served in the Imperial German Army during the First World War.[15] Apparently unhappy with the development of German domestic politics after the war, he immigrated to England in 1922 and became a wealthy and successful businessman in London, where he lived with his wife and young son. After Hitler's takeover in 1933, Spier became an outspoken critic of

German Nazism and the Nazi regime. Spier was involved in the establishment of the British branch of the US-based Anti-Nazi Council (ANC), which in 1936 changed its name in Britain to Focus for the Defence of Freedom and Peace. The Focus group has been described variously as a "kaleidoscopic panel of communist fellow travellers, industrialists, financiers, trade unionists and disgruntled Conservatives" or as "a shadowy group" designed to function as "an All-Party group opposed to Nazism."[16] According to Spier, Focus "was supported by the most representative men and women of the public, spiritual and political life of Great Britain and was formed in order to stem the Nazi peril and to refute the Nazi teaching."[17] Unfortunately, Focus had two strikes against it from its inception. First, only a very few members of the ruling Tory Party joined, and those who did were disgruntled Tories like Harold Macmillan. Second, since many of the leading figures of Focus were of Jewish origin, they could exert only limited influence at a time when Britain's public opinion and leading newspapers were infected by an anti-Semitic temper.

Spier played a major role in Focus as financier and initiator of activities; he contributed the substantial sum of £ 9,600 to the group and was an early supporter of Winston Churchill. When Churchill joined Focus in April 1936, he existed in a political wilderness of his own making through his persistent manoeuvring in pursuit of political power. He had been dropped from cabinet, either for joining cabals or for his attempts to unseat ruling prime ministers, especially Chamberlain. His unpopular opposition to India's independence and his outspoken support for the pro-Nazi and Hitler fan, King Edward VIII, over the issues of the King's marriage and abdication, combined to isolate Churchill in the Tory Party and further diminished his political appeal. During these years, Focus acted as a lobby group in support of Churchill by organizing and sponsoring pro-Churchill rallies throughout Britain. Together Focus and Churchill vociferously and publicly agitated against appeasement of Nazi Germany and vehemently advocated speedy re-armament. However, although Spier was an active participant in these affairs, he nonetheless regarded Focus primarily as a rallying movement around which the moral forces in English public life would gather and through which the conscience of the British nation would marshal its superior moral forces of freedom, justice and peace against Hitler who could mobilize only brutal force and impose immoral oppression. Hitler was therefore bound to lose in the long run. Influential British newspapers supported Focus once its campaign against appeasement and for rearmament gained public support, especially at the time of the huge rally at the Royal Albert Hall in December 1937.

Unfortunately, in 1938, when Spier had an opportunity to become a naturalized British citizen, he failed to go through with the process. The reasons for this failure are not known. On 1 September 1939, Spier and his wife "hastened [to the Home Office] now to offer in the ensuing struggle my services to His Majesty's Government."[18] After their return home, Spier was promptly arrested by two officers of Scotland Yard and conveyed to London's Olympia Hall later the same day. At Olympia Hall Spier was enrolled as Great Britain's No. 2 "dangerous enemy alien" internee. Days before his arrest, Spier recorded that he, personally, had received assurances from Sir Robert Vansittart, Permanent Undersecretary at the Foreign Office and member of Focus, that he had nothing to fear as an alien. In his memoirs, Spier expresses his suspicion that his early imprisonment was the work of anti-Churchillian appeasers, hiding in MI5, who were very well informed about his work for Focus and had always opposed it. His suspicions were apparently reinforced when he looked around and saw "all these Jews from Germany, Austria and Czechoslovakia [who] had fled from the most inhuman and cruel torture...[and] now found themselves at the hand of democracy herded together and classified in the same category with their archenemies." Imprisoned prior to the operation of the tribunal system, Spier nonetheless had high hopes that this "dreadful" mistake would soon be rectified, especially after he received many expressions of sympathy from his powerful friends in Focus, all promising help, including his old beneficiary, the ebullient new cabinet minister Churchill.

In January 1940, Spier appeared before a ten-member Advisory Committee, chaired by the benign Sir Walter Monckton. This committee once again registered at great length and in small detail all the already well-known and public personal data such as his name, date of birth, London address, and business activities and then dwelled extensively on the facts of his German birth and his military service in the Imperial German Army in 1914 as a young man. However, in the end the committee ignored the facts of his Jewishness and anti-Nazi activities and indeed proceeded to dismiss his well-known public work in Focus. After waiting in vain for weeks for the committee's final verdict, Mrs. Spier approached the secretariat of the committee personally and in the process overheard an official's comment: "...he is a Churchill man... no release possible."[19] After this Spier believed his fate was sealed for the time. He remained interned in Category A and spent months in four different camps in England, until in June 1940 he was shipped to Canada on the first boat out, the *Duchess of York*, and ended up in Red Rock, Ontario.

Why Dr. Gustav V. Lachmann was incarcerated remains somewhat of a puzzle. He was seized by London police at his Edgware district residence and, like Spier, delivered to Olympia Hall in early September 1939.[20] Though no record of any tribunal hearing exists, Lachmann was considered a Category A internee. German-born and educated, Lachmann had served as an officer—a Lieutenant—in the Imperial German Army during the First World War and had volunteered for the German flying corps, and thus acquired a lifelong interest in aerodynamics. After the war he studied first at the University of Darmstadt and then at Göttingen from 1921 to 1924. He developed a patent in the field of aerodynamics for the use of "slotted wings." Through this achievement he formed a long-lasting professional working relationship with Sir Frederick Handley Page. During the 1920s, Dr. Lachmann worked as an aeronautical engineer, designer and inventor first in Germany, then in Japan and finally in Britain, where he joined Handley Page Ltd. in 1929. During the 1930s, Lachmann became one of the world's leading aeronautical engineers, winning the George Taylor Gold Medal in 1931 and the Wakefield Gold Medal in 1938. He served as Chief Designer for Handley Page Ltd. and also headed the company's research department. During the Nazi years of the 1930s, Dr. Lachmann, the patent holder for slotted wings, not only successfully sued Germany's Junkers Aircraft Constructor but also actively participated in the design of Harrow, Hampden and Halifax bombers.[21] He married an English woman and raised a family in England.

Dr. Lachmann was interned against his expectations. He was apparently unaware that MI5 suspected him of espionage for both Germany and Japan because he had served as a Lieutenant in the Imperial German Air Force and subsequently had worked in Germany and Japan. What was more reasonable than to behold in him a German-Japanese spy? In its attempt to prove Lachmann's espionage, MI5 intercepted his mail from 1928 to 1936. It was then concluded that "it appears undesirable that a German should be employed in the works of a firm carrying out contracts for the Air Ministry, but...enquiries for over two years have produced nothing to lead to suspecting that he is using his position...to give information either to Germany or to any other power." His boss, Sir Frederick Handley Page, resisted government pressure to dismiss Dr. Lachmann, and while Lachmann was imprisoned in England, Sir Frederick visited him regularly. Lachmann therefore had high hopes for an early release, which however never happened, despite pleas and petitions by Sir Frederick. Lachmann, who continued to work on aircraft design while imprisoned on the Isle of Man, believed professional rivals at Handley Page Ltd. who opposed his "unproductive research work"—and their network of public school pals in high places in Whitehall—connived at keeping him imprisoned, after the Air Ministry had failed to have him dismissed in 1938. Eventually he was dispatched to Canada's wilderness. His family continued to live in London during the war, apparently unmolested.

During internment in England, Lachmann and Spier were fellow inmates in various camps. Lachmann served as camp spokesman in

Lingfield Race Court, where Spier, who managed the canteen, noted that, "apart from other excellent qualities, [Lachmann] possessed a very good sense of humour."[22] Spier and Lachmann cooperated quite often, whether by passing on forbidden newspapers or reliable news, or providing accommodation, or—later in Camp R—preventing bloody mayhem. After the War and his release from internment, the British government agreed to see Dr. Lachmann restored to Handley Page in order to prevent or discourage his emigration to the USA. In 1949 Dr. Lachmann returned to Handley Page Ltd. and resumed his former position of Director of Research. He was a respected member of Britain's Royal Aeronautical Society and was selected to deliver the Society's "Second Handley Page Memorial Lecture" in 1963. There seems nothing in Dr. Lachmann's biography to indicate that he was a Nazi; certainly his Jewish and anti-Nazi fellow inmate did not perceive him as one. There is no record of any political activity by Dr. Lachmann.[23] Perhaps he was just not naturalized.

Dr. Ernst F. Sedgwick "Putzi" Hanfstaengl was first arrested on 3 September 1939 and then much later processed by an Advisory Committee under Sir Norman Birkett in early 1940. Putzi had fled from Hitler's Germany even though he was a very close, longstanding associate of the *Führer*. Because Hanfstaengl saw himself as having exerted a "sobering" influence on Hitler and because he had "helped" such high-ranking diplomats as Sir Horace Rumbold, Sir Eric Phipps and several others during their stays in Berlin, and because as well he enjoyed close contact with Sir Robert Vansittart, he sincerely believed that the combined influence of these highly placed, powerful individuals would rescue him from the clutches of imprisonment. He was wrong. His past Nazi record and ambiguous attitude towards Nazism while in exile far outweighed his inflated opinion of himself. Putzi ended up, quite reasonably, in Camp R.

While Spier, the ardent Churchill lobbyist, and Dr. Lachmann, the well-known aeronautics designer and researcher, were the most prominent individuals placed by the tribunal system among Camp R's future inmates, there were of course others on whom that system had an equally negative impact. Among these were Barons Albrecht von Montgelas and Wilhelm von Richthofen, both refugees from Nazism. Seventy-one-year-old, German-born Otto Slabke, who had resided in Britain since 1870, came to be known as "the father of Camp R." Also included were eleven young Jewish student refugees.[24]

By March 1940, the tribunals had completed the evaluation process and had classified 73,355 enemy alien refugees and residents. Of these only 569 were interned as high security risk under Category A; another 6,782 were regarded as "doubtful cases" and placed in Category B; and the vast majority of 66,002 enemy aliens presented "no security risk" and were placed into Category C, of whom 55,457 were declared "refugees from Nazi oppression."[25] At first glance these numbers seemingly indicate that the tribunal system, despite its observable flaws, on the whole had worked satisfactorily for the vast majority of enemy aliens by March 1940. Such a conclusion assumes, however, that in all these cases the correct decisions were made and that the system actually worked properly, so that, for instance, a Category B person truly belonged in B and not in C or even in A. Many interned refugees and anti-Nazis challenged these assumptions. Spier observed, for instance, that Nazis were released from internment while he and fellow anti-Nazis remained imprisoned. Furthermore, the available evidence suggests a high incidence of inconsistency in the range of verdicts by tribunes whose individual judgements tended to reflect political, regional and social class preferences, preconceptions and, at times, appalling ignorance about current political reality.[26] A few verdicts mirrored the persistent presence of racial and national prejudices that were widely cherished among the civilian and military members of the British ruling classes and that had percolated downward into general public opinion.[27] However, in March 1940 the full consequences of the tribunal selection system were not yet visible, and neither the presiding tribunal chairs nor the affected enemy aliens, refugees, or German nationals had any foreknowledge of coming events and future outcomes.

At the start of the war, Britain's popular press largely ignored the refugees. An occasional editorial mentioned them in the context of general domestic topics such as unemployment, immigration or the spectre of rising anti-Semitism. After April 1940, however, this situation changed, suddenly and dramatically. The once welcomed refugees from Nazi Germany were instantly transformed by the press into "dangerous enemy aliens." This dramatic change was caused by the end of the so-called "phoney war" when Nazi Germany successfully invaded Denmark and Norway in April and thereby pre-empted the Allies' own invasion designed to halt Swedish iron ore shipments to Germany. Subsequently, the *Wehrmacht* (German armed forces) beat back Britain and France's bungling joint military response to this surprise attack. This first Allied failure was followed a month later, in May, by another major Allied military debacle when the *Wehrmacht* in quick succession overran neutral Luxembourg, Holland and Belgium, and also routed the formidable British Expeditionary Force, which fled back home across the Channel, leaving behind almost all its heavy armour and equipment. Next the *Wehrmacht* trounced the vaunted *grande armée* and forced an armistice upon France, which was signed at the historic site of Compiègne on 22 June 1940.

This series of completely unexpected military disasters revealed not only Great Britain's general lack of preparedness for fighting a modern war, but also a high degree of incompetence in its military and political leadership. British troops, some observers noted, "were dumped into Norway's deep snow...without a single anti-aircraft gun, without... supporting airplanes and without a single piece of field artillery."[28] Before these unpleasant new verities were accepted and understood by Britons, the immediate demand was, quite naturally—especially among those guilty of previously advocating appeasement with "Herr Hitler" and Nazi Germany and also among the very practitioners of military incompetence—for answers: how could this have happened; how could these reverses be explained, and who were the culprits behind these defeats? Despite the evidence already available, Britain's Joint

Intelligence Committee explained that the Norway debacle was due to a new phenomenon in modern warfare: the fifth column.

The *Yorkshire Post* was the first paper to identify the fifth column as the culprit responsible for the German success in Scandinavia. The paper's editorial of 16 April explained authoritatively that Hitler's secret agents had formed a fifth column.[29] This simplistic and unexamined, yet most persuasive, explanation was quickly embraced by the rest of the popular press. Within a week British newspapers carried sensational reports directly from the "frontline" by their "special" war correspondents. With the actual fighting between the Allied and German troops still in progress across the border in Norway, these journalists reported from Sweden that treachery and sabotage by the fifth column, rather than incompetent and inadequate Allied preparations, were solely responsible for the Allies' reverses. The actual causes of the failures suffered by British and French military forces were lack of appropriate and adequate equipment, insufficient air and naval support and all of that combined with bungling military leadership at the highest strategic and the lowest tactical levels. These, not any fifth column, were the true culprits of defeat.[30]

Nevertheless, the instant popularity of this fantastic concept of the fifth column with the popular press is not surprising, since it supplied a palatable explanation for these completely unexpected and quite shocking defeats. Gradually, yet increasingly, the popular press unleashed a "wave of panic and hysteria."[31] With the help of government officials and politicians in both Houses of Parliament, as well as the military intelligence establishment, the editors, columnists and journalists of the press spread a mood of debilitating fear and alarm by adopting and proclaiming the fifth column concept. A prominent role in this process was assumed especially by such papers as the *Daily Mail, Daily Express, Daily Sketch, Daily Herald, Sunday Express,* and *Sunday Pictorial*, which only very recently had ardently and vociferously advocated appeasement and had staunchly admired the Nazi regime as the "bulwark" against Bolshevism. Accepting this new concept, without any attempt at verification, such papers could now embrace both the familiar comforts of native British chauvinism and the bourgeoning spirit of anti-alienism and anti-Semitism.[32] With customary fervour and conviction, they now spread suspicion by accusingly linking anti-Nazi and Jewish enemy alien refugees with the new phenomenon of the dangerous, mysterious and ubiquitous fifth column. By this manoeuvre the popular press could deflect attention from its own, very recent pro-Nazi headlines.

On 20 April, the popular journalist, G. Ward Price, once a pro-Nazi Saulus, an appeasement advocate and an admirer of "Herr Hitler," now a patriotic Paulus, directed his readers' attention to a new vision he had suddenly detected: the refugee-fifth column threat! In his column in the *Daily Mail* he called upon his readers:

> Act! Act! Act! Do it now! The rounding up of enemy agents must be taken out of the fumbling hands of local tribunals. All refugees from Austria, Germany and Czechoslovakia, men and women alike, should be drafted without delay to a remote part of the country and kept under strict supervision.[33]

A month later, his colleague, Beverley Nichols, another former ardent appeaser and now a fierce advocate of home front violence, in his regular column in the *Sunday Chronicle* of 26 May 1940 again linked together the refugees and the fifth column:

> The Fifth Column. And what about the spies here? Don't skip this, because you have read before that we ought to have interned the lot. We have not interned anything like the lot. I hate writing this. I have German friends, but I would very willingly indeed see them all, yes all, behind bars, and I have told them so to their faces. Why should we be blown up as we are walking over a bridge, unless it is strictly necessary? Or poisoned by contaminated water, or hit on the head by the local gasworks, as it descends to earth? No, sir. The letters readers send about Germans who

are going free in their own districts would make your hair stand on end. Particularly the women. There is no dirty trick that Hitler would not do, and there is a very considerable amount of evidence to suggest that some of the women—who are very pretty—are not above offering their charms to any young man who may care to take them, particularly if he works in a munitions factory or the Public Works.[34]

It is amazing to note the speed and ease with which journalists and newspapers replaced appeasement and pro-Nazi sentiments with these new suspicions and denunciations of refugees from Nazi Germany both as "dangerous enemy aliens" and—most illogically—as clandestine agents in Hitler's fifth column. Entire influential newspaper chains under the command of their Lords—Rothermere, Kemsley and Beaverbrook—unhesitatingly adopted new sensational and denunciatory editorial positions, replacing appeasement jingles with the patriotic pap of fantastic fear-mongering tales about "dangerous enemy aliens" associated with the omnipresent and omnipotent fifth column. The new editorial line indulged freely in anti-Semitic, anti-German, anti-alien and anti-refugee yarns.

During May and June of 1940, British newspapers regularly published unsubstantiated reports denouncing refugees. One such item reported that English servant girls had observed German servant girls waiting regularly near military installations in order to pick up soldiers and thus "espy" vital military information. Was this act of maiden vigilance inspired by patriotism or by market competition? Another report spoke of flashing lights observed near airports, and yet another spoke of laundry sheets strung up in order to signal enemy aircraft. Enemy alien refugees from Nazi Germany, it was alleged, carefully perpetrated all these acts; none of these incidents, however, was ever verified. Yet increasingly the press demanded, "Intern the lot."[35]

The *Daily Mail*, eager not to neglect the Imperial dimension of the refugee fifth column problem, conveyed to its readers that in Canada, too, the need for vigilance and internment of alien refugees was recognized as the only right remedy for the spectre of the fifth column. In an article, entitled "Canada is all out to win," Miss Alice Hemming reported:

> In Montreal a shopkeeper told me that he is convinced that Hitler drove out the Jews and political opponents with the express purpose of sending *Gestapo* agents among them to the Christian countries that took them in. "Where did so many of them get so much money to live on?" he said. "Poor refugees—huh! All they have to do is to say Hitler was mean to them and we take them in and feed them, and half of them are spies!" Enemy aliens here in Canada and any who did not seem able to behave themselves and appreciate the advantage of life in the New World have been clamped behind barbed wire with the vigour and thoroughness that is typical of this Dominion.[36]

As the campaign in the popular press against the alien refugees gained momentum, even such papers as the *Manchester Guardian*, the *Jewish Chronicle* and the *New Statesman*, usually the few press voices speaking out in defence of liberty and individual rights and stalwart defenders of the refugees until now, succumbed to the anti-alien refugee and fifth column propaganda. The pervasive fear-mongering and denunciation reached even these left-leaning, liberal papers which remained momentarily silent, or—as did the *Manchester Guardian* and the *Jewish Chronicle*—even joined in the call for mass internment, under the convincing though slightly chauvinistic slogan that "when the very life of the nation is at issue" drastic measures were needed. As a result of this constant press barrage, anti-Semitism rose notably among the British public, generally, and within the middle and upper classes, particularly. In May 1940, a Gallup poll showed that support for internment of aliens among Britons stood at 43 per cent, and 48 per cent favoured the incarceration of unfriendly and dangerous aliens. Mass Observation, a public opinion agency, noted that whereas Britain's upper and upper-middle classes traditionally held pro-German views, they were nonetheless always anti-Jewish, and thus were hostile to German Jews. By the end of spring, 1940, as it seems, anti-alienism, anti-Germanism, and anti-Semitism were all acceptable in British society.[37]

Inevitably, the anti-refugee and anti-alien clamour echoed through the chambers of Parliament. In the Commons, right-wing conservative MPs demanded, "Intern the lot," and repeated stereotypical denunciations of refugees. Often these vocal defenders of the realm were affiliated with either the Link Club or the Right Club. The former was known also as the Anglo-German Friendship Association, founded in 1937 by Admiral Sir Barry Domvile. In 1939 it had a membership of four thousand, and in the summer of 1940 it still "defiantly advocated Anglo-German friendship." Captain A.H.M. Ramsay, MP, founded the anti-Semitic Right Club in 1931, relying on a long tradition of anti-Semitism and anti-Bolshevism. Some right-wing MPs even sympathized with Sir Oswald Mosley's British Union of Fascists (BUF). Not long before, these men had spoken fervently for appeasement and frankly hailed "Herr Hitler" and his Nazi stormtroopers as defenders of western civilization against "Bolshevism." Now, with their former ideological and political preferences out of favour, they clamoured for the internment of all alien anti-Nazis and Jewish refugees. In the House of Lords, sitting comfortably among his right-wing peers, Lord Elibank worried about controlling "large number of aliens...who might be utilised by Nazi Germany for nefarious purposes," and about "domestic servants of alien origin," who were "not trustworthy." Lord Elibank offered a unique explanation for Messrs. Petain, Laval and Weygand's recent traitorous cooperation with Hitler: "they went"—he argued—"to the other side to save from communism what possessions they happened to possess."[38]

Of course the refugees had their defenders, too. Labour and Liberal MPs spoke up on their behalf, as did leading churchmen, like the Bishop of Chichester, Dr. George Bell, and the Bishop of York, William Temple. They all supported the refugees, arguing that among the interned enemy aliens were many well-disposed and technically useful Germans and Austrians who should be employed in Britain's war effort rather than held as prisoners. Unlike the political right, the left saw the greatest danger to Britain's security coming from native-born, home-grown, well-heeled persons associated with the Link or the Right Club or Mosley's BUF and not from the alien enemy refugees. One well-informed observer of the British political scene at the time noted, perhaps a trifle sarcastically, that most of Britain's fifth column could be found in the House of Lords. Organized labour, unfortunately, was split on the refugee issue. While some unions assisted their exiled foreign trade unionist comrades, "the TUC [Trades Union Congress] did rather less for their exiled German comrades."[39] Some trade unionists expounded the sentiments of anti-alienism on the grounds of persistent high domestic unemployment, which in January and in May 1940 stood at 1.3 million and 650,000 Britons without jobs, respectively.[40]

As stated above, embracing the concept of the fifth column helped Britons to comprehend recent Allied military calamities. So too did speculations about the potential domestic dangers confronting Britain during the precarious situation in June and July of 1940. And, to be fair, to suspect that Nazi and Fascist sympathizers had helped Hitler's *Wehrmacht* in the rapid conquests of European nations had some basis in logic. For one thing, the political phenomenon of Fascism (or Nazism) was flourishing throughout Europe and also in North and South America. For another, reports and rumours about Nazi sympathizers organizing fifth columns in order to assist Hitler had been widely publicized by exiled leftist critics of Nazism during the 1930s. The unresolved question was, however, who actually were the members of this mysterious fifth column? The answers remained rather vague. Were they recruited from German nationals living abroad, so-called *Reichsdeutsche*, a few of whom were members or sympathizers of the Nazi Party? Or were they native-born citizens, nationals of their own states? For example, were they Norwegians, who followed Captain Vidkun Quisling, proud holder of an Order of the British Empire; or Dutch supporters of Anton Musert; or Belgian followers of Degrelle; or

Frenchmen who were Nazis by personal persuasion, following Laval and Daladier? For the British popular press, military leaders and certain politicians, the answer came promptly. Whether induced by feelings of personal guilt, incompetence, or traditional xenophobia, they seized, almost desperately, upon the presence of refugees from enemy countries and transformed them quickly into fifth columnists and "dangerous enemy aliens." Having identified the culprits and turned them into scapegoats, these spokespersons now demanded *in unison* their indiscriminate mass internment.

Nevertheless, the British government was, in early 1940, divided on the issue of mass internment. An alarmist segment of Whitehall officials, the majority, adhered to the conviction that potential fifth columnists would be recruited from among proven political anti-Nazis and racially persecuted Jewish refugees from Nazi Germany. This dominant majority, which included the Chiefs of Staff, War Office, Joint Intelligence Committee, MI5, the Foreign Office and leading members of cabinet, ignored appeals from important public figures and prominent church leaders. Instead the proponents of mass internment made the astonishing argument, almost in *voelkisch* terms, that "ancestral blood lines would be stronger than political convictions," and that ties of national loyalty and traditions would win out over more recent sufferings caused by bloody racial and political violence in Nazi Germany.[41] The sober-thinking minority, in contrast, reiterated the findings of previous government inquiries, which had concluded that although the refugees would technically be enemy aliens, most of them were nonetheless favourably disposed to their new country in preference to Nazi Germany. The Home Secretary, in support of sober thinking, had expressed his opposition to mass internment as an "inappropriate method of dealing with the problem" earlier and adhered to this position until mid-May 1940.[42] The minority knew that the overwhelming majority of German refugees, who had witnessed Nazi outrage firsthand, were most eager to join and assist in the fight against the brutal Nazi regime.

By mid-May, however, anxieties over military losses, the imminent threat of a German invasion and the insecurity of the realm in conjunction with the continuous barrage by the popular press, politicians, and government officials had transformed formerly welcomed refugees into "dangerous enemy alien" fifth columnists. Public opinion was increasingly ready to accept the mass internment of these dangerous persons in order to secure the safety of the realm.

II

From Mass Internment in Britain to Deportation to Canada

ONCE THE FIRST STEP in the transformation of the refugees from "welcomed" to "dangerous enemy aliens" had been taken, the story of Camp R and its future inmates moves to the next phase: mass internment and then deportation to Canada. This new phase opened with the debate in Britain's House of Commons about the military calamity of the British Norway campaign on 7 and 8 May 1940. Members of Parliament demanded an accounting from the Chamberlain government, during which Prime Minister Chamberlain generously assumed full responsibility for this fiasco and thereby shielded his cabinet minister Churchill. He, as First Lord of the Admiralty, and most importantly as Chief of the Military Co-ordination Committee of the Norway Operation, clearly carried major responsibility and was once again the chief culprit for this disaster, as he had earlier been for the disastrous Gallipoli enterprise of 1915. Now, in 1940, the Norway failure was caused not least, as one contemporary noted, through his "erratic and idiosyncratic methods of conducting the Norway War."[1] At the close of the debate, on 9 May the Chamberlain government suffered a severe reduction in support among its own Tory MPs, almost losing the confidence of the Commons. This near-defeat induced a search for a new prime minister. From the three candidates, Chamberlain, Lord Halifax and Churchill, the latter emerged as the compromise nominee once Lord Halifax, the preferred choice, declined to accept the office. King George VI confirmed Prime Minister Churchill by default on 10 May. After having subsisted as a pariah on the outskirts of English politics for many years, Churchill had finally reached his much-coveted goal, the pinnacle of political power, the Office of the Prime Minister.

Prime Minister Churchill and his newly installed "national" government faced high expectations at home and continuing disastrous military setbacks abroad, since on 10 May the *Wehrmacht* opened its attack on the Allied armies in western Europe. Unable to repel the *Wehrmacht*, the cabinet concentrated instead on the domestic front. At the first cabinet meeting, on 11 May, the fourth item on the agenda read: "Invasion of Great Britain: The Fifth Column." During its deliberation of this item, the cabinet considered the internment of all enemy aliens. While the Home Secretary, Sir John Anderson, valiantly opposed mass internment, his opponents—the Chiefs of Staff, War Office, Joint Intelligence Committee, MI5 and the Foreign Office—exerted immense pressure in favour of mass internment and eventually succeeded in persuading cabinet to implement this measure.

From 12 May to the end of June, German and Austrian-born men, women and children between the ages of sixteen and sixty years (later changed to seventy years), in Categories B and C, were rounded up successively by the local police, first in the restricted areas of the coastal regions and later throughout Britain. Gathered locally by the police, the internees were then handed over to the military for imprisonment. Generally speaking, the individual police officers were courteous and friendly, often assuring the refugees that their arrest was merely temporary, perhaps a matter of days, and would serve to clarify their status. In fact, the police were misinformed due to the secrecy surrounding the sudden roundup of these enemy aliens.[2] By the end of June 1940, 30,000 aliens, men and women, had been interned.

Charged with the task of accommodating this sudden massive wave of internees, the unprepared British Army was simply overwhelmed. The prisoners were placed in unused race courts, sequestered holiday camps, abandoned old factory halls and semi-finished public housing estates. In addition, holiday resorts and hotels on the Isle of Man were once again placed at the disposal of the military and resumed the function of accommodating imprisoned enemy aliens that they had served during the previous war. The hastily assigned new camps shared common features. Most were totally unprepared to receive their assigned lot of internees. Halls and huts, stables and houses were unfurnished, lacking beds or even straw palliasses or tables; chairs or benches and cupboards were missing. The places were dirty, dusty and muddy; old factories were oily, had leaky roofs and were populated by rats, mice and other vermin. Most often these camps lacked sufficient washing and toilet facilities for the number of prisoners assigned. In some camps, tents had to be erected in order to provide additional accommodation and ease overcrowding.

In several camps, food, generally speaking, was of poor quality and insufficient at first, though later both improved. Easing their heavy workload, the over-worked military handed over the internal running of the camps to the internees. Oblivious, it seems, to the fact that pro-Nazis and anti-Nazis and Jews had been placed in the same camp, they ignored the resulting sporadic conflicts between these radically opposed and hostile elements. Here originated the abominable practice of the "mixed camp." In camps where Jews and anti-Nazis constituted a minority, they were subjected regularly to anti-Semitic taunts, insults, threats of physical violence and other forms of harassment; however, when the numbers were more evenly balanced, both sides engaged in mutual physical violence and taunting. Many interned anti-Nazis believed that the British military favoured the Nazis internees, many of whom seemed well connected to the British upper classes and received privileges in the camps from the military, getting parcels, mail and newspapers.[3]

It is important for an understanding of the situation in England to recall that the roundup of the enemy aliens occurred amidst depressing reports of unexpected and disastrous military defeats on the European battlefields and the ever-growing threat of a German invasion. Moreover, the British Army faced rescuing a defeated expeditionary force from Dunkirk as well as recruiting, arming and training new soldiers and re-equipping the old. In addition, public opinion was inflamed by the popular press campaign and by an uncontrolled chorus of super-patriotic voices warning about the nefarious role played by the fifth columnists abroad, which might possibly soon be repeated here at home. All these elements contributed to an atmosphere of panic and hysteria.

The most widely heard and influential of these voices was Sir Neville Bland's. He, a former Minister to The Hague, had fled from his diplomatic post ahead of the victorious German Army and had returned safely to London early in the morning of 14 May. He went directly to see Lord Halifax, his boss at the Foreign Office. Bland reported on his experiences, and Halifax suggested that he write down his story. It was no sooner said than done, and a thousand-word essay, entitled *The Fifth Column Menace*, circulated on the next day among the inner Whitehall crowd of the War Cabinet, War Office, Chiefs of Staff, Joint Intelligence Committee, Security Intelligence Service, MI5, Foreign Affairs and Home Office. Later it was discussed at a cabinet meeting.

Bland linked the ubiquitous fifth column to a brand new German military weapon: the "parachutists." These loathsome and detestable German parachutists, according to eyewitness Bland, were "all boys of 16 to 18 [sic], completely sodden with Hitler's ideas and with nothing else in mind, but to cause as much death and destruction as they could before being killed themselves. They dropped on the roofs of houses, in open spaces—even in private gardens."[4] They were well informed about the Dutch defences and carried with them lists of Dutch officials and civilians. This information, Bland asserted, the parachutists had obtained from German agents of the fifth column, who were German refugees, residing inside Holland. Bland advised that it was better to kill an innocent human than be killed by a German paratrooper. Sir Neville, like Lord Elibank, assumed that the most likely recruits for the fifth column were found "downstairs" among the domestic servants. In fact, however, the anti-alien campaign resulted in physicians, professors and nurses losing their jobs.[5]

The most remarkable aspect of Bland's exhortation is not his fear-mongering and unproven accusations against domestic servants, but the fact that not a single person either within the military intelligence apparatus or the top political leadership or the respectable press corps ever challenged any of his unproven assertions. Bland's essay and radio message not only contributed significantly to the prevailing mood of panic in Whitehall, but also to the rising hysterical temper of the British public. Moreover, his incredible essay was circulated among British diplomatic missions abroad for further distribution as official government information. Bland must be regarded as one of the men most responsible for poisoning the air of public opinion against the refugees and besmirching their true image as refugees from Nazi Germany. First-hand reports, gathered by officials of the Home Office from reliable Dutch officials, "very emphatically" insisted that it was German residents of Holland, the *Reichsdeutsche*, and not refugees, who had assisted the *Wehrmacht* in Holland, thereby disproving Bland's allegations, but these were largely ignored by Whitehall. Instead the British leadership and the press continued to circulate unverified reports about German parachutists being assisted by refugees turned fifth columnists. Months later Sir Neville admitted to possessing no proof for his allegations.[6]

Apparently, only a lone German-Jewish, anti-Nazi refugee, Frederic W. Nielsen, objected to Bland's unsubstantiated accusations. Nielsen rejected the allegations that anti-Nazi and Jewish refugees had helped the advancing Nazi *Wehrmacht*. Writing from inside a

British internment camp to the *Manchester Guardian*, Nielsen observed: "We German emigrants are the avant-garde who fought Hitler long before the politicians of Europe began to comprehend what this man and his regime would mean to the world. For six years, we struggled despairingly to prevent a second conflagration of the world and warned against the fateful policy of appeasement—alas unsuccessfully."[7] Political leaders, the military, government officials, the press and the British public studiously ignored the obvious verity of Nielsen's statement.

The government's own information service under Canadian-born Director of Propaganda in Enemy Countries, Sir Campbell Stuart, failed to provide factual, reliable and accurate information. Instead of clarifying the murky situation, Stuart merely recycled rumours and half-true, exaggerated tales of murder, sabotage, deception and mayhem perpetrated allegedly by enemy alien refugees in the fifth column. According to his official communication, *Operations in Holland*, German paratroopers were moving through the Dutch countryside "disguised as peasants or clergymen, or wearing Dutch [or Allied] uniforms," and were "dressed as ordinary citizens, on bicycles, [as] peasants, priests, clergymen and schoolboys. Some boys were dressed as girls, while real girls were dressed as nurses, servants and so on....They also gave poisoned cigarettes and chocolates to passing troops and civilians."[8]

Why the British military seized upon the phenomenon of the fifth column is understandable, but why they continued to adhere to this fictitious model is less clear—perhaps it was an attempt to conceal and divert attention from past mistakes. By utilizing and feeding the popular panic, the military concealed past failures relating to the Norway campaign. For example, prior to the attack on Norway, they had failed to evaluate and properly process evidence collected by their own air reconnaissance in early March 1940 which showed German army and naval preparations in and around German ports quite clearly. Intelligence, it seems, could be rejected on the basis of whether or not it conformed to imperial prejudices or preconceived notions. This was the virtual world in which apparently the First Lord of the Admiralty, Churchill, lived when he dismissed the *Wehrmacht*'s capability of invading Norway. A further good illustration of this attitude happened on 8 April 1940, when crews of the RAF Coastal Command spotted and reported the German invasion force on its way up to Norway in the North Sea. This visible real evidence was dismissed as "a German ploy in the war of nerves," as was the bombing of the air base at Hatston in the Orkneys.[9] Were these dismissals the reasons for the War Office clamouring so vociferously and persistently for the mass internment of all enemy aliens?

Even though the total collapse of France demonstrated convincingly that mass internment of Jewish and anti-Nazi German refugees could not prevent the political and military demise of a once great nation, Great Britain's top political and military leadership chose to ignore this valuable French lesson.[10] Even after the rout of the Dutch, Belgian and French armies, British military intelligence still accepted and relied on the dubious military intelligence of these Allies instead of its own information. Unbelievable as it seems, British military intelligence was unaware that the fifth columns in Norway, Belgium, and Holland were recruited from among the native-born followers of Vidkun Quisling, Leon Degrelle and Anton Musert, respectively, and not from among German anti-Nazis and Jewish refugees.

Nor was the British military the only agency within the government to accept bizarre information. Cabinet ministers and even MI5 believed and disseminated the most incredible stories. Churchill barely questioned the veracity of the remarks when a member of his cabinet announced that thousands of Nazi agents were operating freely in Britain during the early months of the war, and that two thousand Nazi *Gauleiters* controlled the Republic of Eire. Sir Geoffrey Shakespeare, Undersecretary in the Dominion Office, believed German troops were operating in Holland and Belgium as "gangsters dressed up as nuns or Baptist missionaries."[11] The Joint Intelligence Committee very perceptively identified potential fifth columnists in Britain as German university students and businessmen and "German women who married foreigners, and the German War Graves Commission which provided cover for an intensive connection with Belgian horticultural-ists and florists." Other suspects were persons with "German blood links and German marriage ties," and, of course, persons of "dubious loyalties" who were—quite naturally—hiding among refugees from Nazi Germany.

Prior to the outbreak of war, in 1938, as the refugee wave was at its height, MI5 warned that Nazi Germany was flooding Britain with Jews to create a "Jewish problem," and in 1939 it stated that three thousand German agents operated in Great Britain. Anticipating or perhaps inspiring Lord Elibank and Bland, MI5 warned against the employment of "alien" domestics in the households of civil servants and military officers in the pre-war days. MI5 was especially worried about German-born naturalized English businessmen who employed Irishmen, which they considered a most dangerous combination and a deadly threat to the security of Britain. British security service personnel believed that "ancestral blood" would ultimately suppress the political beliefs that had forced anti-Nazis to flee their homeland and would induce Jewish refugees to forget their recent suffering of real violent and brutal treat-ment by the Nazis and work for the Third Reich.[12]

Critics of MI5 suggested that the agency kept better lists of anti-Nazis than of well-known Nazis living in England. Internee Spier, the fervent Churchillian, accepted this view as fact. The credibility of Spier's view is reflected in the unpleasant reality of the composition of the list of prisoners in Olympia Hall at Hammersmith. In September 1939, the exhibition hall was conscripted as London's designated hold-ing pen for Category A enemy aliens. Here, in September 1939, forty-one prisoners were held, of whom seventeen were well-known political anti-Nazis, another twelve were Jews and twelve were known Nazis. As H.G. Wells, a critic, maintained, "Fascist elements in the British Government had been responsible for the internment of political refugees."[13]

It is noteworthy that Churchill personally, despite facing an overwhelming number of urgent and significant issues, was nonetheless a major driving force behind the government's measure of mass internment and the eventual deportation of enemy aliens as well. At the British home front, he had the perfect chance to demonstrate decisiveness and action by realizing his long-cherished personal goal of arresting all German- and Austrian-born aliens, which he had already advocated as First Lord. On 12 May, Churchill's war cabinet ordered the imprisonment of all male enemy aliens between sixteen and sixty years of age in all coastal areas regardless of their Category status. Three days later, he noted, "there should be a large roundup of enemy aliens and of suspected persons in this country. It was much better that these persons should be behind barbed wire, and internment would be probably much safer for all German speaking persons."[14]

Ostensibly, Churchill knew the pogrom potential of the "public temper in this country" which in case of air attacks might put the refugees "in great danger if left at liberty." On the same day, Churchill supported the Joint Intelligence Committee's proposal of imprisonment of all enemy aliens, since the committee judged all previous measures to be insufficient. The following day, 16 May, all male refugees in Categories B and C were arrested. Churchill was still unsatisfied and suggested that all Category B women should also be incarcerated. On 24 May, while discussing the capitulation of Holland, he observed, "I am...strongly in favour of removing all internees out of the United Kingdom." And on 3 June, he inquired about the progress made in "shipping twenty thousand internees to Newfoundland and St. Helena...is this one of the matters the Lord President has in hand?...I should like to get them on the high seas as soon as possible."[15]

At this time, London and Ottawa were negotiating the deportation of seven thousand internees and POWs to Canada, a move that might have emptied British concentration camps. Was the British Prime Minister's reference to "twenty thousand internees" a joke, as has been suggested? Such a large number does strain belief; however, recent

British measures, such as extending internment, promised to refill the camps with many thousands more new aliens. It is thus most improbable that the Prime Minister was joking.[16]

These remarks by the Prime Minister electrified the ailing Lord President of the Council, Neville Chamberlain. On 27 May, the former super-peace-seeker and much-maligned appeaser was empowered by cabinet to establish a committee for the preservation of domestic security. Officially, the new committee was known as the Home Defence (Security) Executive. Better known as the Swinton Committee, it operated under Chamberlain's exclusive auspices and was chaired by Lord Swinton—an old Chamberlain confidant. Both men had previously been staunch foes of the arch anti-appeaser and political loose cannon, Churchill, but now they worked "with ruthless dedication" to implement their Prime Minister's plans concerning the mass internment and deportation of the new domestic menace, the "dangerous enemy aliens."[17] The creation of the Swinton Committee—on Churchill's personal initiative—finalized an alarming shift in control over the internment process from the Home Office to the War Office. The Swinton Committee was essentially a new expediting committee, "the object of which is primarily to consider questions relating to defence against the Fifth Column and to assure action."[18] This cabinet decision was undoubtedly influenced by external happenings such as the complete military rout and collapse of the Allied forces on the continent, which significantly raised the threat of an imminent German invasion of Britain. The Swinton Committee enjoyed almost unlimited power. It operated independently, free from direct control by either cabinet or Parliament, and its membership was veiled in secrecy. In his memoirs, Viscount Swinton barely mentions his involvement in this committee, claiming that he had only a "minor role in advising the Home Secretary on internment policy."[19]

Within the Swinton Committee, the Chiefs of Staff played a dominant role, arguing relentlessly for internment. On 27 May, the Chiefs of Staff called for "the removal of all refugees to Canada," and demanded that "the most ruthless action should be taken to eliminate any chance of fifth column activities including the internment of all enemy aliens and of all members of subversive organizations. Alien refugees are the most dangerous source of subversive activity."[20] The military's obsessive fear that enemy alien refugees from Nazi Germany would on arrival of the invading Nazi *Wehrmacht* join as fifth columnists is today quite unbelievable. So, too, is the seriousness with which British military leaders argued that refugees from Nazi persecution would support a Nazi invasion force because of old ties of nationality and "blood!" Such viewpoints are astonishing especially in view of the fact that the military had received numerous reports of alleged fifth-column activities which, when examined, proved entirely groundless and could not be linked to refugees. Yet military views remained unchanged, and on 17 June, the security forces advised the war cabinet through Clement Attlee, a Labourite, "that in the event of an invasion a considerable number of such aliens, even those genuinely well-disposed towards the United Kingdom, would in virtue of their nationality help the enemy. Thus there exists even from the refugees from Nazi oppression a present potential danger," Attlee asserted, and he further warned that "a considerable portion of enemy aliens at large at this time seems to us to be taking an unwarranted risk. From a purely military point of view we consider that *all* should be detained forthwith."[21] This insistent belief in the existence of a viable fifth column recruited from "refugees from Nazi Germany" as a military threat to England is as remarkable as the persistent refusal to view and identify native British pro-Nazis as potential recruits for the fifth column in case of a German landing. Befogged by their own myopia, the military therefore called not only for an accelerated and enlarged process of internment, but also, for the first time during these discussions, for the speedy deportation overseas of all interned enemy alien refugees.

Observers, then and now, of the Swinton Committee's secret activities and its secret membership, suspected sinister, anti-democratic forces—former appeasers, admirers of Fascism and Nazism, right-wing, conservative politicians—at work within the British government. Whatever may have been the committee members' long-term objectives, in the end they managed only "to restrict civil liberties, to violate democratic rights," and make important decisions in secrecy and beyond proper public control.[22]

Regardless, by the end of May 1940, as the swelling numbers of arrested enemy aliens, long-term residents and refugees were herded into the hastily arranged internment camps, the problem of their further disposal became a pressing issue for the government. Prime Minister Churchill had raised the issue of deportation as early as 24 May, and the Chiefs of Staff reiterated it a few days later. The scene in London at this time, it must be remembered, was dominated by the military situation which furnished a continuous flow of bad news about Allied military setbacks, the retreat from Dunkirk, the imminent total collapse of France, Italy's possible entry into the war on the side of Nazi Germany and the looming threat of an invasion by the seemingly unstoppable *Wehrmacht*, as well as concern about the potential danger of the interned enemy alien refugees joining up as a fifth column with the Nazi invaders. In addition to these matters, the government faced the problems of providing proper permanent accommodations and essential food supplies while assuring the re-arming of thousands of beaten British soldiers and the training and equipping of new recruits.

While this was the scene in London, in Ottawa, by contrast, tranquillity prevailed. Ottawa's circumstances differed considerably from those of London. In Ottawa, calmness and business, not panic and hysteria, dominated the situation. In organizing the country's war efforts, the Canadian government was absorbed with setting up the British Commonwealth Air Training Plan, the accommodation of British children evacuated for the duration of the war, the mobilization of Canadian industries for war production, and the expansion and arming of the Canadian military forces. Negotiations between Canada and Britain about the deportation of internees were conducted in secrecy. While almost every patriotic British person wanted to see as many of these "dangerous enemy aliens" interned and shipped overseas as quickly as possible, Canadians, generally speaking, were aware of happenings far away but, not surprisingly, were more concerned with their own domestic problems.

Negotiations started when the first official note was exchanged between Viscount Caldecote, Secretary of State for the Dominions, and Vincent Massey, High Commissioner for Canada, in London on 30 May 1940. The note that Massey passed on to Ottawa the next day requested help and explained that Britain held in custody nine thousand interned "dangerous enemy aliens" and German POWs, who together presented a serious burden and a military security risk. Furthermore they tied up urgently needed British soldiers in areas that soon could be the scene of active fighting.[23] Could Canada help, Caldecote asked, and how many internees could she take? On 3 June, in a follow-up letter, Massey reiterated that the incarceration and subsequent deportation of enemy aliens would strengthen British home defence and protect the country against potential fifth columnists ready to aid invading Nazi parachutists. On 5 June, Massey informed Ottawa on behalf of the Dominion Office that the "evacuation of internees has now...become very urgent" and that a Canadian government response was desired "at the earliest possible date and in advance of any decision on refugees and children."[24] The Canadian war cabinet considered Caldecote's latest request, and the first reaction was negative. In the cabinet's opinion, it was "not advisable at present to undertake acceptance" of internees.[25]

Ottawa was genuinely surprised and quite unprepared to cope with this unexpected and unwanted British request. In February 1940, the Canadian cabinet had considered a proposal from a British Columbian fruit grower named Tom W. Stodart, an ex-officer of the King's African Rifles and a veteran of the Boer War. Stodart had suggested bringing German POWs from Britain to Canada. At the time, Canadian officials dismissed Stodart's proposal because it might cause "embarrassment in Britain," and it might be seen as an act of Allied "barbarity" to ship German POWs into the "arctic waste" of Canada, resulting in acts of reprisals against Allied POWs held in Germany. Other objections were increased expenses and the lack of available young, agile and vigorous guards.[26] Four months later, Britain's own request forced Canada to face the same issue again: where could such large numbers of dangerous persons be securely accommodated and on such short notice, especially when the country lacked sufficient barracks to house its own troops?[27]

Despite a genuine sentiment of "Let's help Britain" and in spite of Britain's official entreaties, Prime Minister Lyon Mackenzie King's cabinet hesitated and procrastinated. Indeed, at the meeting of 5 June, the cabinet's concern was primarily about the loyalty of large numbers of Canadian enemy aliens, especially German-Canadians in the western provinces. The spook of the fifth column was present in King's cabinet, even if not actually wandering across the prairie out west. Helpfully, cabinet members suggested alternative destinations for Britain's unwanted dangerous enemy aliens such as New Zealand, Newfoundland, Australia, the West Indies or South Africa.

Dismayed by Canada's reluctant and unhelpful first response, Caldecote send a second note to Massey on 7 June. This time, he pleaded most urgently and ardently for Canada's assistance. Britain, he stated, had twelve thousand internees on hand,

> of whom 2,500 are definitely pro-Nazi in sympathy and allegiance [my emphasis] and therefore are a source of danger in the event, for example, of parachute landings or invasion of the country....In the circumstances, the United Kingdom Government sincerely hopes that the Canadian Government may be pressed to come to the assistance of the United Kingdom by agreeing to receive at the earliest possible moment, at least the internees whose removal from this country it is desired to secure on the ground that their continued presence in the country is bound to be a source of the most serious risk.[28]

Canada, Caldecote continued, could help by receiving "these most dangerous enemy aliens"; Britain would pay for their transportation and maintenance. London's message was plain and simple: help us transfer this "dangerous" and "serious burden" quickly to Canada. In response to further pleas from London, Ottawa asked for "particulars as to numbers and categories of prisoners, whom it is particularly desired to transfer to Canada."[29]

On 10 June, Massey informed Caldecote that the Canadian government was currently undertaking an inventory of available accommodation and

> a decision as to the number which could be accepted would be expedited if the United Kingdom Government would supply particulars as to the numbers and categories of prisoners....the difficulties...of receiving a number of prisoners of war seem to be less formidable than those which would arise from the transfer to Canada of civil internees.

Referring to talks between officials of the High Commission and the Dominion Office, Massey's very long letter continues:

> It is understood that all the German internees, numbering 2,633 persons, whom it is most urgently desired to transfer to Canada, come under category "A" (i.e., persons who have been interned because there is definite evidence of their hostility), and these include persons interned by Tribunals, persons interned at the outbreak of war on account of their personal record, and also those aliens formerly in class "B" against whom further evidence has come to light. Of these...some 350 are Nazi leaders... [and] there are 1,823 German prisoners of war, including 139 officers, whom it is desired to transfer to Canada at the same time as the category "A" German internees.

Massey noted further on "there is nothing to choose between the German internees and the German prisoners of war" with regard to "the urgency of this matter." The letter concludes with this observation by Massey "at to-day's meeting that there still remains the problem of some 10,000 further German internees and some 8,000 Italians who could not safely be left at large...the United Kingdom authorities would wish to make arrangements for the transfer of as many as possible of these groups to Canada."[30]

On the same day, Massey cabled Ottawa emphasizing again the urgency of the transfer of these prisoners to Canada. Massey reiterated, moreover, that "there is nothing to choose from, in their point of view, between prisoners of war and category 'A' internees."[31] On the basis of these exchanges, Canada had no idea that in reality Jewish and anti-Nazi refugees from Nazi Germany would be bundled off and shipped to Canadian shores. Meanwhile, on 10 June, Italy's *Duce*, Mussolini, finally declared war on Britain and France, and Churchill gave the order to "collar the lot!" that resulted in the arrest of all Italian-born males between sixteen and seventy years of age, many of whom had been long-time residents. This command increased the pressure on the available spaces in Britain's concentration camps and greatly enriched the pool of available "dangerous enemy aliens" for deportation. Deportation became an even more appealing solution.

Utterly dissatisfied with Ottawa's response and emboldened by the new circumstances, the Swinton Committee organized the same day a powerful lobby of representatives from the War Office, the Joint Intelligence Committee and the Chiefs of Staff that descended upon Canada House and the resident Second Secretary, Charles Ritchie. They renewed their insistent pleadings and urgently demanded that Canada must accept, immediately, "350 Nazi leaders, 2,633 category A internees and 1,500 Italian Fascists and 1,823 dangerous German ex-combatants."[32] After listening for many days to London's insistent pleas and having received Massey's latest message, Ottawa succumbed later that same day—Ottawa time—and agreed to accept the above consignment. In order to gain more time, however, for completing preparations of the Canadian camps for the reception of these deportees, Ottawa insisted that none of these shipments destined for Canada could arrive before 29 June.[33]

On the very next day, Chamberlain, on behalf of the Swinton Committee, informed the British war cabinet of the Canadian decision which was then used to cajole other Dominions into following suit.[34] After Canada had agreed to receive over six thousand internees and prisoners of war, London sought to exploit Canada's generosity by requesting the acceptance of yet another additional two thousand prisoners.[35] Once the order to assemble internees for deportation reached the British internment camps, the local commandants fell into a state of frenzied activity as they implemented this command. Assembling contingents of internees for transportation overseas in a great hurry, commandants and assisting officers were primarily concerned with meeting required cargo quotas and shipping deadlines rather than human concerns. They used many ploys to obtain their quotas. For instance, they promised the heads of families that if they would agree voluntarily to immediate deportation, they and their families would receive preferential selection of quarters at the new destination, and their wives and children would soon follow and join them overseas. Another ploy was to round up all single and unmarried young men, especially university students and sixteen-year-old apprentices and schoolboys, who were without parental guidance. Of course, many young internees happily volunteered to go abroad in order to escape potential capture by the expected invading German Nazi Army or in search of adventure. Some internees were ready to leave Europe behind and were prepared to trade places with those who wished to stay behind in England.[36]

Among older and married internees, fear and anxiety replaced the earlier depression and despair over their perceived treatment as criminals at the time of their arrest and subsequently as quasi-POWs in the camps, where they were guarded by soldiers with bayonets and kept behind barbed wire.[37] Now they feared renewed separation from family members and the uncertainties of the future, away from England, in unfamiliar surroundings. What new hardships might befall them and their separated families? Should they stay or leave; would deportation mean safety for them and their families? No one knew the answer. They also feared the dangers that might come from German U-boat attacks while crossing the Atlantic. Many were fearful that Britain too would engage in trading refugees for political concessions as the French had just recently done while negotiating their armistice deal at Compiègne.[38] Elderly and sick internees separated from their spouses contemplated committing suicide, and a few actually did.[39]

The practice of trading of places among internees was permitted in some camps, prohibited in others and ignored in a few; however, requests for exchanges of places were officially refused, generally speaking, regardless of the merit of the case. All this private trading of places, often at prices between five to one hundred pounds sterling, served in the end only to aggravate the already existing administrative muddle and confusion. Some internment camps maintained poor records; others kept none at all, both of which made tracing individual internees practically impossible and facilitated the prevailing administrative chaos.[40] The existing chaos caused much avoidable personal hardship and unnecessary costs as release notices issued in London to refugees in transit to the USA were delayed and even lost as internees, even children, were sent overseas. The fact that, generally speaking, British officers managing the internment camps were unaccustomed to dealing with civilians and non-soldiers and especially with the elderly and invalids contributed to this poor state of affairs.

Instead of using the deportation order as an opportunity to distinguish real Nazis from actual non-Nazis, the selection process for deportation degenerated into "a mere juggling of numbers, as if a train timetable were being arranged, and not the disposition of human beings."[41] Others objected to the very process of deportation, being—in the words of conservative anti-Nazi sports journalist, Dr. Alex Natan—driven out of Europe "like a consignment of livestock."[42] An indication of the haste with which Britain seemed to rid itself of the unwanted enemy aliens may be seen also in the fact that three troop carriers, already assigned to carry troops to India, were suddenly re-assigned to the deportation of internees to Canada. This British deportation frenzy kept Canadian military authorities in a state of acute confusion and disorganization for weeks after receiving these deceptively labelled assignments without proper documents of identification.

While British camp commandants were arranging their consignments for deportation, representatives from the Foreign Office, War Office, MI5 and Canada House were meeting at a conference in London on 17 June to settle the final details concerning the shipping of internees and German POWs to Canada. Sailing dates for three ships were set provisionally, and the total number of interned deportees was set at 6,000, subdivided into 2,600 Germans and Austrians of Category A, 1,500 dangerous Italian Fascists, and 1,900 German POWs. Canada asked to send home 500 destitute Canadians. The proposed passenger lists per vessel were 3,000 for the *Duchess of York*, 2,500 to 3,000 for the *Ettrick*, and only 1,500 for the *Arandora Star*. It was agreed that the POWs would carry "Army Form 3,000, W.W.I.P. 236" and "Internees individual cards." "These documents and birth certificates, where available, would be taken to Canada by the escorts, but NOT [emphasis original] Identity Cards, Alien Registration Books, and Ration Books."[43] The accompanying military escort was set at a total of 700 officers and soldiers. Interpreters would be present too and would stay on in Canada. The conference settled questions of food rations and weight of baggage—25 pounds per prisoner—but failed to agree on the issues of camp staffing, money transfers, and control over the different camps, with the Home Office insisting on control over the civilian internees and the War Office asserting its command over the POWs. This impasse required a new liaison level and created more bureaucracy. Embarkation date was set for 24 June.

The first vessel to leave for Canada was the *Duchess of York*, a fast, modern 20,000-ton liner owned by the Canadian Pacific Steamship Line. The *Duchess* carried the entire future prisoner consignment for

Camp R. She sailed from Liverpool, on 21 June, carrying a total cargo of 2,631 prisoners, of whom 2,108 were Category A, including 1,697 German civilian merchant seamen, and 523 POWs.[44] The second ship, the unfortunate *Arandora Star*, a 15,500-ton former luxury liner owned by the Blue Star Line, left Liverpool on 30 June, with a cargo of 479 Category A, B, and C German and Austrian internees and merchant seamen, and 734 Italian "Fascists." The ship was torpedoed on 2 July by U-boat 47 and sank with the loss of over 830 lives. While the British press indulged in its customary hate-mongering war propaganda about selfish Hunnish brutes pushing away elderly Italians and Jews in their rush to the lifeboats, the reality was strikingly different. Surviving Jewish and Italian eyewitnesses reported that due to the skill and diligent efforts of the German merchant seamen under the direction of their Captain Burfeind most of the ship's lifeboats were properly launched and therefore saved the lives of many passengers. The *Arandora Star's* regular crew, in contrast, the same witnesses stated, dispersed to the lifeboats as soon as the ship was hit, leaving the internees to fend for themselves. Of 200 soldiers acting as guards on board only thirty-seven drowned and of a crew of 174 only forty-two. Among the dead were Captain Burfeind and the captain of the *Arandora Star*. Had the *Arandora Star's* crew sent out an SOS immediately, the nearby Canadian destroyer *St. Laurent* could have been on the scene within an hour for rescue operations. As it was, she arrived four hours later after having been informed of the disaster by London headquarters.[45]

The *Arandora Star's* horrendous fate must be noted, since her tragic loss eventually affected the fortunes of all interned refugees as well as the deportees to Canada. The sinking of the *Arandora Star* and the subsequent revelations about the composition of her human cargo produced a startled outburst of questions in Parliament and in the press. It caused the establishment of Lord Snell's inquiry and contributed eventually to a total reassessment of the Churchill government's internment and deportation policies. British public opinion in regard to the mass internment of enemy alien refugees changed, and by the autumn of 1940 the Churchill government published its White Book whose provisions allowed the release of many incarcerated refugees from Nazi Germany.[46]

The remaining two vessels sailing for Canada were *Ettrick*, an 11,000-ton liner owned by the P & O Line, and the Polish owned and manned *Sobieski*, a modern ship. *Ettrick* left Liverpool on 3 July, with a cargo of 1,307 internees of Categories B and C, 407 Italian "Fascists" and 880 German POWs. The *Ettrick* arrived at Quebec City on 13 July, after a brief stopover for engine repairs in St. John's, Newfoundland. *Sobieski* sailed from Greenock on 7 July, with 548 POWs and 985 B and C internees, and arrived at Quebec City on 15 July. By 15 July 1940, Canada had received from Great Britain a total of 7,653 deportees.[47]

Retrospectively reviewing this sad spectacle of mass internment and deportation, one wonders not only how this could have happened, but also who in the end must carry the burden of responsibility. True, all decisions for these actions were taken by cabinet, which was controlled by "the most powerful Prime Minister in British history."[48] Was Sir Winston Churchill therefore responsible? Had he wished to follow a different policy, he could have done so without great difficulty. The available evidence shows that he supported the efforts of the Swinton Committee, and his own remarks indicate his continuous approval of the implementation of mass internment and deportation. His remark relating to the deportation of 20,000 internees overseas must be taken seriously and cannot be dismissed as a mere joke.[49] It has been viewed as such, based on the fact that by 3 June British camps only housed approximately 5,500 prisoners altogether. And yet the British government claimed to hold 9,000 prisoners already on 30 May and on 7 June, 12,000. Even if the number of internees had not yet reached the 20,000 figure, it would undoubtedly soon have reached that point since the Churchill government was willing to intern anyone "who may become a danger or a nuisance" or was a "suspicious character" and was determined to see "that this malignancy [the fifth column] in our midst has been effectively stamped out."[50] With a policy of mass internment, the

Prime Minister knew that the pool of prisoners was bound to increase rapidly. As Prime Minister, Churchill must share responsibility for these policies and their consequences, perhaps even carry the major share. Churchill's well-established reputation today, as Britain's foremost leader in that unhappy and trying time, challenges us to ask whether he could have done more to stem the wave of panic and hysteria that swept over British society in May and June of 1940. Being a great statesman, as Sir Winston Churchill undoubtedly was, does not exclude, it seems, the commission of ghastly mistakes in matters of human affairs.

III

Onward to the New World and
Its Old Problems
Helping Britain in Canadian Circumstances

RELYING ON HER SPEED and the mariner's good fortune, the *Duchess of York* set out on her transatlantic journey without the benefit of either convoy or escorts. However, to the refugees the voyage was sheer agony. Spier recalled his "utter despair" as he first saw the ship, a "Leviathan," arising before him, and he realized this ship would not transport him to the nearby Isle of Man, but overseas somewhere, while he "was pushed forward at the point of fixed bayonets."[1] His assigned berth "was right down at the bottom of the ship, a low and filthy little place which could scarcely accommodate twelve people, but into which were now squeezed over forty." The place was enveloped in a pervasive nauseating smell, a mixture of body sweat and oil fumes. At first, Spier escaped from this smelly, poorly ventilated hole to the dining room to sleep on a table. Later he found a place in the overcrowded cabin of Dr. Lachmann, a fellow internee and alleged Nazi. The overcrowded cabin, designed for six, now accommodated seventeen roommates. The *Duchess's* passengers were, at least, spared humiliating searches and expropriations of their possessions by their guards during the transatlantic voyage. Also unlike other deportees to Canada, the prisoners on the *Duchess* had daily access to the decks and fresh air.

The rumour mills on board the *Duchess* diligently produced fearful and fantastic stories, which circulated among the passengers since everybody on board, whether former Luftwaffe pilots, U-boat crews, civilian merchant seamen, or interned civilians and refugees, freely intermingled. The Nazis, forming the majority, claimed to possess the latest and only reliable radio news on board, and with this they fed the rumour circuit continually. At various times the Nazi rumour mill claimed victory: England has surrendered, the King has fled, Churchill has fled, the Germans have landed in England, the war is over, and Germany has won. The Nazi internees and POWs confidently expected Germany's final victory any time soon, certainly before the ship's arrival in Canada. They were therefore extremely cocky, over-confident and arrogant, according to Spier. In stark contrast, the anti-Nazis and Jews were frightened and distraught. The refugees wondered: would they never escape the reach of Nazism, or was their fate already sealed? Would England's appeasers, like France's, bargain away the refugees' fate and fortune in exchange for some small gain? No one knew.

On 22 June, her second day at sea, after supper, just past 1900 hours, a shooting occurred on the overcrowded ship. Sixteen-year-old Kurt Tebrich—now known as Clive Teddern—gave this eyewitness report years later:

I remember being on deck. As I recall it there were people sitting on deck and the sun was shining. And on one deck higher a British officer came and told everybody to go down below. And people started moving slowly. And suddenly there was a loud bang. And I turned around. There was somebody lying behind me shot through the head because the officer, just to speed up things, took a rifle and just shot somebody. And, of course we moved a little bit more quickly then. And again the usual outcry that he shot somebody and officers and NCO would take the bridge and the engine room and then they would take the ship back to Hamburg and then they'd throw...[sic] you know. And it was very traumatic because we certainly didn't feel safe.[2]

Another youngster, sixteen-year-old Karl Krueger, recalled that the ship's interpreter, Captain Savage,

> got rather excited about getting everybody to go down below. One of the prisoners of war turned around and touched his temple with his finger, suggesting that the captain was an idiot. The next thing I knew was that the prisoner was lying dead on deck. I never found out what exactly happened. Probably one of the guards had shot him—clean through the temple. He was dead immediately. Someone said that the guard was going to shoot above everybody's head, and that the captain had pushed the rifle down. Whoever did it was either a very good shot, or it was an accident.

A third witness was German POW, *Luftwaffe* Colonel Georg Friemel, who eventually submitted this report to the International Committee of the Red Cross (ICRC) in which he allegedly incorporated the testimony of seven additional POW witnesses. Friemel's version stated:

> A mixed crowd of POWs and internees was already going below when the British officer ordered one of the sentries to level his gun and ordered him to fire his gun. Among the prisoners a slight panic arose. The British officer then placed himself behind the sentry and pointed out one of the men. The soldier evidently excited when ordered to shoot, tried to lift his rifle over the heads of the crowd. But the officer pressed down the barrel of the sentry's gun towards the crowd and repeated his order to shoot several times. After the shooting, machine guns were put in place and sentries herded the prisoners below. Casualties were: one dead and ten wounded.[3]

The dead man was Karl Marquart, a civilian merchant seaman. Only two prisoners were wounded.

Spier did not witness the shooting personally; he learned about the event from fellow prisoners. According to Spier these actual witnesses saw a large crowd on deck moving very slowly when ordered below; there was some defiance, and a guard shot, killing one and wounding several others. This incident produced terrific excitement and aroused great passion among the German ex-combatant POWs. Demands were aired for immediate action, such as throwing the British officer responsible for the shooting overboard, burning or sinking the ship. After airing these fancy notions, the German POWs' desire for revenge and severe punishment found expression in "a plan of action unanimously agreed upon, namely to attack and storm the ship's bridge, take over the ship" and sail her to Hamburg. However, this foolhardy scheme was abandoned in the end. Instead a committee of senior *Luftwaffe* officers was elected in order to formulate and present the German POWs' demand to the commanding officer, Major Ayres. As a result the dead man received "a dignified funeral" with the usual "full" military honours.[4]

This shooting resulted in at least one and possibly two by-products. According to Spier, the first was the formation of a triumvirate of "good non-Nazi German civilian internees." They were Dr. Lachmann, Dr. Hanfstaengl and Captain Scharf. These three acted apparently as mediators among the various factions on board and calmed down Nazi hotheads. What role the triumvirate played in preventing the ship's seizure is not clear; neither is what role exactly Spier himself played in the work of the triumvirate; his memoirs depict him as a passive, religious, moralizing background figure rather than as a frontline activist. The second consequence of the shooting may have been that it prevented the execution of the planned takeover of the ship. The plan was hatched allegedly by Konstantin Baron Pilar von Pilchau and like-minded men, possibly before the shooting occurred. However, according to Eric Koch, "it was Commodore Scharf and not the killing that made the Baron and his conspirators desist from their plan to seize the *Duchess of York*."[5] Whether or not it was motivated by the shooting, the plan for the takeover of the *Duchess* was assisted allegedly by the publicly displayed plans of the ship's different decks and cabin outlays and was based on the premise that the experienced German ex-combatants would storm the ship's bridge and other commanding centres such as the engine room, take control of the ship and triumphantly sail homewards to Hamburg or the nearest German-controlled port. The sheer fantasy of this scheme requires hardly any serious comment. How many POWs would have died before even one of the machine guns would be silenced, and even if the seizure were successful, how would the *Duchess* have escaped the Royal Navy? Similar rumours and plans circulated at different times on different ships; none was ever implemented.[6]

Whether the British officer was merely impatient, or had been insulted, or was affected by current rumours about a takeover of the ship by German POWs was never cleared up. The officer concerned was court-martialled. In Churchill's war cabinet, the event on the *Duchess* was tabled as "Mutiny of Enemy Aliens en route to Canada." This incident may explain the rather unfriendly and apprehensive reception the passengers on the *Duchess* received on arrival at Quebec City.

The interned refugee passengers of the *Duchess* shared one bitter complaint with their fellow internees on later transports; they all consistently objected to the apparent better treatment of the Nazi POWs, especially the officers who had been on board the *Duchess* and the other vessels used to bring internees to Canada. The refugees attributed this apparent preferential treatment to latent anti-Semitism prevalent among the British military, rather than recognizing the fact that the POWs, especially the officers, were entitled to a certain standard of treatment guaranteed under the provisions of The Convention Relative to the Treatment of Prisoners of War (in short, the Geneva Convention of 1929),[7] whereas they, the civilian internees, were not covered by any internationally valid and binding convention. Interesting to note is that the German officer prisoners did not share the internees' views. Either because it was an expected routine procedure, or because the ranking German officers were ardent Nazis or committed troublemakers, they predictably and invariably protested to the Swiss consular and ICRC representatives shortly after arrival in Canada over alleged breaches of the Convention concerning their treatment and accommodation on board.

On 29 June 1940 the *Duchess of York* was the first British POW troop carrier to arrive at Quebec City from Britain. After docking, the *Duchess* disgorged her human freight onto the quay and into the care of well-armed and suspicious Canadian soldiers who were ready to cope not only with the expected "dangerous enemy aliens," fifth columnists and German POWs, but also with any disturbance these treacherous Nazis might have planned. Of course, nothing happened. The Canadian soldiers' hostile reception to the *Duchess's* human cargo was in large measure due to British information that the *Duchess* was a "Nazi" ship, loaded with internees of Category A, enemies of the Empire and military security risks, who, moreover, had engaged in "mutiny."[8]

Instead of seeing treacherous fifth columnists trot down the gangway, as expected, the soldiers actually saw unshaven old men and dishevelled young boys, some with bizarre hairdos. Old and young men stood around on the dockside, waiting for someone's instructions on what to do next. The soldiers heard a good deal of shouting in English and foreign-sounding languages, accompanied by excited gesticulation and much running about. Other observers, such as a *New York Times* reporter, ignored the scene of milling human misery and only saw what they had come to see, namely, "skulking, swaggering, arrogant Nazi louts."[9] For the Canadian soldiers the five hundred actual POWs were easier to manage than the large mass of undisciplined civilian internees, since the German ex-combatants were accustomed to the barking of military orders, an internationally recognizable ritual. The POWs were immediately separated from the civilians; officers among them were separated from other ranks, and all POWs disappeared promptly on their way to Camp C, the former Calydor Sanatorium, at Gravenhurst, Ontario.

The process of disembarkation at Quebec, generally speaking, was far less public than the embarkation at Liverpool had been. There

internees and POWs had experienced not only the hectic and disorgan-
ized procedure, which resembled more herding than handling of people,
but also being marched through the streets on the way to the loading
quay and being verbally insulted, spat upon, hit with stones and otherwise harassed by British spectators lining the route. The accompanying
guards had ignored these public outbursts. Such happenings the landed
internees and POWs were spared this time.

After gas masks and swim vests were gathered up, the passengers
of the *Duchess* were processed rapidly, quite unlike later-arriving ships
whose passengers sometimes had to wait for hours before disembark-
ing. Neither were the prisoner passengers of the *Duchess* insulted
and harassed, as happened days later when spirited members of The
Scottish Regiment of Toronto mobbed a dozen Roman Catholic priests
wearing cassocks. Allegedly, these ardent soldiers mistook the priests
for German parachutists who had been captured on the battlefield,
from where they were instantly shipped off to Canada before they had
a chance to discard their battlefield disguises.[10] Nor did military medical officers subject the passengers of the *Duchess* to any demeaning
treatment during the mandatory medical examination. Internees from
the *Ettrick* shared the experience of one medical officer who walked
along the lineup of naked prisoners and used his swagger stick to lift
up prisoners' penises at random, apparently for the purpose of medical
inspection.

Camp R inmates also did not report, although others did, that their
Canadian guards revived the ancient military tradition of ransacking
the personal belongings and luggage of captured enemies. Their possessions were not pilfered either *en route* or on arrival in port or at camp;
neither were their personal belongings expropriated or removed against
receipts that were shortly thereafter often destroyed by the officers or
NCOs who had issued them, usually in front of the robbed internee.
Protest on the spot by the internee, in such instances, was utterly use-
less, since officers and men, in mutual comrade-in-arms support, denied
the incident had happened, even when before a military inquiry.[11]

After the medical examination and yet another search of their possessions and persons, the 1,150 prisoners destined for Camp R were loaded into twenty-four CPR coaches waiting nearby. However before departure some passengers from the *Duchess* succeeded in sending telegrams to different countries and thereby announced their whereabouts, as High Commissioner Massey noted with great concern. How this could happen was never explained.[12] Spier recalled that just before departure each internee was handed a cardboard box containing "two loaves of white bread, cut in slices and wrapped hygienically in grease-proof paper. Besides these there were onions, sardines, one enormous Bologna sausage, pork, beans, jam, fruit, a loaf of cheese, sugar, salt, pepper, etc. a mug and the necessary cutlery."[13] The prisoners could not believe that this provision should suffice only for the next two and a half days.

The train journey of two days and two nights and another half day was uneventful. The train was well guarded.[14] During the day, guards served "two hours on duty and four hours off," while at night they served one hour on and two off. The guards were instructed, furthermore, to "be particularly alert and, while being strict with the prisoners, not to be harsh. They are to ensure that there is absolute and implicit obedience to all orders." The prisoners were not allowed to move about within each coach or from coach to coach, or to stand up; "only <u>one</u> [sic] is to be allowed to leave his seat at the same time for any purpose whatsoever." Prisoners could visit singly, on demand, the doorless washrooms and were "kept under observation" by an unarmed guard. Windows could not be covered during the day to create shading, but might be opened six inches by permission of the commanding officer. Coaches were regularly inspected by an NCO every half hour and by an officer at "frequent intervals." This careful arrangement, which included a medical officer and a medical orderly as well as an interpreter, assured that no untoward surprises might upset this journey to Red Rock.

The journey was uneventful once "an enormous bridge" spanning the St. Lawrence River was crossed, and "the train raced through a countryside of little interest and with no scenic attraction, with a seemingly never-ending flat landscape with enormous lakes repeating themselves again and again leaving behind a rather monotonous impression."[15] This was Spier's unflattering recollection of the rugged and beautiful landscape of the Canadian Shield, with its alternating panorama of impressive trees, mighty rocks and enticing lakes, interspersed occasionally with small, isolated and picturesque hamlets and lonely houses. The food was good and plentiful, and the coaches were clean and comfortable, with plenty of hot water for tea or washing, quite unlike the British troop carrier they had just left behind. The remainder of the *Duchess's* cargo of civilian internees were sent to Camp F, Fort Henry at Kingston, Ontario and to Camp T at Trois-Rivières, Quebec.

Cut off from all communications with either Canadian civilians or guards, without newspapers or radio news, the landed civilian internees destined for Camp R sensed that the welcome mat had not been spread out for them. This observation did not trouble the "enemy merchant seamen" (EMS) very much. However, the small group of Jewish and anti-Nazi refugees were shocked and disappointed as they realized that they were not welcomed as fellow fighters in the struggle against the menace of Nazism. All Red Rock–bound inmates had apparently not the slightest knowledge about the general political situation in Canada against which their incarceration would now unfold.

During June 1940, Canada's government and society had to cope with issues and concerns similar to those in Britain, such as the presence of very large numbers of resident aliens. Public anxiety was excessively stimulated by such issues as the questionable loyalty of these immigrants to their new country and the potential emergence of a Canadian version of the dreaded, ill-defined, all-powerful, omnipresent fifth column. The wide shroud of deep secrecy, which in the beginning enveloped the negotiations between London and Ottawa over the deportation of internees and POWs to Canada, assisted the cabinet of Prime Minister William Lyon Mackenzie King in managing these and other significant domestic political problems without extensive public exposure.

By keeping the official Tory opposition in darkness over the ongoing negotiations, the government gained time to consider the implications for domestic politics of the British request for help. The Tory opposition, having recently been trounced in the federal election of March 1940 by the Liberals, was preoccupied with vociferously demanding the formation of a Canadian "national government" in imitation of Churchill's resuscitated British version. Unaware of the flow of urgent requests for help from Britain, Canada's Tories, it seems, were absorbed with pestering the Liberal government with questions on the implementation of Britain's scheme to evacuate English school children to Canada. Since the availability of shipping presented the major obstacle to this project, and since London controlled shipping, the Canadian Liberal government was really unable to satisfy the opposition's irksome demands for action. Moreover, Churchill opposed the evacuation scheme as "defeatist."[16] More importantly, Mackenzie King's government was fully preoccupied with the details of implementing the country's war efforts within the peculiar parameters of Canadian federal politics.

A major domestic political concern for the federal government was the avoidance of a divisive debate over the issue of conscription, which would threaten Canada's precarious national unity. Success in these troublesome circumstances required the achievement of a political equilibrium, carefully balancing on one side the demands of a vociferous, entrenched and dominant Anglophone establishment of voters, who clamoured for unconditional, all-out Canadian support for King, Country and the British Empire, and on the other side the expectations of an equally vocal and ardent group of Francophone voters, who agitated against any involvement in an "English" war to save the King and the British Empire. Although remote from the turmoil of war, Canada nonetheless experienced the repercussions of the rapidly changing events in Europe in the summer of 1940. Surprisingly, Nazi Germany had demonstrated its might and its mastery of modern warfare. The Nazi menace had become a reality. Mackenzie King, for example, could imagine Hitler's armed forces leaping from Norway to the Faroe Islands to Iceland and from there to Greenland and on to Labrador and Newfoundland right into Canada. Canada, he realized, was still ill-prepared to meet these possible and terrible challenges.[17]

Against this background of potentially divisive political contro-versies, Mackenzie King's cabinet had little incentive to share widely its initial concerns about Britain's request for help. Canada's initial procrastination in response to British pleas was caused primarily by domestic concerns. First was the sheer surprise about the request and second its scope. The cabinet was simply reluctant to accept the additional burden of organizing such a large-scale enterprise as find-ing accommodation and provisions for both guards and this sizeable number of dangerous men, at this stage in Canada's war preparations, especially in view of the uncertainty about what to do with Canada's own suspected hostile "aliens." Plainly speaking, the government was quite unprepared for this influx of internees and POWs. Moreover, Mackenzie King and his cabinet colleagues were keenly concerned about protecting Canada's hard-won sovereignty and independence from Great Britain's tutelage and interference. Almost obsessively, they feared and suspected Whitehall plots against Canada's autonomy.[18] These suspicions were not entirely fantastic, as we shall see. Distrustful of British intentions, Ottawa was fiercely vigilant in protecting her internal social security, domestic economic situation and overall stability. The cabinet hoped to control, if not banish, Canadian unem-ployment by the strict application of restrictions on immigration and the unwavering maintenance of health regulations.

Viewed from this Canadian perspective, the British request to transfer thousands of "Austrian and German dangerous internees," who under Canadian laws were illegal, unqualified and inadmissible immigrants, looked very suspicious. Perhaps Britain was exploiting an apparent emergency situation of "military risk" in order to bypass Canadian laws? Or was Britain again merely following historical precedent and exporting her undesirable domestic problems to the colonies? The Mackenzie King cabinet wondered what would happen to these internees once hostilities ceased. Would they be returned to their country of origin, as POWs were under the Geneva Convention of 1929, or would they become a burden to Canada, as unwanted immigrants? These lingering doubts and suspicions in the cabinet explain why Ottawa was more willing to accept German POWs than civilian internees. The POWs would return home at the cessation of hostilities; the interned dangerous enemy aliens, on the other hand, might possibly present a complex legal problem for Canada after the war.

Nevertheless, domestic security during the war was a foremost concern. Cabinet members were well aware of the country's nervousness and worry about domestic enemy aliens and the potential of a local fifth column. Mackenzie King personally noted such concerns with regard to the potential dangers posed by these imported dangerous enemy aliens. He wondered what these English assessments and their categories really meant.[19] In Canada, as in Great Britain, the spook of Hitler's fifth column marched unverified through the pages of the press and haunted the speeches of MPs in Parliament, just as they haunted the minds of other Canadians. Eager to inform their readers of what they needed to know about the European war situation, Canadian newspapers reprinted unverified, hoary tales about fifth columnists and their nefarious deeds and supplied updates on British counter-measures. Canadian readers learned from their newspaper that every Briton who lived near an airport and employed an "alien" nanny was urged by the British authorities to register her with the local police, since she might be a camouflaged fifth columnist, ready to murder her employer and his family and then rush instantly to assist the incoming German Nazi parachutists. Clearly the message was that fifth columnists lurked everywhere and were murderous, but detectable and controllable.

In Canada's Parliament, patriotically inclined MPs, like their right-wing British colleagues, engaged freely in fear-mongering by reciting uncritically the fantastic yarns they had gathered from reading the British papers about dangerous enemy aliens and the pernicious fifth column. Impressed by the example of his English role model Churchill, R.B. Hanson, leader of Canada's Tory opposition and MP for York-Sunbury, advocated ardently for imitating Britain's mass internment policy, which in Canada meant that citizens should also pay attention to "pinkos" in the universities and among Christian preachers.[20] MP Alan Cockeram's speech in Parliament on 21 May 1940 conveyed a trace of Canada's homemade hysteria. Speaking for all "red-blooded Canadians," Cockeram, MP for York South, urged the government "to turn its attention to the activities of communists and other subversive elements" and to incarcerate them as well. Cockeram, looking at the broader picture, naturally, from his perch in Parliament, showed no concern for the fate of individual Canadian immigrant citizens, all of whom he blanketed with his unfounded, generic accusation. Unaware of France's recent blunder and uncritically embracing Britain's current hysteria, he was willing to repeat the fiasco of indiscriminate mass internment and its associated despair and misery for individuals.[21]

On 3 June the super-patriotic Tory opposition, ever eager to keep Canada free and safe from enemy aliens, enquired in the House of Commons what the government intended to do with the "more than fifty Germans,...all of whom were born in Germany, but now hold British passports," who, according to a *Globe and Mail* report, had arrived at the port of Quebec from overseas and planned to stay in Canada. In his reply, the Minister of Mines and Resources, responsible for the Department of Immigration, T.A. Crerar, stated, "The story *is entirely incorrect and without foundation in fact* [my emphasis]. There were three refugees with American visas who disembarked...and they are on their way to the United States." The Minister concluded his statement with a general admonition that "stories of this kind...

naturally have a disturbing effect upon the people" and that dealing with them consumed valuable government resources.[22]

Later, on the same day, during the debate reviewing the *Defence of Canada Regulations*, the Minister of Justice, E. Lapointe, acknowledged the receipt of a telegram from the Fraser Valley Mayors and Reeves Association of British Columbia, which Liberal MP, G.A. Cruickshank for Fraser Valley, had handed to him. Responding in the House, the Minister acknowledged that he had received many similar resolutions "from all parts of the dominion" and that he had instructed "the committee on enemy aliens to review the defence of Canada regulations [sic]." The committee, having "carefully" considered the suggestion to intern all enemy aliens of military age, "unanimously reached the conclusion that it could not at present recommend the internment of all enemy aliens." He summarized the committee's reasons thus: First, the necessity for mass internment in the public interest "was not at present apparent." The police authorities were satisfied that enemy aliens were registered and that they had sufficient information available concerning enemy alien activities. Second, guarding and maintaining internment camps and "providing for the dependent families of the 16,000 aliens now registered" would require a "very large" expenditure. The internment of "all persons of German origin or German descent, whether naturalized or not," meant the incarceration of 495,000 persons. Third, among the 16,000 registered aliens were many who were alien only in a technical sense, by place of birth, and who "did not adhere in sympathy to the cause of the enemy." Fourth, the committee recognized that many enemy aliens lived on farms in remote areas, in isolation, "where possibilities of sabotage or civil disorder were practically negligible."[23]

Reading the statement by the Minister of Justice, one wonders what drove some Canadians, common folks and political leaders, to forward to the government those outrageous demands that set aside longstanding traditional notions of law, justice and order. What was the evidence suggesting that the present situation was so volatile as to require the incarceration of Canada's third-largest population segment? Such a measure seemed more reminiscent of the practices indulged in by totalitarian European regimes than of the practices engaged in by a democratic government allegedly adhering to the traditions and procedures of English Common Law. Surely, the past conduct of these immigrants, especially naturalized and long-time residents of Canada, ought to have sufficed to prove their loyalty or disloyalty to Canada, if not perhaps to King and Empire. It seems that sensational fear-mongering and witch-hunting were as successful in Canada, far removed from the tumultuous European battle zone, as they were in Britain. Many Canadians apparently failed to differentiate between alien-born and descendant generations of long-time resident Canadian citizens and the very real Nazis in their midst, whether foreign-born, imported or home-grown. Nor, obviously, did the concerned patriotic MPs understand the negative impact their fanatic and racist proposals could have.

Like their panicky and hysterical British contemporaries, these Canadians, guided by hyper-patriotic political leaders and journalists, opted for the simplistic notion of the enemy alien fifth column and refused steadfastly to explore the question of who actually would be the members of Canada's fifth column. Were they recruited from naturalized German-Canadians, or from German-speaking, German-born landed immigrants, or from German-descended minorities, such as the Mennonites or the Hutterites or Sudetens? Or other minorities, like Ukrainians, French Canadians, or Italians? Would Canadian-born nationals supply recruits for Canada's fifth column, as had been the case in Holland with Musert's followers, and in Norway with Quisling's? Perhaps the circles around Adrien Arcand's National Unity Party or William Whitaker's British Empire Union of Fascists (later Canadian Union of Fascists) and similar rightists would have offered more likely candidates than foreign-born immigrants.[24]

Fortunately, Canada's Parliament also heard other voices concerned with domestic security which reported on the results of the newspapers' unbridled nationwide campaign of suspicion, unsubstantiated accusations and racial hatred against immigrants and Canadian citizens of German, Austrian (Ukrainian), Italian and even Chinese origin. The well-known member of the Co-operative Commonwealth Federation (CCF), M.J. Coldwell, MP for Rosetown-Biggar, decried the riots, military and civil insubordination, and the total incompetence or unwillingness of Canadian military and civilian authorities to intercede during two days of riots in Regina, Saskatchewan.

Rioting began on the evening of Thursday, 16 May, when between eighty and one hundred soldiers, cheered on by civilian onlookers, stormed first to the Ukrainian Labour Temple, ransacked it and then went on to the German-Canadian Club and finally to the Austrian Kitchen. This rampaging military mob looted and did $3,400 worth of property damage. Military officers standing nearby did nothing to stop the rioting soldiers. Both the mayor and the chief of police of Regina refused to interfere with the patriotically inspired vandals. Encouraged by the inaction of their superiors, the rioters returned next day and resumed their patriotic work by demolishing first the Metropolitan Hotel, then the Regina Hotel, then the office of *Der Courier*, a Canadian-German language newspaper, and finally Fuhrmann's butcher shop, adding substantially to the previous day's property damage. On Saturday, 18 May, the local chief military commander finally acted and imposed a curfew. The Regina riot ended promptly. However, on 19 May, a Sunday, some twenty to thirty soldiers, on leave in Saskatoon and Estevan, were seized by patriotic activism or boredom and proceeded to vandalize a few Chinese-owned cafés. In Toronto anti-German and anti-Italian actions provided similar opportunities to blow off nationalistic steam and demonstrate racist patriotism.[25] Indeed, the Royal Canadian Mounted Police (RCMP) had worried about the possibility of just such outbreaks of anti-alienism. In its *Security Bulletin* the Force warned that the anti-alien campaign of Canadian newspapers amounted to sponsoring and fomenting class and race hatred. The *Bulletin* also noted that mining companies wished to fire all alien workers, but instead of doing the deed themselves, the companies preferred that the RCMP remove these foreign-born persons simply by interning them.[26]

These Canadian manifestations of anti-alienism seem surprising in a country with a long tradition of open European and restricted Asian immigration. Perhaps it was an affliction, like the notion of the "white man's burden," only found in a small segment of the population. Why did anti-alienism break out in Canada at this time? Was this anti-alien hysteria just a manifestation of latent racism, or an expression of economic stress? Was it another means to stimulate enthusiasm for the war? Or was it just an expression of anxiety about the future? Perhaps all these factors were at work; certain it is that Canadians demonstrated that they too, just like others, harboured traits of irrationality, perversity and degradation in times of national stress such as war. It is into this New World atmosphere with old problems of anti-alien hype, traditional patriotism and nationalism, and virulent racism that the inmates of Camp R were introduced.

In anticipation of war and in response to legitimate concerns over national safety and security, the Canadian government had in the late 1930s established committees and subcommittees charged with reviewing policies and examining existing legislation such as the *War Measures Act* of 1927—originally proclaimed in 1914—and such other related matters as censorship, shipping regulations and the treatment of enemy àliens living in Canada. The subcommittee "on the treatment of Enemy Aliens on the Outbreak of Hostilities" submitted its first report in January 1939. This report perceived Hitler's Germany as Canada's most likely future enemy and therefore proposed the internment of all male Germans of military age living in Canada. In addition, the report urged the incarceration of members of two Nazi organizations, the Nazi Party (NSDAP) itself and the German Workers Front, Deutsche Arbeitsfront (DAF), which represented all German workers after the abolition of all existing German trade unions after 1933, as well as the incarceration of all naturalized enemy aliens suspected of disloyalty and posing a security risk. The result of all this labour was that the government proclaimed the *Defence of Canada Regulations* on 3 September 1939.

The *Defence of Canada Regulations* granted the government arbitrary powers over all residents in Canada, citizens and non-citizens. Suddenly, thousands of ordinary German, Austrian, and, later, Italian immigrants, living peaceful and productive lives, were declared enemy aliens and had to register with the local police, facing the prospect of instant arrest and internment without trial on a mere suspicion of disloyalty or on being regarded a security risk on the basis of neighbourly denunciations, unsubstantiated suspicions, or membership in alien cultural clubs or organizations. These legal cultural organizations were often classified officially as Nazi or Fascist, even though most members gathered there to indulge freely in nostalgia and memories, to speak their native languages and dialects, and to provide economic help and advice. Occasionally, however, Nazi representatives used such gatherings to convince young German males to register for service in the *Wehrmacht*. When war broke out, those arrested in the first wave by the RCMP were regular folks: farmers, farm workers, artisans, labourers, unskilled workers, bakers, butchers, tailors, hairdressers, shoemakers, waiters, musicians and a few professional men. The second wave of arrests, in the summer of 1940, yielded similar results. By the end of 1940, the provisions of the *Defence of Canada Regulations* eventually produced 1,200 German, German-Canadian, Italian-Canadian, Canadian Fascist, Communist, and trade unionist internees as well as other "undesirable" leftist elements.[27]

This dramatic and drastic action by the Canadian government was partly provoked by the widespread belief that there flourished a far-flung pro-Nazi conspiracy in Canada. Leftist opponents to Nazism had fostered this belief during the 1930s. After hundreds of Canadians were imprisoned under the *Regulations*, however, the authorities soon realized the inappropriateness of this rash act and began a gradual program of release of interned Canadian citizens. At the end of the war, in 1945, only eighty-nine Canadians were still interned. The number of arrests was very small compared to the 16,000 non-naturalized German immigrants living among the third-largest Canadian population segment. In a similar story of gradual moderation, the RCMP had speculated earlier in 1940 that "a very large number of [German aliens were] sympathetic to [the] Nazis" and that potentially one hundred thousand Italian-Canadians were Fascists. Later on, with greater knowledge of the facts of the alien situation in Canada, they drastically reduced these hyper-inflated numbers.[28]

On 19 June, in response to quarrelsome questions in the House of Commons from the Tory opposition on Canada's seemingly dilatory handling of the British scheme of overseas evacuation of children, Prime Minister Mackenzie King lifted, quite unexpectedly, the veil of secrecy from the ongoing Anglo-Canadian negotiations about the deportation of British enemy alien internees and German POWs to Canada. The Prime Minister announced:

It is quite true that the British government made representations with regard accepting evacuated children. They also made very strong representations to us about their desire to have us accept interned aliens and German war prisoners. There has been considerable communication back and forth in this matter....The wishes of the British government are these; in the matter of preference they are anxious that we should take first of all interned aliens, secondly that we should take German prisoners of war in Britain, and thirdly that we should then consider the matter of evacuation of children. The reasons they give in this connection are that the interned aliens in Great Britain may be in a position to help direct parachutists in the event of a bombardment of the British Isles which they are expecting hourly. They also feel that the German prisoners of war they have there require a great deal [of troops] by way of protecting them, [troops that] should be available for the protection of the British Isles themselves.[29]

Mackenzie King's statement in the Canadian Parliament temporarily stirred up diplomatic concerns from the United States and Switzerland, both of which were acting as Protecting Powers for the United Kingdom and Germany respectively. Objections from the United States included concerns over the status of Britons interned in western Germany being shipped eastward to less suitable quarters; fears that Canada would become a leaky holding pen for a mass of troublesome, dangerous, potential illegal emigrants to the USA; and concern that the presence of German prisoners of war presented a danger.[30] Eventually, these concerns grew, and Canada had to assure American officials that strict watch would be kept on all detainees in Canada. Switzerland was concerned with whether or not the deportation of German POWs to Canada across the Atlantic war zone violated the terms of the Geneva Convention of 1929. (It did not.) Most importantly, however, the Prime Minister's announcement not only succinctly summed up the official diplomatic exchange of cables hurriedly criss-crossing the Atlantic between Ottawa and London. It also signalled an end to discussions and heralded the arrival of 1,150 men and boys in Red Rock on the shores of Lake Superior in about two weeks' time.

IV

Getting Ready

Acquisition and Administration of Camp R

THE PROCESS OF ACQUISITION of the property for the future internment Camp R started as early as 5 June 1940, long before the embarkation of its future inmates in Britain. While the diplomats in Ottawa and London were still negotiating the details of the pending deportations, Canadian government officials were already busily engaged in locating, evaluating and preparing several internment camps in Ontario and Quebec. In general, the process of acquisition of the properties for these new camps started and proceeded quite uneventfully, but this was not the case with Camp R. In this case, the process followed a meandering course of negotiations until an agreement was finally reached just in time for the arrival of the first ship, the *Duchess of York*.

Despite their initial hesitancy in responding positively to London's pleas for help, the Mackenzie King cabinet nevertheless instructed the Director of Internment Operations, Brigadier-General Edouard de Bellefeuille Panet, to prepare a report on the availability of appropriate and sufficient accommodation for the internees and POWs and for the guards. As soon as he received his instructions on 5 June, General Panet contacted different federal and provincial departments, among them the RCMP, the Ministry of Justice and the Department of Agriculture and Forestry, concerning the availability of suitable internment camp facilities. He received many replies promptly. The Ministry of Munitions and Supply, under C.D. Howe, provided an inventory of two thousand two hundred idle and unused factories and mills, which were readily available for internment purposes.[1]

Also in response to General Panet's request for information, the Secretary of the Government of Ontario, H.C. Nixon, offered Ottawa, in a letter dated 12 June, two provincial prison facilities.[2] One was an industrial farm complex in Northeastern Ontario at Monteith, in addition to which there were "three prison camps on the road project between Hearst and Long Lac" in the same vicinity. The other complex was also an industrial farm and a former prison for juvenile delinquents at Mimico near Toronto. Furthermore, Nixon made available old Fort Henry at Kingston. Eager to help the war effort, Mr. Nixon also advised that Italian internees could be employed on road construction, namely, the completion of the Trans-Canada Highway across northern Ontario. Another provincial Ontario Liberal minister, Paul Leduc, suggested to Panet that abandoned pulp and paper mills at "Red Rock, Sturgeon Falls and Espanola" were available as suitable locations for internment camps.[3]

In his letter to the Secretary of State on 27 July 1940, Panet wrote, "You will recall, no doubt, we had some difficulties in reference to this property having been first advised by The Honourable H.C. Nixon...and also by the Honourable Paul Leduc that the property would be available for internment purposes."[4] The process for the acquisition of the Lake Sulphite Pulp and Paper Company property at Red Rock began on 14 June. This property had all the right attributes from Panet's viewpoint: existing connections to electricity, sewage and potable water link-ups, and railway access. This site was situated near the Canadian Pacific

Railway (CPR) main line, was large enough and ready to house 1,150 prisoners, had its own local power supply, had easy access to sewage and water facilities, and could be readied in two weeks at a cost of only ten thousand dollars.

However, what seemed at first an easy and straightforward acquisition turned into a protracted process of bargaining. The Lake Sulphite Pulp and Paper Company had been in bankruptcy proceedings since 1938; although its receiver, George S. Currie, Chartered Accountant, Montreal, was agreeable to facilitating the transfer of the property to the federal government, the liquidators suddenly espied more profitable opportunities lurking on the wartime horizon. Just when Panet learned to his delight, on 18 June, that the planned camp could accommodate an additional 750 prisoners in a 30,000-square-foot (3,600-square-metre) mill building, thus raising the camp's total capacity to 1,900 prisoners, the liquidators began lobbying several federal ministers in pursuit of their profiteering interests.

Unperturbed by patriotic sentiments and supported by their provincial and federal political friends, the bankrupt capitalists argued that the company had "a definite deal to put the plant into active operation" and to obtain orders for the production of ammunition from the American government or, alternatively, for the manufacture of cellulose from the British. They claimed, moreover, that the mill complex at Red Rock would sell for $4.5 million. Temporarily, Panet was forced to abandon his plans for Red Rock and instead relocated Camp R to the unused site of the Standard Underground Cable Company in Hamilton, Ontario. By 19 June, however, Panet's original plans for Camp R were back on track. Having confronted the Lake Sulphite Pulp and Paper Company's chief political advocates, Peter Heenan and R. Sweezy, the Honourable C.D. Howe encouraged Panet to proceed with the original plans, since the Red Rock plant would not "be utilized for the next ten years."[5] Meanwhile, the Hamilton alternative suddenly collapsed, and the Red Rock option became once again the preferred location for Camp R. On Saturday, 22 June, in Toronto, the Crown, represented by Lieutenant-Colonel Goodwin Gibson, Real Estate Advisor, and the liquidators reached a final agreement with the assistance of the Court, which stipulated:

a. That the Crown had immediate access to the premises (at Red Rock);
b. That on request for the purpose of sale or production, the Crown must vacate within thirty days; and
c. That a rental be reached on "a fair and reasonable basis" between the two parties.[6]

It is interesting to note here that despite the urgent need for the property at Red Rock, the federal government proceeded most cautiously in the case, first, in order to gain access to the site at the lowest cost possible, and second, to avoid expensive expropriation procedures in which the Court usually favoured the defendants. The precarious situation then existing, namely, the urgent need for accommodation of the incoming cargo of the *Duchess of York* with 2,600 deportees, is reflected in a letter that General Panet wrote a month later, on 27 July, to the Secretary of State: "It was essential to occupy the plant at any cost as we had then no other facilities available to lodge the prisoners of war and internees arriving from Great Britain."[7]

At the same time as the troublesome negotiations over Camp R went on, Panet secured, with much greater ease, the sites for several other internment camps and was therefore able to present, as early as 19 June, a plan for the allocation of the expected internees and POWs to the available Canadian camp locations. Panet's list distinguished between permanent and temporary camps. According to this plan, six permanent camps and a temporary one were located in Ontario and four temporary ones in Quebec. In Ontario, the first camp at Mimico/New Toronto, a former industrial farm utilized for the rehabilitation of delinquent youth, was considered "very suitable" for the expected "350 dangerous Nazi leaders," who, on the advice of their British jailers, were to be kept separate from the rest of the internees. Next was old Fort Henry at Kingston, which, until the outbreak of the war, had served as an historic site, a museum, and a tourist attraction, and was to receive 500 enemy aliens. Another batch of 1,783 would go to Camp R at Red Rock. The fourth camp was the vacant Calydor Sanatorium at Gravenhurst, which was valued as a first-class facility, eminently suitable for the 139 German officer prisoners, who were entitled to POW accommodation a cut above "other ranks" of military prisoners, according to the Geneva Convention of 1929. In addition, Calydor would receive a further 300 "other ranks" POWs. The unused paper mill at Espanola and the former provincial jail for juveniles at Monteith were made ready to accommodate future shipments of prisoners, as number five and six, respectively. The Exhibition Grounds at London, Ontario were designated as a temporary camp and would house 1,500 Italian Fascists.

In Quebec, the first of these temporary camps was on St. Helen's Island (future site of Expo '67), near Montreal, which would accommodate 384 Italian Fascist prisoners. The second camp, the Exhibition Grounds at Trois-Rivières, could house 1,000 enemy aliens, and a similar number could go to each of Cove Field Barracks on the Plains of Abraham, Quebec City, and old Fort Lennox on the Île aux Noix, the third and fourth camps respectively. Eventually, in October 1940, permanent camps were located at Farnham and Newington, near Sherbrooke in the Eastern Townships of Quebec. At Little River, near Fredericton, New Brunswick, a former work relief camp from the Depression days was restored as an internment camp. In addition to these new camps, there already existed a camp at Petawawa, Ontario, and another one at Kananaskis/Seebe, Alberta. Both were former forest training stations, which would house Canada's own civilian internees.[8] Earlier proposals to use Sable Island, Grosse Isle and one of the Magdalen Islands as camp locations were abandoned.

The Directorate of Internment Operations first used a simple system of single-letter identification for each of the internment camps. For instance, the location at Red Rock became Camp R; the Calydor

Sanatorium was Camp C; old Fort Henry was Camp F, and Monteith was Q, while Mimico was known as Camp M. In 1941, the Directorate introduced a more sophisticated numerical system of identification. The camps received a number composed of the military district number and an additional digit. In Military District No. 2, Calydor became Camp 20, Mimico Camp 22, and Monteith Camp 23. Old Fort Henry became Camp 31, being located in Military District No. 3. This system prevailed until the war's end. Neither the former nor the latter system prevented the enemy from knowing the locations of Canada's internment camps.

On the same day as the contract between the federal government and the bankrupt owners of the Lake Sulphite Pulp and Paper Company was signed in Toronto, the Ministry of National Defence in Ottawa ordered the Commanding Officer of Military District No. 10, Winnipeg, to pre-pare Camp R to be ready for 30 June to receive its consignment of British deportees. Three days later, on 25 June, Brigadier H.J. Riley, Officer Commanding Military District No. 10, Fort Osborne Barracks, Winnipeg, ordered the Fort Garry Horse to prepare Camp R, as the property was now being referred to in official correspondence, for the reception of pris-oners of war by 29 June. As barbed wire fences were being erected around the future enclosure, the Township of Nipigon issued, on 27 June, a "dis-tress warrant" against the tax-cheating Lake Sulphite Pulp and Paper Company in order to collect outstanding property taxes.[9]

The administration of Camp R in structure and procedures adhered to well-established rules and regulations designed by the military and appropriate for such a military installation. The Camp Commandant, Lieutenant-Colonel Raymond Barrat Berry, exercised absolute con-trol over all aspects of the camp's operation. Security guard duty was assigned to "The Fort Garry Horse, Canadian Active Service Force [CASF]," under Commanding Officer, Lt.-Col. S.J. Cox. At the time the Fort Garry Horse, CASF, consisted of twenty-seven officers and 464 other ranks.[10] Berry had at his direct command an administrative staff com-plement of five officers and 35 other ranks. The officers were Adjutant, Captain W.M. Johnston, Quartermaster, Captain E.F. Stovel, Medical

The Fort Garry Horse arriving, July 1940. *[Private collection]*

Officer, Captain Dr. A.A. Klass, British Army Intelligence Officer, Captain K. Kirkness and civilian interpreter, S.A. Warkentine. By all accounts, Berry was a stern and strict chief. He was not quite satisfied with every one of his staff officers, primarily because he had no say in their individual appointments. Berry judged his Adjutant lacking in imagination and initiative, and his Quartermaster as medically unfit. Berry expressed to Panet his strong opposition to the appointment of "job seekers" to positions of officer for which they lacked the "qualifications necessary to do this work."[11] Visiting military inspectors, however, evaluated the performances of all staff officers at Camp R as "satisfactory." True, the first visiting inspector noted, the Adjutant had difficulties in recruiting competent office personnel, yet the Orderly Room was "well run," keeping different kinds of registers and

Arrival of the Veterans Guard, 1940. *[Private collection]*

all sorts of records concerning pay matters, including "P/W [prisoners of war] accounts."[12] He also observed that the Adjutant was "not very aggressive or energetic,...[perhaps] a little afraid of his job." The Quartermaster was judged "anxious to do good work,...energetic and keen." The Medical Officer was very highly praised, being "very keen" and having assembled an excellently equipped hospital. The British Intelligence Officer knew his work and was "keen," as was the Interpreter.

During the early weeks of operation, Camp R, like other internment camps, experienced a military command phenomenon, the so-called "dual control" issue. This phenomenon had perhaps two causes: a) seniority of rank dispute and b) overlapping and ill-defined jurisdictions of the Canadian Active Service Force—the fighting army—and the Army's

Provost Division—the policing army. A memorandum of 19 August 1940 noted that "the relation between the Camp Commandant (CC) and the Officer Commanding the Guard of Internment Camps has been under review," especially in situations where the Officer Commanding the Guard was senior in rank to the CC. The memo reiterated that the CC "is responsible for the safe custody of Internees and the administration and discipline generally [and] must be invested with the necessary authority. Consequently,...the CC will be considered the senior officer in the camp."[13]

The issue of "dual control" was finally settled, it seems, by a further circular to "All District Officer Commanding, Officer Administering Canadian Provost Corps, Officer Administering Veterans Guard of Canada" which in five separate Appendices set out the respective "duties and responsibilities" of all officers concerned. Appendices D and E, respectively, enumerated the duties and responsibilities of the "Camp Commandant Internment Camp" and "The Officer Commanding a Detachment of Veterans Guard of Canada at an Internment Camp."[14]

At Red Rock the issue of "dual control" arose from the fact that Lt.-Col. Cox was senior to Lt.-Col. Berry, who only very recently had been elevated to this rank. Although Berry was actually the Camp Commandant, and therefore officially and theoretically undoubtedly in charge of all the camp's accoutrements, nonetheless his junior rank excluded him from command of his policing regiment, the Fort Garry Horse, CASF. The Director of Internment Operations, General Panet, described this implausible division of command, on his first visit to Camp R: "this is unsatisfactory. The CC must be the senior officer and recognized as such. The guard must perform its duties according to the instructions issued by the CC. Dual control will not be successful."[15]

The presence of two commanding officers at the same rank apparently caused conflict, creating tension and stress within the local military set-up at Red Rock. "Dual control" in practice meant that while Cox's troops provided regular sentries for all shifts, day and night, CC Berry was obliged to "request" assistance from Cox for the performance of escort duties and other routine services such as military maintenance work, strengthening the barbed wire fences around the enclosure, doing repair work on the watchtowers or any additional duties that required extra soldiers. Since Cox's regiment was in training as a regular army outfit, seeking to achieve proficiency in battlefield combat skills, fixing barbed wire fences was, understandably, not a high priority for the commander of the Fort Garry Horse, CASF.

Real difficulties with "dual control" arose over issues of military discipline at Camp R. Berry's authority did not apparently extend over the conduct of soldiers from Cox's outfit, and since Cox failed to perceive the need to punish his soldiers for such breaches of discipline as pilfering, vandalism and fraternization, tension and friction determined the relations between the two commanding officers and their respective staffs. Although General Panet lamented the existing situation of "dual control," he could not change the reality of the regular army's exclusive control over the military ranking system. Colonel Watson, the first regular visiting military inspector, also noted, in his report of 16 August 1940, "evidence of friction between the camp staff and the guards," adding that "it is difficult to see how this can be avoided where there is dual control." Watson observed that the prohibited practices of fraternization and pilfering remained unpunished, and he acknowledged that in the existing circumstances "little could be done since the *regular* army troops are not under Colonel Berry's command [my emphasis]."[16] Although, Watson wrote, "both the camp commandant and the officer commanding The Fort Garry Horse disclaim any responsibility," nonetheless he "anticipated that [Cox]...may have to take some disciplinary action."[17]

During August 1940 the issue of "dual control" stirred up a lively discussion within the upper command ranks. This problem had emerged in other camps such as Calydor and seems to have been linked to escape attempts by POWs.[18] On 21 August, the Adjutant-General suggested that the "system of control" needed to "tighten up" and "the relationship and responsibilities of personnel employed in connection with Internment Camps" required clarification. It was proposed to create a

The Fort Garry Horse in summer dress uniforms.
[Courtesy of the Red Rock Historical Society]

unified command by placing the Officer Administering the Canadian Provost Corps, Colonel P.A. Puize, in complete charge of all aspects of "security" of all internment camps, exercising full command over camp staff and guards. Brigadier K.J. Oran, Judge Advocate General, proposed to the Adjutant-General that, in order to eradicate the problem of "dual control," the Director of Internment Operations and his staff, "who are members of the Militia, could be called out and placed on Active Service thereby putting them in the same category as other officers serving in the Canadian Active Service Force as far as status and pay and allowance are concerned."[19]

This change would have placed the Director and all his subordinate officers in the Internment Operations under the control of the Minister of National Defence and directly under the Adjutant-General. The Minister of National Defence, Ralston, joined the discussion, but he was less concerned with command structures and more interested in such practical measures as counting prisoners, irregular enclosure patrols and better means of identification, which might help in preventing escapes. Escapes aroused anxiety in the public, who eventually would seek to allocate political blame.[20] In due course the issue of "dual control" was resolved by the passage of time, which in the case of Camp R saw at the end of August 1940 the arrival of and assumption of duties previously held by the Fort Garry Horse under Lieutenant-Colonel Cox by the Veterans Guard of Canada under Major V.P. Torrance. Elsewhere a similar process simplified the command structure.

Absolute in authority locally, Colonel Berry nonetheless stood last in a long chain of control extending all the way from Ottawa to Winnipeg to distant Red Rock. As a result, Camp Commandant Berry was a very busy person.[21] He had to ensure that all orders and instructions coming from Ottawa through Winnipeg to Red Rock were not only conveyed promptly and properly to the local officers and then to the troops guarding the camp, but were also fully, speedily and competently implemented. It was his responsibility to ensure that all his subordinate officers executed all functions of their various offices, ranging from the simple administration of their individual units to the maintenance of discipline, health and morale among their subordinates, from providing the soldiers with proper training to overseeing the soldiers' performance of their assigned duties. Moreover, Berry was responsible for issuing all orders that were necessary to ensure the efficient operation of the camp. Highest-ranking among his concerns were the prevention of escapes through regular daily inspections of buildings and grounds, the enforcement of non-fraternization and the effective and efficient posting of sentries around the compound wherever and whenever necessary.

In addition to the maintenance of discipline and the operation, administration, and training of his own staff, Berry was also

Veterans Guard Charles Stanley Gallop with dog, 6 July 1941. [LAC-ee006611165_s1]

responsible for the officers and soldiers of the Veterans Guard. The security and safeguarding of the prisoners and the observance of the Articles
of the Geneva Convention of 1929 that were relevant to Canadian POWs
and Class II civilian internees also formed part of his duties. He had to
develop, revise and enforce appropriate standing orders for the camp,
devise a suitable plan for dealing with escapes and supervise the execution of a myriad of detailed instructions and orders. Berry was indeed a
very busy man who was responsible to the District Officer Commanding
(DOC), Brigadier H.J. Riley, for his staff, the Provost detail, the Veterans
Guard and the imprisoned internees in his care.

Riley was the Officer Commanding Military District No. 10 in
Winnipeg, and therefore Camp Commandant Berry's immediate
military superior. Riley served in two distinct capacities: first, as a

transmitter of orders from the Director of Internment Operations in Ottawa, and second, as a supervisor under whose auspices Berry carried out the execution of his duties and implementation of his responsibilities. The District Officer Commanding had absolute control in the execution of measures "in regard to the custody and security of prisoners of war and internees."[22] Furthermore, he had to inspect frequently the camps in his district and "detect and correct weaknesses, investigate and report escapes and prevent recurrences." He "has authority over all camp personnel, arranges training, [and] is responsible for local administration and discipline," and he advised the Adjutant-General on the staffing of camps. The Military District commander dealt, moreover, with all "outside" matters.

Of course, the District Officer Commanding cooperated with all his superiors. This transmission link in the command chain sometimes caused delays in communications between Red Rock and Ottawa. Here at the very top stood the special committee of the war cabinet, which determined policy and set directions for the Canadian internment process. Just below in the command hierarchy stood, jointly, the Departments of National Defence and of External Affairs, which together guided the operation of the internment camps through the Directorate of Internment Operations under the authority of the Director. These last three agencies were responsible for the implementation of government policy concerning security, maintenance, discipline, and the physical and mental welfare of all Canadian-held internees and POWs. The Director of Internment Operations under the supervision of the Department of National Defence was responsible in particular for providing soldiers and armaments, for managing the logistics of shelter, food, recreation and health, and for the complete provisioning of the prisoners in their enclosures. The Director of Internment Operations reported to the Secretary of State on all matters of an international character that arose from the detention of international civilian internees and German POWs. This included all relations with the United Kingdom, with Switzerland, as the Protecting Power of German interests, and with the International Committee of the Red Cross, as the guardian of the Geneva Convention of 1929.

A brief sketch of the personalities of the few men primarily responsible for the administration and operation of Camp R seems now most appropriate. First of these was the Director of Internment Operations in Ottawa, Brigadier-General Edouard de Bellefeuille Panet, aged fifty-nine, who was greatly respected by everyone whether his superiors or his subordinates; even his prisoners spoke highly of him.[23] All praised him as a fair person. Panet, a resident of Montreal and a descendant of an old and most distinguished French-Canadian family, participated actively in the cultural and charitable activities of Montreal, where he was well-known not only for his friendly and likeable disposition, but also for his readiness to help the helpless instantly. A visiting, high-ranking British government official observed: "[Panet's] personal charm and commanding stature, the breadth of his sympathy, the sincerity of his smile, have conquered all ranks in Canada. To serve with him is to have the privilege of meeting the incarnation of French Canada."[24] Before his appointment as Director, General Panet enjoyed far-ranging military and civilian experiences. During the First World War, he served in different positions with the Canadian Army overseas, last as staff officer with the First Canadian Division. In 1918, Panet received the Order of the *Légion d' honneur* from France. After returning to civilian life, he served first as Comptroller of Quebec's Liquor Commission from 1921 to 1925, and then transferred to the CPR, where he headed the Department of Investigation until he was appointed Director of Internment Operations on 4 September 1939. He was without any doubt a most conscientious Director of Internment Operations, "a human and perceptive individual." After one of his personal inspection tours of a Quebec refugee camp with an extraordinarily large number of youngsters, one of the young boys wrote in his diary that "he [Panet] did a lot of things to our benefit."[25] Recognizing an acute shortage of writing paper, Panet personally arranged for an increased supply of writing paper to this camp. Once the true character of the British-imported internees emerged, Panet was among the first to inform a British War Office official in early August 1940 that among the "dangerous enemy aliens" were "large numbers of schoolboys, college undergraduates, priests, rabbis, etc....It is considered that these people should not have been sent to Canada." In recognition of the new situation, Panet proposed to his superiors a radical reorganization of the enemy alien internee camps into refugee camps as genuinely self-governing republican institutions, with a drastically reduced military presence inside and outside these specially designated camps. Of course his imaginative and timely suggestion was rejected by his military superiors in the Department of National Defence. He retired as Director on promotion in the fall of 1940 and died in 1977.[26]

Next in line of command was Colonel Hubert Stethem, aged fifty-two, who first served as Assistant Director and then as successor to Panet in the autumn of 1940. Stethem was in almost every respect the very opposite of Panet. He exhibited "all the qualities of a fearless and tenacious soldier," and these military attributes were well illustrated by two remarkable incidents in his career. One goes back to July 1914, when young Lieutenant Stethem charged bravely with six Royal Canadian Dragoons under his command into a crowd of 10,000 strikers and their supporters, including women and children, in downtown Fredericton, New Brunswick, only to be beaten back by the crowd, which forced his retreat in humiliation with bleeding horses and men. In the words of the official historian of the Royal Canadian Dragoons, Stethem performed "one of the most foolhardy cavalry charges in the annals of Canadian military history."[27]

The second incident happened in April 1941 at the time of the notorious Angler escape by German POWs.[28] When he heard the news of this wicked deed, Director Stethem was engaged on business in downtown Toronto. He dropped everything, assumed his Colonel's role and rushed north in his Oxford shoes and spring attire in order to take personal command of the operation and participate personally in the recapture of the twenty-seven escaped POWs. True, at the time, the Colonel was totally unfamiliar with the local terrain, the climate and the type and numbers of the available troops. After his subordinates, without much input by the Director, had accomplished the recapture of the POW escapees, Stethem returned to Toronto completely exhausted and seriously ill, but triumphantly content, having done his duty once again.

Some subordinates depicted Stethem as a leader; most often, however, he was perceived as a driver of subordinates, a stickler for details, a domineering authoritarian who caused anger and annoyance rather than inspiring dedication and commitment. Under his leadership, the camp was not a cheerful place to work. His telephoned comments and orders to the camp commandants were peppered with such pithy, morale-boosting phrases as "Twist their tails all right" and "[Your] men make insufficient use of their rifle butts." Stethem "disliked, despised, and distrusted them [the internees]. They were just a lot of 'sick headaches' to him, and, during the war, any time spent on them was a waste of time."[29] Stethem regarded the internees as having "no interest in the present life and death struggle in which we are engaged. They are self-centred and would not turn a hand to help along a British victory, and the claim that they are refugees from Nazi oppression has, they feel, placed them into a position whereby they can demand anything."[30]

He strongly disapproved of the War Prisoners' Aid Committee of the Young Men's Christian Association (YMCA) and anyone who sympathized with the interned refugees. In return, the Jewish and anti-Nazi refugees perceived him, if not as an outright anti-Semite, as lacking humanity and an understanding of their plight. Commissioner Paterson described Stethem as "a mixture of shyness and disappointment...responsible for an unusually ungracious personality and manner....It was exhilarating to find that anyone could be ruder than an Englishman on his travels."[31] Saul Hayes, Secretary, who regularly dealt with the Colonel, saw Stethem as the embodiment of "the ignorance of the military mind."[32]

Stethem, a native of Kingston, lectured at the Royal Military College as a professor of Military Organization, Administration

and Law before he was called to the internment directorate in early September 1939 to assist in upholding the Articles of the Geneva Convention of 1929. He resigned due to illness in September 1941 and died in 1944. His successor was Colonel Hubert Streight, a lawyer from Winnipeg working in the District No. 10 Headquarters. The then-serving Assistant Director, Lieutenant-Colonel G.B. Bouchard, continued in his supporting position.

The third person of importance, perhaps the most influential figure, was Lieutenant-Colonel Raymond Barrat Berry, the Camp Commandant of Camp R. He was in his late fifties. Unfortunately, no information on his civilian life could be found in various provincial archives, Library and Archives Canada, the History and Heritage Section of the Department of National Defence or the Canadian Legion national office. The explanation for this lacuna of information may be the fact that Berry had served as an officer in the British Army during the First World War, had immigrated to Canada after the war, and was a reserve officer when called on to command Camp R. That Berry is not a phantom is proven by the recorded comments of Spier, Panet, Riley and Watson as well as references in various reports on Camp R and in correspondence written by Berry. Former prisoners in his care described him later as a "straightforward soldier," more concerned with security and discipline than with the dispensation of justice. Internee Spier recalled that Berry was not altogether happy with his command at Red Rock. In conversation with Spier, Berry pointed out that the separation of Nazis from anti-Nazis in Camp R and "the latter's early release was not only a matter of elementary justice, but would also save him a lot of trouble and facilitate his task of keeping peace and order inside the Camp....The sooner I get rid of you [the anti-Nazis and Jews], the better I like it." In his memoirs, Spier very perceptively sums up Berry's dilemma. Having listened to Berry, Spier wrote, "I realized what a simple administrative job it was to perform the duties of a

< Lieutenant-Colonel R.B. Berry, Camp Commandant.
[Courtesy of the Red Rock Historical Society]

Commandant of a War Camp consisting only of men caught in battle or some other military engagement. But I also realized what a worrying and awkward job it must be to do justice in a Camp like ours."[33] Berry practised a peculiar notion of justice: he imposed the same penalty of solitary confinement on all participants in a fracas—victims and perpetrators alike. His superiors in Ottawa in the Directorate of Internment Operations regarded Colonel Berry as "competent," effective and efficient, and overly concerned with the "unsuitability" of Camp R for internment. In the view of his fellow officer and frequent military inspector, Colonel Watson, Berry would have preferred commandeering a camp of regular POWs in the midst of unspoiled wilderness.[34] In the memory of Red Rock's long-time resident, Lloyd Roy, who was nine years old in 1940, Colonel Berry was "the man driving around the camp site on a motorcycle with a sidecar."[35]

A fourth person who deserves notice is Dr. Alan Abraham Klass, BA, MD, FRCS, LLD, the medical officer in Camp R.[36] Klass and his four assistants, all well-trained interned German-Jewish medical practitioners and surgeons, were responsible for the physical and mental health of several hundred officers and soldiers of the Veterans Guard of Canada, attached to the camp, and for the imprisoned 1,150 men and boys in the enclosure. By all accounts, Dr. Klass was a truly remarkable man, who earned unconditional praise from Canadian military and international medical inspectors and most significantly in the homeward-bound letters of inmates of every political *couleur*. At his well-equipped hospital in the wilderness of Red Rock, Dr. Klass used X-ray equipment in the performance of his work, which included hernia and appendix operations and other complex medical treatments. Dr. Klass cared for the general welfare of the soldiers by conducting regular inoculations against typhus and by controlling and treating other contagious and troublesome afflictions such as syphilis.

Dr. Klass was born in the southern Imperial Russian city of Ekaterinoslav in 1907. Seeking a better living, free from the regular threat of anti-Semitic pogroms, his artisan family with eight children

Veterans Guard out for exercise. *[Courtesy of the Red Rock Historical Society]*

came to Canada in 1914 just before the First World War and settled in Winnipeg. There he attended elementary and high school and moved on to the University of Manitoba where he first obtained a BA and then an MD in 1927 and 1932. In later years Dr. Klass earned professional distinctions from the University of Edinburgh, his first Fellowship of the Royal College of Surgeons in 1937, and his second in 1945.

At the outbreak of war, the 32-year-old Dr. Klass, a resident of Winnipeg, volunteered and joined the Royal Canadian Army Medical Corps (RCAMC) and served as Chief Medical Officer at Camp R from its opening day to its closure. Here he placed the welfare of *all* his patients above the principles of rigid military discipline. In the case of one very seriously injured internee, a victim of anti-Semitic violence, Dr. Klass persuaded Commandant Berry to countermand his original order of solitary confinement in order to assure proper treatment of the injured man. The eye-injured man was taken to the hospital, and Dr. Klass was able to save the prisoner's eyesight. Always ready to extend his knowledge of medical phenomena, he noted an astonishing increase in the individual and collective weight of the inmates in Camp R. The weight gain figure for the inmates amounted to 4.5 tons, collectively. Dr. Klass wrote to his colleague, Professor Thompson, at the Medical School in Winnipeg, asking for advice on setting up an appropriate statistical survey for studying this phenomenon. Unfortunately, it is not known if this study was ever completed. After the closure of Camp R, Dr. Klass continued his service with the RCAMC in England and participated in the D-Day landing in June 1944. On the first day of the invasion he established the first operational field hospital in the landing zone.

On his return to civilian life in 1946, Dr. Klass resumed teaching at the Medical School of the University of Manitoba and practising medicine in Winnipeg. In collaboration with other doctors, Dr. Klass established the Mall Medical Group, a clinic offering medical services for a prepaid fixed fee, which served as a forerunner of the widely used American Health Maintenance Organizations (HMOs). Dr. Klass was a popular and well-respected medical practitioner, known for his kindness and compassion and for his skill as a surgeon. During the early 1970s, as chairman of the Manitoba commission on drug costs, he recommended the introduction of the first pharmacare program in Canada, which was later implemented. As a professor in the Faculty of Medicine at the University of Manitoba, Dr. Klass enjoyed the respectful admiration of his students as an effective and inspiring teacher and the professional recognition of his colleagues as an active researcher and author of many professional publications. In addition to his numerous academic and professional research activities, Dr. Klass wrote popular books on the abusive and greedy practices of the pharmaceutical industry. In 1973, in recognition of his many achievements, the University of Manitoba awarded Dr. Klass an LLD. He died at the age of 92.

Captain Kenneth Kirkness, the camp's Intelligence Officer, is another person of importance in Camp R. He was an officer in the British Army and was assigned to Camp R as liaison and Intelligence Officer. He received not only well-deserved high praise from his Canadian superiors, but also contributed constructively to the running of the camp by developing the practice of monthly Morale Reports. Whether Kirkness originated the idea of these reports, which were based on examination and censorship of the prisoners' outgoing and incoming mail, "on interviews, conversations and observation," is not certain. Uncertain about his venture, Kirkness asked to be "informed whether a monthly report of this nature is of value" or "would be desireable in any different form."[37] They were welcomed by his superiors and were widely circulated. In civilian life Kirkness was a writer and translator. He disappeared without a trace on his way back to Britain in May 1941, just as suddenly as he had appeared in July 1940. He published his first monthly Morale Report in August 1940 and the last in March 1941. Kirkness and his assistant Interpreter Warkentine had close contact with the inmates on an almost daily basis. The first Commanding Officer of the Veterans Guard of Canada at Camp R, Major V.P. Torrance, in civilian life a realtor, was promoted in January 1941 and appointed Camp Commandant of the newly opened POW camp at Angler, Camp 101.[38]

Without the old soldiers of the Veterans Guard of Canada, the successful operation of guarding Canada's numerous internment camps in 1940 would have been a very difficult and additional burden on the Canadian Active Service Force (CASF), commonly known as the Canadian Army. The soldiers of No. 10 B Company of the Veterans Guard of Canada played a significant and essential part in the smooth operation of Camp R.[39] On 26 August 1940, a contingent of the recently established Veterans Guard of Canada replaced the Fort Garry Horse, CASF, which returned to its Manitoba barracks. The arrival of the Veterans contingent signalled the end of "dual control" at Red Rock.

Veterans Guard route march. Photo taken west of Roadhouse Tavern.
[Private collection]

Canada-wide, a similar general transfer of military functions from army units to companies of the Veterans Guard of Canada also occurred at other internment camps. The Veterans Guard unit stationed at Camp R consisted of ten officers and 310 other ranks.

The origin of this new military corps can be traced back to concerns first raised by the leaders of the Canadian Legion over the state of home security as early as 1938. Legion leaders proposed the creation of an auxiliary body of ex-members of the Canadian Expeditionary Force (CEF) into a national organization operated on a civil defence basis by the Department of National Defence. The Legion leaders saw that the purpose of this new national organization could be in the provisioning of guards, protecting essential installations against sabotage, and preventing potential public disorders. The Canadian government responded reluctantly and dilatorily despite the Legion's ardent and energetic agitation. By conducting a nationwide survey of First World War veterans, the Legion collected an impressive response of 80,000 names of persons who were willing to serve the country, if needed. Legion leaders eagerly proposed additional organizational details, types of uniforms, rank hierarchy and pay rates for the utilization of this patriotic military *levée en masse*. They found support for their scheme from understaffed provincial police forces and even the RCMP. Rising tension in Europe's international relations and perceived threats to the British Empire energized the Legion and its allies, and finally the federal government agreed to hire Special Constables under the control of the police. With the outbreak of war came rising demands for combat soldiers and the subsequent need for auxiliary military troops capable of performing non-combat functions such as providing guard personnel for military installations vulnerable to sabotage.

The culmination of the Legion's agitation, one might say, came on 23 May 1940 in the House of Commons when the Minister of Pensions and Veterans Affairs announced the formation of a "Volunteer Force for the Protection of Military Property and Other Necessary Purposes." An order of cabinet issued on 24 May 1940 initiated the establishment of the new Corps, originally known as Veterans Home Guard, consisting of twelve companies of 250, all ranks, each under the command of a Major. Soon, by January 1941, the number of Corps had grown to 15 and finally to 29 companies "with a total strength of 206 officers and 6,360 other ranks."[40] Recruits for the Corps had to be veterans of the First World War, less than fifty years old, who were physically and mentally fit. In some Military Districts, the rush to join the Corps was overwhelming, while in others recruitment was disappointingly slow. The motivation for joining up fluctuated from one extreme to another.

At Saskatchewan's recruitment centres, they ran out of proper uniforms, and at first the new soldiers had to wear armbands over their civilian dress to signify their new military status. Some men enlisted because the persistent Depression had kept them long enough unemployed and in a state of involuntary leisure, idleness and poverty. For them enrolment in the Veterans Guard was the quickest and easiest way of upgrading their lifestyles. Others were bored working on the farm or at their regular factory jobs; they sought adventure. A few missed the camaraderie of the military life during the "Great War"; very likely, they had never become fully reintegrated into civilian life, and here was their chance to escape back to the comforts of the old soldier's life. A few saw an opportunity to escape the vicissitudes of domestic life. Many tried to enlist in the regular army, but were rejected for one reason or another, and the Veterans Guard offered a substitute. There were also those anxious to fight and die for King, Empire, and Country, especially against "the Huns," whether led by "Kaiser" or "Führer." Several had personal motives; they sought to utilize their previous experience in German POW camps during the first war. Almost all who came were enlisted initially, even those over fifty-five, until gradually many were eliminated for lack of discipline and fitness, perpetual drunkenness or similar disabilities.

The first commander of the Veterans Guard was Colonel H.R. Alley, who commanded the Corps until September 1944, when he voluntarily resigned. Colonel Alley was a conscientious officer who measured the performance of his officers and soldiers by high, perhaps slightly idealistic standards in order to eliminate the Army's and the public's perception of the Home Guard's military inferiority. This perception was reflected in the Corps' nickname "Alley Cats." Colonel Alley hoped to overcome this popular stigma by having high expectations for his officers, who had to be "sober, trustworthy, resolute, energetic and resourceful." They needed to meet, furthermore, "a reasonable standard of education, and manners" and have a strong sense of duty and responsibility. Moreover, he encouraged them to care for their NCOS and soldiers by getting to know them personally and becoming aware of their family situations. Naturally, officers had to assure that their charges were well informed about their duties and well trained in handling their weapons.

In order to improve further the public's perceptions of the Corps, Alley advocated and finally succeeded in obtaining the Army's consent for sending one company of Veterans Guard to London, England, in order to assume guard duties at the Canadian Military Headquarters. Overseas service was seen as a sign of recognition and distinction. Other Veterans Guard companies saw overseas service in Newfoundland, the Bahamas and Nassau, and British Guiana. In each of these locations the Canadian veterans protected important and vulnerable military properties such as port facilities and industrial complexes. At home, the Veterans Guard was primarily deployed in the guarding of internment camps for POWs, civilian internees or refugees. Regardless of where the Veterans Guard served or what their specific duties were, they acquitted themselves with honour and distinction, through efficiency and effectiveness under non-glamorous circumstances.

In June 1943, at the apex of its existence, the Veterans Guard of Canada numbered 451 officers and 9,806 other ranks. In addition, the Corps counted 43 reserve companies with 183 officers and 3,765 other ranks. Nonetheless, despite Colonel Alley's various efforts to improve the Corps' image, when he was replaced by Colonel J.M. Taylor, the Corps' nickname merely changed to "Taylor's Toothless Tigers," on account of the Corps' badge showing a Scottish tiger. In view of the service rendered, both nicknames were inappropriate and undeserved. On 31 March 1945, the Corps still counted an overall active strength of 8,453 officers and men, and reserve strength of 1,937. The Corps was disbanded in March 1947.

At Camp R, the primary duty of the Veterans Guard was to assure the security of the inmates, the prevention of escape and the maintenance of good order and discipline in the enclosure. In practical terms, it meant guarding and escorting prisoners and preventing escape by means of tunnelling, hiding in vehicles, absconding from work details, or attempting breakouts. Commanded by their own officers, the Veterans Guard nonetheless stood under the direct command of the camp commandant. At Camp R, the Veterans Guard manned the guard-house, which controlled direct access to and exit from the camp area, the compound and the enclosure. At all times, three sentries manned each of the five watchtowers that surrounded the enclosure, and each watchtower was equipped with a machine gun. Eighteen sentries served in each night shift, patrolling outside the enclosure's perimeter barbed wire fences.

Camp R had a special unit of enclosure "police" called "provosts." A provost sergeant who was assisted by a number of men led this provost police force. All were selected with "great care" from the Fort Garry Horse by the camp commandant, "for work inside the wire compound or enclosure." The provosts were armed with blackjacks, "hidden from view," and whistles, the former to be used only in self-defence. This police force was responsible for "constantly patrol[ling]" the enclosure, day and night. Provosts were to observe the inmates' compliance with camp rules, prevent illegal assemblies, detect escape preparations or the prohibited production of alcoholic beverages, and report on morale or catch snippets of conversations with potential subversive implica-tions for the security and "good order" of the camp. "Any infractions and subversive or suspicious acts [had to be reported] promptly to the Camp Commandant." Their special attention was drawn to the preven-tion of escapes, and they were urged "to study questions pertaining to escape and familiarize themselves with methods employed." They were to read "in detail" the Directorate's "Notes on the Prevention of Escape of Prisoners of War."[41]

The life of the Veterans Guard at Camp R was regulated by the routine of a twenty-four hour cycle of work and rest: a whole day's duty followed by a day off-duty. Life was quite monotonous, interrupted only by regular drill and training periods. Each soldier had to know the relevant standing orders that set out in careful details his many

CN supply truck with some local residents, near the guardhouse. *[Private collection]*

responsibilities in various daily routine situations and also in case of extraordinary occurrences. In addition, soldiers were trained in the use of rifle and bayonet, map reading and the handling of a light machine gun. Camp R's armament included Vickers machine guns and Lewis guns, and sufficient ammunition for the regular firing practice that was recommended to intimidate the inmates. The older medium Vickers machine gun was water-cooled, recoil-operated, tripod-mounted and fed by a belt with 250 rounds of .303-inch calibre, and had a rate of fire of 500 rounds per minute. In contrast, the somewhat newer, but still obsolescent First World War–era Lewis light machine gun was air-cooled and gas-operated, with a horizontal drum magazine with forty-seven rounds of .303-inch calibre and a rate of fire of 500 rounds per minute.[42] Often the soldiers' training included the use of hand grenades and tear

A view from a watchtower with a well-maintained Lewis gun.
[Courtesy of the Red Rock Historical Society]

gas grenades for crowd control. Later the Veterans Guard was trained in judo, boxing and first aid. Eventually, lectures on discipline, methods of searching, contraband detection and general guard responsibility were added. Initially, Camp R's Veterans Guard needed intensive training in vigilance and coping with the geographic peculiarities of the camp ground with its trenches, culverts and ditches and the unused machinery scattered around the former construction site. In addition, soldiers were expected to maintain their uniforms in order to present a clean and neat appearance always.

Normally, soldiers had little direct contact with the inmates, except when working as a provost or together with them in the guards' kitchen or mess, at the Red Rock Inn in the Officers' Mess, or on other fatigue details, or when escorting them to and from the daily shower parade, sports activities, swimming or ice hockey parades. Fraternization was strictly forbidden for everyone: officers, NCOs and soldiers. Talking to the inmates was forbidden except for the communication of orders. Any exchange of money, gifts, souvenirs, newspapers, magazines or letters or any agreement to requests for such items was strictly forbidden and punishable. Only the camp commandant or his deputies were allowed to communicate directly with the inmates.

The Veterans Guard were housed in the twenty houses standing on the property of the Lake Sulphite mill ground. These quarters were crowded and furnished with double bunk beds, tables and chairs. The comfort level of the soldiers apparently barely exceeded that of the inmates. The recreation facilities for the guards in the camp were primitive and Spartan at best. Guards were left to unlimited conversations about sports, women or family affairs, card games, reading, job talk and limited drinking. The nearby Village of Nipigon, eight kilometres on foot along the CPR tracks, or fifteen kilometres by road, offered only a handful of bars and cafés as entertainment attractions. The Lakehead's twin cities, Port Arthur and Fort William (now Thunder Bay), a hundred kilometres west, on the other hand, had plenty of real and varied amusements to sell in bars and bordellos, in cafés and diners, movie theatres and dance halls. There the entertainment tended to be lively and energetic; therefore Berry was forced periodically to post the names of selected establishments and entertainment centres and declare these "off-limits" to the soldiers from Camp R. In December 1940 the off-limit list advertised these names: Devon Café, Diamond Café, The Candy Kitchen Restaurant, Twin City Winery, Kimberley Hotel, Stanley Café and the Popular Café.[43] (Not one of them exists today.) No reasons were given for these prohibitions. When random venereal disease parades revealed the presence of this affliction among the Veterans Guard, condoms were issued to all. While this prophylactic measure might have placed a damper on the more cautious of the many who sought entertainment among the various pleasures locally available, it apparently did not restrain those more daring and venturesome.

At Camp R, as elsewhere, the Veterans' life was routine and monotonous, far removed even from the small pleasures of small communities. Red Rock was an isolated hamlet in the backwoods of Northwestern Ontario. It was a hard life for the old soldiers. Faced by prolonged routine and little change in their soldier's life, the Veterans were vulnerable to a certain staleness that could decrease their keenness and alertness. In order to combat this condition, the Veterans Guard units assigned to each camp were regularly rotated every four to five months, and underwent a month of training before returning to regular guard duty once more. The available records for Camp R do not show the occurrence of any dramatic or unusual incidents of any sort between Veterans and internees during the sixteen months of operation, although occasional fraternization did occur.

V

Settling In and Sorting Out

AFTER THE LONG AND RELATIVELY comfortable but quite uneventful train journey from Quebec City across half of Canada, the imprisoned internees arrived at their appointed destination, Camp R, in the early morning of 2 July. The officers and soldiers of the Fort Garry Horse, waiting on the earthen platform of the Red Rock railway station, were pumped up not only by war propaganda and sensational news reports in the media, but also by official communications from the Directorate of Internment Operations. They sincerely believed that these men dismounting from the train were dangerous enemy aliens, treacherous fifth columnists, saboteurs and captured POWs. They knew that these imprisoned men had been shipped out to Canada by Britain for easier safekeeping because they represented a grave military security risk. By guarding these dangerous prisoners, the soldiers knew that they were assisting the homeland, Great Britain, in time of great peril, when facing the threat of an imminent Nazi German invasion.

The Fort Garry Horse leaving to meet train with prisoners. *[Private collection]*

Official communications on these matters appeared in the circulars General Panet sent to the commanding officers of Military Districts 2, 3, 4, 5, 7, 10 and 13. On 28 and 29 June 1940, he alerted the camp commandants about the incoming shipment of deportees: "We have a very bad lot to deal with," he warned. "Most of these prisoners are desperate, and will, no doubt, stop at nothing to escape." Underlining this warning, Panet quoted Captain J.P. Kemp, the British Liaison Officer who had accompanied the internees, claiming—incorrectly—that "during the voyage [of the *Duchess of York*] one [of the prisoners] was killed, three were wounded and another committed suicide." Panet warned the camp commandants of their very difficult and important task. Internees were to be stripped "to the skin" and "very carefully scrutinized." Clothing was to be searched on arrival in camp in order

Arrival at Camp R, July 1940. *[Courtesy of the Red Rock Historical Society]*

to find "lists showing the names of Gestapo agents, which it is of the greatest importance to obtain" and which "the Intelligence Service of England knows that some" of the prisoners would carry. The final paragraph of Panet's circular continued to reflect the near-hysteria about the incoming internees that was prevalent in the Directorate at the end of June 1940, when Panet wrote, "I would like also to draw your attention to the possibility of Nazi and Fascist sympathizers, from across the border, attempting to drop arms and machine guns, and even parachutists, to these prisoners, by means of aeroplanes. Remember that this is the chief reason why Great Britain is sending these prisoners over here. Some of our Camps lend themselves to this more than others, but it is important not to disclose the location of any of them."[1]

For many prisoners the arrival at Red Rock was a harrowing experience. Arriving in the early morning, the group of 1,150 was met by heavily armed soldiers who assembled and counted the prisoners before marching them off "into a virtual wilderness" towards a barbed wire enclosure two kilometres distant. The enclosure stretched along the shoreline of Nipigon Bay. A main road led to the mill building from the hamlet and railway stop. Eugen Spier, the only known memoirist of Camp R, who arrived on 2 July 1940, later recalled being met at the entrance by "fierce and vigilant soldiers with rifles and fixed bayonets ready to charge at us at any moment; others with army revolvers held their fingers at the triggers ready to shoot instantly."[2] The prisoners' belongings were searched once again, and then they were led to "huts" that would house 28–30 prisoners each.

The hutments inside the enclosure were originally built to house construction workers on site and were placed very close together, thus leaving practically no free space inside this holding pen either for assembling the inmates for roll call or for providing recreational space for playing sports. On entering the huts, the prisoners noted that the twenty-eight army-style double bunk beds were without bedding, blankets and pillows. Chairs, tables, benches and cupboards were also missing for the first two days. The large dining hall and the kitchen, both located at the bottom of the camp slope near the Bay, had neither cutlery and dishes nor pots and pans, respectively.[3] It took the organizing skills of the Canadian military only two days to correct these deficiencies and to procure a dozen missing stoves. Obviously, Camp R was not entirely ready to welcome its new tenants, but unlike some other Canadian internment camps its sanitary facilities sufficed and were in excellent working order from the very beginning.[4] The camp area and the compound covered the space south of Trout Creek and up to and beyond the mill building; the creek flowed from Mount How in the west, eastwards into Nipigon Bay.

The huts were surrounded by three-metre-high barbed wired double fences, and four five-metre-high watchtowers were placed around the

Veterans Guard outside the guardhouse at Trout Creek Bridge.
[Courtesy of the Red Rock Historical Society]

enclosure. The newly erected Red Rock Inn, designed originally to serve as quarters to the Lake Sulphite Pulp and Paper Company's local and visiting managers and officials, was also found near the enclosure, and it served the needs of the local military officers. Yet, despite the security, prisoners were informed upon first arrival that the screen-covered windows should not be approached; they were not allowed to leave the huts unless instructed; and they were not to approach the door, as "the soldiers on guard had been given instructions to shoot with intent to kill without any further warning immediately [if] we appeared in the vicinity" of any opening. To reinforce this point, shortly after Spier and his 1,150 comrades were introduced to what he described as "a third-rate jungle prison," shots rang out; someone in an accompanying hut had apparently approached a window. "An officer," he recalls, "came into our hut, cautioning us in very definite terms, that anyone who approached the window or the doors was liable to be shot. So we sat down on the floor stretching our tired bodies in expectation of what was to come."[5] Spier's forlorn reminiscence reflected the essential elements of the prisoners' new, sobering and disappointing Canadian reality. Prisoners found themselves in "a situation similar to that of kidnapped persons dragged into the wilderness, thousands of miles from home, torn away from our friends with nobody to ransom us."[6]

Every Canadian internment camp consisted of these component parts:[7] First, there was the "military area," which included the entire zone over which the camp commandant exercised full jurisdiction. Private airplanes were forbidden to fly over this area, and vessels could not venture into it without authorization. Second was the "camp area," which designated the space in which the stationed troops moved about freely without special permission, while civilians needed passes as they did also for the military area. Third, "the compound," was the actual camp, or "the Camp proper," in which were located the quarters of officers and soldiers and also various buildings and installations used by the troops and required for the operation of the camp. The fourth part, "the enclosure," housed the prisoners and was the *raison d'être* for the camp. The enclosure formed part of the compound and was often confused with the compound even by superior officers. The fifth, "the yard," was the recreation area.

However, while officially Camp R was off-limits to all unauthorized persons, the local children apparently enjoyed access to and played in the camp zone.[8] In addition to the mill building, the Inn and the twenty semi-finished houses, the camp area included a hospital, recreation huts, a kitchen and dining hall for the troops, repair shops, a pump house with a chlorination equipment shed, and garages. Camp R, however, was not, as some authors have incorrectly asserted, an "unused mining camp," nor was it located in "Nippigon [sic]."[9]

A good view of the wire. [LAC-e006611163]

Once settled in and having absorbed the first shocking surprises of their new situation, Spier and his fellow prisoners found time to record descriptions of the camp's surroundings.[10] Spier's personal observations and description caught the pristine wild surroundings of Camp R, but they also reveal prisoners' misinformation about the camp's geopolitical location. The American border was at least 150 kilometres southwest of Red Rock, at the Pigeon River Border Crossing, and not across the lake from the camp, as prisoners seemed to think. While the inmates inside the enclosure settled into the new camp routine, spending time and effort on establishing new, intangible but very real, boundary lines among themselves—sometimes as old friends, sharing a common past in Britain, and sometimes as old foes—the local military authority, from

Commandant Berry and his staff down to the officers and men in the lower ranks, underwent a process of getting to know their charges.

In the absence of necessary official identification documents from Britain, and in the light of such official Canadian information as Panet's circular, this evidently was a very perplexing experience. Obviously, the very large number of young apprentices, the 15- and 16-year-old schoolboys and the slightly older university students, whose spoken English "was so damn good," could hardly be the ferocious Nazi parachutists the British military had announced and the Canadian newspapers had warned about. And neither, really, could the old men be parachutists. The large number of sailors explained that they were actually civilian merchant mariners and not soldiers of the *Kriegsmarine*. Moreover, all prisoners showed an astonishing and appalling lack of military bearing and discipline, which one would naturally associate with German soldiers trained under the Prussian-Nazi military system. Of course every inmate presented his own peculiar identity. They all denied they deserved the label of "prisoners of war." The inmates saw themselves as Jews, anti-Nazis, refugees, and German nationals, as civilian internees and interned merchant seamen. Only a small number admitted and professed, proudly and defiantly, their Nazi sentiments.

Puzzled, the Canadians asked: if you are a Jew, an anti-Nazi, a refugee from Hitler's *Grossdeutschland*, why are you then fighting for the Nazis? And if you are not a Nazi, why are you in prison? Before these questions could be answered satisfactorily, it was best to be "on guard," to observe and apply the prescribed standing orders as they related to these prisoners. Listening to the contradictory claims of the inmates only caused confusion, for who could believe any of it? None of their confusing tales could be verified. All that military officials knew, whether in Ottawa or in Red Rock, was that the prisoners at Camp R were dangerous enemy aliens who presented a military security risk and had been classified by British tribunals as Category A—enemies of Great Britain—and were part of "a very bad lot."

Into this confusing situation, Spier injected himself as he modestly reported in his memoirs: "I was asked to try to obtain an interview with the Commandant," in order to be granted canteen privileges of purchasing cigarettes, tobacco, chocolates, etc. "and to get access to our money."[11] Spier, unfortunately, did not say who of his fellow inmates asked him to initiate this first contact with Berry. It would seem likely that he was encouraged by Dr. Lachmann, or by Ship Captain Scharf and others who possessed credit accounts and with whom he had previously collaborated as canteen and account manager in Lingfield and in other English camps. Perhaps he also hoped to obtain a chance to send a letter or cable to his family in England.[12] Spier's first direct personal encounter with an officer guard—and vice versa—is quite illuminating. In the course of his conversation with the officer, Spier recalled:

> I heard to my greatest surprise and horror, that he was told that all of us were either parachutists, airborne Nazi troops dropped in civilian clothes on English soil, or the remainder of us belonged to a secret Nazi organization set up in England for the purpose of supporting landing airborne troops. He also stated that I was caught red-handed and made a prisoner with the others at the recently attempted invasion, which according to his information, had failed, and was completed defeated and wiped out, and in consequence of which we were made prisoners.[13]

Spier tried to explain "our real position" and assure the officer that "he was quite wrongly informed and that we were definitely the victims of, to say the least, a gross misunderstanding."

As Spier and his co-internees were discussing these disturbing disclosures based on false information and inflammatory war propaganda, their "discussion came suddenly to an end, when a detachment of soldiers entered the hut led by an officer who held a whip in one hand and a revolver of frightening size in the other. Ordering us to assemble in abreast [sic], he directed us with the help of his whip and at the point of his revolver from the hut through the Camp to a fairly large-sized building." Once inside the dining hall the prisoners "were pushed nervously with the butts of [the soldiers'] rifles." Both officers and men, Spier noted, displayed "nervousness and excitement" during these herding operations.[14] After all was this bad lot not crack parachutists?

In due course Spier was granted his interview with cc Berry, who received him "in the open, just outside the barbed wire, accompanied by a bodyguard consisting of a few soldiers. He received me in what could be described a business-like, confidence-inspiring way." Berry inquired who Spier was and what he wanted, and Spier explained that in England he had been the "Internees Canteen Accounts" manager and that he carried with him a statement certified, "by the English officer in charge, showing the amount due to each internee." In response to Spier's requests, Berry produced a telegram from the War Office in London asserting that "due to enemy action these remittances were delayed" and that the same applied to the absence of the internees' luggage and their belongings "which we were promised would travel with us." Spier of course took this opportunity to inform cc Berry "who we actually were" and that "we were neither caught red-handed on the battlefield, nor on the supposed landing from the air as parachutists, and that all these stories were libellous inventions and blatant lies."[15]

Having delivered his view of the reality of the situation, Spier proceeded to enlighten Berry about "the opposing parties inside the Camp" and proposed not only to separate Nazis from anti-Nazis, but also to release the latter as "a matter of elementary justice" which would save Berry "a lot of trouble and facilitate [Berry's] task of keeping peace and order inside the Camp." According to Spier, Commandant Berry responded with great frankness to Spier's suggestions: "The sooner I get rid of you, the better I shall like it." This first encounter between an inmate and the chief local jailer was quite inauspicious. It is impossible at this late date to say if this meeting inaugurated a process of enlightenment for cc Berry and his staff about the true nature of their charges.[16]

Even while the nature of the prisoners was an item for discussion, another aspect of the prisoner-guard relationship was slowly developing. Although the initial officer guard did not accept Spier's explanation that they were not "crack parachutists," he made a suggestion "that we should let him have some of our military decorations, swastika emblems or any other Nazi emblems, as his friends were most eager to get some of these as souvenirs."[17] For many, such offers for "a real swastika," while enticing in the prisoners' penniless position, "was of little or no value since we could buy nothing with it here in this wilderness." However, these items were useful in attempts by prisoners to communicate with others. Spier mentions that some officers allowed exchange of these "souvenirs" for permission to contact other recently captured prisoners in other huts "without being shot." They were also exchanged in barter for "cigarettes, tobacco, chocolate, writing paper etc."[18] News of the arrangement spread among the prisoners, and the contact also allowed for Spier to inform his co-internees about the situation, namely how they had been "libelled and labelled as parachutists," so they all understood the "militant attitude and alertness of the Guard."[19]

Who really were the inmates of Camp R? The official Canadian military record, dated 21 September 1940, listed 1,142 inmates inside Camp R's enclosure and in addition counted one absent escapee, two mentally ill internees in the hospital at Port Arthur, and five internees already returned to Britain in August 1940. Four of the returnees were members of the German consular staff at Reykjavik, Iceland, who should never have been interned in the first place under the prevailing rules of international law. They had been arrested originally "by mistake," as the British claimed, and were then shipped again "by mistake" to Canada. The fifth returnee was Dr. Erich Paul Meissner, who was needed for war work back in Britain. He too should never have been jailed.[20] The total added up to 1,150 prisoners. Swiss diplomats, representing either the International Committee of the Red Cross (ICRC) of Geneva or the Protecting Power, produced varying accounts, one numbering 1,146 inmates and one giving an inflated total of 1,186.[21] These diplomatic reports, unfortunately, do not offer any explanation of how their data were collected. It can be assumed with certainty that the military record was based on the daily roll calls.

There are no precise statistics available concerning the distribution of age, nationality (ethnicity) and occupation among the inmates of Camp R. On his first visit to the camp, General Panet observed the large number of "boys under eighteen" as the most obvious characteristic of the camp, as well as a large number of young adults. Indeed 144 were under age eighteen, and 197 persons were under twenty. The youngest inmate was fifteen years old and the oldest was seventy-one. There were nine seventeen-year-olds and three sixteen-year-olds in the camp. Panet's impression of this "youth factor" in the camp prompted him to make his original proposal to open up a special camp just for youth under eighteen. His suggestion, however, failed to get the necessary approval and support from his political and military superiors. Although several general references were made to the presence of older men in camp, one can safely assume that their share of the total camp population was less than 20 per cent.[22]

Based on self-identification, these nationalities lived in the enclosure: 1,099 Germans, four Poles, one Spaniard, one Yugoslav, one Norwegian, one Czech and 38 stateless ex-Germans, totalling 1,045 persons. Other calculations offered these numbers: 80 (or 82) anti-Nazis, subdivided into two Jews, 40 merchant seamen and 40 civilians; 100 boys and 120 pro-Nazi youths, as well as 700 "enemy merchant seamen" (EMS), 82 "South African" Nazis, 62 civilians and 40 ship captains, totalling 1,186. One report identified a group of "172 Poles and Jews," including 78 Jews. Yet another source sets this group's number at 178. One source listed 850 EMS, 120 non-refugees and 180 anti-Nazis, Jews and members of the International Seamen's Union, totalling 1,150 men.[23]

Not only do these varying statistical groupings not add up correctly, but they also do not ever reveal the basis on which the author(s) constructed their concepts or their numbers. Who, for example, was a Pole?

A person of Polish ethnic origin born and living in the then-German provinces of Silesia or Posen, or a German citizen living in Poland? Who, for instance, constituted the group of 172 or 178 Jews and Poles? If the Jews numbered seventy-eight, did this figure include the eleven Jewish schoolboys "from Scotland," originally classified as "C," but now securely lodged in an "A" Nazi camp? Were there 98 or 100 Poles altogether in the camp?

Unfortunately, no source provides definitive numbers describing the exact size and composition of any of these various subgroups. Not surprisingly, Jewish and anti-Nazi internees refused to have any contact with the Swiss Consuls, representing the ICRC, whom they regarded as representatives of Nazi Germany. Their position, understandable as it was, did not facilitate the gathering of reliable information and statistics. Whose numbers can one trust? These data only provide indicators rather than reliable figures. Furthermore, they tell us very little about the inmates as groups, as communities. What can be asserted with absolute certainty, however, is that Camp R did not at any time lodge either pilots of the *Luftwaffe* or U-boat captains and crews. Notwithstanding local and regional folklore, Camp R was exclusively an internment camp for civilian Prisoners of War.

Readily perceivable is that the camp's aggregate of inmates fell into two distinct yet numerically quite unequal segments, the mariners and the non-mariners. The number of mariners was undoubtedly the largest, at approximately 770. In contrast, the non-mariners numbered only about 375 men. Furthermore, this second group was divided into smaller subgroups, each with distinct social and political attributes. These diverse, unequal groups were forced to co-exist in an enclosed area of roughly one square kilometre. A closer look at each of these groups may assist in understanding the social and political dynamics that operated, or failed to operate, in Camp R.

The mariners were German civilian merchant seamen designated as Enemy Merchant Seamen (EMS) in the official terminology, and included ship captains, ship officers and crews who had previously manned German luxury liners and merchant vessels. The British automatically placed all the mariners with Category A civilian internees. The EMS had been captured by the British in many different ways. Some were taken from German merchant ships anchored in British or Commonwealth ports or in ports under British control at the outbreak of war; others were captured on the high seas, especially the luxury liners, as these ships attempted to run the British blockade on their way home to Germany from North and South America, Africa and Asia. Several were taken prisoner during the Norway campaign while working as crew on German supply ships.

Captain Kirkness described the EMS as "in themselves decent, simple, happy (in so far as it is possible for a man behind barbed wire to be happy) men [sic]."[24] The seamen came with different social backgrounds. The vast majority of the EMS had completed eight years of elementary schooling, from age six to fourteen, under the then-existing German school system. Captains and officers, in contrast, had completed either six years of high school education, from age ten to sixteen, or had graduated with the *abitur*, after a nine-year course of study from age ten to nineteen. The levels of skills varied widely among the EMS, who ranged from unskilled sailors to highly skilled cooks, headwaiters, machinists and navigators. A large number of fifteen- and sixteen-year-old boys had been apprentices, working as cabin boys or cooks on the luxury liners, learning the necessary skills of their future vocations as ship stewards or ship cooks. The forty ship captains and an undetermined number of merchant marine ship officers among the EMS "were of quite superior type and largely anti-Nazi." They were widely respected by their crews and exercised a certain degree of authority within the camp. Unfortunately, no evidence exists which would allow identification of ship crews in Camp R.[25]

The numerically much smaller non-mariner group of approximately four hundred was very diverse socially and professionally. Within this group were primarily German- and Austrian-born citizens; however, some may have had different ethnic and national affiliations such as Czechoslovakian, Polish, Galician and Sudeten.[26] Some Germans were long-time residents of Britain where they had achieved success in professional and business careers. Crucially, they had failed to become naturalized before 1939. Many were embittered, puzzled and depressed about their treatment by the English. Most had no sympathy for the Nazis in Germany. Quite a few had served in the German or Austrian Imperial Army as young men during the First World War, and many of them had likely been officers. Some may have been liberally minded German patriots. Half the prisoners in this non-mariner group were interned Jewish and anti-Nazi refugees from Nazi Germany, and a group of approximately one hundred consisted of professed Nazis and their sympathizers.[27]

German- and Austrian-born Jews in Camp R numbered perhaps 78. They came from all walks of life, from business and the professions; were journalists or academics, or ordinary workmen; most were either elderly or very young schoolboys, apprentices and university students. Ronald Stent includes in this group ten *yeshiva* youngsters and their teacher.[28] There were possibly thirty to forty religious Orthodox Jews in this group. At the time of their arrests, many Jews were in transit to other destinations, awaiting their visas or the call-up of their quota number in order to emigrate to Palestine, the United States, different countries in South America or various locations within the British Empire. Camp R's four medical doctors came from this group.

More important and certainly more troublesome than the social distinctions among inmates were their political divisions. These presented unbridgeable schisms and dominated camp life, determining and sometimes disrupting the daily relations between the inmates, especially during the first six months of the camp's operation. While CC Berry, his administrative staff and the officers and soldiers of the Veterans Guard of Canada, looking in from the outside, saw the inmates in the enclosure, collectively and primarily, simply as "prisoners of war," Intelligence Officer Kirkness was, in contrast, almost an insider. He enjoyed a closer, more comprehensive and nuanced view of the inmates and reported a perceptive analysis of their political divisions. Kirkness, perhaps more than any other officer, knew the temper of the inmates in the enclosure.[29]

The vexatious political issues that divided the inmates arose from contemporary, national, domestic and international politics. In Camp R, the adherents of the dominant *Weltanschauungen* confronted each other directly. On one side stood the proponents of Fascism and Nazism, and on the other, the supporters of Liberalism, Democracy, Socialism and Communism. General Panet noted the existence of these sharp political distinctions on his first visit to the camp at the end of July. Having scrutinized eighty-three outgoing letters written by inmates since 23 July, Kirkness noted, in his first Morale Report of August 1940, one common complaint shared by both Nazis and anti-Nazis: their mutual abhorrence of living together in one and the same camp. On the basis of this early information Kirkness predicted perceptively that sooner or later this intense hostility towards each other would lead to "incidents of more or less serious nature." While his September and October Reports, generally speaking, mentioned the prevailing political tension in the camp, it was not until his November Report, No. 5, that he offered a more detailed analysis of the political scene in the enclosure. For example, Kirkness discerned that:

> Camp R is a "mixed camp" which means that there are present both kinds of Germans. Those who are *for* [sic] Hitler and those who are not. Although this sounds a quite simple and clear-cut division, in Camp R, the "mixture" is by no means a straightforward one of two ingredients. The "Hitler" group can be divided into (a) radical, out-and-out National-Socialists, (b) recognizable but mild supporters of National-Socialism, (c) those who are National-Socialists, not from conviction, but for personal convenience, and (d) those who are secretly opposed to Nazism, but who purposely conceal their opposition for fear of bringing ruin upon themselves and their relations. The Anti-Hitler group contains no less than fifteen distinct types of prisoner. It contains genuine refugees; near-Communists; political

fugitives; police fugitives; adventurers; Devisenschieber;—currency
smugglers [sic]; International Trade Unionists and, possibly, a few Nazi
agents in sheep's clothing.[30]

Kirkness's idiosyncratic tabulation deserves a closer look.
Unquestionably, his first subgroup of the pro-Hitler bloc included
of course the band of 82 "South African" Nazis and a small group of
German nationals such as Pastor Fritz Wehrhahn and Baron Pilar. The
"South Africans" were a group of German merchants, professionals and
journalists, living in the former German Imperial African colonies, who
had been gathered up by the British, interned, then taken to England
and from there shipped off to Red Rock. They were older men "of good
education and considerable experience of the world," in Kirkness's
view, and "on this account they exercised a fairly powerful, out of all
proportion to their numbers, influence on the camp life." All were committed radical Nazis. They particularly influenced the younger EMS,
who were politically inexperienced and lacking in worldly wisdom. The
chief instrument of their influence and success apparently was Edwin
Guelcher, an experienced and notorious Nazi leader and journalist from
former German South West Africa—now Namibia—who assumed from
the very start the influential function of the camp's sport-*führer*. The
"South Africans" rivalled the authority of the ship captains among the
seamen.[31]

The bulk of the pro-Hitler bloc were the large crowd of fellow
travellers, members of Kirkness's subgroups (b) and (c), those who
opportunistically and obediently, and perhaps unthinkingly, followed
the dominant political current of opinion in the camp. This large group
was recruited from the merchant marine. In the opening weeks and
months, the camp's ruling opinion was decidedly shaped, whether
deliberately or accidentally, by rumours and bits of speculative information about decisive German military victories, an imminent German
invasion, the expected collapse of Britain, and an eventual German
victory, followed by a quick and glorious return home to Nazi Germany.

Easily influenced and generally uncritical, ill-informed and confused about the current political issues and the military progress of the war, the men in this lot were resentful and angry about their imprisonment and their present situation, and perhaps even ridden with feelings of guilt about their inglorious capture and enforced inactivity, while elsewhere the big actions of the day were being carried out without them.

These men, especially the younger EMS, had not only experienced at least six years of education under Nazi rule and Nazi propaganda, but had also witnessed the actual and impressive improvements in German life such as the elimination of mass unemployment and the restoration of German prestige abroad. They were aware of the international acquiescence, even approval, of the Nazis' many achievements.[32] In their trusting naïveté, these achievements were uncritically accepted and perceived as causes of national pride. In these years, before the horrors of the "final solution" and the Holocaust were being executed, the Nazi terror against German Jews was seen quite often by most other Germans as aberrations perpetrated by zealots of the *Sturmabteilung* (SA) rather than the implementation of the Nazi Party's ideology of racial purity and Nazi government policies. It remains open to speculation whether these young men, anxious to please and conform, were essentially Nazis who were exhibiting their rekindled patriotic and nationalist feelings or were just venting their temporary frustrations through vulgar anti-Semitism and acts of juvenile bravado.

By December 1940, it seems political fervour and anti-Semitic outbursts had diminished noticeably; and following their transfer to other camps after the closure of Camp R, this EMS crowd remained tranquil and politically uninvolved. In different circumstances, they would very likely have happily followed different leaders and different directives. But for now it sufficed that these young men, while in Camp R, followed the popular Nazi sport-*führer* Guelcher and the other radical Nazis and participated, emotionally and unthinkingly, in singing such provocative Nazi songs as the *Horst Wessel Lied* ("The Horst Wessel Song," the official Nazi anthem), *Und Heute Gehoert Uns Deutschland und Morgen die*

Ganze Welt ("Today only Germany Belongs to Us, Tomorrow the Whole World"), and *Und Wir Fahren Gegen Engeland* ("And We Journey Against England").

In his tabulation of the "Types of Internees" in Camp R, Kirkness placed the "total number of Nazis [at] 951" and explained that "this is the number of those whom one must consider (in the absence of any proof to the contrary) as Nazis or supporters of the Nazi Regime. They are not necessarily members of the Party, or a sub-organization of the Party." Kirkness's loose definition of Nazi would include every German national who was not Jewish or a political refugee; a German patriotic Christian, practising silent resistance to Nazism, would obviously not escape Kirkness's label.

Spier's observation that he found willing workers and assistants without any difficulty, even among those who were labelled officially or by fellow inmates as fierce and ardent Nazis, to help him in the operations of the camp canteen or to perform personal services for him, supports Kirkness's opening assumption that the sailors were basically decent men if freed from such evil "influence" as exerted by Nazi leaders. A two-page, typewritten letter composed many years later by an unidentified former young EMS inmate of Camp R still reflects the basic elements of naïveté and uncritical simplicity characteristic of the political perceptions held among the EMS crowd in the camp.

The writer offered several interesting recollections about his internment experience in Britain and at Red Rock, perhaps with fading or distorting memories. He came over on the *Duchess of York* to Quebec City, not Halifax as he claims, on 29 June, and not on either 1 July or 30 June. He recalled encountering some anti-Nazis, whom he and his fellow EMS regarded as traitors "since our country was at war." He could not remember "any German Jews being in the camp." In Britain, he was imprisoned at Lingfield, which he mistakenly regarded as an exclusive, special EMS camp, where he was treated as a civilian internee, and where he met for the first time Dr. Lachmann, the camp spokesman there. Since he had already graduated from German high school, he was exempt from

attending compulsory school courses for all internees under eighteen, and instead he served as "runner" to the English camp commandant. The EMS prisoners resented the new Canadian label that re-classified them as "POW, Class II," after having been informed about their new status on arrival at Camp R. He claimed that their civilian clothes were taken away on arrival and that instead they were given the official uniform, an action that actually occurred months later. He dismissed summarily Captain Scharf's benevolent role and sought to downplay his position within the camp. He confirmed that the soldiers of the Fort Garry Horse were ready to use their rifles and bayonets should the slightest infraction of the camp rules occur. His old pro-Nazi sentiments were still alive in his letter and perhaps prevented him from recalling nastier events such as the beatings of Jews and anti-Nazis in the camp.

Not much can be said about subgroup (d), the secret opponents but passive followers, except that they were captives of their own fears, especially in regard to the danger to their relatives in Nazi Germany. Although the threat of reporting unpatriotic and disloyal behaviour in internment camps to Nazi Party agencies at home, including the *Gestapo*, was widely used, no evidence has emerged so far that these threats in fact were ever actually executed. However, this blackmail device successfully intimidated many.[33] In Camp R, the members in this subgroup existed in a condition of political and moral unease and inactivity, since they were unable to resolve their feelings and their fears, one way or the other.

According to Kirkness's analysis, the anti-Hitler contingent of openly outspoken anti-Nazis was numerically very small—perhaps altogether only 200 adherents—and was far from presenting a united political front. In reality, it seemed, this group was a crucible in which "quite a lot of tension and bickering" prevailed, producing endless

< One of the watchtowers with members of the Fort Garry Horse.
[Courtesy of the Red Rock Historical Society]

arguments, not only about cherished political principles but even about the trifles of everyday existence between doctrinaire leftists and pragmatic refugees. It can be assumed that, as in other camps, the Jewish contingent was split not only along religious lines but also into secular political sections of Zionists and anti-Zionists.

Kirkness's count of "no less than fifteen distinct types" in the small anti-Hitler segment is as remarkable as it is peculiar, especially since this group included seventy-eight Jewish refugees. Descriptive as his labels appear at first glance, they reflected more accurately Kirkness's prejudices and perhaps those of certain levels of British society.[34] When he describes anti-Nazi Germans as "political fugitives"—illegal runaways, rather than refugees—and the German Jew and anti-Nazi trying to bring his valuables out of Nazi Germany, like the Frankfurt book trader, as a "currency smuggler," one wonders whom Kirkness placed in the "police fugitives" group—those escaping the *Gestapo*? And who belonged to his unmentioned additional eight subgroups? Apparently, the anti-Hitler contingent did not enjoy Captain Kirkness's wholehearted approval.

Kirkness's anti-Hitler contingent included not only all German- and Austrian-born Jews and anti-Nazis refugees, but also the small and politically distinct group of members of the International Seamen's Union. These men of German origin were all staunch anti-Nazis who had declared themselves "stateless" after 1933, and had been working as crew members on neutral ships from which they were forcibly removed and assiduously collected by the Royal Navy after the war's outbreak, on order of the First Lord of the Admiralty, Churchill. By arresting these left-wing anti-Nazi seamen on neutral ships, the Royal Navy acted in flagrant contravention of international law. It is interesting to note that while neutral Brazilian and Japanese ships were regularly subjected to these illegal searches, US ships were not, apparently to avoid annoying and reminding Americans about historic incidents of British high sea piracy, thereby spoiling the fruits of ardent British anti-Nazi-German propaganda seeking to influence the American public.

These international unionists called themselves "Bolsheviks" and, like their political opponents in the camp, made the best of a bad situation. Unlike in other internment camps such as Cove Field Barracks, and later Newington and Farnham, all in Quebec, and Little River, New Brunswick, where Communist cells either controlled or at least exerted considerable influence on camp affairs, Red Rock's small cell of Bolsheviks seemed not to have exercised any influence whatsoever on camp life. The local Red Rock communists enjoyed the free and good food, but objected strongly to unpaid, fatiguing work.[35]

According to Spier, who lived in the same hut with these left-wing sailors, they regarded themselves as victims of the warring international capitalist systems. They were angry since their British and Canadian capitalist captors ignored their well- and long-established anti-Fascist record, since many of them had already fought against the Fascists in the Spanish Civil War and had voluntarily abandoned their German nationality long before capitalist Britain and Canada joined the anti-Nazi forces. Of course these unionists fitted well into several of Kirkness's sub-categories such as "near-communists," or "the international unionists."

In the summer of 1940, Kirkness estimated that the split between pro-Nazis and anti-Nazis in Camp R stood in a ratio of 85 to 15 per cent, and at the year's end 80 to 20 per cent.[36] He characterized the attitudes of these two main elements towards each other as extremely hostile; they viewed each other with "horror and loathing," and "to say [that they] are not on each other's visiting lists is to make a substantial understatement." Kirkness thought that the "mixture" in the camp was dangerous and explosive. The official view of the Canadian military authorities was that all inmates were Category A internees and that all of them were "dangerous enemy aliens." It did not seem to matter to the Canadian military that the minority of Jews and anti-Nazis in that "mixture" inside the enclosure were confronted by a vast majority of civilian merchant marines who were dominated by a band of radical Nazis. In the refugee camps of the east rumours abounded that

Camp R was a very dangerous and frightening place, a "gigantic" and fearful camp totally in the grip of Nazi violence. However, while the political divisions greatly burdened Camp R's daily routine, especially the interactions between anti-Nazi and Jewish inmates, camp life, was determined also by other factors such as standing orders, sports and education, cultural and hobby activities.

VI

Camp Life at R under Standing Orders

PART OF THE SETTLING-IN PROCESS for the inmates involved absorbing the rhythm of life in the new camp and becoming accustomed to a different set of standing orders and rules. This process started very early on with the inmates facing a totally unexpected and dangerous situation. Expecting every kind of trouble from these "dangerous enemy alien" prisoners of war, the sentries had strict orders to shoot in case of unauthorized assembly, which during daytime meant that prisoners were forbidden to congregate in groups larger than three or to stand at or near windows and doors. This order presented a serious danger for the prisoners, especially during night time, since the sentries also had orders to shoot at anyone attempting to leave a hut or move around in the enclosure. How were prisoners to act in case of sudden sickness of a fellow prisoner?

This perilous situation existed at Camp R, because unlike other camps, Camp Commandant Berry ordered that prisoners were not to be locked in their huts at night, due to the many fire hazards in the camp. In these first weeks, therefore, it could happen that if an inmate stepped out in search of help, shots could ring through the night. In case of illness, inmates were eventually instructed to stay inside the hut and attract the sentries' attention by banging against the hut door and shouting for help. In time this dangerous arrangement was amended, and the new standing order thereafter decreed that an inmate dealing with a night emergency would open the hut door, wave a flag and shout "Doctor, doctor." It is amazing that in these early, jittery nights or even in later, regular nights, no prisoners were mistakenly shot by their alert guardians. The military's general apprehension in these early days, fed by propaganda and incorrect information, led them to expect that these incarcerated Nazis might at any time create mayhem and seek to escape. The alert sentries would avert and deter such attempts by shooting at any movement inside the enclosure, especially during darkness.[1]

An important step forward in normalizing the operation of Camp R was the appointment of a "camp leader." On 13 July, Berry selected and appointed "Commodore" F. Oskar Scharf as "man of confidence" in accordance with the provisions of the Geneva Convention of 1929. Who was Oskar Scharf? He was one of the forty ship captains in the EMS cohort. Among them, however, he was the most respected and influential member in this group. The unofficial title "Commodore" reflected his status as a captain *extraordinaire*, having served as "the Commodore of the biggest German passenger ship, *Europa*," a luxury liner on the Hamburg-New York run of the North German Lloyd Shipping Company.[2]

Scharf was a Roman Catholic, a fifty-five-year-old "white-haired figure" with an "ever quiet and friendly voice."[3] He was internationally and domestically well-known and a respected person who knew many of the leading Nazis personally, but he was not one of their followers. In fact their disapproval of him and his disagreements with them had lost him his command of the *Europa*. On 11 April 1940, at the time of his capture by the British during the Norway campaign, he was captain of the *Alster*, a small supply ship, *en route* to Narvik. At the British internment

"Commodore" F. Oskar Scharf—the camp leader—and other prisoners watching a sporting event. *[Courtesy of the Red Rock Historical Society]*

camp Lingfield, Scharf met Spier and other future fellow inmates such as Dr. Lachmann, Baron Pilar, Count Montgelas and Dr. Hanfstaengl; the latter he already knew from his *Europa* days. At Lingfield, Scharf apparently "did much by his quiet diplomacy to ease tension between the [hostile] groups."[4] In conjunction with Dr. Lachmann and Spier, Scharf was credited with dissuading Baron Pilar from his foolish scheme to seize the *Duchess of York* on her way to Canada. Kirkness had this to say about Scharf in his report:

A man of fine character. Officially a Nazi, he does not impress one as being the type of man who dabbles in politics. He probably is a loyal servant of the existing German regime, but one would expect him to serve with equal faithfulness a government of any other political hue. He commands universal respect in the Camp and he possesses the confidence of both Nazis and anti-Nazis....As master of the *"Europa"* he has met most of the leaders of the Nazi Party. He describes these meetings in a most interesting way. In conversations, he frequently mentions the War, and bases his hopes in diplomatic action (possibly initiated by the President of the United States) to put an end to bloodshed and destruction.[5]

Kirkman's decision to label Scharf a "Nazi" instead of simply "German" illustrates his imprecise definition of this term, especially in view of the fact that the radical Nazis, who would have preferred a different person in the role of "man of confidence," rejected Scharf as camp *Führer.* Having failed to remove him, they tolerated him. The minority considered him "a decent man and a non-Nazi," one who was able to maintain enough order in the camp to limit the violent outbreaks by the radical Nazis. Scharf's personal skills and experience succeeded in gaining him general acceptance throughout the camp.

A fellow inmate and former chief officer, apparently on the *Europa,* offered this comment to an acquaintance in New York State on Scharf's regime in the enclosure: "Everything here proceeds a long [sic] a normal course. Captain Scharf runs the compound in the same efficient manner as for all those years he ran the 'Europa.' It is a special satisfaction to me to observe the high degree of respect and confidence which Captain Scharf enjoys both inside and outside the compound."[6] According to Spier, "Scharf successfully supported our plea to have our sleeping quarters separated from those of the Nazis, and also endeavoured to arrange that we would take our meals at different times from the Nazis. In consequence of his representations, the anti-Nazis were given a separate row of huts."[7] In cooperation with Spier and Dr. Lachmann, Scharf also arranged with Commandant Berry to provide a kosher meal for the Jewish inmates on Yom Kippur. Scharf was "universally respected" and was the only camp spokesman at Camp R during its entire period of operation. In October 1941, Scharf was transferred to

Camp 130 at Seebe/Kananaskis in Alberta, where he was again elected camp spokesman.

In May 1944 Scharf was selected by a medical commission for repatriation to Nazi Germany via Camp 23 to New York, then Algiers, then Barcelona, where the exchange took place, and finally to Marseille. What happened to Commodore Scharf after his repatriation is worthy of consideration at this point. He was chosen by ninety repatriated civilian internees to deliver a "Thank-you address" at their welcome-home ceremony in Stuttgart. In a personal letter from the Reichs-Ministry of Foreign Affairs, Scharf received high praise from German and Swiss diplomats for his work in the internment camps. He was praised for maintaining "the high standard of morale and discipline" and, as well, for

> the contact which still connects your men with you beyond life in camp, [which] are all proof for your [personal] sacrifice and unreserved devotion of your person for the acknowledged difficult task of caring and leading more than 500 men during long years of internment behind barbed wire. In this regard special attention must be directed to the trying circumstances under which this work was performed by you in Camp R during 1941.

In conclusion, the Ministry noted that "the good understanding with the foreign authority, which shaped the camp conditions, is undoubtedly essentially your achievement and that of your assistants."[8] After thanking him again for his work in the Canadian internment camps, the Ministry next requested that Captain Scharf submit a report on his experiences during his internment and repatriation.

The Ministry's effusive laudatory letter to Scharf produced a highly critical and condemnatory response from the Ausland-Organization (AO) of the Nationalsozialistiche Deutsche Arbeiter Partei—National Socialist German Workers Party (NSDAP), an agency primarily concerned with the supervision of the Nazi Party's branches operating in foreign countries. The AO perceived itself as the Party's foreign affairs office and regarded the Reichs-Ministry of Foreign Affairs as a nuisance and rival. This letter scheduled a rendezvous for Scharf with the *Gestapo* in order to undergo "an exhaustive state police investigation" and respond "to extraordinary strong attacks on his camp leadership which are being made by all trustworthy inmates who have returned home from internment."[9]

In Nazi style, the attack was based on anonymous accusations without any specific details. Since the Reichs-Ministry was, indirectly, also being criticized by the AO-NSDAP, in its own defence the Ministry's staff defended Scharf. They cited not only German diplomats but also Swiss diplomats speaking on behalf of the ICRC or the Protecting Power in high praise of Captain Scharf as frequently re-elected "man of confidence" and *lagerführer* in the most trying circumstances. The German Embassy in Bern, transmitting the Swiss Consul's report on Camp R of 16 October 1941, added this comment: "[Consul] Preiswerk reported that despite the shortcomings of Camp R he had formed a good impression and in this regard pointed out the excellent relation which existed between the camp spokesman Scharf and the camp administration." Preiswerk observed that thanks to Scharf's personality he was able to gain a hearing before the camp administration for all legitimate wishes of the internees. The Ministry questioned the Party's assertion of many critics by pointing to the actual small number of eight returnees from Camp 130, yet conceded that even the best of camp leaders face discontent.[10]

The available archival files unfortunately do not reveal what happened ultimately to Captain Scharf. His report, which reached the Ministry a month later, was very carefully constructed; it criticized the "enemy" actions at the time of capture of the unarmed ship *Alster* and praised Scharf's own "correct" behaviour in the camps. Lavish praise was given to the various aid organizations such as the German and Swiss Red Cross, the YMCA, German-American, Brazilian and Argentine aid groups and the German shipping companies. Scharf downplayed the violent incidents of October 1940 as some "EMS beat[ing] up (*verpruegelten*) the Jewish hospital personnel." Reading his report, one gains the impression that Scharf had been cautioned and that he wrote down what he could surmise might be expected. He noted the enemy's "correct" treatment but never forgot to praise the NSDAP. He stressed the positive and he ended with "Heil Hitler." One can readily agree with Stent's assessment: "His whole report is an obvious attempt to please his masters" and save his skin.[11]

The authority of the camp spokesman, the internees' "man of confidence," was set forth in a standing order issued by the camp commandant. Under its provisions the camp spokesman dealt with all complaints arising among the inmates and by inmates against any member of the military. In fact, the spokesman reported all relevant matters happening in the enclosure to the commandant, going through the provost sergeant who passed his reports on to the duty officer. Furthermore, he was entitled to request interviews with the commandant or to speak with international representatives of the Protecting Power or the ICRC and through them submit requests and petitions. An additional task for the camp spokesman was the supervision of the hut "elders." The spokesman "supervised" the activities inside the enclosure and "controlled" the appointment of assistants such as camp clerk, mailman, cooks, etc. While the German military POW camps such as Gravenhurst, Medicine Hat, Lethbridge and Angler sometimes maintained large administrative bureaucracies inside their enclosures, at Camp R this was not the case.[12] At appropriate occasions, the spokesman and his assistants were also in charge of the distribution of gift parcels and similar mailings.

The duties of the hut elders were light but numerous. These hut leaders, the standing order announced, were to "be appointed by the Internees in each sleeping hut; [they were] responsible for discipline [and]...cleanliness" in and around the hut; for keeping an inventory of all hut articles such as pails, brooms, etc., maintaining these in good order and available; and for keeping the fire buckets filled with water.

They reported any complaints from inmates to the camp spokesman and any "unusual occurrences or any breach of discipline" to the provost sergeant; they ensured that tables and floors were scrubbed and bedding aired weekly and that beds were made properly each morning. Each hut had to appoint day and night shifts that had complete responsibility over the firing of the six stoves in each hut. The night shift also had to ascertain that a properly shaded light near each stove was lit all night.[13]

These arrangements may lead one to believe, at first glance, that the internal administration of the enclosure at Camp R was in the hands of the inmates. As the overwhelming majority of the camp's inmates were German by active citizenship, it is not surprising that Scharf's assistants were German, but it is somewhat surprising that they were all pro-Nazi. No representative of the anti-Nazi and Jewish minority was apparently included in the internal administration of the enclosure. Nevertheless, in the opinions of Spier and Kirkness, as well as the Swiss diplomats, camp spokesman Scharf did an excellent job in difficult circumstances by keeping hostile sentiments from exploding regularly into senseless, bloody and violent eruptions. It must be emphasized that the camp spokesman had absolutely no disciplinary powers over his fellow inmates, and neither had the hut elders. The camp spokesman's authority arose mainly from the personal respect and moral authority which he enjoyed among his fellow inmates and which he was capable of exerting. Important to remember also is that all responsibilities for the administration of the enclosure rested in Commandant Berry's hands. Scharf was in every way the Camp Commandant's creation.

This is how Swiss Consul General Ernest Maag, Representative of the ICRC, perceived not only the relationship between Scharf and the camp's military authority, but also the general atmosphere in the enclosure after his first visit in August/mid-September, 1940:

The representative of the prisoners can confer without hindrance with the military authorities and as a matter of fact, the reporter had the impression that at this camp the relation between authorities and prisoners is more liberal and truly democratic than *at any other camp* [italics mine]. But this does not seem to interfere with the discipline at this camp...any suggestions made by the prisoner's representatives to the military authorities are promptly investigated and the wishes of the prisoners are being granted whenever reasonably possible. The Detaining Power as represented by the commander has no complaints about the conduct of the interned men.

Consul General Maag finally added this remarkable observation to his report. He thought that Captain Scharf and his assistant, Konstantin Baron Pilar von Pilchau, deputy spokesman, "seem to do a very good job in keeping up the morale of the prisoners." Maag failed to mention here young W. Lueddeke, the camp clerk, who, like the Baron, was a professed Nazi. This detail notwithstanding, the Swiss certainly conveyed their high esteem of Captain Scharf as camp spokesman to the German government.

Konstantin Baron Pilar von Pilchau was a handsome Russian-born Baltic aristocrat.[14] The Baron had served as a young officer in the Tsarist army during the First World War. In the days of Imperial Russia, he had already discovered a personal preference for the Russian radical racist right and supported the Black Hundred movement before 1914. In exile in Germany, he associated with the early German Nazi movement. Before the outbreak of war in 1939, he lived in England working as the representative of the German shipping company Norddeutscher Lloyd. He was Britain's first civilian internee at Olympia Hall, where Spier joined him as No. 2. Baron Pilar was a fervent Nazi and anti-Semite with well-polished social manners. In England, he was camp *Führer* at Clacton Camp, but was soon dismissed by the local commandant.[15] In Camp R, he remained true to his ideological convictions as an anti-Semite and an acknowledged, but affable, Nazi. In acting as the assistant camp spokesman, he perhaps sought to control spokesman Scharf or to give the radical Nazis a share in the internal administration of the inmates in the enclosure.

Captain Kirkness described him as:

> a man of middle age, tall, distinguished in appearance....A man of the world; cultured; courteous; a good conversationalist; shrewd; difficult to read and estimate. An active man, with organizational ability and business acumen, he plays a capable and prominent part in the internee organization. He is a man of unlimited discretion. What he thinks of German politics it is difficult to discover. At the same time, what evidence there is, points to his being a fairly enthusiastic supporter of the Nazi cause. Not for one moment that one imagines him a convinced believer in German ideology; rather he gives the impression of being a man who is a Nazi because that seems to him the best policy.

Despite Kirkness's favourable commentary, Baron Pilar was a fervent believer in the Nazi ideology. His daredevil actions betray that fact. Fellow inmates travelling with the Baron on the *Duchess of York* accused him of being the initiator of the foolhardy plan to seize control of the *Duchess* and bring her back to Hamburg. Had Captain Scharf, Dr. Lachmann and Spier failed in dissuading the others from pursuing this fantastic scheme, a massive bloodbath would have been the result, as unarmed men sought to take over well-placed machine guns and the heavily defended ship's bridge. After the closure of Camp R, the Baron disappeared from the records, ending up perhaps in Camp 70, the Nazis' last meeting place in Canada. About young Lueddeke, who originally hailed from Hamburg, relatively little is known. Kirkness wrote this in his November Report: "a well educated young man from the former German colonies. He is at present occupied as a clerk in the office of the Camp Leader."[16] What function exactly clerk Lueddeke performed in the camp office is not known. Later Lueddeke also fulfilled the function of the canteen steward.

The administration of the enclosure proceeded on various levels. Although Spier portrayed himself as a background figure, just a spectator, more passive than active in Camp R, nonetheless he was the first to establish contact with Camp Commandant Berry, and thus began to disseminate the new truth about the nature of Camp R's inmates. Spier was therefore one, if not perhaps the first and leading, informant, one of many refugees who helped to reveal the great British deception of Canada. Since Spier already knew such important inmates as Scharf, Dr. Lachmann, Count Montgelas, Dr. Hanfstaengl and Baron Pilar from their joint incarceration in such camps as Olympia Hall, Clacton and Lingfield, as well as from the *Duchess*, his views and opinions most likely continued to influence administrative affairs in the enclosure in some ways. Without any direct evidence, one can only speculate about the inter-personal cooperation of these diverse personalities, though one can assume that it was less visible in Camp R than it had been in British camps previously. Spier assisted in separating Nazis from anti-Nazis at Camp R and helped to maintain open communications with the camp leaders. Scharf obviously enjoyed the Commandant's trust and was capable perhaps of limiting the excesses the Nazi faction and its supporters might have contemplated, although he could not completely prevent their daily pranksterism, harassment and bullying. In his endeavours Scharf was certainly assisted by the oppressed minority. Spier and other anti-Nazis always spoke highly of Captain Scharf.

Important as the trouble-free function of the internal administration of the enclosure was, nonetheless it formed only one aspect of Camp R's overall operations. Daily life at Camp R differed little from life in any the other internment camps in 1940. Camp routines were almost identical everywhere: wake-up, followed by morning roll call, then various parades or free times. Interspersed throughout the day were breakfast, lunch and supper, and the afternoon saw a repetition of the morning schedule. The day ended with evening roll call and lights out. Everywhere camp life unfolded daily under strict and rigid military discipline and rules. These camp rules were known as the standing orders that were usually posted in English and German inside the enclosure in every camp.

In Camp R, standing orders not only controlled every aspect of the inmates' existence but also regulated the conduct of the guards vis-à-vis their prisoners. Standing orders determined the operation and the life rhythm of Camp R. Different standing orders carefully outlined in great detail what actions needed to be implemented by officers and soldiers, when and how. It was every soldier's duty to know the particular standing order that applied to the task currently executed by him. Camp R's standing orders were carefully prepared, issued and revised by Berry and his administrative staff as inadequacies or deficiencies were discovered in the existing standing orders over the course of time. Amendments could also be initiated by instructions from the Military District Headquarters in Winnipeg and the office of the Directorate of Internment Operations in Ottawa. Updating the camp's standing orders was one of the commandant's many responsibilities.

Updates and revisions were, in part, necessary because standing orders were designed from a strictly military perspective and ignored any civilian viewpoint. According to Spier the very first standing orders were Draconian. However, once the camp's military command had formulated a clearer picture of their "prisoners," these first standing orders were gradually amended to suit the new reality. The revised standing orders set forth in detailed instructions what should be done concerning most situations imaginable. Standing orders governed the tasks of the "bridge guard" and of "sentries [for the] internee compound"; they detailed how to respond to "fire [alarms]" and how to "escort prisoners." The "officer i/c of guard" had his standing order of five short articles, outlining his duties and responsibilities. In contrast, the standing order "for general alarm"—concerned with escape—covered two foolscap pages with fifteen major articles and an additional twenty subsections, setting forth every conceivable operational function.[17]

The standing order covering the escort of prisoners—one guard to four prisoners—required ten articles and four subsections. According to the order, the escort officer had to prepare a list of the prisoners to be escorted, note their registration numbers, and then list all the escorting soldiers and record the times of departure and return. In addition, the order spelled out whether a particular escort needed to be accompanied by an officer or only by an NCO. The order also explained where the sentries had to be placed—geographically—while on march in relation to the marching column of prisoners; what constituted appropriate behaviour for sentries generally, and in case of escape—just fire three shots in quick succession. Calling a warning first apparently was unnecessary in August 1940. Fraternization was prohibited while on escort duty. Sentries were encouraged to note their prisoners' outstanding physical features. Being on escort duty was not, it seemed, an easy job. Of course, many former inmates are pleased to relate stories of "incapacitated" (drunken) escorts, and their weapons, being safely returned to camp by their charges.[18]

The guard in charge of the bridge entry to Camp R required a standing order of eight articles. At first the bridge guard required only one man on duty, but later two NCOs and four privates were called for. Instructions to the bridge guard were to stop all incoming and outgoing cars and persons. All persons had to give their names and state the purpose of their visit. Before proceeding they had to receive the commandant's permission to enter the camp; all luggage and parcels, in or out, had to be inspected. No one could enter the camp area without permission unless showing the Red Card pass. Cars with military officers were also stopped. Civilians seeking entry were escorted to the officer, or to the Lake Sulphite Pulp and Paper Company official, awaiting them. During the emergency of an escape, no one could enter or leave the camp area. The main guard managed the soldiers leaving the camp area. No soldier could leave camp after 2200 hours without a pass; those returning after 2200 hours had to report to an NCO, who collected all passes from returning soldiers and registered their time of return. Those without passes would be specially noted and listed. Soldiers, moreover, had to be properly dressed before being allowed to leave camp. The guards themselves were advised that they must be "fully dressed for action with Webb equipment on and rifles loaded. Fifty rounds of ammunition [were to] be carried by each man."[19] The soldiers on guard duty were issued flashlights that were to be readily available at all times.

Sentry duty was regulated by thirteen articles, which re-enforced the principle that sentries existed in order to prevent prisoners from escaping, tinkering with the wire, signalling to outsiders, or causing disturbances at any time. The sentries' main purpose was to shoot and then report such incidents. In order to safeguard against any attempt to escape from the lakeside, a powerful searchlight was set up on the dock and manned like a watchtower.

The standing order dealing with an outbreak of fire explained in thirteen articles the process to be followed: at the time of the discovery of a fire the "alarm" was to be sounded by the bugler, then the officer in charge of the Guard was to seek either to extinguish the fire or to confine the blaze; simultaneously the Officers' Mess was to be called and all officers were to be summoned to their assigned stations. The camp car was to bring officers to the flagpole area; the guard officer was to be in charge until the camp commandant or his designated officer appeared; all soldiers were to stand-to, fully dressed, in their huts; platoon officers were to inform ranks about the nearest hydrant and how to use it; a number of soldiers were to proceed to the location of the fire after having received instruction on hydrant locations or the use of hand extinguishers. Exits of all buildings were to be checked. Practice fire drills were to be held. The order reminded all that fires require immediate response and reactions that are dictated by circumstances rather than rules and instructions. Interestingly, this standing order did not refer either directly or indirectly to the prisoners.

The standing order on camp life governed the existence of the inmates in Camp R most minutely. First proclaimed on 9 July 1940, this standing order had then only sixteen main articles and twenty-five sub-sections. Subsequently, this order was amended and extended twelve times—four times in August, seven more times in September and once again in October 1940. The order spelled out the daily routine for the inmates from first roll call in the morning to "lights out" in the evening. Both the morning and evening roll call took place inside the huts, since the available open space in the enclosure was insufficient for the assembly of everyone in one place at the same time. Independently, two NCOs counted the assembled inmates in each hut and then reported their score to the attending officer. If the two scores did not tally a recount occurred. Apparently, outside of one escape, roll calls proceeded frictionlessly in Camp R.

A regular day in Camp R started with wake-up at 0630 hours. Roll call was at 0730 hours, and thereafter breakfast was served in two shifts. Next were scheduled the daily parades: for unpaid fatigue work and paid work, if available; for sick visits to the camp hospital; for showers or washing laundry; and for the distribution of clothing. Those not on any parade could enjoy their free time. The morning's work was interrupted by dinner at noon, after which a similar rhythm as the morning's unfolded for the afternoon. In summer, the daily rhythm ended with supper at 1800 hours followed by the evening roll call at 2030 hours. In autumn and winter roll call was at 1930 or 1915 hours, depending on sunset. Lights were out at 2200 hours, in all seasons. From lights out to reveille, smoking was forbidden inside the hutments.

The standing order on camp life, furthermore, prohibited the possession of a variety of useful utensils such as large knives, scissors, sticks, tools of any type, pieces of iron or metal or any "materials which would facilitate escape," and of course that also included cash. Inmates were warned that if they attempted to "pass" through the flimsy barbed wire fence surrounding the enclosure or walked away from the enclosure unescorted through the gate, they would be cautioned and then fired upon.[20]

Regular weekly clothing parades were scheduled on Tuesdays from 0900 to 1130 hours and 1330 to 1600 hours. This parade gained in significance after Berry prohibited the wearing of the prisoners' own personal civilian clothes and ordered the wearing of the official Canadian-designed prisoner's uniform. The official uniform was of blue denim cloth for the jacket and shirt, each of which had a bright red round patch on the back, at shoulder height, and denim trousers with a bright red stripe running down the side of each pant leg. The policy on wearing this prisoner's garb was not standard in all camps. In some camps inmates were allowed to wear their own civilian clothes until these wore out. In other camps the rules demanded prisoners wear this much-despised garment. Supposedly, this order was issued as a measure to prevent escapes from Camp R, but whether these outfits were designed to humiliate the wearers or to provide better shooting targets for the sentries is open to debate. They did not prevent or reduce escapes by internees or POWs. The wearing of this prisoner's uniform was universally resented by all prisoners, whether internees or POWs. Commissioner Paterson described it a "clown's uniform"; others called it a "circus outfit." Prisoners saw it as an assault on their human dignity.[21]

The standing order on camp life severely limited the social activities of inmates. They were not to "converse with any person unless permission of the camp commandant has been given."[22] Conversation among prisoners was permitted. While card playing was allowed, gambling of any kind was prohibited as was the production, consumption or possession of alcohol. These prohibitions were not always strictly obeyed since the occasional illicit still was discovered, much to the chagrin of its customers who might well include soldiers. Inmates were urged not to waste food, and it was also strictly forbidden to take food from the kitchen or the dining hall to the sleeping hut. However, inmates found ways to bypass this restriction.

Discipline and cleanliness were the watchwords for the camp. The enclosure had to be kept clean and orderly, free from disused paper and cartons and other refuse. Inside the huts, the order decreed that bedding, consisting of two woollen blankets, a pillow and mattress, had to be aired once a week. Later, this was to be done twice weekly.

Prisoners unloading ice. Their shirts and coats had a round red patch sewn on the back to make escape attempts more difficult. Though not its intent, many observed that it would also make a good target for the guards.
[Courtesy of the Red Rock Historical Society]

The blankets had to be neatly folded and towels, wet or dry, stashed between them. Electric fixtures could not be removed or altered, and cardboard or paper could not be used for lampshades. The inmates had to obey and execute all orders from officers or soldiers promptly; disobedience in any form, the order stated, was to be dealt with by force of arms first and punished later. Inmates must know the camp rules and follow them.

The standing order also gave explicit instructions to the inmates on marching. To and from work, they were to march in an orderly manner, properly acknowledging officers passing by and obeying all orders from the escorts promptly. The standing order on camp life provided also for the wellness of the inmates. Twice-daily sick parades were held from 0900 to 1100 hours and again from 1500 to 1600 hours. Times for recreational activity spanned practically the entire day, from 0800 to 2045 hours in the summer and from 0800 to 1700 hours in the winter. According to the standing order, the maintenance of orderly conduct, good discipline and proper cooperation would govern the granting of privileges to the prisoners. No evidence has emerged indicating that in Camp R soldiers or NCOs abused their authority and tyrannized over inmates by excessively strict, petty-minded enforcement of rigid disciplinary rules.

Food played an essential part in the life of any prisoner. Its scarcity or plenitude can affect mental and physical well-being as well as morale, and the inmates of Camp R were no exception to this observation. Once pots and pans arrived at Camp R, the former chefs from German transatlantic luxury liners, who previously had cooked sumptuous, multi-course dinners for an international sea-faring clientele, now took over from the Canadian military cooks and prepared the prisoners' meals in accordance with German taste. Apparently stewards, dressed in their white linen uniforms, served the meals in two shifts. Since both the quality and quantity of the food provisions were good, the meals served were excellent and plentiful. It has been said that the inmates ate better than their guardians. The best supporting evidence in this regard comes from the prisoners' own correspondence to their loved ones in Nazi Germany or in the internment camps back in Britain. They recorded individual gains of twenty to thirty pounds during the early weeks. As mentioned earlier, the Morale Report of Kirkness noted a collective weight increase by inmates of 4.5 tons following their internment in Canada.[23]

At Camp R, morning roll call was followed by a healthy and appetizing breakfast which consisted of these basic ingredients: "eggs, German beefsteak or bacon, tea, white bread, porridge with a rich creamy milk, sugar, jam or marmalade."[24] At lunchtime the German cooks served a German main midday meal—dinner—of soup, never the same soup two

One of the dining halls and kitchen in background

View of Camp R looking north. Handwritten caption says "One of the dining halls and kitchen in background." [Courtesy of the Red Rock Historical Society]

days in a row, good quality meat dishes, well-prepared vegetables in the German style of that period, a variety of potato dishes and a sweet dessert. In the evening, at supper, a three-course meal was provided. On all tables, Spier reported, were placed extra dishes with uncooked vegetables, chopped onions, grated carrots and raisins. The servings were generous, and inmates took extra slices of bread with condiments to their huts for snacks. Every afternoon hot water was available for tea-making. There were no complaints about the quantity and quality of the food served at Camp R. In comparison, at Cove Field Barracks, Camp L, the menu consisted of bacon, jam, bread, butter, tea for breakfast; soup, stewed steak, roast beef, braised cabbage, potatoes and bread for dinner; and cold beef, cheese, cold veal, bread, cocoa and tea at supper. In either case, it was certainly a far cry from English camp cuisine, which had impressed with salted herring, overcooked cabbage, mushy peas and potatoes.[25]

The inmates reflected the excellence of the nourishing meals not only in the visible accumulation of poundage individually and collectively but also in the laudatory reports of the visiting Red Cross representatives. These weighty results were not attained through extra rations, since the internees were supplied with the same level of rations as their Canadian captors, known as "depot troops" in the parlance of the Geneva Convention of 1929. Perhaps it was due entirely to the difference between the caring preparation of trained professionals and the indifferent preparation of semi-trained army cooks, with their task-oriented military approach to the mere feeding of a mob of hungry soldiers with the appropriate quantity of calories.

While the provision of plenty of good food on a regular basis was a primary concern for prisoners, they were equally concerned about the availability of water. Potable water is a life necessity. A plentiful supply of raw water is also necessary for the maintenance of bodily cleanliness. However, despite the camp's proximity to the masses of water in Nipigon Bay and huge Lake Superior, the provision of raw water was not a job easily accomplished by the military engineers. Shower parades were scheduled for Mondays, Wednesdays and Fridays from 0900 to 1500 hours. Since the shower hut was located a short distance outside the enclosure, the shower parade required the inmates, thirteen each time, to leave the enclosure and march under escort to the bathhouse to take their showers. Both the Veterans Guard and the inmates used the shower facility, so the demand on the shower was enormous. After the transfer of a large number of inmates in January 1941 to other camps in eastern Canada, however, the shower schedule was amended to Mondays, Wednesdays, Thursdays and Fridays from 0900 to 1130 hours and from 1330 to 1530 hours. On Saturdays only the morning shift was available. Wednesday morning shift was set aside for washing laundry. In order to cope with demands and avoid disputes, Berry

The central sports field. *[LAC-e006611164]*

decreed: "Maximum Bathing Limit 5 minutes." The Swiss Consul, in an
early report, calculated that under the old schedule if each individual
had three minutes to shower, a total of seventy-eight persons could be
cleansed per day and 234 weekly, and that every inmate could expect
a shower every eighteen days.[26] Luckily, these men were most likely
all old-fashioned Europeans, culturally pre-conditioned to respect the
cost of the natural resources involved, for whose hygienic well-being
one thorough weekly bath normally sufficed. Otherwise, without
these strict rules, the Veterans Guard might have faced daily shower
pandemonium.

As soon as the inmates of Camp R had adopted and adapted to the
new daily routine, they began to pursue the development of such camp
activities as sport, education, the arts and sundry hobbies in order

to fill the available hours of "free time and leisure." These activities served a vital function in a well-managed camp since they prevented the development of such debilitating syndromes as idleness, monotony, boredom, claustrophobia, restlessness, dissatisfaction and depression. The presence of any of these afflictions encouraged declining morale, rising insubordination and unrest. Several factors could contribute to their presence. The camp administrative routine, while necessary for the proper operation of the camp, could yet contribute, as a routine, to the camp's dysfunction. All of the above syndromes were very much dreaded by the camp military authority, the internal administration of the enclosure, and individual prisoners. Consequently, in different ways they all cooperated to deny these syndromes an active presence in the camp. At Camp R, the local military did what it could, within its limited means, to encourage sport activities by setting aside hutments and creating outdoor sport space and to support any initiatives the inmates took up. Moreover, the local military welcomed contributions from the War Prisoners' Aid Committee of the International YMCA and from the ICRC, regardless of Col. Stethem's negative view of these agencies and their work. Once an appropriate environment had been created with the assistance of the local military, the inmates did their part in beating back these feared syndromes through a wide range of organized activities.

Sport activities were very important and most popular in Camp R. Most inmates, especially the EMS, were young and eager, and had been accustomed to performing daily work before their incarceration and enforced idleness. Enforced inactivity was stressful, and sports offered an outlet. In the absence of any data, it is not possible to assert with certainty the extent of participation in general or specific types of sport or the inmates' actual preferences. What is certain, however, is that sport activities began some time before educational work did.

> **Prisoners practise gymnastics.** *[Courtesy of the Red Rock Historical Society]*

Without any recreational space inside the enclosure, the younger, sports-minded crowd, on the initiative and under the direction of coach and sport-*führer* Guelcher, happily and willingly, and with the blessings of the commandant and sundry visiting military superiors, began the construction of a recreational area "northeast of the railway track" outside the enclosure. Here the inmates were able to play soccer and handball, stage boxing matches, engage in gymnastic exercises on parallel bars, practise "building human pyramids" and pursue a variety of other sports between 0800 and 2045 hours in the summer and between 0800 and 1700 hours in winter. Photographs taken at the time certainly illustrate the inmates' fitness and enjoyment. A contemporary witness, Lloyd Roy of Red Rock, then nine years old, in April 2002 still remembered watching the building of a human pyramid of "seven men stories high."

As previously stated, Edwin Guelcher was a notorious, longstanding, ardent member of the NSDAP both during the democratic Weimar Republic before 1933 and in Nazi Germany after 1933, as well as following his emigration to the former German colony of South West Africa.[27] In Camp R, Guelcher delighted the young, robust and idle EMS, the radical Nazis and their sympathizers, and also the local Canadian military officers and the visiting military leaders and inspectors with his sport acumen and *Führertum*—leadership. In Camp R, Guelcher assumed the role of initiator of sport activities and instruction and, of course, coaching. In everyone's view Guelcher, the Nazi, assumed the function of an outstanding morale builder—or was he providing *Wehrertuechtigung* (military training)? What more could one ask for? Ex-*Oberleutnant* Guelcher magically banned idleness and boredom and lifted morale, and perhaps fostered physical fitness as a prerequisite for military fitness.

Guelcher was Bavarian by birth, fortyish, small and wiry in stature, a former German Imperial Army officer turned pilot during the First World War. After the war, in 1918, he joined the right-wing *Freikorps* movement and boasted of his involvement in the gruesome murder of

Dr. Rosa Luxemburg and Karl Liebknecht in Berlin in January 1919.[28] Both of these persons were leading figures in the postwar German revolutionary movement and were founders of *Spartakus*, forerunner of the German Communist Party. Guelcher also participated in the abortive radical rightist Kapp-putsch in 1920.

In the mid-1920s, he emigrated to the former German colony of South West Africa, today known as Namibia, which was then administered by the government of the Union of South Africa under a League of Nations mandate. Before the outbreak of war in 1939, Guelcher had been a farmer and later in 1938 worked as a journalist and editor of the *Swapokmunder Zeitung* in the small town of Swapokmund. A contemporary, though not an unbiased observer, described Guelcher's work in Swapokmund in these terms: "The officers include men like Oberleutnant G_____ [sic], who has a facile pen and expresses himself violently in the Nazi sheet."[29] Apparently, Guelcher was in the thick of Nazi activities in South West Africa, which were controlled from Nazi Germany, and were designed to advocate and seek a re-union with the Reich similar to what Germany achieved in the case of the Sudetenland. He criticized the government of South Africa's policy of assimilation of the races, which in his view threatened political stability and led to the progressive "proletarianization" of the blacks, their "bolshevization" and complete demoralization. Instead, Guelcher argued, the "legitimate masters of the land"—the German farmers who were setting the standards and were the bearers of culture—must resume the education of the blacks and turn them into pliable and usable support labour for the further development of the land. In Guelcher's view, the government of the Union of South Africa had no reason to be proud of the result of its native policy.[30]

In 1939, the government of the Union of South Africa considered Guelcher "politically very dangerous." Having been arrested on the blockade runner SS *Adolf Woermann* by the British, he was sent to the United Kingdom. There he first gained notoriety as a Nazi troublemaker in the detention camp at Seaton. Dr. Hanfstaengl saw him as an agent of Dr. Josef Goebbels, Nazi Minister of Enlightenment and Propaganda, and labelled Guelcher "the little demon." Guelcher was described by Kirkness as "thin-faced, with very sharp features, and eyes uncommonly close set. Despite his distinctively grim appearance he is the possessor of a very keen sense of humour."[31] Suspected of being one of the instigators of the anti-Semitic disturbances in the camp, Guelcher was never seen or caught in the front ranks, nor did anyone in the local camp military apparently know about his Nazi pedigree or his racist views and longstanding commitment to right radical extremism. In May 1945, after the news of Adolf Hitler's suicide reached the camp that lodged Guelcher, he organized a "memorial service" for his venerated *Führer* during which he extolled in the bombastic style of the NSDAP the *Führer*'s many "excellent and star-like qualities."[32]

Guelcher's popularity at Red Rock was based entirely on his role as sport instructor, coach and organizer of sport activities. This modern re-incarnation of nineteenth century liberal German nationalist *Turnvater Jahn*, and contemporary disseminator of *deutsch-voelkische* ideology *à l'esprit de Freikorps*, delighted the Canadian military, who were looking for ways to keep the latently restless busy as well as to keep the camp's young EMS inmates physically active and occupied. Guelcher not only organized the construction of outdoor recreation space and built gymnastic equipment such as parallel bars and a boxing rink but also started programs of gymnastics and boxing. Nothing further is known about his later career in Canadian internment, after his return to England, or in Germany after his return from internment in 1946 or 1947.

Sometimes Camp R's sport activities had a serious purpose for the participant. After winning the camp's trophy in boxing, the champion, a young EMS, wrote his girlfriend back home that he was seriously considering embarking on a career in boxing on his return home to

> Prisoners kept active with various athletic competitions. *[LAC-e006611160]*

Guards look on during a sporting event. *[LAC-e006611159]*

Germany. In the summer of 1940, Commandant Berry allowed swim
parades. Batches of 100 males, from a group of 400, either stark naked
or sparsely dressed—to impede escape—enjoyed a refreshing plunge in
the cold waters of Nipigon Bay under the watchful barrel of a Lewis
machine gun. In winter, the inmates were granted the privilege of playing ice hockey outside the enclosure near the lakeshore. Unfortunately,
1,100 hopefuls had to share thirty pairs of used skates. Arrangements
outside the enclosure placed a tremendous extra burden on the guards,
who had to escort prisoners on shower and laundry parade and also on
sport parade for soccer games, swimming and hockey. Unfortunately,
very little information is available on the internal organization of the
camp's sport activities. Spier recalled that political factors divided
the sport participants and that the boxing clubs carried the label

"Germania" and "Kondor." One can assume that competitions formed a regular part of the sport routine, but it is not known how many soccer or hockey teams existed, or whether teams were formed on the basis of hut locations, or age, or former ship crew affiliation. Were there prizes awarded and what kind of prizes? Many details remain a mystery.

Surrounded by this cult of the body, internee Spier reflected on the Nazi spectacle of sports and offered this observation: "Mental decay very often enhances in a spectacular way the physical conditions of a person to such a degree as would be unobtainable under normal circumstances." He drew a parallel between the Nazi promotion of the cult of body culture and obsession with racial physical beauty and the "Greek idolatry of physical culture and beauty," which, in his opinion, had heralded the downfall of Greek civilization. He anticipated a similar historical repetition and felt calmed by his analysis and consoled in his temporary misfortune.[33]

The lack of space for recreation and the inadequacy of sport facilities were noted by General Panet on his first inspection visit to Camp R at the end of July. During his short visit, Panet met with Swiss-born site manager, Mr. Hurter, who lived on the premises of the Lake Sulphite Pulp and Paper Company at Quebec Lodge and very amicably discussed the space problem with the latter. In the course of their conversation, Panet suggested a solution and both agreed to the creation of a recreation area. Hurter placed company dirt and a tractor at the disposal of the military camp administration for levelling an area "west of the compound [sic] across the road."[34]

Specially appointed inspectors like Panet, who were either military officers or high- ranking RCMP officers and leading professionals in the prison system, periodically inspected Camp R, as they did all other Canadian internment camps. These inspectors assessed all aspects of the camp operation, not just the sports facilities. They examined the condition of buildings and equipment, the functional efficiency of the administrative staff, and the operational fitness of the troops guarding the enclosure. They evaluated training, conduct, discipline, alertness, morale and cooperation of the soldiers. A very important factor in their inspection was the "security" of the camp. Copies of the military inspectors' reports went to the Director of Internment Operations, the Commanding Officer of Military District No. 10 and of course to Commandant Berry.

The first inspection, actually more a brief visit, occurred approximately three weeks into Camp R's operation. General Panet arrived at Red Rock on the evening of Friday, 26 July 1940, and left early the next day. During his short personal visit, Panet nonetheless made some astute observations and drew important conclusions that affected the camp's ultimate future. Surveying the camp's layout and construction, Panet observed that the internees' huts were "most comfortable," but unfortunately were built far too closely together, and being of wooden construction, in case of fire it would be "practically impossible to save any of them." Recognition of this acute potential fire hazard became a recurrent theme in practically all subsequent inspection reports. Panet recognized, moreover, a further major deficiency of Camp R: its "security." In fact, the fire hazard and the problem of security were closely linked together. In case of a fire, the 1,150 inmates would have to be evacuated immediately from the enclosure to a safe but open and unfenced area nearby. Guarding such a large number of prisoners in an "insecure" area would constitute a major security hazard. How could escapes be prevented from this very large number of prisoners with the small number of soldiers in the tumultuous and confusing circumstances of fire and mass evacuation?[35]

It is important to realize that when Panet and other military representatives discussed the problem of "security," they had only one notion in mind: the prevention of escape by POWs, whether individually or in large numbers. For this they would use all the legitimate means at the Army's disposal. In his report to the Secretary of State, Panet used only two words to describe the camp's security: "Not satisfactory." The barbed wire fences were too weak, he noted, the wires being fastened to 2x4 posts, and the fences did not run in regular straight lines but in accordance with the geographic lay of the terrain. In some places the fence was too close to the prisoners' huts and in others too flimsy. In Panet's judgement, this entire fence arrangement was too weak to withstand a deliberate massive rush by the prisoners. The two machine guns available were Vickers models, not Lewis guns. Panet recommended the immediate acquisition of Lewis guns, and he advised the officer commanding the Fort Garry Horse to schedule periodic shooting practices in order to intimidate the prisoners with the presence of these deadly guns. However, Colonel Cox's Adjutant—Col. Cox was on leave at the time of Panet's visit—cautioned that this advice could not be followed since there was not enough ammunition available. Panet gave orders immediately to remedy this deficiency, and he suggested considering the use of non-lethal gas grenades for "crowd" control.[36] The containment and suppression of riots or disturbances inside the enclosure—that is, the maintenance of "good order and discipline"—was only a secondary concern to the military. The prevention of escapes was primary.

A further serious deficiency Panet noted was the absence of any opportunity for paid work for the prisoners at Red Rock. He declared that Camp R was therefore "not satisfactory as a permanent camp." This important observation by Panet became a regular refrain in future reports and seems to have influenced from the start the process of decision-making concerning the long-term future of Camp R. Regarding the absence of paid work and the resulting lack of money among the inmates, Panet offered several remedies. First, he advised Berry to utilize the government's start-up fund of $1,148—one dollar for each prisoner—in assisting prisoners to purchase "necessities" collectively, if all prisoners would agree to this solution through the camp spokesman. Second, he advised Berry to encourage prisoners to engage in hobbies and the production of handicraft goods and then to permit them to sell these products through the army canteen against credit coupons. In later years this very idea was successfully practised in the big western POW, Class I camps from 1943 to 1946.

Panet also suggested replacing Camp R with two new camps to be built further east of Nipigon. When these camps were eventually constructed in the autumn of 1940, they became known first as camp "X" and "W" and later were numbered Camp 101 at Angler/Marathon and Camp 100 at Neys, respectively. In his conversation with Mr. Hurter, Panet proposed that opportunities for paid work could be made available by thinning out the forest in the vicinity of the camp and on the plant site, thereby producing firewood and fence posts.[37]

It is interesting that Panet did not opt to employ Red Rock's inmates in the construction of the unfinished highway between Longlac and Hearst, as the Canadian Legion, Port Arthur and Fort William branches, and also the local of the British Empire Services League at the Lakehead had suggested in letters to the Minister of Defence, Ralston, as early as July 1940.[38] Observing the large number of "boys under eighteen" in Camp R, Panet noted in his report that the prisoners in Camp R constituted a "mixed lot," consisting of five groups, "boys under eighteen, Nazis, anti-Nazis, Jews and communists." Panet proposed to open up a special camp just for youth under eighteen, but this suggestion failed to get the necessary support from his political superiors. Other minor defects that Panet noticed were more easily corrected, such as the insufficient number of fire buckets, two instead of six; or the improperly coloured work clothing, denim blue instead of army khaki. A surprise discovery was that two camp gates, blocking the railway spur line running through the campsite, had no locks.

At the end of his visit, Panet was very pleased with his inspection of the soldiers of the Fort Garry Horse. They were "a fine young-looking lot of men" and "very smartly turned out," and they appeared "very efficient, indeed" as regular soldiers go. However, it took them eleven minutes to "turn out the guard." They had misconstrued the order. If pleased by the soldiers, General Panet was not at all impressed by the inmates' appearance. In his view, which was shared at the time by many other officers on inspection tours of other civilian internment camps, especially those holding refugees, the internees at Camp R needed "more discipline." For example, they must "pay proper respect to officers" and "stand at attention" in an officer's presence; they must touch their hats when walking past an officer and on encountering an officer; and when marching under escort, the soldier in command should give the order "eyes right" or "left" depending on the situation. Obviously, what these German and Austrian civilians needed was the administration of a strong dose of old-fashioned militarism. Despite these weaknesses, however, it is fair to conclude that Camp R was, for the most part, both well-ordered and well-guarded. Of course, there were exceptions.

VII

Issues in Camp Life

Stresses and Opportunities

DESPITE ALL ITS CAREFULLY DEVISED standing orders, Camp R's military administration could not avoid facing various minor and major issues in the course of time which reflected particular or even peculiar needs or demands of the inmates. Whether these idiosyncratic requests arose from legitimate concerns or evil motivation mattered very little initially. They were issues that had to be dealt with. In part, the emergence of these problems signified that participants in the camp's operational existence pursued objectives that varied according to their roles. For example, the military's primary task was the incarceration and safeguarding of the prisoners. On the opposite side, the prisoners could respond with defiance, strikes, boycotts, demands, and ultimately with escape. The inmates could claim rights and privileges on the basis of international agreements such as the Geneva Convention of 1929, even though this Convention only selectively applied to them. The local leadership of each participating party, foremost the camp commandant and the inmates' spokesman, had to confront and resolve the issues resulting from these conflicting objectives.

General Panet's brief inspection visit, surprisingly, did not lead to a discussion of the camp's first dispute between the camp's military administration and a substantial segment of the inmate population, the Nazis and their sympathizers. This provocative dispute, it seems, did not entirely disrupt ordinary camp life activities, which included unpleasant and threatening behaviour on the part of the Nazis towards the anti-Nazis as well as more pleasant routines, such as launching sport activities and educational work or pursuing hobbies and cultural work. The dispute between military and Nazi started as part of the settling-in process during early July when camp life had barely achieved a semblance of routine. The interned Nazis started decorating the insides of their huts by hanging up Hitler pictures and German flags. The local military authority promptly responded and ordered the removal of this offensive German national paraphernalia. The Nazis promptly turned this prohibition of displaying German national emblems in their huts into an issue and, not surprisingly, protested officially. On 25 July 1940 they requested that Scharf, as camp spokesman, present an official protest to the Swiss Consul. He, as the Representative of the Protecting Power, was to appeal to the Canadian government to lift this ban against the "legitimate" display of pictures of German national leaders and German national flags or other German patriotic insignia inside their huts. The Nazis claimed that these displays expressed and demonstrated "their natural national sentiments."[1]

The ensuing controversy, between the Nazis in Camp R and the Director of Internment Operations in Ottawa, over the hanging of photographic images of the inmates' leaders was fought, it seems, with such dedication and intensity that one might assume that the issue involved the hanging of real men rather than mere images. This picture-hanging problem, the request and the resulting prohibition, was not foreseen by the original framers of the Geneva Convention of 1929, and therefore its resolution necessitated discussions in Red

Rock, Winnipeg, Ottawa, London, Geneva and, I suspect, Berlin; it is certain that the Directorate, External Affairs and the Swiss Consul General considered the matter in Canada. The Nazi prisoners at Red Rock assisted in this debate by insisting that in British camps such displays were permitted. But this claim was of no avail in Canada where Canadian-made rules prevailed, and Panet would not budge in this matter. He decreed, "the buildings in which they [the interned Nazis] reside are Canadian Government Quarters and it is not proposed to permit pictures of Adolph Hitler, German flags, or emblems to be displayed or flown in any Canadian Government Quarters, regardless of who may be occupying same."[2] Plainly spoken, Panet told his prisoners that their huts at Red Rock were public government buildings and that, therefore, no pictures of Hitler could be displayed in what essentially were the detainees' private bedrooms. By early September 1940 standing orders had been amended to state: "No emblems or insignia of foreign powers with whom Canada is at war will be exhibited in any hutment of the compound [sic]." In addition it was ordered "the singing of songs of a political character and the recital of lyrics of a political character is prohibited."[3] These decisions caused tremendous resentment and anger among the Nazi element in the camp. But to what extent this first incident inflamed the atmosphere in the enclosure it is impossible to ascertain.

In connection with this controversy, it is interesting to note that less than a year later, the circumstances for hanging Hitler in a picture frame in a Canadian internment camp had drastically changed. In exchange for permitting Allied soldiers imprisoned in Nazi Germany to hang their King, Nazis were allowed to hang their Hitler and other national political paraphernalia in Canadian camps. These balsamic concessions to the respective national and patriotic spirits were obtained through the implementation of the wholesome principle of reciprocity and the provisions of the Geneva Convention of 1929.

A more important issue for both inmates and the camp military administration was the matter of work, both unpaid mandatory fatigue and voluntary paid work. The performance of fatigue work was a daily task by which inmates in all camps were confronted and which was dreaded by every prisoner. Unpaid mandatory fatigue work included camp maintenance work, road repairs, burying garbage, cutting and chopping firewood and similar labour. At Camp R, internees were obliged to perform unpaid fatigue work under Article 34 of the Convention.[4] Fatigue work was universally disliked. The impecunious merchant seamen in Camp R were accustomed to getting paid for their labour and rejected and resented this aspect of camp life. The Bolshevik sailors absolutely abhorred the very notion of working for no pay for capitalists. All missed their regular pay from Germany. They needed money desperately to buy such necessities as tobacco, soap, toothpaste, toothbrushes, razor blades and other hygiene products, as well as such occasional comfort products as chocolate, candies and cookies. Both Nazi and Communist seamen were united in protesting this practice, but to no avail.

Voluntary paid work, in contrast, was in high demand and was rarely available at Camp R. The camp military favoured the concept of paid work and viewed the lack of paid work as an unsolvable problem. Even with the best of will, there was very little that could be done at Red Rock to provide paid work either within the military zone of the camp or in the wider Red Rock vicinity. There were no opportunities available for paid work in regional agriculture or forestry, in industry or mining, or even in road construction. None of these activities flourished in the vicinity of Red Rock: local agriculture and pulp cutting were carried out on too small a scale.

In due course the absence of paid work gave rise to serious complaints by the inmates, not only to Commandant Berry but also to the Representative of the ICRC. The sound waves of these protests, stirred up in Red Rock, were eventually heard in Ottawa. The unavailability

> **Prisoners cutting firewood.** [Courtesy of the Red Rock Historical Society]

of paid work on a voluntary basis was perhaps the most significant concern that faced the military at Camp R because the lack of money, certainly in the early months, affected everyone, not only the notoriously flat-broke EMS but also the wealthier inmates whose credit accounts had not been transferred from Britain. Lack of money stimulated the rapid development of manufacturing and then of illegal trade in souvenirs, handicrafts and carvings between soldiers and inmates. Legal paid work offered several advantages. First, work of any kind kept the inmates occupied and diverted them from less desirable ventures like escape or rioting. Second, paid work, at the rate of twenty cents per man, per day, saved money for the government since the inmates could earn the small sums necessary to purchase hygienic necessities and some luxury items. Earning money would certainly stretch the one-dollar-per-prisoner emergency fund that the government had on account in the Bank of Montreal at Schreiber. Third, paid work improved or maintained good morale. As early as August 1940, Colonel Berry and Captain Scharf discussed the need for paid work. On behalf of the inmates, spokesman Scharf argued that all work done by prisoners at Camp R should be declared paid work. With the help of the Swiss Consul this matter was passed on to the Directorate of Internment Operations in Ottawa for further direction and decision. The Directorate, however, rejected this request.

Solving the issue of work appeared simple, on first sight, but it was not. Indeed it was complex; it raised many supplementary questions, all of which deserved answers. The first set of questions requiring clarification and definition were: What in fact constituted "fatigue work"? Article 34 defined "fatigue work" this way: "Prisoners of war shall not receive pay for work in connection with the administration, internal arrangements and maintenance of camps." The next question to be clarified was: What did the concept "camp" mean, i.e., did it mean only the "enclosure" or the entire "camp zone"? A second set of questions was: Were they, the inmates of Camp R, "prisoners of war" or were they not? Were they merely "internees" or not? The German-speaking inmates were accustomed to the simple and straightforward German distinction between *Kriegsgefangener*—a disarmed, surrendered, captured ex-combatant, a prisoner of war, and *Internierter*—a civilian enemy national incarcerated by one of the belligerents. This was a simple, clear and easily understood differentiation. The German nationals in Camp R found the Canadian pronouncements concerning their status as captives in Canada puzzling at best and totally confusing in the end. And so, it seems, did members of the Canadian military and the Swiss consular staff. The simple word "internee," as Commissioner Paterson observed, was "absent in Canadian law of custody."[5] In place of a simple concept, the Canadian government preferred the use of the rather opaque classifications of "Prisoner of War, Class I and Prisoner of War, Class II."

The anti-Nazis and Jewish interned refugees found the Canadian practice of labelling them "prisoners of war" highly offensive, inhuman, and degrading. On their arrival at Camp R, one of the Canadian officers told all the prisoners that according to a Canadian government decision their status was "Prisoner of War, Class II" and that the qualification "Class II" was merely for identification to distinguish them from members of the German or Italian armed forces. This was undoubtedly an ingenious, but hardly truthful, explanation of their status. If they were prisoners of war, they would be protected under the Geneva Convention of 1929, plain and simple, yet they were later told that this was not the case.

The discussion about the status of prisoners of war, based on the Geneva Convention of 1929, started originally among the small group of ship captains and ship officers who asked Commandant Berry why they were not treated as "officers" when according to the Convention "officer prisoners of war" were exempted from performing such duties as work and fatigue labour. As a lengthy period of incarceration loomed on the horizon as the summer of 1940 faded, more and more elderly and physically less fit inmates began to look for answers to these questions. In comment, Kirkness observed, "No great importance is attached to such discussions in themselves, especially as only a small minority is concerned. They are not likely to lead to breaches of discipline, or even to a bad atmosphere in the camp." Kirkness noted further: "None of the prisoners expects to receive pay for any work done within the prisoners' enclosure; but almost without exception the men consider that they are entitled to payment for some of the work and fatigues performed outside the barbed wire. It is asserted that the Convention refers to work in the camp; there is no mention of a 'camp area.' There is argument therefore as to what comprises a camp area, and how the boundaries of a camp are demarcated."[6]

On 20 March 1941, Colonel Stethem, who had in the meantime visited Camp R, answered all questions arising in conjunction with the issue of work in a lengthy letter to Berry. Stethem's letter, almost nine months in gestation, is worth considering at length. It provides many details and reveals not only important government policies vis-à-vis Canadian and foreign civilian internees and prisoners of war, but also illustrates Stethem's thinking and the formalistic care with which he operated. Concerning the concept of "camp" Stethem advised Berry to discuss the issue with Captain Scharf "in view of the fact that a communication has just been received from the Consul General of Switzerland which...gives a definite decision on the conception of the word 'Camp' as mentioned in the Geneva Convention of 1929, and provides the information requested by Captain Scharf."[7]

The term "prisoner of war," former professor Stethem went on to lecture, was used in the technical sense. Simply put, it was because the term was used in both the Convention and the *Defence of Canada Regulations*. Both documents indicated that when applying these legalities to Canadian civilians, they might be interned as "prisoners of war," and by extension the term included civilian internees. Therefore in drawing up the *Defence of Canada Regulations* the one expression "prisoner of war" was used in the technical sense, and the expressions "POW Class I" or "POW Class II" were stipulated in the *Regulations* for use where it was desired to distinguish combatants from civilian internees.

Stressing that the classifications were used only to differentiate between ex-combatants and internees, Stethem provided several examples to illustrate this point. If a particular regulation applied to both classes of POW, only the term "prisoner of war" was used. However, if only a combatant was meant then the label "POW, Class I" was applied. Stethem emphasized: "It was not intended that the words 'Class I' or 'Class II' should be used in any way except for definition in the Regulations."[8] Then Stethem explained that a further reason for granting the privilege of the title "prisoner of war" was that it confers free postal privileges. Furthermore if civilian internees were not classed as POWs it might still be possible to arrange with the postal services in Canada to carry their mail free of charge within Canada. For international mail to other co-belligerent countries a similar situation might also be arranged, but the same would not be possible with neutral countries to which mail might be sent or have to be forwarded through. In effect he was pointing out that the Buenos Aires International Postal Convention exempted "prisoners of war" from postal charges, but it did not grant this to the mail of civilian internees.

After this condescending epistle on the postal advantages of being a Canadian POW, Class II under the homemade *Defence of Canada Regulations*, Stethem acknowledged that an internee was not, however, quite entitled to the full protection and benefits of the Geneva Convention of 1929. Moreover, in singling out Scharf on the "free mail" issue, Stethem exhibited a touch of personal irritation since Scharf corresponded extensively with his many international friends who lived mostly in the USA or in other neutral countries. Stethem concluded with the delivery of a further clarifying and negative judgement, namely, that interned merchant marine ship officers were not "officer prisoners of war," only civilian internees or POWs, Class II to whom Article 22 of the Geneva Convention of 1929 did therefore not apply. Article 22 exempted officer POWs from all work and just happened to be one of those many articles of the Convention Canada had eliminated in its writing of the *Regulations*.

Stethem concluded by offering, "If Captain Scharf is not quite clear on the points which he has raised, this office will be glad to afford him further information, or he may forward another communication to the Consul General of Switzerland through this office." This short paragraph illustrates perfectly well Colonel Stethem's many personal qualities upon which Commissioner Paterson had more to say in his report.[9] His letter to Berry and indirectly to Scharf and all inmates was straightforward in its clarification of the concept of "camp" and in the definition of paid work, though from the viewpoint of an impoverished EMS in Camp R, the fine distinction between cutting down trees and cutting the same trees into firewood may have seemed just a trifle Jesuitical and legalistic. Stethem's official explanation regarding the meaning of the Canadian term "prisoners of war" seemed confusing and obfuscating. He explained nicely that Canada had its own homemade rules, but offered no clarification as to why the customary distinction between POW and internee was dropped in favour of the cumbersome terminology "POW, Class I" and "POW, Class II."

This peculiar innovation was devised primarily perhaps to meet domestic exigencies in order to bypass all legal hassles arising from *habeas corpus* legislation, which for centuries had safeguarded an individual's rights against arbitrary arrest by the state. This issue would certainly have arisen at the outbreak of war when the Canadian government was most anxious to incarcerate Canadian-born citizens and those of enemy alien origin whose loyalties and sympathies were suspect. This interpretation arises from Col. Stethem's reference to the *Defence of Canada Regulations*. Once declared a "prisoner of war," a person was now under the unrestricted control of the state by means of the Army, regardless of whether or not there existed any actual proven basis for imprisonment. Stethem's point was more elegantly and succinctly put in a memorandum of 15 July 1940 by the Judge Advocate General who stated, "An internee is a prisoner of war under the Defence of Canada Regulations [sic] and on being interned is in legal custody and according to the International Convention having application to the treatment of prisoners of war such internee becomes subject to the laws, regulations and orders enforced in our own armed forces."[10] Initially, if incarcerated under the articles of the *Regulations*, a Canadian citizen could be declared a "prisoner of war," which placed that individual under the protection of the Geneva Convention of 1929. Nonetheless, once imprisoned that civilian was then subjected to specially devised laws and rules which placed that individual under military jurisdiction and thereby denied any recourse to traditional legal rights of protection against arbitrary arrest and protection of the Convention.

For the prisoners in Camp R such obfuscating legalistic arguments were frustratingly contradictory. All internees fell under the rules of Canada's Army and the homemade *Regulations* as soon as they landed in Canada. When internees, especially refugees, appealed to Canadian sovereignty, as in the case of appeals for release, Canadian authorities always insisted that the internees, as British captives, were subject to British jurisdiction and that Britain's permission was therefore needed in order to alter their status. The Privy Council Order, P.C. 4121 of 13 December 1939, stated clearly and unambiguously in Article 2 that "enemy aliens interned as prisoners of war under Defence of Canada Regulations [sic] are not entitled to the special rights and privileges accorded to those prisoners of war defined in Articles 1 and 85 of the International Convention" of 1929. Civilian internees in Canada existed in a quasi-legal limbo, and the inmates of Camp R were part of this uncertain arbitrary system. Their fate had been decided, and it was up to them to cope with the arbitrarily imposed conditions.

In spite of these disputes which in a way happened "off stage" for the ordinary inmate, daily life in Camp R went on. In addition to sports, education—though second in popularity—nonetheless occupied an important and intrinsic part of camp life. Classes and lecture courses began soon after arrival with the active help and encouragement of Dr. Jerome Davis, an American citizen and volunteer, representing the War Prisoners' Aid Committee of the YMCA. He helped by donating large quantities of pencils, writing paper, exercise and textbooks, paints, blackboards, chalk, paint brushes, art supplies, ink and other teaching materials to what he described as a "very elaborate plan for classes and studies."[11] A severe scarcity persisted in the supply of textbooks written in German. Many teachers resorted to writing their own textbooks. From October 1940 to April 1941, seven different language courses were taught in Camp R. Four sections in English were offered from October to March, varying in hours from twenty-four to six per month and in enrolment from eighteen to five students. French was taught in three sections in the same time period for twelve hours monthly and showed enrolments of ten to four students. Spanish and Russian stood next with two and three sections, respectively. Spanish enjoyed a steady enrolment of ten students attending twenty-four hours monthly and Russian with four students present for twenty hours monthly. Swedish attracted only two; Dutch, seven; and Norwegian, five; they had the smallest enrolments. In addition, ten courses offered such practical and technical subjects as navigation, mathematics, mechanics, engineering, wireless operation, wireless technique, electro-technique, shorthand and American geography. Enrolment in the technical-practical courses was on the whole higher; fifty students enrolled in wireless operation, twelve in electro-technique; thirty-four in mathematics and only five students in engineering. These courses required a real commitment by their participants. Seventy to eighty-seven hours monthly of attendance were required in mathematics—in February 1941, one hundred and four hours of attendance were demanded. Forty hours of attendance were expected from those enrolled in the machinist and navigation courses. Teachers for all these different courses were recruited from among qualified and interested inmate volunteers. In general, Camp R's educational activities grew in popularity in the period from October 1940 to April 1941, with enrolment rising from 157 to 368 students, and number of hours taught from 330 to 654, respectively.[12] On the successful completion of their courses, participants received a certificate signed by the teacher of the course and the camp spokesman in the hope that their academic studies and training would receive recognition from established educational institutions in the homeland.

The participation rate of nearly one-third of all inmates in the camp's education program was low in comparison to other Canadian internment camps where the rate was as high as 50 per cent. As a group, the EMS of Camp R were sport-inclined and intellectually and culturally challenged, perhaps due to their social background and previous class conditioning. Unlike elsewhere in other internment camps, it seems, the curriculum at Camp R was not focused on meeting prescribed high school examinations for "middle standard" or "maturity," or on preparing students for examinations to obtain qualifying certificates for positions of First Ship Mate or Ship Engineer. Only the Jewish group in Camp R organized courses that were designed to meet the needs of young schoolboys and the standards of English high schools. For the Jewish youngsters, in religious training, general and special courses were organized, suitable to meet their needs and requirements.

From the evidence available, it seems that cultural and entertainment activities started late in Camp R. Whether the delay in launching cultural activities was due to the absence of appropriate housing, to demand, to the social and political divisions in the camp, or to the educational and intellectual interest levels of the inmates must remain an open question. The space offered within each hutment sufficed for playing chess, card and board games, but not for table tennis. Perhaps the inmates collectively felt there was no need for other cultural and leisure activities, and in any case the camp lacked such a physical facility as a large recreation hall. The unavailability of space for cultural entertainments such as concerts or theatre performances persisted for quite some time. Eventually, arrangements were worked out and hutments became available to accommodate some of these activities. Nevertheless, whereas eastern Canadian internment camps fairly quickly developed a vigorous and lively cultural and intellectual life and atmosphere after arrival of the inmates, little of a similar kind apparently happened at Red Rock. In the absence of any evidence to the contrary, it must be assumed that the inmates at Camp R produced neither a camp newspaper nor any poetry or other literary works and songs. However, Kirkness cited an internee letter excerpt in his Morale Report No. 5 of 26 November: "Last month we held an exhibition of handicrafts, and put on show model ships and aircraft, boxes, vases, and pictures."[13] If they did create any other artistic creations such as paintings and drawings, none have survived, not even the pornographic drawings of nude women that allegedly one artist supplied regularly to the guards.[14] At other camps, the inmates published camp newspapers regularly; at Farnham, it was called *Stacheldraht* (*Barbed Wire*), and at Little River, it was *Die Andere Seite* (*The Other Side*). These newspapers discussed current political topics, world affairs and internees' concerns.[15] Considering the social and political composition of Camp R's inmate population and its official classification as a "Nazi" camp, it is possible that the local military hesitated in making the necessary concessions that might have fostered journalistic and other creative activity. In comparison with other internment camps where the Jewish inmates took the lead in creating a lively intellectual and artistic atmosphere, the small Jewish contingent of Camp R hardly influenced the camp's cultural affairs.

Entertainment received a mighty boost when Dr. Davis with the assistance of the War Prisoners' Aid Committee acquired a piano first, and later a film projector and a regular supply of films for the camp. It is interesting to note, in conjunction with the latter activity, that thereafter the Veterans Guard, inmates of every political *couleur*, and local youth and residents, in the middle of a fierce war on the actual battlefields and the virtual campaigns of ideological political and war propaganda, were able to share the joys of a Hollywood movie show—a feature film with comics—peacefully and harmoniously together in the mill building adjacent to the enclosure once weekly for approximately two hours.[16]

A cultural highlight at Camp R was listening to "Putzi" Hanfstaengl's renditions of Wagner or Chopin on the newly acquired camp piano. Dr. Ernst Franz Sedgwick "Putzi" Hanfstaengl was a character totally different from the other inmates, even from Spier or Dr. Lachmann. Hanfstaengl was unique! He was flamboyant and controversial, a one-time member of the Nazi clique around Hitler and then a "refugee" from the same gang.[17] Hanfstaengl was a German-born and Harvard-educated German citizen. Among his rich and powerful friends in Germany and the USA, Hanfstaengl was better known by his nickname "Putzi," which was a term of endearment from his baby days, meaning "cute little fellow" in the Bavarian dialect. Calling this two-metre-ten (six feet four inches) tall man "Putzi," in later years, seemed a bit incongruous. The Hanfstaengl family was well connected on both sides. Paternally, Hanfstaengls had served not only as privy counsellors to both the Royal Houses of Wittelsbach and Saxe-Coburg-Gotha, but also to the pre-1917 Bavarian aristocracy. Since 1880, the Hanfstaengl family had operated an internationally well-known chain of art shops with outlets in Munich, Rome, London and New York, which special-ized most successfully in the photographic reproductions of famous and treasured paintings. Before the First World War, "Putzi" had managed the family's American boutique-shop, known as *Hanfstaengl-Kunstsalon* on 5th Avenue, No. 45, New York, where he met and socialized with such famous men as Charlie Chaplin, Randolph Hearst, Woodrow Wilson, Arturo Toscanini, Pierpoint Morgan and Henry Ford. From his student days at Harvard University (1905–1909) and through his membership in the Harvard Club (1908), he counted among his personal friends Theodore Roosevelt, Jr., Franklin Delano Roosevelt, then a Senator for New York, Walter Lippmann, T.S. Eliot, the humour-ist Robert Benchley, and also future Bolshevik and later hero of the fashionable far left, the bourgeois American "salon-Bolshevik" and notorious journalist, John Reed. On his mother's side "Putzi" was con-nected to leading figures in America's revolutionary and military past and to Boston's social best; his mother was a direct descendant of the Sedgwick-Heine family, which had provided well-known American mil-itary leaders.

The outcome of the First World War ruined "Putzi" Hanfstaengl. As a result of the German defeat, he was forced to sell his half-million-dollar business for a mere eight thousand dollars to his American competitors. In 1921 he and his American wife and their newborn son Egon returned to Munich. Through an American friend from Harvard who was then the American Military Attaché in Berlin, Hanfstaengl was introduced to a rising and popular orator and leader of a minor political party, the NSDAP, in Munich. He was impressed by Adolf Hitler's simple analysis of Germany's litany of contemporary political problems—the undeserved imposition of war guilt by the victors, the exorbitant reparations, occupation, and crippling territorial losses imposed on them by the Versailles "*Diktat*," and the threat of the Marxist-sponsored class struggle and the bolshevization of the German Reich through trade unions, social democrats and Communists. Hanfstaengl sought to meet Hitler privately in November 1922, and soon joined Hitler's inner circle, becoming a close and enthusiastic associate and advisor to the evolving *Führer*. Indeed the entire Hanfstaengl family—mother Catherine, sister Erna, and brother Edgar— adored Munich's current fashion, the popular and rising right-wing nationalist agitator and anti-revolutionary rabble-rouser. Under the Hanfstaengl family's social tutelage, the lower-class, shy and socially backward Hitler acquired new useful social skills and polite manners as well as invaluable contacts with generous financial supporters and future adherents to his cause. In exchange for adding titillation to this high-society coterie, as their very own salon-fascist, Hitler gained recognition and acceptance among the upper bourgeoisie of Munich and Bavaria.

Hitler, a very moody person, needed "Putzi," an accomplished piano player, in order to assuage the budding *Führer's* mental and emotional stress during the beginning days of the Nazi movement. Hitler greatly enjoyed "Putzi's" renditions of Wagner—*Tristan and Isolde*, *Lohengrin*, *the Meistersingers*, *Liebestod*—and also selections from Chopin, Richard Strauss, Schumann, Bach and Beethoven. These selections "Putzi" played, according to his own testimony, "with an all too emphatic Lisztian fortiori and romantic élan." After these wonderful performances *Führer* Hitler felt mentally restored and at peace. It is difficult to judge "Putzi's" talent; his foes dismiss him as a dilettante, while others are full of praise. Perhaps one may see in him a forerunner of the later popular American piano performer, Liberace.

"Putzi's" ambition was to educate Hitler not only socially, or as *Sturmabteilung* comrades put it "to seduce Hitler to champagne and lovely ladies," but also politically, especially in world and international affairs. In Hanfstaengl's view Hitler and his close associates had very narrow visions of the world, a Central European rather than a world-embracing perspective; Hitler and his entourage's vision of the world was as limited as the view an infantry soldier in his trench has of the objectives of the battle being fought. He dismissed the Nazis' anti-Semitism and racial ideology as silly and infantile. Hanfstaengl participated actively in the planning and preparations of the events leading up to the abortive Munich putsch in November of 1923. Still active in the discussions and negotiations immediately prior to the march on the *Feldherrnhalle* on 9 November, he did not, however, join in the actual march and the shoot-out. When the putsch aborted, he, like the *Führer* and many other valiant *Kaempfers*, fled the scene and Munich and quickly crossed over to the safety of nearby Austria. Hitler, however, went into hiding in "Putzi's" summer home in Uffing at the Staffelsee, near Munich. Here Mrs. Helene Hanfstaengl, "Putzi's" "blond American wife," whom Hitler coveted, persuaded the future *Führer* not to commit suicide and instead to surrender peacefully and bravely to the Bavarian police.

Once political and social tranquillity returned to Munich, so did Hanfstaengl. He visited Hitler regularly in the latter's new temporary lodging in nearby Landsberg prison. After Hitler's release, "Putzi" fancied himself as the *Führer's* advisor and spokesman on foreign affairs. Certainly within Hitler's entourage this presumption by the wealthy, well-educated, much-travelled and cultured Hanfstaengl was quite justified, especially in regard to American matters. Hitler utilized him in this capacity on several occasions very successfully and to financial advantage. However, as Hitler dedicated himself to rebuilding the Nazi Party, Hanfstaengl's contacts with him weakened, but never broke off entirely. By 1931, Hanfstaengl was again a constant companion of the *Führer* during election campaigns or on financial begging trips across Germany. In January 1931, Hitler elevated Hanfstaengl to the position of Auslands-Presse Chef of the NSDAP. In 1942, during dinner at the *Führer's* Headquarters, Hitler treated his table companions with stories about "my Foreign Press Chief, Hanfstaengl's rapacity and avarice." In those days, Hanfstaengl was trying hard to sell Hitler's articles to the highest foreign bidder in order to earn lots of money for the ever rapacious as well as impecunious and spendthrift *Führer*. However, that fact was not part of the *Führer's* delightful table tale.[18] After the January 1933 Nazi assumption of state power, Hanfstaengl was increasingly marginalized; the *Führer* was very busy and no longer needed "Putzi's" private entertainment to relax. Numerous new rival advisors were crowding around the *Führer* as well.

While in good standing with the Nazis, Hanfstaengl claims he saved various people from incarceration by the *Gestapo*. Eric Koch states that Hanfstaengl saved "many Jewish lives" during those years.[19] According to "Putzi," he fell foul of Himmler, Goering and Goebbels, who had planned his assassination. He was able to foil their plot and fled to Switzerland in February 1937, where his son Egon was soon to join him, and then they both proceeded to England. His wife had divorced him in 1936 and was safely back in America. While in British exile, "Putzi" told various versions of his experiences around the *Führer*, but somehow never found time or opportunity to denounce Hitler or to reject the Nazi regime publicly. In fact, "Putzi" often announced that he would be the next *Führer*. In 1939, Hanfstaengl apparently was ready to return to Nazi Germany in response to invitations from Hitler, but he insisted on receiving first a personal apology and security assurances from Hitler. When these were not forthcoming, he remained in the UK. In England, Hanfstaengl was approached, but was "not willing to work for Britain as an anti-Nazi propagandist." Hanfstaengl met Spier at the Olympia Hall in London, and subsequently they shared the accommodations at Lingfield Race Court and many other internment camps until they ended up together once again in Camp R at Red Rock.

In Camp R, some inmates appreciated the fifty-two-year-old Hanfstaengl for his virtuosity on the piano. Others, however, distrusted him for his ambiguous and ambivalent views and attitudes relating to Hitler and Nazism. In the days at Lingfield internment camp, "Putzi" actively participated in the celebration of the *Wintersonnenwende*, the winter solstice—the Nazis' pagan substitute for Christian Christmas— by reciting passages from the Nordic saga *Edda*. At Camp R, however, Hanfstaengl stayed in the background; eventually he became *persona non grata* with the Nazis, especially after they discovered in February 1941 from reading American newspapers that Egon Hanfstaengl—a one-time mandatory *Hitlerjunge*—had enlisted in the US Army Air Force. His father wished him well in his American military career and reminded him of his great and famous American military ancestors General John Sedgwick and General William Heine.

In the summer of 1941, Hanfstaengl was granted the privilege of viewing his own personal papers and of being visited by Mr. Donald Keyhoe, a representative from the Hearst chain's *Cosmopolitan* magazine, in order to discuss a pending contract for his memoirs and his apparent refusal to write while interned at Red Rock. Moreover, Mr. Keyhoe planned to clarify whether Hanfstaengl had entered similar contracts with other magazines. This interview required the approval of the British government and was strictly controlled in terms of duration and type of issues under consideration. When the event occurred, time was very limited, a military officer was always present, only English was spoken, and the issues considered were limited to the contract. No questionnaire was permitted, and excluded were any comments or questions designed to elicit references to "Putzi's" past, which Keyhoe might have used in preparation of articles about Hanfstaengl. Moreover, any article written by Keyhoe needed to be submitted to Ottawa and London prior to publication. One wonders whom the authorities trusted less, Keyhoe or "Putzi"? The discussions about contracts with *Cosmopolitan* or the *New York Times* dragged on into December 1941, after Pearl Harbor Day, and Keyhoe pleaded with the Canadian and British authorities to let Hanfstaengl publish his writings now that the USA was at war too.[20]

In October 1941, Hanfstaengl was transferred to Fort Henry, Kingston, Ontario, from where he was eventually released into American custody on the request of his old pal and Harvard Club friend, President Franklin D. Roosevelt. "Putzi" was transferred to Washington by Roosevelt's advisor John Franklin Carter, and there he lived near Washington under a form of house arrest. In his memoirs, Hanfstaengl claimed that he acted as advisor to his old Harvard buddy Roosevelt on German and Nazi affairs. In 1947, Jay Franklin, aka John Franklin Carter, a "confidential" contact person for President Roosevelt, published an interesting book, entitled *The Catoctin Conversation*, with an introduction by Sumner Welles, which pretends to present actual conversations between Roosevelt, Churchill and Hanfstaengl. Welles neither confirmed nor denied the authenticity of these conversations; they were plausible, he implied. When "Putzi's" transfer to the United States became public, Ottawa received a handwritten letter from "Mrs. Arthur Goadby" (Joanna M. Goadby) of Charlottesville, Virginia, protesting his "release," arguing that she knew "Putzi" and knew he was a spy for Hitler.

In 1944, despite his American intrigues, England demanded Hanfstaengl's repatriation.[21] It seems the English believed, like Mrs. Goadby, that Hanfstaengl still had contacts with the Nazis because he had once been an ardent supporter of Hitler. Of course, looking over Dr. Hanfstaengl's career and public actions, one might ask how deeply he was committed to the Allies' cause. The British kept "Putzi" incarcerated until 1946. When he was released, he returned to war-ravaged Munich. After the war, his name was found on a *Gestapo* list of persons destined to be shot after a successful Nazi invasion of Great Britain. The *Daily Express* published this list in its issue of 11 October 1946.

Whether bystanders, inmates or officials, all regarded Hanfstaengl as unreliable and untrustworthy. Critics called him "an essential bohemian," Hitler's "playboy," or an arrogant, unrepentant and effeminate Nazi. His son saw him suffering from "polygamous impulses." Against these negative views stand the facts that Hanfstaengl consistently rejected and condemned Nazi anti-Semitism as a lunacy, that he fled Nazi Germany in 1937, and that he never joined any Neo-Nazi activities after his return to Germany in 1946.[22] His failure to condemn Nazism unequivocally nevertheless left doubts about his views and position.

Nothing is known about theatre and concert performances being staged at Red Rock, except a passing reference prohibiting a "variety show," which may have been staged in the opening weeks of the camp and was subsequently forbidden, perhaps on account of its tendentious character. The standing order on camp life specifically prohibited the staging of theatre and variety performances, unless pre-censored and permitted by Berry.[23] Was only one performance staged, and if so was this first performance too risqué for Canadian taste in the 1940s, or was it politically objectionable? Did Berry's insistence on his prior approval stymie the creative imagination and talents of inmates? These questions remain unanswered for lack of evidence. Likewise, one knows that the camp choir and orchestra performed at least once at the German inmates' Christmas party.

Neither an easy nor a ready explanation is available as to why in Red Rock, unlike elsewhere, the creative energies of the inmates were apparently so completely absorbed by physical activities. They were diverted at best into the manufacture of saleable souvenirs or into sports and at worst into harassment of the Jewish and anti-Nazi minority. Perhaps the pool of talent in the camp was too small, or too old, or too young, or the social, cultural and educational mix inappropriate and inadequate. Perhaps the political divisions absorbed most creative impulses.

Camp life also included many facets of little importance to the camp community as a whole, but which was nonetheless of significance to individual inmates. Excerpts from inmates' letters provided by care of Captain Kirkness give a glimpse of what also was going on in Camp R during the first three months from July to September.[24] In August the inmates' letters seemed primarily concerned with the reality of finding themselves in the enforced company of their political foes. Mutual dislike found expression in many letters. A second recurrent complaint lamented the lack of space for recreational and sports activities. These deficiencies were supplemented by complaints about the lack of tobacco goods. The elderly and better-educated prisoners grumbled about the lack of newspapers, magazines and books.

In September the letters indicated that the inmates were pleased by "the excellence of the food," which occasionally recalled unpleasant memories about English cooking and led to unfavourable comparisons with English camp food. "The food is good and plentiful. The only thing we miss is the variety of vegetable we have been used to in the past. We never see fruit in season, such as strawberries and cherries: but, of course, we don't expect that. We don't get salads, but there is white cabbage and new potatoes. We also get fish, e.g. halibut and freshwater fish. There is plenty of butter," wrote ship captain A. Weiss to his wife in Hamburg.

With September came colder weather and increased pessimism. Many of the "South Africans," who suffered from malaria and other tropical ailments, dreaded the coming of winter with its suspected "Siberian climate." During August and September a most remarkable shift was noted in "the rather pronounced optimism" displayed by the Nazis in the early days of their internment in Red Rock. Already towards the end of August their optimism was "less apparent." Fewer inmates still believed that the war would be over in a few weeks, and many now acknowledged the prospect of remaining in Canada for the winter. Several letter writers were concerned about the "severity of the bombing raids over Germany." In Kirkness's view the excerpts taken from the letters of the "National-Socialists" still reflected "considerable optimism" and expected confidently "a quick Nazi victory" before Christmas. Whereas previously the Nazis had scheduled victory in

May, then July and even August, now it was September going on to December. Increasingly it seems a willingness to face a long war was spreading among the faithful. Regardless of external developments, camp life even of the faithful like Baron Pilar went on routinely. As he wrote to his wife in London: "my days are well occupied. I am again giving lessons as in Lingfield. Also I am taking a lot off Captain Scharf's shoulders, which means that I have plenty of writing and talking to do." Censorship had become more severe; as a result, many inmates' letters were rejected, and this act increased resentment among inmates. In connection with the inmate's letter-writing habits, Kirkness observed, "It is clear that morale increases in ratio to the amount of work and recreation which the internees receive. The men who occupy most of their time with work and sport write the best letters. The worst letters are written by the Jews, who rarely work, or play, but appear to spend most of their time in political discussions." Kirkness noted, "in general, there is a fairly friendly atmosphere in the camp" despite the tension between "two intensely hostile groups." Neither Kirkness nor the letter excerpts indicate whether the "fairly friendly atmosphere" resulted from such recent developments as regular mail delivery from the USA and the establishment of a camp library, a shoe repair shop and a carpenter's shop.

VIII

A Canadian Conundrum

Deception, Anti-Semitism, Paterson Mission

and Partial Solutions

DURING THE PERIOD FROM JULY to September 1940, life in the enclosure at Camp R was unfolding more or less as it was expected to do under the guidance of multiple standing orders, regulations, and the relevant Articles of the Geneva Convention of 1929. During this time, as well, increased contact between prisoners and Commandant Berry and his staff eventually revealed the true nature of the inmates. As early as 10 July, General Panet heard from Camp R that about 200 of the newly delivered prisoners were refugees from Nazi Germany, Jews and true anti-Nazis. Ostensibly they were friends of the Allies in the fight against Nazism and certainly not Nazi POWs or enemies of the Allies. At about the same time, Under-Secretary of State for External Affairs, Dr. O.D. Skelton, who apparently was petitioned directly, received several auto-biographical statements from refugee internees in Camp R.[1]

Obviously these prisoners were not what they were supposed to be. Moreover, observing the schoolboys and elderly men, it became increasingly obvious that they were utterly passive militarily and incapable of posing a military risk to anyone's national security. They were not the crack elite parachutists that had been promised. Observing the situation in Camp R, one could readily conclude that the camp scene illustrated Canada's conundrum in microcosm: a small group of perhaps 200 unwanted, unexpected, potential Jewish-German-Austrian immigrants had been mistakenly categorized and then deported and dumped in Northwestern Ontario. What was to be done?

The process of enlightenment unfolded in Camp R much as it did in other Canadian civilian internment camps housing the recently unloaded "dangerous enemy aliens" from Britain. The local military camp authorities in Quebec and Ontario rapidly realized that they were guarding not dangerous Nazis and fifth columnists, but mostly Jewish and anti-Nazi refugees from Nazi Germany, schoolboys, students, rabbis, professors, professionals and artists.[2] Soon the realization of the true situation spread from the camps to the central government agencies in Ottawa, and awareness arose that Great Britain had engaged in a great deception of the Dominion of Canada over the true nature and character of these interned "dangerous enemy aliens" and "Nazi leaders" who needed to be deported to Canada. Instead of military security risks, Prime Minister Churchill's government had dispatched to Canada, according to British records, a bounty of 2,108 German or Austrian Category A, single male internees, including circa 1,700 enemy merchant seamen, an additional 2,290 Category B and C Germans and Austrians, 407 Italian civilian single male internees and 1,948 genuine prisoners of war, making a total of 6,743.[3] Most (85 per cent) of the German and Austrian civilian internees were refugees from Nazi Germany.

Ottawa's first response to the news from the various internment camps was astonishment: what was received was not what was expected. Subsequent responses have led historians to conjecture whether Ottawa was anti-Jewish, anti-Semitic or just anti-refugee.[4] Such inferences often require fine distinctions. Anti-Jewish attitudes discriminate against Jews on religious or ideological grounds, while anti-Semitism does so based on racism; and anti-refugee attitudes are nativist in origin, but also are coloured by racism, making each hard to differentiate. Close analysis suggests that Ottawa's reaction actually contained a mixture of all three.

It seems that from the very start of negotiations between Ottawa and London at the end of May and beginning of June 1940, not all the facts were given regarding the true nature of the deportees to be transferred to Canada. Ottawa's recurrent requests for clarification and amplification on who was coming implied a degree of concern and perhaps suspicion. The first, though unofficial, recognition by a Canadian diplomat of Britain's successful deception of Canada came from Charles Ritchie, the Second Secretary at Canada House in London, on 16 July 1940, when he entered the following illuminating passage into his private diary:

> I hear the ferocious internees whom the British government begged us on bended knee to take to Canada to save the country from nefarious activities are mostly entirely inoffensive anti-Nazi refugees who have been shovelled out to Canada at a moment's notice where they may have a disagreeable time, as our authorities have no files about them and will not know whom or what to believe. Part of the trouble is due to the fact that the Home Office and the War Office seem barely on speaking terms.[5]

Two weeks after the *Duchess of York* had landed, one day after the last troop carrier arrived in Quebec harbour, five weeks after the Swinton lobby descended upon him with their urgent hysterical request for help and almost one month after the crucial London Conference of 17 June at which he was Canada's representative, Ritchie very perceptively summarized the existing situation. Britain's deception of Canada was coming to light as information from the various internment camps filtered back to Ottawa, forcing the government to face a changed situation and an unexpected conundrum.

Though Canadian officials never raised the issue of deception publicly, nonetheless diplomatic communications soon aired the matter in London. On 22 July, High Commissioner Massey wrote a long letter to Viscount Caldecote, Secretary of State for the Dominions, in which he revisited the negotiations carried on between them in early June. "A number of questions," Massey wrote, "have now arisen regarding the internees transferred to Canada which appear to require some further clarification."[6] He complained that Britain had indeed deliberately withheld information concerning the true identity of the deportees and their dangerousness. Massey assured Caldecote that he did not want to re-hash past details, but stated that the Canadian government still did wish clarification of the assertion from the United Kingdom government that "these particular internees...constitute a most serious danger in the case of an attempted German invasion." Drawing attention to Caldecote's letter of 7 June, which explicitly claimed that "2,500 are definitely pro-Nazi...and therefore a source of danger in the event... of parachute landings," Massey reminded his British colleagues "the Canadian government only accepted this responsibility [for safeguarding the internees] in view of this urgent request of the United Kingdom Government." Massey continued: "Moreover, the internees arrived in Canada without any individual dossiers or records which might enable the Canadian authorities to judge of the political views and past history of the internees in question." Furthermore, Massey informed Caldecote that Canada House in London received daily inquiries alleging that the enemy aliens "are innocent internees of anti-Nazi sympathies." This view, moreover, Massey pointed out, was now expressed even by the Home Office, which had told him "that a number of internees sent to Canada are, in their opinion, in fact innocent internees." Massey requested clarification and stated that "if it should, in fact, prove that a very substantial number of the civilian internees transferred to Canada should be regarded as innocent refugees from Nazi oppression, *the Canadian Government would be faced with responsibilities of a character which they had certainly not contemplated when they consented to receive these internees* [my emphasis]" who in the words of Churchill's government were "a source of most serious risk." The italicized phrase in

Massey's letter highlighted Ottawa's conundrum. Ottawa had accepted in good faith three shiploads of allegedly dangerous people and now ended up with thousands of unwanted and undesirable potential immigrants, who, in addition, turned out to be Jews. What had landed in Canada was "very far away from the kind of men Canada had been led to expect."

A military officer framed the surprise situation this way: "No definite information as to the character of these internees was available in Canada and it was thought that they were all POWs." This surprise created a problem: what to do with these undesirable, non-dangerous persons, Jewish refugees, whose admission Canada had refused steadfastly over the past decade?[7] On 30 July, London replied and now declared suddenly that neither the "Fascist Italians" nor the German and Austrian internees in Categories B and C were dangerous anymore. This was quite a reversal. London now explained that "the prospect of invasion not only made it necessary to intern large numbers [of] Germans and Austrians...but made it desirable that as many as possible of the internees, and especially the more dangerous elements among them, should be sent overseas."[8] A common refrain of British requests for assistance was that the internees were "potentially dangerous persons in areas which may soon be the scene of invasion."[9] Indeed British diplomatic correspondence left the impression that London was keener on shipping out civilian internees than military POWs. This attitude seemed present in Lord Snell's Inquiry Report and in Chamberlain's report to the cabinet on the Swinton Committee.[10] Since Britain's mass internment was launched "owing to the exigencies of the military situation," all enemy aliens whether in Category A, B or C would be shipped out. According to official British government communications, Canada had received only "dangerous enemy aliens." No explanation was offered why these once dangerous enemy aliens had suddenly ceased being a danger or being "bad characters."[11] Always a tad sanctimonious, London advised Ottawa to keep "Category A internees" in separate camps from the other now non-dangerous internees and the still dangerous POWs. Not even then did London officially admit that most of these same dangerous enemy aliens had always been just plain Jewish and anti-Nazi refugees. One may well ask whether Great Britain ever really did have "350 Nazi leaders" in detention? Indeed it is interesting to note that British government correspondence avoids references to "refugees" or "Jews" or "anti-Nazis" in its discourse.[12]

Despite repeated requests, Ottawa did not receive any identification documents for these imported prisoners for many months. For the longest time British explanations for this failure invariably proved false. Caldecote claimed, for example that, but for the sinking of the *Arandora Star* these identification documents would be in Canada. However, it was soon established that the British military had no reliable records of who actually sailed on this ill-fated ship, and that certainly she could not have carried the *entire* documentation for all four ships, since neither the *Ettrick* nor the *Sobieski* had been loaded at the time of the *Arandora Star*'s departure.[13] Equally questionable is whether or not Canadian officials were ever properly briefed by the British government on the meaning of the Categories A, B and C or on the nature and function of the entire tribunal process. And if so, would such explanations really have enlightened Canadian officials about the tribunal process which landed Spier in Red Rock or had Jewish schoolboys declared Category A internees?

Two separate and accidental incidents suddenly exposed the scope of Britain's mismanagement of the whole deportation procedure and further revealed the process of deception. First was the tragic sinking of the *Arandora Star* by a German U-boat off the west coast of Ireland on 2 July with the loss of 700 lives. The second was the revelation of the sufferings refugee passengers endured at the hands of the accompanying British guard, officers and soldiers, *en route* to Australia on the liner *Dunera*. An immense public outcry after the first incident forced the Churchill cabinet to set up an inquiry into the *Arandora Star* disaster under Lord Snell on 12 August. However, Lord Snell, charged "to inquire into the method of selection of the aliens," exonerated, first, the War

Cabinet, which had pressed for speedy deportations, and second, the military, which also had operated under great time pressure and implemented sloppy and haphazard selection procedures.

The military had executed its orders on the basis of inaccurate lists supplied by MI5. Snell upheld the official Churchill government's tale that only "dangerous characters" of German or Austrian origin—never Jews and anti-Nazis—boarded the doomed vessel, and that the Italians, too, were "bad characters" and Fascist Party members. Admittedly, in case of the Italians mistakes were made; extreme time pressures did not allow disentangling misspelled names and mis-selected deportees. Such a mere "list error" was "Signor Anzani, who had lived in England for twenty years and was the well-known Secretary of the Italian Section of the League of the Rights of Man." Another list error, not mentioned by Lord Snell, was Mr. P.M. Salerni, a well-known aircraft engineer much wanted by Lord Beaverbrook and his Air Ministry for his recently invented aircraft transmission device.[14] They both drowned, unmistakably.

The story of the suffering of passengers on the *Dunera* is tangential to the story of Camp R. It is therefore mentioned here only because it, like the sinking of the *Arandora Star*, played an essential part in forcing the Churchill cabinet to change its attitude towards interned enemy aliens. And this fact did, in the end, impact the fate of the Jewish and anti-Nazi refugees in Camp R. Details revealed of the horrendous *Dunera* incident seized the attention of the British public. Mounting public pressure through newspaper reports, editorials and parliamentary inquiries forced action from the government. Consequently, the Churchill cabinet published a first White Book at the end of July, which presented some eighteen categories under which interned aliens could seek to obtain release from their unjust incarceration. Thereafter additional categories were added, and by November 1940, twenty-three categories offered release opportunities.[15]

These fundamental changes in Britain's policy on the treatment of interned enemy alien refugees in the autumn of 1940, it must be noted, happened in the context of two important developments. First, Britain's military fortunes drastically improved; second, the public's mood recuperated. The imminent threat of the much-dreaded German invasion had passed; the air battle over Britain had been won, and the United States was helping with Lend-Lease arrangements and fifty pre-owned destroyers. The public once again regarded Jewish and anti-Nazi refugees from Nazi Germany as capable of contributing to the war effort.

The general awakening of British conscience moved London finally to dispatch the internees' long promised personal identification documents to Ottawa. These documents continued to recite the deceptive official version of past events, maintaining that internment and deportation were the result, first, of thoughtful classifications of enemy aliens into Categories A, B and C by British tribunals and, second, of urgent demands by the War Office on military grounds and because of security risks. These facts had necessitated the hurried and harried deportation of these most dangerous and risky Germans and Austrians. The documents never spoke about deporting Jews or refugees, only about Germans and Austrians or Italians. The British authorities admitted that in the rush of events and pressures of time errors were committed, but only a few, and some Category B and C internees were shipped off accidentally. These few—who actually numbered many hundreds— might be innocent refugees. These innocents should be held in different camps from the Nazis, the British suggested self-righteously, forgetting of course their own practice of operating mixed camps. Unfortunately, this British information never explained how an ardent, well-known and committed Churchill lobbyist and supporter like Spier was classified "A" and how eleven schoolboys ended up in Red Rock with several hundred civilian sailors who were also, and perhaps correctly, evaluated Category A. The great deception, it seems, was continued and rationalized by excuses.

In Britain in the late summer and autumn of 1940, incarcerated enemy alien refugees were freed under the provisions of the new White

Book. In Canada, in contrast, confusion prevailed over the issue of what to do next with these unwanted internees. Ottawa believed that if it solved its conundrum unilaterally in the simplest and most obviously humanitarian way by immediately releasing all schoolboys, university students, rabbis, priests, elderly academics and old men, this action might stir up domestic political unrest. Ottawa had other reasons for uncertainty as well. Chiefly, no one in Ottawa really seemed to know what the British tribunal classifications actually meant: how credible were the internees' own stories; how dangerous were these enemy alien refugees; and finally what were the legal consequences of setting them free in Canada? Could Canada even legally free these internees? Had Britain not declared at the Conference of 17 June her unwillingness to cede full control over the internees and over the POWs to Canada?[16] These internees were still legally Britain's responsibility, and Canada could hardly release them unilaterally. Without clarification of the refugees' true security status and explicit legal consent from Britain, the way forward was blocked. Help was needed.

In September 1940, Ottawa requested the physical presence of a London representative who could help sort out the imported mess of the hapless internees, victims of fear, hysteria and panic, of incompetence and callousness, and of racism. The Churchill government agreed and eventually sent out "a responsible official, who would be qualified to advise the Government of Canada as to the degree of danger of the different categories of internees."[17] This person was Mr. Alexander Paterson, "His Majesty's Commissioner of Prisons in England and Wales" for the past twenty-five years.[18]

The Paterson Mission, which covered 18 November 1940 to 6 July 1941, served two distinct ends. First, it was to extract Great Britain from the mess of its own creation, the mass deportation of "dangerous enemy aliens" who were overwhelmingly German and Austrian-Jewish refugees from Nazi Germany. Second, Paterson was to assist Canada in sorting out the refugees. During his eight months in eastern Canada and the USA, Paterson worked most diligently and imaginatively not only in Ottawa and the various eastern camps, but also in Washington in order to devise and implement various proposals and procedures. On arrival, he contacted numerous Canadian ministers and their officials, as well as various Jewish and Gentile community leaders and officials of their respective relief organizations. He worked closely with the Directors of Internment Operations, first the open-minded and outgoing General Panet and then the disappointing Colonel Stethem.

Preceding Paterson's arrival, the Directorate had already initiated a process of separating Jewish and anti-Nazi refugees in Categories B and C from Nazi elements by sending the former to newly constructed and organized camps in eastern Canada by the early fall of 1940. This initiative greatly aided Paterson, who visited every one of the five eastern civilian internment camps set aside for refugees. These new refugee camps were Camp A located at Farnham, Camp N at Newington, Camp I at Île aux Noix, Camp S on St. Helen's Island, all in Quebec, and Camp B at Little River, New Brunswick.

Paterson achieved many successes. Almost immediately he succeeded in alleviating the mental distress internment caused many refugees. Frequently visiting the camps and speaking freely and privately with the inmates, spending countless hours interviewing refugees, Paterson succeeded gradually in unravelling the tangles of their misery. He eased the sense of injustice, resolved numerous wrongful tribunal categorizations and advised refugees on how to apply the new and numerous regulations of the British White Book to their individual cases. He even restored some hope to their lives.[19] In this regard, Paterson was quite successful: in December 1940, 287 refugees returned to England; in February 1941, a further 274, and finally 330 followed in June.[20]

The impact of Paterson's visits is well documented by young Harry Seidler, interned at Camp N, who noted in his diary: "Paterson brought the air of the civilized world outside" into the camp. Seidler was delighted to hear once again a "gentleman's correct English" instead of "the horrible Canadian dialect."[21] In one very sad instance, Paterson finally brought relief to a long-suffering shy seventeen-year-old German-Jewish teenager whose repeated requests to have his broken eyeglasses repaired were callously ignored by the local military chain of command, and therefore the teenage lad had been unable for five long months to read his mother's letters, to write to his family or to read books or newspapers. By the time Paterson discovered this state of affairs the boy had become much disturbed, psychologically and emotionally.[22]

Paterson's encounter with Max Otto Ludwig Loewenstein, now known as Marc Lynton, is worth a brief mention even though this tale does not directly involve Camp R, because it nonetheless illuminates the general circumstances confronting Paterson and perhaps explains why he never found time to venture north to Red Rock. Loewenstein found himself imprisoned in Camp L, Cove Field Barracks, and offered these comparative observations. Whereas English soldiers "were both incurious and utterly ignorant of who we might be, and proved to be friendly, indifferent, quite courteous and staggeringly incompetent," in contrast, Canadian soldiers "were tough, smart, very efficient, and generally rather hostile." Lynton later recalled that he learned these lessons about internment: "1. Everyone impinges on everyone. 2. Dignity and privacy dominate reality. 3. Activity makes optimism. 4. Some one must lead initiate, and keep doing so, people just mill about and get discouraged."[23]

During the course of his interview Loewenstein found out that he and other members of the Cambridge gang had been released in early June 1940, but due to the inefficient administrative system prevailing in the British camps, the Home Office did not know in what camp he was and then concluded that he and the others had been shipped out with the *Arandora Star* and eventually and logically declared them "dead" and so informed their next of kin. And inmate Loewenstein sat illegally in Camp N at Newington, trying to return to where he should have never left.

Paterson achieved his greatest success in advising the Canadian government to separate the administrative operations of internment camps for refugee internees from all other Canadian and imported civilian internees and POWs. This advice was accepted by the government and implemented on 25 June 1941 by P.C. 4568 with the creation of the new office of a Commissioner for Refugees and the appointment of Colonel R.W.S. Fordham, who was a lawyer and "a man of wide sympathy, strong character, and most charming personality."[24] Fordham was placed directly under the Undersecretary of State, Dr. E.H. Coleman, while Colonel Stethem would continue as Commissioner of Internment Camps administering all non-refugee and POW camps under the auspices of the Directorate of Internment Operations.

Since Camp R was officially Category A, it did not come under Colonel Fordham's new refugee jurisdiction. R's small group of suffering Jews and anti-Nazi refugees remained outside the new administrative regime and had to wait until March 1941 before being interviewed. By then they had already been transferred to compatible eastern Canadian refugee camps in January 1941. Apparently Paterson used his influence in Ottawa and thus contributed to the transfer of the Jewish refugees to Camp N.[25]

Paterson succeeded also through continued personal contacts with the military, especially at the local level, to obtain slight amelioration of camp routine. Paterson had great hopes, in 1941, as had Panet a year before, that a new administrative regime might abandon or at least lighten the excessively military atmosphere in the newly designated refugee camps. Unfortunately, the Department of National Defence decided to continue its system of rigid military discipline based on armed guards, bayonets, machine guns and barbed wire in the refugee camps. This questionable regime of military discipline is illustrated by these silly practices: (a) forcing inmates to fold used wet towels for the sake of neatness into their bed blankets, and (b) insisting that the camp commandant entering a hut be accompanied by two soldiers with fixed bayonets.[26] Commissioner Paterson thought that the refugees needed schoolmasters rather than military officers. He recognized that better brains were often inside the enclosure than outside. In his view "a Canadian tends to be a man of rigid and unimaginative mind, and therefore not well-suited to taking care of sensitive and temperamental human beings" such as the "perky schoolboys and bespectacled professors" in the camps.[27]

About Canadian camp commandants, Paterson remarked that although some had been prisoners of war themselves during the First World War, they lacked the ability to comprehend the refugee camp atmosphere and "find it curiously difficult to understand the inner working of the minds of the men in their charge."[28] Not surprisingly, as his report recalled in details, he failed to convince the Canadian military to abandon its military regime. Why exhibit all this formidable military rigmarole? Who among the refugee inmates needed intimidation; the few temporarily illegal Communists inside? They would soon be allies. In the preceding twelve months no refugee had tried to escape from any eastern Canadian camp. Obviously, the inmates wished to assist the Canadian war effort. Yet the Department of National Defence, its minister especially, and the local military in charge of the refugee camps were unwilling to abandon or incapable of changing the offensive military command routine in the management of affairs in refugee camps.

A further achievement, indeed a major victory seen from the perspective of the refugees affected by it, was Paterson's success, with the assistance of many helpers, in obtaining eventually the release in Canada of hundreds of young Jews, students and workers. He was able to mobilize religious leaders, Jewish and Gentile agencies, politicians and the press. The *Halifax Herald* and the *Winnipeg Free Press* wrote supportive articles on the issue. And gradually public opinion was changed. An important role was played in this affair by the American entertainer and singer Ruth Draper who successfully secured the release of her Canadian-detained Italian protégé by means of her personal acquaintance with Prime Minister Mackenzie King. King's direct intervention in the release process was used cunningly by Paterson to effect the subsequent liberation of hundreds of young Jews in Canada.[29] Generally speaking, however, all these intriguing and successful efforts completely bypassed the refugees in Camp R.

Unfortunately, for the small group of Jewish and anti-Nazi refugees imprisoned in far away Camp R, in Northwestern Ontario, Paterson's many blessings remained distant rumours only. For many valid reasons, Paterson never found time or opportunity to venture forth and visit Red Rock. Being very busy in eastern Canada and in Washington was one reason; another was the fact that this relatively small group of refugees was classified as Category A and was viewed therefore with suspicion by everyone, even by their Canadian fellow Jews. Believing that *all* inmates in Camp R, including the alleged refugees, had been properly placed into Category A by British tribunals, deterred Paterson and others from coming forward to help. Furthermore, all these inmates had been shipped over on the *Duchess*, the first ship, which according to British government evidence carried the most dangerous enemy aliens.

Paterson also experienced failures. His most important setback was his failure to overcome the opposition of the American Legion and similar right-wing groups to the opening of the US border to permit the re-unification of Jewish families, parents and children. Four times he visited Washington and conducted protracted, but unfortunately abortive negotiations with different political leaders, government officials and public agencies. The dominant political influence exerted by super-patriotic American legionnaires intimidated the Roosevelt government which decided not to allow legitimate Jewish persons, with previously issued visas, mostly youngsters seeking to rejoin their parents, to immigrate to the United States.

Paterson and many others looked into different schemes to enable young Jewish refugees to enter the USA legally from Canada, or via Newfoundland or Cuba, and he invested months of hard work and scarce financial resources. All these plans come to naught. "The American government did not want them."[30] This was due to a small vociferous group of determined American anti-Semites who wrapped themselves in the camouflage of patriotism and abused their political power in a democratic system to bestow misery upon hundreds of individuals and families.

Against this tragic failure stands of course Paterson's dramatic repatriation of almost one thousand interned refugees from Canada. With this accomplishment, Paterson ended the episode of the great deception. What is remarkable is that the Churchill government never officially and directly admitted this great deception nor its incompetence and mismanagement of the deportation process. Moreover, Prime Minister Churchill never expressed regrets over the deception to Canada, his staunch ally. Not even in his voluminous postwar writings did Sir Winston find time and space to express regrets over the utter disregard for Jewish and anti-Nazi refugees' human rights or for inflicting incalculable and unnecessary human anguish and suffering on these already victimized persons. Of course this is only a minor matter among the big and grandiose issues of war and affects only the lives of a few thousand ordinary people. Perhaps Churchill's memory of the past became blurred or extremely selective, as happened in the House of Commons in August 1940, for example, when he declared that personally he had always thought the "threat of the fifth column" exaggerated.[31] It is true that the war cabinet took the decisions concerning mass internment and deportation, but equally true is that Churchill dominated the cabinet.

In any case, the presence of widely dispersed anti-Semitism within Canadian politics and society complicated Ottawa's conundrum and hindered its quick and effective solution. Government and military circles, from cabinet level down to the ordinary sentry in the camp, all wrestled with the problem of how to manage and perhaps resolve the problem of the landed "dangerous" enemy alien internees who had suddenly become innocent refugees and potential immigrants, but who as Jews were considered "undesirable and unassimilable."[32] Undoubtedly, this issue of ethnicity influenced the process of decision-making and the execution of new policies. Ottawa's state of confusion was reflected in its hesitation to deal directly and promptly with the new situation once Britain's deception had been established and was unquestionably affected by its awareness of the widespread existence of racial and economic anti-Semitism in Canadian society.

The prevalence of Canadian anti-Semitism was reflected in the practice of admission quotas for Jewish students to medical and law schools or to the professions. Publicly displayed restrictions on access—"Gentiles Only"—to beaches and parks further underlined the dominant anti-Semitic attitude.[33] In response to public demands from farmers, trade unionists, professionals and business men, Ottawa had carefully regulated and restricted all immigration into Canada during the 1930s. Jewish refugees from Nazi Germany found no exceptions in these rules. Even the Jewish passengers on the ill-fated ship St. Louis were refused admission to land in Canada despite the pleas and support from influential Canadians.[34]

The Mackenzie King cabinet was aware of and shared the public's anti-Semitic sentiments. Mackenzie King, personally, was not free from anti-Semitic views and was very much aware of strong anti-Semitic feelings in Quebec, which were presented in cabinet by Ernest Lapointe, Minister of Justice, and other Québécois ministers. King believed that a release en masse of Jewish interned refugees in Canada would endanger Canadian unity and strengthen separatism and disrupt the country's war efforts. Ottawa feared Canadian public reactions to setting aside existing Canadian immigration laws and rules, which had framed the inhuman anti-Semitic, anti-refugee immigration policy of the 1930s, especially in the circumstances of an already existing national hysteria about suspected fifth columnists, saboteurs and multitudes of allegedly untrustworthy resident aliens of German, Austrian and Italian origins. Certainly, the right-wing press had already accomplished much in arousing national hysteria.[35]

Some Ottawa officials were firmly opposed to the release of the Jewish internees, regardless of pleadings and entreaties from anyone; Jews were unwanted. Perhaps the most adamant, vociferous and influential representative of this circle and the most formidable obstacle was F.C. Blair, Director of Immigration. Blair, who was described by Saul Hayes, Director of United Jewish Refugee and War Relief Agencies as "a very devout and righteous [Christian] believer," was a blatant anti-Semite and at the same time a zealous defender of Canadian laws designed to keep refugee Jews out of Canada and the country stable and sound.[36] But there were others, like Dr. O.D. Skelton, Under-Secretary of State for External Affairs, who, right at the outset, advocated positive action, namely, the release of all refugees in Canada.

Civil servants and military officers in Ottawa were not the only ones confused by the situation. Jewish leaders and officials of Canadian Jewish relief agencies were also confused. Initially, Canadian Jewish leaders were unaware of the true character of the deportees from Britain. Canadian Jews believed that Nazis were masquerading as Jews.[37] They were alerted by the contradictory information they received about the newly arrived internees from the Canadian government and from Jewish agencies and relatives in Britain. Officially, the landed civilian deportees were classified Category A, B and C, but all were deported from Britain as dangerous security risks. On arrival the deportees themselves, however, insisted that they were genuine anti-Nazi and Jewish refugees, and some even argued that they were incorrectly placed in Category A, especially those in Camp R. Canadian Jewry was confused and suspicious: who really and truly were these people? Canadian Jewish leaders could not risk supporting enemy aliens, foes of Britain, possible fifth columnists or worse Nazi spies; if they mistakenly did this, such an act could potentially destroy their credibility and thus all their efforts concerned with saving European Jews from the clutches of Nazism and, worst of all, might provoke outbursts of anti-Semitism.[38]

Officials of the Canadian Jewish Congress eventually agreed that they would help those interned refugees in Categories B and C, incarcerated exclusively in camps in the eastern parts of Canada, but not those Jews in Category A—in Camp R—who were considered Nazis and enemies of the British regime. Stanley Goldner, assistant to Hayes, for instance, considered the Jewish inmates in Camp R as pro-Nazi.[39] These concerns certainly influenced discussions between Commissioner Paterson and Jewish representatives when considering action concerning the refugees. This decision by the Congress certainly affected all seventy-eight Jews in Camp R negatively. For the foreseeable future, these members of the anti-Hitler bloc were consigned to life in "the little Third Reich on Lake Superior."[40]

Canada's military, being directly responsible for the incarceration of the imported "dangerous enemy aliens," was the first government agency to face the new reality. Initially, of course, nothing changed in the operational reality of the internment camps. The German POWs, who had been separated from the civilian internees right after landing in Quebec, were not affected by the discovery of Britain's deception. In regard to the civilian internment camps, the military's initial response was an instinctive reaction, namely rigid and strict adherence to existing regulations; it simply carried on its assigned duties from day to weeks to months, following established routine procedures until new orders were issued in Ottawa. In the purview of the Army all inmates of internment camps were POWs.

In accordance with the existing rules and regulations, every camp administration and its local contingent of sentries from either the Army, "The Permanent Force," or the Veterans Guard of Canada were guarding "Prisoners of War, Class II" and not specifically civilian internees, certainly not refugees. These "Prisoners of War, Class II" were subject to military discipline, requiring well-armed guards with bayonets and machine guns and barbed wire fences. That was the message coming down right from the top to the local soldier. For example, at Camp R, an officer addressed the inmates at arrival and declared: "Now you are POWs *from a failed invasion* [my emphasis], so let me have your decorations. I pay high prices."[41] At another camp, the commandant announced to the assembled internees: "I am not interested if you are pro- or anti-British! You are not refugees, but POWs, Class II under the laws of Canada."[42] Colonel Watson, on an inspection tour of

Cove Field Barracks in August 1940, was appalled when he heard the inmates of Camp L referred to as "refugees from Nazi Germany"; in his view, they were only POWs.[43] The interned refugees regarded themselves as essentially civilian individuals, and therefore rejected and resented the military ambience imposed upon them by their captors. Internees also feared that this new designation implied Canada's willingness to exchange them and thus send them back to Nazi Germany in the event of an armistice or a peace treaty.[44]

Misunderstandings and misperceptions between the military authority and the interned refugees determined the atmosphere of their mutual relations. The application of Canada's official but opaque classification of POW, Class I and POW, Class II caused problems with guards as well as inmates. The distinction between the two classes, one an ex-combatant Nazi and the other a non-combatant Nazi, was often too subtle for an ordinary soldier on duty. They were all imprisoned German Nazis who were all dangerous. From the perspective of the interned Jews and anti-Nazis, however, to be referred to commonly and openly as prisoners of war and to be subjected in their private existence to military discipline seemed not a foolish annoyance, but an insult and injury. They were persecuted victims of Nazism, innocent men and boys who suffered an illegal and wrongful incarceration. To be made into Prisoners of War was harsh and incomprehensible to individuals who included an internationally renowned professor, a well-known anti-Nazi journalist, a "perky" schoolboy, a Jewish refugee, a Rabbi, and a Bolshevik international unionist, none of whom had committed any offence or had ever been tried and found guilty in a proper court of law.[45]

During the early weeks, when uncertainties about the prisoners' status arose, officers and soldiers were unwilling or incapable of recognizing the new, changed circumstances as they discharged their duties. In Camp R, it was especially difficult for guards to distinguish Nazis from anti-Nazis; they all looked alike to the guards, and they usually spoke German among themselves, but most importantly, they all were in Category A. Nevertheless, compared to other camps, the inmates at

Red Rock lived free from harassment by their guards. This was true even in the days of the trigger-ready soldiers of the Fort Garry Horse. There exist no reports of cruel treatment of inmates by soldiers at Camp R, although there do from other camps.

Differentiating between genuine Nazi prisoners, interned German nationals, known anti-Nazis, refugees, and Nazi sympathizers was not an easy undertaking for Canadian military authorities. Their lack of knowledge about recent history of domestic political developments in Germany was as lamentable as that exhibited by the British tribunal establishment earlier. Jews were identified relatively easily, since they denounced everything and everyone German as Nazi. From the perspective of the Jewish internees, it seems, only Jews were refugees. Eventually, these differences manifested themselves in such actions as the camp leadership of (refugee) Camp N refusing to accept thirty-five anti-Nazis who were being transferred from Camp F.[46] What was the military to think of an internee who longed to return to Germany after Hitler and his regime had vanished? Was he a loyal ally, a genuine anti-Nazi; could an anti-Nazi question the Allied bombing of German civilians and cities? Sorting out these contradictions was challenging; perhaps the guards would have agreed with the popular Anglo-Saxon saying as expressed by the Governor of the Isle of Man: "a good German is a dead German!"[47]

Of course the Directorate and the local camp commandants and staffs were not immune to anti-Semitism. It is impossible to establish how widespread these sentiments were among officers and soldiers, though records abound of incidents that indicate the presence of anti-Semitic attitudes in individuals at given times. General Panet, most benign and favourably disposed to the internees, offered this observation: "These [Jews] are the most troublesome of all. They beg to be fed on kosher food—they are unusually dirty and untidy and generally speaking cause more bother than all the others."[48]

On tours of inspection of various camps, officers found the inmates sloppy in appearance whether in the enclosures or on marches to and from work; the prisoners were totally lacking in military bearing, even neglecting to greet officers when passing by. In the opinion of one officer, "the internees...are all Jews...and they definitely need severe discipline....They are disposed to be sullen and uncooperative, as well as dirty."[49] Not uncommonly, local camp authorities ordered Jewish refugees to work on fatigue parades on the Sabbath. Some Veterans took pleasure in telling their Jewish prisoners who objected to working on the Sabbath, "We will make you work."[50] This attitude was especially difficult to comprehend for the small group of Orthodox Jewish scholars among the internees. The Jewish scholars objected strongly to the performance of any work, in principle. Their religious lifestyle induced them to avoid the physical in preference to religious-intellectual labour. Obligation to work prevented them from reading, studying and contemplating their prayer books. The military authorities had difficulties in sympathizing with this view of life.

At Camp R, the soldiers of the Veterans Guard were more dismayed than confused and disliked the Jewish inmates. According to Spier's testimony, this is because, as the soldiers understood the situation, Hitler had defamed and disgraced the Jews and yet the Jews were ready to do Hitler's dirty work. How could they? In general, in Camp R the soldiers seemed unfriendly to the Jews and friendly, soldier-like, to the Nazis.[51] This impression, first formed in England, persisted among the interned Jewish and anti-Nazi refugees even in Camp R, where they believed that despite the Nazi elements' deplorable activities, the officers and soldiers guarding them actually gave preferential considerations to these Nazis. Generally speaking, Canadian officers and men preferred guarding genuine Nazi soldiers—POWs, Class I—to guarding interned civilians. Guarding enemy soldiers was uncomplicated; the rules were simple and easy to interpret and to apply. Furthermore, these POWs were soldiers, accustomed to orders and instructions and less argumentative, and thus more ready and prompt to obey.

Handling Jewish refugees, who were "sensitive and temperamental human beings," required too much patience and skills other than barking orders. At least Commandant Berry, who would have preferred guarding real German soldiers, did not express his disappointment in the manner of his colleague, Commandant Campbell, at Camp Q, Monteith. Campbell ordered the new arrivals to clean out the guards' latrine and allowed his drunken sentries to fire pot shots at the prisoners' huts and tents during the night.[52] Berry expressed his displeasure only orally in conversation. Compared to Camp Q, in Camp R life was almost tranquil.

Finally, a general observation about these disturbing events and experiences: Many of the interned Jewish and anti-Nazi refugees, especially among those who returned to Britain, blamed Canada for their misfortunes.[53] Their intense negative reaction is understandable. Coming to Canada, far from hysteria and panic and the fear of invasion prevailing in Britain in the summer of 1940, the internees expected not only a less restrictive camp environment, but also their eventual release. They were after all victims of Nazi persecution and refugees from Nazi Germany. Moreover, many were ready and willing to fight for freedom and democracy, if given a chance. Furthermore, had their British captors not intimated future release during the rush to meet their shipping quotas?

Instead, on their arrival the refugees were treated as POWs and then incarcerated in enclosures, surrounded by double barbed wire fences and heavily armed troops with machine guns and bayonets, and placed under strict and rigid military discipline. For the longest time, the refugees' pleas for recognition of their true status and for different treatment were simply ignored by both the Canadian military authorities and the civilian federal government. In coming to Canada the interned refugees had different expectations from those they had had in Britain. There they perceived themselves as being at home, near their families, in familiar and friendly surroundings; they had hoped for a brief internment. Coming to Canada, they expected recognition as refugees from Nazism, release, and freedom. They deeply resented the treatment they received from the Canadian military authorities. They resented being in foreign surroundings, away from home, and being treated as prisoners of war rather than refugees. And why were those who were willing to assist in Canada's war effort not released into freedom? The small group of Jewish and anti-Nazi refugees held in Camp R shared these views.

The military at first hesitated to abolish the mixed camps and separate Nazis from anti-Nazis. Undoubtedly, the most decisive failure of the military and political leaders in the Department of National Defence was not to implement the sensible advice Brigadier-General Panet, and Commissioner Paterson, had proffered in the fall of 1940, and April 1941, respectively, namely the demilitarization of the refugee internment camps, the abandonment of the machine gun and bayonet culture as well as the rigid military discipline and command language. The refugees often regarded their camp experiences and the delays in their release as manifestations of Canadian anti-Semitism, and their highly critical attitude is therefore understandable.[54]

What is surprising, however, is that refugees, when discussing the historical subject of refugee internment, place the blame for refugee misery entirely on Canada instead of Great Britain, the mother country of the original evil.[55] It is worth recalling that it was Britain that initiated the tribunal system, and it was Churchill's war cabinet that decreed mass internment and then mass deportation to Canada. Second, the Churchill cabinet deliberately failed to disclose accurate and full information about the so-called "dangerous enemy aliens" it had rounded up. Third, Britain's incessant pleading for help prompted the Canadian government eventually to accept as many of these "dangerous," "military security risk" deportees as Britain wished to dispatch. Surely, it was the responsibility of British authorities to ship out only those whom it regarded as a threat to its security. How was the well-known German Jewish anti-Nazi and long-time English resident and Churchill lobbyist Eugen Spier included? Fourth, Britain refused to acknowledge its original mistake of incarcerating the bona fide refugees from Nazi Germany. Britain would eventually advise Canada as to their actual harmlessness, set others like them free at home and thereby encourage their release in Canada. Of course Canada's management of the refugee conundrum does not present an unqualified success story either.

It seems both Koch and Paula J. Draper, in analyzing Canada's response, downplay not only the ever rising numbers of dangerous enemy aliens presented by Britain, but also the mounting urgency portrayed. In the end the responsibility for sending innocent refugees, Category B and C internees, to Canada must rest with Great Britain, since Britain was in complete control of every aspect of deportation from the selection of deportees to the shipping.

A humorous incident happened as a result of Churchill's mistake, which illustrates Britain's incompetent handling of the deportation: after the internees' identification documents finally arrived from England. Canadian officials discovered that two hundred prisoners were in Canadian internment camps without any official identification whatsoever and that they now possessed two hundred documents without any detainees attached. What better detail to demonstrate the extent of Great Britain's mismanagement of the deportation process?[56]

It seems likely, considering the facts, that from the very start of the deportation process, the Churchill government, guided by the Swinton Committee, was keenly interested in sending *all* interned enemy aliens abroad.[57] As early as 24 May 1940, Prime Minister Churchill declared, "I am strongly in favour of removing *all* internees out of the United Kingdom."[58] On 3 June, he inquired in cabinet if the Lord President [Chamberlain] had "the case in hand" of deporting 20,000 internees to Newfoundland or St. Helena.[59] Koch believes this number of internees was not available at that time and therefore could not be taken seriously. Draper however states that Britain had interned 23,000 men and 3,000 women by mid-May. In fact, the number of "dangerous enemy aliens" eligible for deportation rose continuously in the urgent pleas for help Viscount Caldecote forwarded to Canada. First, there were "at least 4,000 internees," on 7 June;[60] next there were 9,000 and then

12,000.[61] In his address to cabinet on 11 June, having received assurances of assistance, Chamberlain confirmed that Canada's acceptance of 7,000 internees and POWs "would be enough to put all the *really dangerous characters* [my emphasis] out of harm's way."[62] Furthermore, Lord Snell's Inquiry Report into the fiasco of the *Arandora Star* clearly reiterates the view that the government intended to deport overseas *all* categories, not just "A." After the sinking of the *Arandora Star*, the Lord President, Chamberlain, reported to cabinet that "every effort—on the direction of the Prime Minister—had been made to send as many internees abroad as possible."[63]

IX

Other Aspects of Camp Life

Inspections, First Escapes, Religion, Mail

GENERAL PANET'S SHORT VISIT AT THE END of July 1940 may be regarded as the first inspection. It proved uneventful, though it established the camp's temporary usefulness and its long-term deficiencies and liabilities. The next inspection occurred about two weeks later and was conducted by Lieutenant-Colonel Hugh de Norban Watson over a period of several days. His lengthy and detailed inspection was of a general nature rather than designed to resolve specific problems as others attempted later on. He covered every aspect of the camp: the location, the buildings, the guards, the administrative staff and their work, the inmates, and their enclosure. Arriving on the evening of Saturday, 9 August, at 2130 hours, Colonel Watson spent the next morning and several days surveying the compound and camp area; in the process he inspected, inside and outside, every building and hut.[1]

His first observation was that Camp R occupied an "unfavourable site." Next, he remarked perceptively that many of the internees now held by Canada might soon be returned to England in the wake of the newly emerged agitation, both in England and in Canada, over the deportation fiasco and the unfolding discovery of Great Britain's deception of Canada about the true character of the aliens who had been shipped overseas. The need for operating Camp R might therefore only be temporary, he concluded. As he wandered about the site, Watson observed that the camp's numerous military buildings were too widely scattered and that therefore too much time was spent in covering the long distances between the Orderly Room, the Supply Stores, the Quartermaster's office, the Officers' quarters, the Officers' Mess located in the Inn, and the administration and commandant offices housed in the mill building. He queried the efficiency of this far-flung set-up. However, he awarded high praise to the camp staff for their efficient and effective administration of the camp. Their individual and collective efforts to operate Camp R had overcome all obstacles even in the face of shortages of trained staff and inadequate supplies. He praised both Captain Kirkness and Mr. H.A. Warkentine, the civilian interpreter, for their excellent work and suggested that their censorship activity required more assistance from other staff members.

Watson disapproved of the joint use of the camp hospital by the Canadian troops in one wing and by the prisoners in the other. He warned that the armed sentries, who guarded the hospital, could be rushed and disarmed by the prisoners. The beds in the inmates' hospital wing, he noted, had no pillowcases. At the time of Watson's inspection of the hospital, one case of typhoid and one of tuberculosis were being cared for. Lavish praise was awarded quite deservedly by Watson upon the medical officer, Dr. Klass, for his keenness and for the excellence of his equipment, which included an X-ray apparatus, as well as for his accomplishments in performing hernia and appendectomy operations in the camp hospital. The health of the soldiers under the care of Dr. Klass was very good; inoculations against typhoid and smallpox were administered regularly to all members of the camp community; there were VD parades and condom distributions to the Veterans Guard. Moreover the Dental Corps operated a dental clinic "for the Guards first and emergency treatments and extractions amongst the P/W who are inclined to expect far more dental treatment then they are entitled to."

Unlike General Panet, who got on well with Mr. Hurter, the resident manager of the Lake Sulphite Pulp and Paper Company, Colonel Watson did not. Hurter, it seems, was frustrated and angry, and repeatedly presented new evidence of daily pilfering by the members of the Fort Garry Horse to the visiting Watson, who himself was unable to remedy the situation. Watson also noted that Berry had no staff car at his disposal and had to rent a car for ten dollars a day should he wish to travel on military business to nearby Nipigon or to the more distant Lakehead, as the twin cities of Port Arthur and Fort William were then called; and if he wished to travel by train a similar, very cumbersome procedure had to be followed to obtain railway vouchers. Inside the camp area, Berry moved about by motorcycle with sidecar. Eventually, Camp R received its own staff car and a 1.5-ton truck. By March 1941, Camp R enjoyed the use of a transportation detachment of one staff car, three station wagons, one two-ton stake truck, three one-and-a-half-ton lorries, one three-ton lorry, one diesel tractor and two motorcycles with sidecars.[2]

On the issue of camp "security," Watson offered an abundance of criticisms and suggestions. He was mostly concerned over the presence of Canadian civilians freely intermingling with the military throughout the environment of the camp. These civilians presented a formidable security risk in his view. Most important for Watson was the fact that the camp military had no authority over these workers. Their only identification mark was a numbered disc issued by the plant manager. These twelve civilian workers, employed by the Lake Sulphite Pulp and Paper Company, performed needed repairs and maintenance work throughout the entire camp area. Watson's great security concern here was that the internees could take these civilian workers hostage, assume their places and attempt to escape. Moreover, the civilian

Guards with some citizens of Red Rock. *[Private collection]*

workers could be used to smuggle letters and messages in and out of the camp on behalf of the inmates. These circumstances, Watson judged, presented serious security hazards.

Then there was the issue of the camp telephone party line. In those days the party line telephone system was widely employed, low in cost, and the most profitable communications technology in operation. This technology necessitated sharing the camp's military line with eighteen civilian telephone line subscribers, who could all listen in as military communications, some secret, some confidential, and most ordinary, were transmitted. Moreover, every incoming or outgoing camp call, Watson observed, passed through the civilian manager's office telephone switchboard. In Watson's view, this was a most objectionable breach of security. Canadian civilians, perhaps of alien origins, could be listening in on sensitive military discussions. Watson's proposed solution to this challenge was modern and progressive: build a separate, private line for the camp. He objected, furthermore, to the existing situation in which the camp's military administrative staff worked in close proximity to Hurter's civilian staff, who were able to listen in on military conversations, the two groups being separated from each other only by a thin plywood partition. He raised similar objections concerning the Guard Room, which was far too close to the huts of the prisoners, who were thus able to listen to the radio news.

Not unexpectedly Watson also turned his attention to the "camp fences," another issue of security. He dismissed them as "a very flimsy affair." He warned that whole sections of the fence could be dragged away by some determined prisoners. The existing weak fence required too many sentries, eighteen for one night shift alone, he noted, and yet despite this large number the sentries could not guarantee security in bad weather conditions. Watson regretted that the prisoners could not be locked up at night on account of the fire hazard. He shared Panet's previously stated concerns. The lighting of the compound was, in his view, inadequate. The terrain created too many "dark shadowy areas," and the closeness of the hutments added others; all of these could aid escape. Moreover, he noted, prisoners could easily throw a rope across the electric power lines feeding the overhead lights in the enclosure and, by dragging the power lines down, create total darkness in the compound. He called for the installation of floodlights and for more hand-held searchlights with grip handles to be made available to the guards.

With regard to prisoner welfare, Watson noted that fifty cents each of the government fund had already been disbursed among the prisoners in the first month of the camp's operation in order to cope with their impecunious state. In order to foster work, he advised acquiring working tools such as shovels, axes, crowbars and wheelbarrows, because these would help in the construction of more recreation areas outside the enclosure, one of which was near completion and just needed a wire fence to encircle it. He also suggested the acquisition of tailors' and shoemakers' tools and machines and the establishment of workshops for their use. It seemed the camp had a great need for this skilled work. Watson solicited the help of the visiting Swiss Consul for sports equipment, including footballs, and reading materials. In this connection, it is interesting to note that the Directorate issued orders which strictly prohibited American organizations such as the Philadelphia-based *Kyffhaeuser Bund* and the associated *Kyffhaeuser Kriegshilfswerk* (a war aid committee) from carrying out welfare work in conjunction with Red Cross agencies in Camp R or in any other Canadian internment camp.[3]

Like Panet, Watson complained about the apparent lack of military behaviour among the inmates. He wanted to see proper respect for the officers from the internees. When the commandant entered the enclosure or a hut, Watson advised, a provost guard should precede the commandant, calling the inmates to attention. Indeed, Watson called for a larger number of provosts who would patrol the "compound" during the day and "enforce cleanliness, tidiness and good behaviour." Provosts inside the enclosure, recruited from the regular soldiers of the Fort Garry unit, should not be armed, but should carry "billies" or sticks and a whistle. Colonel Watson's and General Panet's comments on the appearance of the camp's inmates illustrate the Canadian military's widespread disappointment with their imported civilian wards, who did not turn out to be Prussian-drilled, fiendish and dangerous, but just ordinary civilians, some of whom were anti-Nazis and Jews and most of whom abhorred mindless and rigid military discipline.

During his inspection visit, Watson encouraged Berry to set a cleanliness standard for the enclosure; in exchange for upholding this standard, the commandant could grant the inmates a swim parade in the hot summer days of 1940. After some discussion with a very reluctant troop commander, Colonel Cox, who looked upon this proposal strictly in terms of security and escape and extra work for his men, the parade was eventually implemented. Four hundred men, in groups of one hundred, under the watchful barrel of a Lewis machine gun, were allowed to swim in Nipigon Bay. They wore either swim trunks or nothing in order to enhance security and impede escape. This venture was a tremendous success in the experience of all, including Colonel Cox, according to Watson. The camp military liked it because it was a change in routine and occupied the prisoners' time; moreover, it was a privilege, which could be withdrawn as a disciplinary measure if necessary. The inmates liked it because it refreshed them and gave them something to do; it broke the routine and, not unimportantly, it eased the pressure on the shower facility.

In the conclusion of his long and detailed report, Watson summarized his findings:

1. Camp R was unsuitable as a permanent camp; the fire hazard could not be eliminated;
2. the enclosure fences were too weak;
3. no paid work was available;
4. water intake was not frost-proofed;
5. lighting was inadequate;
6. military offices and stores were too widely scattered;
7. necessary improvements would be too costly to make;
8. all commanding officers disliked the existing conditions; and
9. continuous friction existed with Hurter.

Watson mentioned in his report that the office of the Swiss Legation in London, England, acting as the Protecting Power, had ordered its Canadian branch office to inspect Camp R in order to verify reports about the existence of "unsatisfactory conditions," prompted by complaints which four former inmates had submitted after their release. These were the work of the four returned German consular internees, who were falsely arrested by the British at Reykjavik at the outbreak of war and mistakenly send to Canada. With regard to the inmates of Camp R, Watson finally asked the Directorate for clarification of the status of the inmates: were they A, or B and C category?

Added to his report, Colonel Watson presented a secret confidential appendix commenting on the camp's staff officers. In this confidential assessment, Commandant Berry emerged as a competent, efficient and cautious officer, who would have preferred to operate a "regular" POW, Class I work camp somewhere in the Canadian bush, populated with less troublesome inmates and in uncomplicated circumstances. Berry, Watson continued, was unhappy with his Adjutant, Captain Johnston, and his Quartermaster, Captain Stovel. Watson regarded the former as "not very aggressive or energetic and...perhaps a little afraid of his job at present," and the latter as one who, although "anxious to do a good work...perhaps relies a little too much on his Camp Q.M.S. [Quartermaster Sergeant]." Time and experience would correct these weaknesses. About Captain Kirkness, Watson wrote that "he was keen, knows his stuff" and should be used to teach his skills to others.

In his inspection report, Colonel Watson considered at length the troubling subject of "dual control," which Brigadier Panet too had noted briefly in his report. In Watson's view dual control caused serious friction between the camp administrative staff and the officers and troops of the Fort Garry Horse. All sorts of avoidable extra problems arose, as he noted; delays were common in responding to requests from the camp commandant for action, whether these were for additional escorts and sentries or for soldiers to do maintenance and repair work on the fences or the watchtowers.

Delay was also common in the execution of orders once issued or the implementation of camp policies and standing orders. In cases involving fraternization and bartering by soldiers of the Fort Garry Horse who were on sentry or provost duty with inmates, Berry could do "very little" since the unit was not under his command. Most significantly "dual command," in Watson's view, interfered with the maintenance of discipline among the troops. As has been noted, Mr. Hurter, the manager, accused the soldiers of pilfering and stealing; he also accused them of illegal entry into buildings and of setting fire on the company dock, causing damage in the plant and to the property of the Lake Sulphite Pulp and Paper Company. Although Berry was in charge of Camp R, he was not the senior officer; therefore he could not issue orders to Lt.

Colonel S.J. Cox, commander of the Fort Garry Horse. In the case of the manager's complaints and requests for compensation, Berry maintained that he carried no responsibility and therefore passed on all such complaints and requests to the Military District No. 10 Headquarters at Winnipeg. Camp Commandant Berry was not able to persuade Colonel Cox to take action against his men. Watson's conclusion was that there must be only *one authority* in camp. The solution to this intractable problem came with the arrival of the Veterans Guard of Canada later in August.

Other inspections followed Colonel Watson's. On 6 September, a special inspection team of Colonel P.A. Puize, Commander of the Canadian Provost Corps, T. Daun, Deputy Commissioner of the RCMP, and G.T. Goad, Warden of Dorchester Prison in New Brunswick, arrived.[4] They were charged with the thorough examination of all camps with the primary objective of espying ways to prevent escape.

By early September, at Camp R, six escapes had been attempted, of which one had been successful. The first escapee was Heinz Eichler. He ran away from a work party at 1530 hours on 30 July 1940 and was recaptured at 1930 hours the same day within the camp area. In early September 1940, Louis Mueller, Heinz Domnick, Josef Gedanitz and Walter Lautenbach were caught as they were tunnelling their way out of the enclosure. The one successful escape came on 19 August, when "Don Manuelo" Fischer disappeared. "Don Manuelo" was Spier's name for Manfred Fischer, a German-born sailor by vocation and an adventurer by inclination. During the Spanish Civil War Fischer had fought as an officer in the International Brigade against Fascism and had gathered personal experiences of Spanish, German and French concentration camps, all of which he had successfully escaped. He was a widely popular person in the camp among the non-Nazis and was always radiantly cheerful, a physical fitness fiend with a flamboyant, magnetic personality—a charismatic individual. His absence was noted at the evening roll call at 1900 hours, and it was assumed that he had absconded either from a fatigue work detail or from a shower parade.

An escape tunnel that the prisoners dug under their huts. It was discovered before they could make their getaway. [LAC-e006611166_s1]

Indeed he had concealed himself inside the bathhouse in a closet with the assistance of friends, had dressed in his ordinary civilian clothes and had succeeded in departing from the camp without detection. Twenty-five minutes after roll call, the RCMP and the police forces of Fort William, Port Arthur and Nipigon had been alerted. On reports of sighting the fugitive by local residents an intensive search of the surrounding area and shoreline was conducted. According to the military's description, Fischer was "thirty years old, with reddish brown hair, blue eyes, a scar on the left side of his face, with a crippled left index finger, two tattoos on his left arm...dark shade of sallow complexion" and was 1.70 metre tall. Despite this excellent description, Fischer was gone for weeks and then months with everyone thinking that he had succeeded in escaping. He had!

Fischer had crossed into the then neutral United States and expected that his request to join the battle against Fascism would be appreciated and approved by the neutral and freedom-loving Americans; instead he was arrested while travelling on an American train. The Americans, apparently being as sympathetic as some of their Anglo-Saxon cousins towards enemy alien refugees, especially of the left or Jewish persuasion, gave "Don Manuelo" a choice: be returned to non-democratic Fascist Spain, or to Nazi Germany, or to the democratic, Fascist-fighting Dominion of Canada. He wisely chose Red Rock, crossing the US–Canada border at Fort Frances and arriving back to Camp R on 3 November 1940.

In returning Fischer to belligerent Canada, the United States acted in violation of Article 13 of the Hague Convention on the Conduct of Land Warfare of 1907, which stated "that a neutral state shall leave a fugitive at liberty" and that the right of asylum must be granted.[5] The Americans of course, as we have seen, were anxious to avoid an influx of unwanted foreigners, whether anti-Nazi German, Austrian, Italian or Jew—they might be Communists. And, indeed, this one was.

In pursuit of their mandate, the prevention of future escapes, the inspectors Puize, Daun and Goad insisted that all civilian clothes be taken away from the inmates and that all prisoners wear the much-despised prisoner's uniform, consisting of a denim shirt and jacket with a large round red patch on the back and denim pants with a wide red stripe on the right leg. They believed that this simple measure might hinder, if not prevent, future escapes. Had not Fischer escaped wearing his own civilian clothes? The inspectors also examined the camp's roll call procedure and proposed a new double-check method. Under the new arrangement two NCOs, one following the other, would separately count the inmates, who had lined up in two rows inside their hut. Then each NCO would hand in his count separately to an attending officer, who would check and verify both and, if correct, pass them on to the Orderly Officer, who would pass them finally to the Adjutant. They suggested, furthermore, adding an additional count "at unstated hours"

One of the watchtowers. *[LAC-e006611161]*

and making inmates wear numbered discs. Another measure to prevent
escape, they suggested, was to increase the number of provosts constantly circulating among the inmates in the enclosure. The provosts'
weaponry should be upgraded, they urged, from billies to baseball bats
and axe handles.

Relating to the issue of civilian workers and escapes, the visiting
inspectors proposed that the civilians should sign in and out and say
their names as well. This practice would force individuals to speak;
thus accents could be detected, demeanour be observed, and time for
additional examination be gained. Like Watson, the inspectors feared
prisoners could kidnap civilians, exchange clothes and assume their
identities in order to escape.

Again the major concern was the issue of security. All the old criticisms concerning the deficiencies of the enclosure fence were rehashed. They agreed that Camp R had "the worst [terrain] we have yet seen... it was exceptionally bad." To improve security, they recommended a Lewis or Vickers machine gun in each of the five watchtowers surrounding the enclosure. They approved the camp's basic armour; the soldiers were armed with .303 Ross rifles, and most officers owned their own pistols or revolvers. In addition to an increase in the number of provosts working in the enclosure, they recommended the use of shotguns for sentries. They approved the night guard routine of eighteen sentries who at fifteen minutes intervals reported to their neighbour "All is well!" and were checked by a sergeant, by the Regimental Sergeant Major, and by an officer making the rounds. However, they noted that strong winds, blizzards and storms decreased the efficiency of this arrangement.

The inspectors recommended opening a gymnastic hut, acquiring recreational and work tools, adding a medical officer, and establishing an internees' canteen. The recreation room for the troops, the inspectors recommended, should be relocated in the mill building, and the camp office should be moved to the basement of the Red Rock Inn. This move would maintain the proper distance between soldiers and their leaders. To improve the sentries' efficiency in the watchtowers during the winter months, it was suggested that a small heating shelter be constructed at the bottom of each tower, that the floodlighting be standardized and that the old double fences be replaced with one single ten-foot-high fence reinforced with a proper overhang and concertina wire. Finally, the inspectors suggested replacing the worn-out cookers in the camp kitchen with new, better equipment requiring less maintenance. The proposed alterations, at a total cost of $8,000, were implemented.[6]

The inspectors awarded high praise to the troops guarding Camp R, who were supplied with ten officers and 320 soldiers of other ranks by the Veterans Guard of Canada in September of that year. While the inspectors were generally satisfied with the Commandant's staff of five officers, one civilian interpreter and thirty-five other ranks, they judged the Veterans Guard as "alert, keen and conscious of their duty," but in need of more "active training." What exactly was meant by this term, the inspectors never spelled out. However, they suggested improvements in escort practice; criticized the habit of letting rifles lie about on beds, tables and chairs or lean against walls rather than setting them in rifle racks, and ordered stricter controls and searches of outgoing vehicles. They urged, furthermore, that the Veterans Guard practise rifle and machine gun firing more often on the nearby range. They noted that one officer and two NCOs were attending an advanced skill-training school in Ottawa. The inventory of inmates showed a complement of 1,142 Category A internees, plus five returned to England, two in medical care and one escapee.

In addition to these Canadian military inspections, representatives, both of the International Committee of the Red Cross (ICRC) of Geneva and of the Protecting Power, which was Switzerland, regularly visited Camp R and examined the implementation and execution of the articles and provisions of the Geneva Convention of 1929. Swiss consular staff members, stationed in Montreal and Toronto, regularly fulfilled these two distinct functions. They were concerned not only with whether or not the application of Canada's modified domestic regulations concerning "Prisoners of War, Class II" conformed to the articles of the Convention, but also with inspecting the general conditions in the camp. The representative of the ICRC reported on, among a number of other factors, the suitability of the geographic site and the climate of the detention camp for POWs. Did the physical layout of the camp meet the requirements of the Convention with regards to hygiene and minimum comfort in bedding and food, and with regards to mail privilege? They listened to complaints from the camp authorities as well as from the inmates. The ICRC inspector reported in detail on the physical, mental and dental health of the inmates, and noted educational opportunities and deficiencies, as well as the particular lack of paid work in

Veterans Guard route march. Photo taken in front of the tea house.
[Courtesy of the Red Rock Historical Society]

Camp R. The ICRC inspector's reports went first to Commandant Berry
for his attention and perhaps immediate corrections, then to Foreign
Affairs, next to Geneva, and eventually to Berlin.[7]

Generally speaking, there were no complaints over breaches of the
Convention raised by any of the different representatives or by any
segment of the inmates in Camp R. Such complaints as those over the
display of Hitler's picture and national flags by the radical Nazis did
not fall under the rules of the Convention and were settled in negotiations on the basis of reciprocity among the belligerents. Requests
for the establishment of a canteen were handled locally and by the
Directorate. Berlin was informed only about the end result. Complaints
about delays in mail deliveries, going out or coming into camp, were

beyond the power of the Swiss to solve, but were duly passed on to Ottawa, London and Berlin. The relationship between Berry and the Consuls—Consul General, Mr. Ernest Maag from Montreal, representing ICRC, and Consul, Mr. John Oertly from Toronto, representing the Protecting Power—seem to have been excellent. Consul Oertly, who visited the camp as early as 12–14 August, had no complaints about the camp's geographic characteristics—650 metres above sea level, continental climate—or about the operation and administration of the camp. On his 14 September 1940 inspection, he noted that the international standards were being met, the inmates' beds and beddings were standard army issue, and that "the food was of excellent quality and was plentiful."[8] Both Swiss inspectors acknowledged the excellent hygienic facilities despite the temporary nature of Camp R and judged the camp's administrative climate as "more liberal and democratic" than in the eastern internment camps. They noted that censored local newspapers were available to the inmates and that mail arrived more regularly; however, they continued to lament the lack of a camp radio and the absence of a canteen for the inmates. They noted with surprise that only one copy of the Geneva Convention of 1929 in English and one in German were available in Camp R.[9]

The Swiss consular representatives were aware of the tension between the *Reichsdeutsche* majority and the Jewish and anti-Nazi minority in Camp R. The Swiss Consuls, whether representing the ICRC or the Protecting Power, were not, however, in any position to influence or stop the anti-Semitic harassment engineered by the Nazi faction in Camp R. Maintenance of discipline and good order in the enclosure was the job of the Detaining Power, of Canada, and in this particular instance of the camp's military authority. The Jewish and anti-Nazi minority in the camp, unfortunately, refused on principle to speak to the Swiss as Representatives of the ICRC. This fact did not help the situation. The minority group mistakenly identified the neutral Swiss ICRC representative as a German substitute and did not differentiate between the ICRC and the Protecting Power representative. It is true that Swiss representatives in the early weeks of the incarceration hysteria in Britain had passed names of refugees on to Nazi Germany, believing that since they were treated as POWs, they were genuine POWs. The refugees hoped that their rebuff of the Swiss would demonstrate to the Canadian government that "we are *not* German citizens of Nazi Germany; we *are* anti-Nazis!"[10] No evidence exists which shows that this ploy worked. It proved, however, very satisfactory psychologically to those otherwise helpless and maltreated internees who used it in practically every Canadian internment camp.

Dr. Jerome Davis, representing the War Prisoners' Aid Committee of the YMCA, also visited Camp R regularly. His concerns were limited to the mental health of the prisoners as reflected in their cultural, social, educational, leisure and religious needs. The religious needs of the inmates were not neglected in Camp R. Lutheran, Roman Catholic and Jewish worship services were offered on a regular basis. A zealous Nazi resident in the camp, Pastor Wehrhahn, once chaplain to the German diplomatic staff in London, looked after the Lutherans' spiritual needs, while a local Jesuit, Father Charles J. Carrell, came out from Port Arthur and cared for the Roman Catholics.[11] The thirty or forty Orthodox Jews, unfortunately, were without a Rabbi, but not because the Canadian military denied requests for rabbinical service.[12] As early as 12 July 1940, inmate No. 43065, Benedikt Rappoport, wrote a letter to Chief Rabbi Dr. Maurice Eisendraht of Toronto and asked for help and support of the small Jewish group in Camp R. Rappoport reported that "thirty-six" Jewish refugees were in camp and that this small number of Jews found themselves in an especially awkward position among more than 1,000 Nazis. "While their interest is represented by the Swiss Embassy... our Jewish interests are not in any way represented since we Jews are no more recognized as German subjects, in fact the majority of us were never German citizens, we all are genuine victims of Nazi oppression... we Jews find ourselves in a desperate situation...be grateful if you could possibly arrange for us to have a personal interview with you or one of your representatives in order to discuss all matters so vital to us. We sincerely hope for your kind protection and assistance...."[13]

Rappoport's letter achieved results. On 12 August, the National Executive Director of the Canadian Jewish Congress and of the United Jewish Refugee and War Relief Agencies in Montreal, Saul Hayes, wrote to Panet and asked whether "the few Jews in Camp R are as badly placed as Mr. Rappoport indicates." Panet replied, on 26 August, and restated the official Canadian position: "the internees at this camp (Camp R) were transferred to Canada as Category A," and "until we have been advised otherwise by the British Authorities" no other alternative classification was available. Panet indicated that the government was considering the existing situation in all civilian internment camps and was prepared to find a remedy. Meanwhile, Panet agreed to provide the services of a Rabbi. "We see no reason," he wrote, "why the spiritual welfare of these internees should not be ministered by a Rabbi and if you would let me have the name of a Rabbi you have in mind, instructions will be sent to the Camp Commandant to admit him to the Camp for this purpose." In appreciation of Panet's efforts, Mr. Hayes assured Panet in an undated reply "that we will obviously not lift a finger to bring aid, assistance and comfort to anybody whose allegiance to the British Crown is suspected."[14] However, Hayes inquired shortly afterwards, "if you would be kind enough to let me know the town nearest to camp 'R,' I will let you have the name of the Rabbi who would give spiritual ministration to those at the camp." On 7 September, Lieutenant-Colonel Minns from the Directorate of Internment Operations informed Hayes that the nearest town was Nipigon, and "the nearest large cities are Port Arthur and Fort William." In February 1941, Hayes and his associate in Winnipeg, Louis Rosenberg, were still discussing the issue of assistance to the Jews in Camp R. Of course by this time events had moved on, for in January 1941 Camp R's last Jews were transferred to new "refugee" camps in eastern Canada.

Though the status of the Jews in Camp R remained unaltered, some amelioration of their situation was accomplished with the help of Captain Kirkness. Inmate H. Glaser thanked Kirkness in an undated letter for arranging "to celebrate our festival in keeping with the spirit of the time and tradition." Apparently, Kirkness had written to Rabbi Solomon Frank of Winnipeg, who in turn forwarded such "comforts" as cigarettes and tobacco. Glaser gives the number of Jewish inmates in Camp R as 40.[15] It is interesting to note that the Directorate of Internment Operations advised the Congress that the nearest Jewish community was in Winnipeg, some eight hundred kilometres away. Apparently neither the military nor the Canadian Jewish Congress was aware of the proximity of a Rabbi in the nearby flourishing Jewish community in the Lakehead. However, in February 1941, Mr. Hayes once again confirmed the hard-line stance of the Congress: no help would be given to Jews in Category A, even if placed there incorrectly in the first place. This was a matter of policy and reflected the continual concern that indeed Category A Jews might be Nazis.

Unlike the Canadian Jewish Congress, another Jewish organization sought contact with the few Jews in Camp R in a less cautious and more direct manner. In October 1940, the Zionist Organization of Canada, in its zeal and perhaps impatient with the more careful approach of the Congress, sent individually addressed postcards and other "printed materials" to different inmates in Camp R, having assumed on the basis of their names that they were of Jewish background. In fact the recipients of these mailings were actually Gentiles and some even "very anti-Semitic," according to Stethem's reprimanding letter of 7 November 1940 to the Canadian Zionists. As the military saw the situation, "Correspondence from your organization, addressed to anti-Semitic Gentiles, only tends to add fuel to the fire of mutual hatred."[16] It is unclear whether indeed this mailing contributed to the riotous occurrence in Camp R in early October 1940. The correspondence between Hayes and Panet and the rebuffing of the Zionist organization illustrate the difficulties faced by those who were attempting to help Jews in Canadian camps.

Due, in part, to the religious differences—orthodox, reformed and liberal—among the Jewish internees, it took some time before services suitable to their various needs could be organized from within the camp's Jewish community. Moreover, harassment from the Nazis in camp added other obstacles. At first the small religious group held their Sabbath prayer meeting in a hut adjacent to Guelcher's boxing school; later a separate wooden shed was found outside the camp area, and prayer meetings were held there.

Religious sentiments sponsored two rather remarkable events in camp life. December 1940 witnessed the celebration of both Christmas and Chanukah in Camp R. This indicates that religious sentiments were alive among the German nationals, even the Nazis and their supporters. Of course these two festivities occurred separately, but their co-occurrence presented in these trying circumstances an exceptional moment of harmony. A highlight in the local camp life at this time of the year was unquestionably the visit to the camp by Dr. Davis on 24 December and his staying for Christmas Eve. He attended both events and left personal reports of each. About his attendance at the Chanukah celebration, Dr. Davis wrote, "At 2:30 in the afternoon I attended a celebration of the Non-Aryan [sic] group which was made up of Jewish Orthodox prisoners who will soon be transferred to Camp N. They had songs and speeches, take-offs on camp personnel, and the various prisoners in this group distributed the Christmas packages and apparently had a royal good time."[17] Spier reported that camp spokesman Scharf had offered gifts of sweets to him for the Chanukah festival, but on behalf of his fellow Jewish inmates he refused to accept this offer.

The camp's next celebration turned out to be a traditional German Christmas celebration, despite the local Nazis' dominant influence in the camp. A year earlier, by contrast, at Camp Lingfield, the Nazis had staged a Nordic-Nazi version of Weihnachten/Christmas by reciting Nazi poetry and slogans, standing around a huge blazing fire and singing Nazi songs. Dr. Haenfstaengl had contributed to that celebration by reciting passages from the Nordic saga Edda. Camp R's festivities also included addresses from Captain Scharf, Commandant Berry and Dr. Davis, the singing of *Weihnachtslieder* by the camp choir and a concert by the camp orchestra. (By July 1941 the camp had a brass orchestra and a schrammel orchestra). This is the only time these two cultural groups are described as cooperating. The celebrations even moved Spier, who commented favourably on these happenings; in his view the Nazi atmosphere in Camp R had lessened since the October and November outbursts. The camp also put up a huge Christmas tree, but it is not clear which segment of the camp sponsored this exhibit, the troops or the inmates.

Christmas and Chanukah celebrations provided momentary joy and much needed pleasures, as well, perhaps, as pleasant reflections and memories. The inmates experienced similar emotions when receiving and sending mail, activities that for most inmates constituted an emotional and pleasing highlight in their daily camp routine. These postal pleasures presented the foundation of many prisoners' psychological wellness, it seemed. Mail supplied the inmate with the only reliable source of news from the outside, about the outside, even when it was outdated by weeks and months. Mail broke the routine, interrupted idleness and temporarily re-connected the prisoners with their separated families; mail eliminated at least for a moment their worries about their families. Such worries, during the long intervals that elapsed between the dispatch and the receipt of a letter or postcard from overseas, could cause emotional devastation.

The absence of reliable news was a depressive aspect of camp life. It opened of course the floodgates to all sorts of rumours. This was especially true during the first weeks and months of the camp's operation, when not even censored newspapers were available and almost no mail was coming into the camp. The Nazi element among the prisoners had exploited the news blackout in England, and again on board the troop transporter, by pretending that they had received the latest news by illicit radio transmissions. They spread the most frightening rumours among the Jewish and anti-Nazi refugees about England's defeat and surrender, and raised the prospect of having to return to Nazi Germany. They continued this practice in Canada.

Within the first week of arrival in July 1940, all inmates were allowed to send the obligatory postcard of seven lines in order to communicate their new address to their immediate families. Thereafter, mailing privileges and practices were regulated by an extensive standing order of thirty-six major articles and an additional thirty subsections of regulations. Under these rules an inmate was allowed to write one letter weekly, later amended to three letters, and four postcards monthly. Each letter, written on a prescribed form, was limited to twenty-four single lines, later increased to thirty-four; the official postcard had seven lines. Letters must be written in "plain language," either in English, French or German. Mail had to be addressed in a prescribed way; the content of each letter must be private or relate to personal business affairs and must be directed to one person or family only, with whom the prisoner had previously corresponded. In their letters and postcards inmates could not cite any quotations or poetry or refer to books, music, poetry, drawings, politics, camp or army matters, or fellow inmates. Unacceptable too were criticisms of Canada, its government and policies, officials or agencies, and references to other camps. The censor could delete untrue statements and could detain letters or postcards and even cancel mail privileges altogether. Newspapers could not be received by mail; neither could cables or telegrams be sent. No mail was exchanged between internment camps in Canada. Prisoner mail was sent free of charge.

An amended version of the standing order controlling the mail privilege was issued on 10 March 1941. The new edition was six foolscap pages long, had thirty-eight major articles and a further thirty-nine subsections. The new edition repeated the old regulations, but gave explicit instructions for addressing mail coming from Germany going to Canadian-held German prisoners. It prohibited mailing letters to foreign governments, soliciting assistance for release from Canadian internment. Prepaid cables could now be sent to the United Kingdom and the United States.

Whereas return replies from persons living in the United States arrived shortly after the original dispatch, responses from Europe to letters mailed in July had not even yet arrived in September 1940. The first parcels from the United States reached the camp as early as August. These postal delays had many causes. For example, letters written in English were processed more quickly by the censors than those in German; administrative foul-ups slowed down the mail; and then there were the problems of restricted shipping capacity and priority and of postal overload. Censors wielded absolute power and could retain mail for a variety of violations: conveyance of false and malicious information about the Allies, suspicious language, even humour.

Of course all these outside problems mattered little to the inmate with plenty of free time on his mind and soul, fretting and anxiously waiting for news from his loved ones. Receiving mail was always a joyous occasion, even when thirty-eight letters arrived all at once, as happened to Spier, even when the news was already quite dated. In time, mail delivery improved and the interval between out and in grew shorter; while mail from the United States travelled in spans of a week or two, European mail, whether from England or Germany, took a month or two, whether sent by self-paid airmail or not. If the mail service was slow, the British Army beat even that record, for it took nine months before the prisoners of Camp R finally received their twenty-five-pound kit bags from Great Britain.

Inmates were strictly forbidden by standing order to send so-called "godmother" mail. Under this mysterious label emerged the fact that censors had caught on to the practice by prisoners in some camps of writing letters to unrelated persons in neutral countries, such as the United States and various South American countries—Brazil, Argentina and Chile to name a few—under the fictitious greeting of "my dear godmother." By this ruse they were trying to bring these strange persons into their close family circle of postal correspondents. In reality, however, these foreign addresses were correctly suspected by the Canadian military intelligence of assisting in the preparation of escapes and thereafter of providing further help, or of gathering information about camps or, conversely, of conveying illegal information to inmates. There exists no evidence, however, that any prisoner at Camp R either sent or received "dear godmother" mail.

Some inmates in Camp R found the limitations on their correspondence most irksome and depressing. Captain Kirkness's monthly Morale Reports and the Swiss Consuls' commentaries reflected repeatedly the inmates' complaints over long delays in mail delivery and in receiving return mail from overseas. These reports note the negative impact these delays had on the mood of individuals and the morale of the collective. In view of the fact that inmates, generally, claimed that the mail privilege, its delivery and its dispatch, constituted a very important element of their daily camp existence, contributing to high morale and wellness, it is therefore both interesting and revealing to look at statistics that Captain Kirkness collected on that very point for the month of February 1941. By that time the camp had lost most of its Jewish and anti-Nazi components, numbering approximately two hundred persons; the total camp complement was thus about 950 persons. This is what he found:

Number of letters and postcards written in February 1941:	3,148
or approximately 3 per person	
Prisoners who did not write	315
Prisoners who wrote one letter	146
Prisoners who wrote two letters	144
Prisoners who wrote three letters	104
Prisoners who wrote three letters and one postcard	111
Prisoners who wrote three letters and two postcards	92
Prisoners who wrote three letters and three postcards	77
Prisoners who wrote three letters and four postcards	148

Only about 7 per cent (148) of the prisoners made use of the full mailing privilege, while 33 per cent of the total number of inmates did not use the mailing privilege at all.[18] Do these intriguing statistics support arguments made earlier about the low educational, social and cultural level of the EMS crowd? Or do they evidence a climate of discouragement, of perceived powerlessness, in the camp? Were any other factors at work? It is difficult to interpret such data without more context, especially when collected over only a single month.

Camp life had its moments of joy and disappointment such as receiving mail and missing out. In addition inmates had access to organized group activities such as education and sport, and had the "freedom of the enclosure" to pursue their own individual inclinations, especially after the withdrawal of the combative soldiers of the Fort Garry Horse.[19] Inmates could take a leisurely stroll, back and forth along the lakeshore fence, or even climb up and down the narrow lanes between the huts. They could visit each other and exchange the latest news, or more likely rumours and camp gossip; they could stay home and clean their huts, if it was their turn, or they could sign up for any of the leisure and recreation parades. In addition inmates could apparently meet and chat in coffee houses, where perhaps they could choose their companions according to political stripe.[20] Or they could attend to their hobbies of painting or drawing, if paint and paper were available. Others pursued the lucrative production of handicrafts and carvings for sale as souvenirs. The need for finding accommodation for hobby workshops was seen as an urgent necessity already by General Panet on his July visit to the camp. Hutments were, accordingly, provided for the hobbyists and the producers of souvenirs. Space was also found for housing a modest camp library, consisting of some twelve hundred privately owned books. Prisoners of course could use their time for studying for their courses, or could read books and newspapers, when the latter became available. Prisoners could not, however, change their sleeping quarters without the commandant's permission.

But every day every inmate faced an insoluble problem, a real challenge: coping with the absolute lack of privacy. At first everyone in the hut and in camp was a relative stranger to one another. Everyone's story was new and interesting. Very soon, however, everyone had told his story and had heard everyone else's story. Soon everyone knew each other's gestures, habits, thoughts and feelings, viewpoints and opinions, even idiosyncrasies, some pleasant, some annoying. What one really wanted was to be alone, to be by oneself. Familiarity spread and so did boredom, and indifference crept into personal relations. The monotonous routine of camp life coincided with the monotony of one's social life. "There is just no variety at all—every day roll-call, meals, another roll-call, bed. You lose your sense of time."[21]

Confined to the enclosure at Camp R, a person's movements were severely restricted; inside the hut, the relatively small space reinforced the absence of any private space. In the hut lived fifty-six persons, day and night, almost always together, day after day, weeks on end, one month after another, never alone, always in company. Even the most private and natural human acts had to be performed with an audience standing nearby, even if inattentive. Since everyone knew everyone, inter-personal contacts no longer provided much emotional or intellectual stimulation.

Hopelessness sometimes replaced boredom; perhaps annoyance set in. All prisoners experienced those feelings to some degree; some coped, others did not; some tried to escape, and some became sick or even insane. Some inmates of Camp R escaped their loneliness by joining others in the harassment of the weak minority. Young persons usually found the camp atmosphere most enjoyable; no one really was there to be in charge of them, and they enjoyed this freedom from direct supervision. The conditions were slightly reminiscent of holiday camp. However, this freedom could degenerate to the level where

< There was plenty of free time at Camp R.
[Courtesy of the Red Rock Historical Society]

Jewish youngsters in some of the other internment camps perpetrated such cruel practical jokes upon their elderly camp companions that one inmate called them "sadistic."[22] No such acts, however, were reported from Camp R.

The camp routine encouraged idleness among individuals unless a person participated in such time- and energy-consuming activities as sports or the pursuit of learning or a hobby. Even activities such as smoking, reading newspapers and listening to the radio were considered powerful counterforces against idleness. The constant demand for "smokes" by prisoners and their outside caretakers often arose from the men's desire to cope with idleness rather than from a desire to nourish an addiction. Using tobacco by filling a pipe or rolling a cigarette, and then smoking the same, all consumed time. Shortages of "smokes" and tobacco and the absence of newspapers and radio were perceived as true disasters because they all added to the rise of prison-claustrophobia. Spier found his "escape" in religious contemplation and reflections.[23] Jews and anti-Nazis together found theirs, generally speaking, in endless debates; and the merchant sailors found theirs in sports.

Besides boredom and familiarity, there were other sources of irritation as well. A severe blow was struck against the hopes of interned Jewish and anti-Nazi refugees in Camp R by the prohibition of visiting relatives in other camps and vice versa. A similar devastating strike was the announcement that no wives were allowed to visit. Old British promises proved false. How far these and other factors contributed to the outbursts of violence in the camp is open to speculation. But violence there was.

X

"The Little Third Reich on Lake Superior"

AS HAS ALREADY BEEN MENTIONED several times throughout this story of Camp R and its inmates, the entire camp life as it existed within the enclosure, with all its multiple activities, was affected by the underlying tension between the pro- and anti-Hitler blocs. This most troublesome factor dominated not only the ongoing daily relationship between inmates, but also pervaded all activities whether sports, education or entertainment. These strained interactions between the two sides had existed since they first encountered each other in the mixed camps of Britain; they persisted on board the *Duchess* and resumed their ugly role in Camp R until the separation of these two hostile groups was implemented in the late winter of 1940–1941. Up until then Camp R was officially known as a "mixed Nazi" camp. Included under the "Nazi" label were not only eleven Jewish schoolboys, but also the small group of adult anti-Nazis and Jews, whom British tribunals had misplaced in Category A. Officially, there should not have been any trouble among these so-called Category A Nazis. In reality, however, as

the local military very well knew, daily incidents of anti-Semitic harassment and political chicanery occurred and made life for the minority
almost unbearable. Especially dramatic were two violent incidents that
took place in October and November of 1940. In the eastern Canadian
refugee camps, Red Rock's abominable reputation as an oppressive
place inspired Koch's memorable and appropriate epithet, "the little
Third Reich on Lake Superior."[1]

It is surprising that in this charged atmosphere of political and
racial antagonisms, as reported primarily by Jewish and anti-Nazi
inmates, major brutal outbursts of violence did not occur on a daily
basis. During the opening days of the camp, perhaps, everyone was
preoccupied with settling in, and the Nazi element, collectively, were
busy hanging Hitler's portrait and decorating their huts with national-
istic paraphernalia. None of the various early visitors and inspectors,
whether Brigadier Panet, Colonel Watson, or even Consul General Maag
of the ICRC, reported any manifestations of unrest or anti-Semitic
harassment during their visiting periods. Panet, in July, observed the
political divisions among the prisoners; Watson, in August, did not.
Did Consul General Maag misjudge the situation due to his inability to
speak with the camp's Jews and anti-Nazis, or did he view the constant
anti-Semitic hassle as non-threatening and unruly behaviour, a daily
unwelcome annoyance? The War Diary shows no relevant entries: did
Consul General Maag and Commandant Berry both fail to assess the
seriousness of the situation sufficiently?

Captain Kirkness had already written in his Morale Report of
August about tension in the enclosure. He did not list any particular
daily or recurrent incidents, but spoke in general terms. "In general," he
commented, "there is a fairly friendly atmosphere in the camp—however, there will always be tension while there are two intensely hostile
groups."[2] In fact Kirkness repeated this general observation in later
reports. In his September and October Reports, Kirkness observed that
the internees' morale was in "progressive decline." He saw the cause for
this in the German aerial attack on Britain. The Battle of Britain had

inspired, among the pro-German inmates, an "unshakeable confidence in a swift German victory." When, however, the expected victory did not materialize, "disappointment is giving way to surprise and a degree of doubt," Kirkness noted. Astute observers among the prisoners, such as G. Noffke, writing to his wife, accepted the reality of a long internment: "the war doesn't look like ending, and it seems that we shall be here another winter." Kirkness added this characterization of the situation:

> Impatience and uncertainty have engendered a spirit of restlessness in the pro-Fascist group, while worry and uncertainty have provoked a similar spirit among the anti-Fascists, who in Camp R constitute about 20% of the total number of internees. This condition among the anti-Fascists has been further aggravated by the Governmental decision to classify them—ignoring the possibility that many of them may be, and no doubt are, genuine refugees—as Category A. The outward and visible sign of this unhealthy undercurrent of feeling are "incidents" and attempts at escape.

At the same time, however, Kirkness commented that "in other respects moral[e] is good, owing to continued improvement of the conditions in camp." More internees, he stated, were able to purchase tobacco and "additional comforts"; in addition, censored newspapers were now available and mail from Germany was finally arriving.

Another witness, inmate Spier, offered a different view of camp life at this time. Not surprisingly Spier stressed what he saw as the Nazis' impudent arrogance towards the Jews and the anti-Nazis, whom they ridiculed and denounced as "the vanguard of democracy" in the camp. In the early weeks, he observed, the Nazis had displayed their customary cockiness, bragging about Germany's very near final future victory, and they had underlined their confidence by preparing and posting a large sign on one of the huts reading, "To Be Let By September 1940." This was a new form of harassment of a more subtle and enervating kind, an attempt at subverting the spirit of the anti-Nazi minority. It annoyed the camp military, who wished the sign removed until Spier apparently advised Kirkness against this action. Bored by inactivity, the younger EMS were quite easily led and willingly joined such provocative activities as taunting, shouting anti-Semitic slogans and uttering intimidating threats of physical violence. The EMS, enveloped in the comfort of peer pressure, felt strong and boisterous, encouraged by the clique of Nazis around Guelcher, Baron Pilar and Pastor Wehrhahn.

This is how Spier perceived the camp's anti-Hitler groupings: there were "the so-called Bolsheviks, the international seamen, the democrats, the intelligentsia, and the members of the International Brigade."[3] All were anxious and eager to help Britain subdue the Nazi regime. Lachmann let Spier have *Hansard* at night to read to anti-Nazis. Spier describes somewhat exuberantly the atmosphere in camp growing more confident among the anti-Nazis, as news of the August debates in the House of Commons concerning the injustices and mistakes of deportation forced the Churchill government to reconsider its policies and actions. Simultaneously, Spier claimed, the Nazis grew "more restless...and their impatience to return to Europe and join in the apparently victorious air battle over England became more and more wildly manifest, and made them lose the last bit of self-control."[4] It was in this situation that the October riot occurred. Spier also attributes the escape of Mueller and Rauschenbach to this situation and seems to embellish it as "part of an organized conspiracy" by the Nazis. Spier suggests that the Nazis hoped the camps' guard troops would be dispatched on searches of the surrounding area in response to the escape and thus provide the remaining "Nazis an opportunity for a wholesale dash for liberty."[5]

The Nazis also perpetrated so-called practical jokes. When Berry granted the small Jewish community the privilege of being served kosher food on Yom Kippur, some Nazis working in the kitchen replaced the specially ordered kosher meal for Yom Kippur with a pot of fried bacon. Enjoying their dominant influence due to their overwhelming numbers, the EMS, providing the bulk of the pro-Hitler faction, complemented such stupid pranks with annoying the anti-Nazis by singing provocative and obnoxious Nazi songs. The small Jewish group was especially targeted in the early days with a continual raucous disruption of their religious services by the EMS holding "noisy boxing training exercises" in an adjacent room.[6] This constant harassment and personal bullying succeeded in continuously disrupting the camp's routine and tranquillity. Koch sums up the situation appropriately: "it was impossible for any opponent of Hitler to live in peace within a compound dominated by a pro-Nazi majority."[7] It is not surprising therefore that Camp R had the reputation of a dreadful place among refugees in eastern camps.

Using his very limited authority, camp spokesman Scharf was able, apparently, to prevent major outbursts of violence between the warring sections during the first three months. On the initiative of the Jewish and anti-Nazi faction, according to Spier, Scharf persuaded adherents of both blocs to move into separate huts and thus, by limiting daily contact, substantially reduce the possibilities and incidence of unfriendly friction and physical violence. For this as well as other similar measures, Scharf required, of course, the full and official backing of Commandant Berry because, first, it was forbidden to inmates to move from one hut to another without the Commandant's permission; second, the Nazis, who had already protested against Scharf's selection as camp spokesman, would have resisted; third, the spokesman simply lacked the power to enforce such an order. Spier was convinced that the Nazis were determined to unseat Scharf by provoking unrest and turmoil through their continuous anti-Semitic behaviour.

While camp spokesman Scharf, with his limited power, was unable to suppress all political and racist harassment in the enclosure, the local military, whose responsibility it was to maintain law and order, was seemingly oblivious to the atmosphere in the enclosure. It cannot be determined with any certainty that Berry administered Camp R's enclosure on the principle that "what happens inside the fence is the Germans' affair," although there is some evidence that this attitude prevailed in military POW camps, with the result that the highest ranking soldier might simply be picked by the commandant and appointed as spokesman.[8] No reports exist that provosts detected, stopped or punished perpetrators of harassment in Camp R. Yet tension was ever present. It might rise to the surface and explode at any time for any reason. And on 1 October 1940, it finally did.

On that day, a small group of Nazis went to the hospital allegedly for treatment. On arrival they proceeded to beat up the two Jewish doctors in attendance, Drs. Hans Novotny and Leo Seewald, and the two German orderlies, Otto Stalski and H. Ehrecke, and for good measure smashed the medical equipment. In the course of his subsequent local investigation, Berry reported:

> Certain members of the Nazi group proceeded to the compound [sic] hospital for treatment on the first of October 1940. An Anti-Nazi member of the hospital staff referred to them as Nazi Swine and adopted a threatening attitude with the result that a fight ensued in which two orderlies and doctors were injured.

"[The] Anti-Nazi Group," Berry continued,

> claims that this was a deliberate attack made by members of the Nazi party wishing to take over control of the Compound Hospital by intimidation, which of course is ridiculous as the Compound Hospital is under the supervision and authority of the Camp Medical Officer....I do not consider the statements submitted by either group should be accepted as evidence in an effort to arrive at a just decision, and I am therefore awarding all parties concerned the same punishment. These people would willingly perjure themselves to place the blame on the other side.[9]

In the absence of any reliable and independent eyewitnesses, other than the participants, it is impossible to reconstruct what happened precisely, other than that beatings and injuries were inflicted. Koch argues that the sentries outside the hospital either ignored the disturbance inside or did not hear the shouts for help from those under attack or from inmates who had rushed to the scene, also shouting for help. Apparently only the provost sergeant came to the rescue of the doctors and the orderlies.[10]

In a separate memorandum to his immediate superior, Brigadier Riley, at the Winnipeg Military District Headquarters, Berry claimed that "the incident [offered] conclusive evidence that if people who are definitely Anti-Nazi are interned with Nazis, a situation is bound to arise which will be impossible to cope with, and which will ultimately bring about the most serious complications." He concluded with an urgent request "that immediate steps be taken...to rectify this intolerable situation." These remarks and Berry's actions reflected his frustration and annoyance with this incident and over the continuous disturbances of the camp's tranquility for which he blamed both groups. He saw the root cause for this riot in the mixed character of the camp, an opinion shared by the Intelligence Officer, Captain Kirkness, who already had predicted this kind of disturbance in his August Report. Berry, however, was not concerned with justice; he saw only instigators and perpetrators of this violent fracas who needed punishing; all were guilty, aggressors and victims. In response to Berry's judgement of assigning to all participants the same punishment of seven days solitary confinement, the anti-Fascist few staged a hunger strike, which was ended a few days later after Berry promised to advance arguments for their transfer to a separate camp with his superiors.

Scharf reacted swiftly to this violent fracas. On the very same day, he called together the enclosure's imprisoned German nationals and addressed them.[11] Addressing them as "My Young and Old Comrades," Scharf's speech was a masterly rebuke of the Nazi rowdies; it criticized them in terms of their own professed standards of discipline and adherence and respect for a "Führer." Reminding the camp Nazis of their violation of the much adored "Führerprinzip," Scharf went on to depict their action as harmful to the name of the fatherland and the spirit of the Lagergemeinschaft, the camp's sense of "community," a local off-shoot of the Nazi concept of the wider "*Volksgemeinschaft.*" Scharf's admonition did not eliminate anti-Semitism and anti-Nazi harassment completely from Camp R, but it seems to have calmed tempers temporarily. Perhaps the bulk of the EMS, young and old, realized they had a lot to lose. However, Scharf's action annoyed the Nazi element in the camp sufficiently that after his repatriation to Nazi Germany, perhaps in 1944, Scharf was invited to a *Gestapo* interview and faced the charge that he had been too friendly towards the Jewish and anti-Nazi inmates in the camp.[12]

The Nazi element organized its response by 3 October in a letter—in English—addressed to "The Commandant, Internment Camp R, which is here reproduced in full:

Sir,

We, the undersigned, beg to draw your attention to the following facts

Since tis [sic] camp was established we have endeavoured to help Capt. Scharf two respects. In the firsdt [sic] place, to keep order and good discipline in the camp in spite of the fact that men with completely different outlook were herded together here under the aggravating circumstances of internment, on the other hand to make the Canadian authorities see eye to eye with us in regard to this fact, i.e. the impossibility of establishing lasting peace and order amongst these naturally hostile elements, Germans and Refugees from Germany

For three months nothing happened—neither from the side of the Canadian authorities with a view to segregate Germans and Refugees, notwithstanding Capt. Scharf's repeated representations, nor inside the camp, but under the smooth surface of things the situation grew from bad to worse. It is an impossibility to keep a crowded number of men together behind barbed wire fences looking at each other with the deepest distrust and aversion, deeper than it could exist between national enemies. This state of things is about to bring about a violent explosion sooner or later.

The explosion occurred on the 1st of October. We feel convinced that this event was due to the incessant provocations of our men by the refugees, especially so by the behaviour of the Jewish surgeons who had succeeded in transforming the camp hospital into a nearly exclusively jewish [sic] institution. The final clash then came when the surgeons appointed an individual who had betrayed his own comrades in an English camp, as medical help in the hospital and when some of the Jews employed there used insulting language towards German sailor patients. The violent outbreak of our fellow internees' indignation was perfectly spontaneous, had not been prearranged in any way whatsoever and the whole affair developed so suddenly that Capt. Scharf was given no opportunity either to prevent it or to settle the matter in a different way. We wish to point out expressly that this outbreak of public resentment should not be taken as a sign of lack of authority on Capt. Scharf's part whose authority we all fully acknowledge and indisputedly [sic] obey. When the question about the culprits for this event was put before us we felt that we all were in a certain way morally responsible for it. In expression of this common feeling and with the intention of assuming responsibility the hut leaders of all the huts of groups II, III and IV stepped forward. We might mention that all the men who actually were in the hospital at the time of the happening at once volunteered to report but were held back because we felt that the responsibility really was ours.

We wish to reaffirm again this attitude that we and with us all the internees of groups II, III and IV are fully prepared to share the consequences of what has happened. We are prepared to take the consequences on us and declare at the same time that Capt. Scharf has our full confidence and all orders he will give us will be obeyed. Without intending to defend the violence of the happening we beg to consider in judging these that they were caught in the last sense by a situation which a priori was dangerous and bound to lead to trouble—a situation which is not our fault—and that men who have been held behind barbed wire for over a year cannot always be judged by normal standards.

We beg to remain, Sir, Yours faithfully.

signed by thirty-six persons.[13]

This letter is a masterly expression of the Nazi spirit that the Nazi leaders in Camp R were apparently able to impose on their German fellow national internees. By reaffirming Scharf's authority as camp spokesman, they made him, by implication, marginally co-responsible for what had happened. In affirming his innocence, they also implied his failure to know what was really going on. The thirty-six signatures, among them Guelcher, Pilar, Stuessel, Beissel and Lachmann, reflect a degree of unanimity that suggests the use of suppression and intimidation to achieve *Gleichschaltung* (bringing into line). Placing a cover of collective moral responsibility on all, even totally uninvolved bystanders, they applied a standard Nazi practice—used in such Nazi affiliations as the *Arbeitsdienst*, *Deutsche Jungvolk* and the *Hitler Jugend*—which declared the entire group "guilty" and thereby in this instance prevented any punishment, since the Geneva Convention forbade collective punishment. The letter also exploited, it seems, the local camp administration's misgivings about operating a mixed camp.

Following the October outbreak of violence, Kirkness noted,

> the atmosphere in the camp has continued, unfriendly; and the anti-Nazi element feels itself to be a helpless and persecuted minority.... Recently the anti-Nazi group has displayed a tendency to various forms of passive resistance to authority and has become rather soured and difficult to handle. This may be attributed to two principal causes: (a) The announcement that all internees in Camp R are Category "A" Aliens; (b) The decision that all internees will be obliged to wear internee clothing, which is described as "Prisoner of War uniform." In the case of (a), this is keenly felt, since the majority of the group are with little doubt genuine refugees.[14]

Whatever measures were taken, their immediate effects lasted barely a month. On 5 November, another violent fracas erupted between Nazis and anti-Nazis. This time three Nazis—Heinz Ebert, Karl Salewscky and Willi Horkheimer—attacked Dr. Max Bruenn, Heinz

Thelen and Fritz Wolf. Although no details of this disturbance are found in the available records, nonetheless the assault caused severe physical injuries. In an unrelated incident, fighting broke out and inmate Walter Ruckersberger was so badly beaten up that he suffered a "considerable bleeding eye injury." He was rescued from solitary confinement, which Berry had once again imposed on both parties, by the timely intervention of Dr. Klass who thereby saved Ruckersberger from permanent loss of sight.[15] Following this latest incident, Berry asked Headquarters of Military District No. 10 "for instructions regarding procedures to be followed in the case of assault and injury of one internee by several others," especially when "ordinary summary punishment" will not prevent future incidents. Berry suggested "that the prisoners involved be tried by a Military Court under provisions of Section 64, *Regulations Governing the Maintenance of Discipline among and Treatment of Prisoners of War*, P.C. 4121, December 13, 1939" or by civil court of criminal jurisdiction under Section 63, since the victim "was quite badly beaten...in the assault causing bodily harm." In response to Colonel Berry's inquiry, Captain H.N. Streight, the District's Assistant Judge Advocate General, asked the Judge Advocate General in Ottawa for further advice since he, Streight, felt "intimidated" by the relevant Articles 60 to 62 of the Geneva Convention of 1929. The Judge Advocate General assured Winnipeg in its reply that if they proceeded with this case, the Ottawa office wished to receive the pertinent documentation and would then undertake to inform the Protecting Power.[16] It is not known if any action was taken subsequently.

What exactly the underlying tangible and intangible causes of these two violent outbursts were is difficult to establish with any certainty. Many factors undoubtedly contributed. By the end of the summer many prisoners, pro- and anti-Hitlerites, were depressed by the uncertainties of their personal fate and future. The mood of the interned German nationals, especially the Nazis, had been very high, buoyed up during the summer months by German military successes that led to exaggerated expectations of an early final German victory. They therefore exhibited an arrogant, aggressive and antagonistic attitude towards "the traitors," the Jews and anti-Nazis. Their taunting was more than ever unbearable to their victims in these circumstances. As time went on, however, military fortunes changed. By the end of September, the threat of a German invasion had vanished and the *Luftwaffe* had failed to bomb Britain into submission, and now the much-feared Canadian winter was coming. As high hopes for victory and a quick return home faded, so did arrogance, and the sign "To Be Let" outside one hutment disappeared. Instead frustration and anger began to emerge, focusing on other minor common irritants. Kirkness observed that the "easy confidence and cheerful optimism" among the interned German nationals "have unobtrusively vanished and have been replaced by 'quiet resignation.'" Yet Kirkness also noted that this "substantial change in opinions" has not "appreciably altered" morale or "shaken confi[d]ence in the 'Fuhrer,' who—it is believed—will accomplish his purpose in his own time, and in his own way."[17] Euphoric expectations disappeared and cockiness weakened as final victory eluded the *Führer*'s grasp in 1940. Yet they were still confident in the *Führer*'s ability to seize a future victorious outcome. At the same time the imprisoned internees increasingly began to accept the reality of a long war and a lengthy incarceration.

According to Kirkness, declining morale led to a slackening of political activism, generally, and led "progressively" to spreading doubt, disappointment, anger, restlessness, resentment and helplessness. Furthermore, with the coming of winter and its "Siberian climate," a new reality suddenly loomed before the internees. The prospect of winter worried the "South Africans," especially those suffering from malaria. An additional contributory cause might have been General Panet's final decision to prohibit the display of Hitler pictures in the prisoners' huts. This decision coincided with other depressing discoveries that caused tremendous resentment. There was the order that every prisoner must wear the despised regulation prisoners' uniform, the "circus outfit"; the lack of mail from England or Germany; the growing

Camp R, winter 1940–1941. *[Courtesy of the Red Rock Historical Society]*

constant coldness inside the non-winterized huts; the lack of reading lights in the huts as the days grew shorter, and the announcement of stricter mail censorship rules ahead. It is impossible to determine how far these and other irritants, shared by all inmates, Nazis and anti-Nazis, contributed to the tension in the camp during October and early November.

Jews and anti-Nazis had their own special worries. At first, they were concerned about the fate of their families left behind in England, facing the immediate threat of a German invasion, the collapse of Britain and a possible British sell-out *à la Compiègne*. And after these dangers dissipated, the refugee inmates at Camp R were dismayed to learn, in September, from Canadian officers, that their wives and children would not be permitted to join them as British officers had promised in June. Many refugees had volunteered to go to Canada on the basis of that promise. In Camp R, they wondered too when they would be transferred to a separate camp for anti-Hitlerites. They were very disappointed to learn that visits from friends or relatives in Canada or the United States were cancelled. The Jewish and anti-Nazi group felt helpless and persecuted. They fiercely objected to their new status as "Prisoners of War, Class II" and Ottawa's confirmation of their status as "Category A" prisoners. Were they now victims of New World Canadian anti-Semitism? The camp reminded them daily what they had escaped from, but was there no end in sight to their sufferings, their persecutions?

From the military's point of view the violent disturbances of October and November as well as the continuous turmoil were the direct result of the mixed camp set-up at Red Rock. Camp R showed conclusively that this concept did not work. While the practice of mixing antagonistic groups together in one camp had worked for the British military, perhaps since the groups were more equally matched numerically, it did not work in Canada. Captain Kirkness had said so repeatedly, and now Berry pointed out that "mixing" produced "an intolerable situation" which sooner or later would find release through individual prisoners in some sort of emotional and bloody explosion of tension and stress. Moreover, the disturbances demonstrated that the soldiers of the Veterans Guard were incapable of assuring either the prisoner's personal safety or discipline within the enclosure. Perhaps they did not care; perhaps that sort of safety was not their concern; perhaps they were not trained for this. Yet the enforcement and maintenance of discipline and good order over the inmates inside the enclosure was the sole responsibility of the Canadian military in accordance with the Geneva Convention of 1929, Articles 18–20, to be implemented by the local camp commandant, his administrative staff and the officers and soldiers of the Veterans Guard of Canada.

This new reality was well expressed in camp secretary Lueddeke's letter to his mother in Hamburg: "Spirits here are not very rosy.

However, let's keep our chins up—I haven't given up hope yet."[18]
Towards the year's end, by Christmas, political tension in Camp R had
lessened considerably; although hostility still existed between the two
groups, violent incidents no longer occurred. As Kirkness noted, Jews
and anti-Nazis at first tended to discuss politics endlessly in order to
cope with their concerns. The EMS crowd, on the other side, played
sports, an activity more to the liking of Canadian Army officers. By
March 1941, however, Kirkness noticed in his reports a "progressive
decline of political interest," which he believed was achieved without
resort to special measures by the local military authority. In fact by
this time the process of sorting out Nazis and anti-Nazi and Jewish
refugees had also finally reached Camp R. This meant that the camp
Nazis had lost their local scapegoats upon whom they could vent their
fears, their anger and frustrations. Other improvements, such as better
mail delivery, better dental service, regular movie presentations and a
return of hopes that the war would be over by the coming summer, all
contributed to the new "good atmosphere [prevailing] between guards
and POWs, [with] remarkably little complaining."[19]

Anti-Semitic violence and harassment were unpleasant, even brutal,
interruptions of the routine of camp life; another source of interruptions was the escape of prisoners. Camp R, just like every other camp,
had a plan ready to cope with escape. In accordance with Camp R's
"Recapture Plan," the camp siren would send out its long warning
wail accompanied by the bugle's sounds. While the siren alerted the
neighbourhood to the dangers associated with escapees, the bugle summoned all soldiers and officers to their posts and alerted all and sundry
in the camp to what had occurred. The Veterans Guard were called
into action, while the inmates wondered who had dared to break out
and whether they would succeed. At Camp R, the sounding of "general
alarm" frequently disturbed routine during the period from July 1940 to
October 1941, announcing numerous though usually unsuccessful and
unspectacular escapes.

The trio of Puize, Daun and Goad had hardly completed its tour when, on 16 September 1940, Fritz Fuchs wandered away from a work detail and was gone for seven days. On the day he was retrieved, 23 September, Herbert Cohn, a Jewish internee, was betrayed while he sought to tunnel his way to freedom in order to join the Canadian Army in the fight against Fascism. Spier maintained that a Veterans sentry had suddenly disappeared from sight as the tunnel collapsed under him, and this accident ended the escape attempt. By the end of September, Internment Operations instructed all District Headquarters to implement additional regulations in order to prevent future escapes. Concerning the Veterans Guard of Canada, camp commandants were ordered to "remove and dispose" of all soldiers "found unsuitable." Next, the Guard were to be thoroughly trained, including range practice with small arms, and receive shotguns. A bugler would "sound all routine and other calls." Furthermore, it was suggested to install camp telephone systems and to review standing orders. Most remarkable was Instruction 5, which stressed that:

> respective responsibilities of guards and Camp Staffs will be clearly defined. Instructions on all matters concerning internment camps will emanate from the District Officer Commanding. The Commandant of the Internment camp will be treated as the Senior Combatant Officer in so far as the Internment camp is concerned and he will be responsible to the District Officer Commanding.
>
> The Officer Commanding the Veterans Guard will come under the direct orders of the Commandant of the Internment Camp for all purposes, except internal administration and discipline of his unit.[20]

With this, the ugly visage of "dual control" was finally pushed aside.

Then on 4 October, Ernst Mueller, a stateless leftist, and his nineteen-year-old pal, Rudolf Rauschenbach, escaped while working at the Red Rock Inn. They were recaptured later that evening in a shack on the west side of nearby Mount How, on the Arolas' homestead "seven miles away from camp," at 2200 hours. It was a very dark night with heavy rain falling when a lone soldier came upon them. In the process of capture, Mueller was shot twice, once in the stomach and then in the head, while surrendering and shouting, "Don't shoot—I have a family." Whether fear, carelessness or darkness induced Private J.R. Moar to shoot and kill Mueller was never established; the subsequent inquiry cleared Moar of any wrongdoing and of negligence. Local folklore has it that Colonel Berry instructed the searchers to shoot first and then call "Halt."

Lloyd Roy, late of Red Rock, also provided an account of this tragic incident, based on soldier Moar's own story told to the Roy family, who had befriended Moar. Roy, nine years old at the time of the inci-dent, was assisted by the memories of other family members, when he recorded the following:

> On 4 October 1940, mid-night raining heavy very dark, soldier alone came
> upon POWs in steambath, given away by fire smoke, Rudolf Rauschenbach
> (16) yrs was pushed out by Ernst Mueller soldier called Mueller to come
> out hands on head, he did not, Moar looked in shack and saw Ernst
> halfway out vent told to halt then shot in right hip, still trying to get out
> soldier shot again this time in back of head. My dad saw Mueller's face
> reconstructed and was then paraded to Red Rock station and shipped to
> Port Arthur, from there repatriated to Germany at end of war. We were
> told J.R. Moar was jailed in brig in Winnipeg and died 2 years later from
> this shooting. This fact confirmed by letters from soldiers writing to us
> from home in Winnipeg.
>
> Signed: Lloyd Roy.[21]

One minor factual difference exists between Mr. Roy's account and history: Mueller's corpse was buried first in Port Arthur cemetery and later transferred to Kitchener-Waterloo Woodside Cemetery where all German POWs and internees who died in Canadian captivity are interred.

A former inmate of Camp R left this brief account:

> As far as the shooting of Mueller goes, I can only say what Lauterbach [sic],
> who was the only witness to the shooting, told me. He said that when the
> guard approached them they were resting under a pine, when they got
> off the ground as ordered, the guard shot Mueller claiming that Mueller
> tried to pick up a rock to hit him with. Since Mueller as far as I know was
> a stateless person, having legally denounced his German citizenship prior
> years, there was no international outcry about this affair.[22]

Both accounts of this tragic event exonerate the side of the witness and
implicitly blame the other. What actually and exactly happened cannot
be established for lack of other eyewitnesses.

Erich Weisser and Bruno Schwaiger decided to escape during
the unusually cold night—"the temperature was 15 below zero
[Fahrenheit]"—of 17 January 1941. A strong northerly blizzard was
blowing as well. Their absence was discovered at the morning roll call
at 0730 hours, and immediately the standing order concerning escape,
the "Recapture Plan," was invoked. The siren sounded, the bugle blew
and the Veterans Guard soldiers and officers assumed their assigned
posts and executed their predetermined duties. Picquets were sent to
the towns of Dorion and Nipigon to control the railways and to the Port
Arthur-Geraldton highway. Commandant Berry was informed first and
then the dog handler and his well-trained dog, North. Next, the camp
staff telephoned the RCMP detachment in Fort William and then the
one in nearby Nipigon; thereafter, the provincial police and the CNR
police detachments in Port Arthur, who in turn contacted their agents
at Port Arthur, Hornepayne and Long Lac; next they called the CPR
police units in Fort William and Sudbury.

Unfortunately, Camp R did not have any usable description or
photos of these two fugitives as they had of Fischer, requiring these to
be ordered from Ottawa. Having completed these important telephone
calls, the staff contacted the Director of Internment Operations in

Ottawa and finally the Headquarters of Military District No. 10 in Winnipeg. Simultaneously picquets were set up on all roads and highways leading out of the area. At the camp, the Bridge and Main Guard was increased in numbers, as were all others. The ford across the creek was guarded, search parties were formed, and the machine gun truck was readied for action. All officers were on their assigned posts, having been picked up previously by the station wagon at the Inn and taken to the flag post area of the camp. The standing order advised the guards not to trample down the escapees' tracks, to secure clothing belonging to the fugitives, and to transmit name, age, internee number, weight, general description, colour of hair and eyes, tattoos and language(s) spoken to all search agencies. The search for the two escapees was hampered not only by the bitter cold and the blowing snow that prevented search dog North from demonstrating his skill and finding a trail, but also by the lack of photographs of the fugitives.

Schwaiger was recaptured, nonetheless, that morning at 1015 hours in Port Arthur, and Weisser that afternoon before 1500 hours some twelve miles outside Port Arthur. Everyone was reunited at Camp R at 1800 hours. Internment Operations in Ottawa was very critical of the subsequent inquiry conducted by the Headquarters of Military District No. 10 concerning this last escape. Again the records do not reveal the outcome of this inquiry. A surprising fact emerged, however: the two escapees had accumulated sufficient Canadian funds, namely $1.93, to purchase railway tickets from Red Rock to Port Arthur.

The Schwaiger and Weisser escape in January 1941 exercised the "great alarm" procedure as it had been perfected over time and by experience. Previously in Camp R, a most peculiar flaw existed in its communication system. In the early months when the "great alarm" procedure was first implemented, Nipigon's nearby RCMP unit was the last to hear about the emergency. This was due entirely to the communications technology then available. In 1940, no direct telephone link existed between the camp and the local RCMP station. Therefore the established procedure required that the camp staff call the

International Hotel in Nipigon and ask the proprietor, Mr. Fazio, a man of Italian origin, to hire a taxi and drive over to the RCMP station and inform the officer on duty to contact the camp immediately. The staff was ordered under no circumstances to ever divulge any details to the hotelkeeper. No record exists to testify to the efficacy of this process.[23]

In March 1941, Ernst Schipper tried escaping for the second time and failed again as he did on his first attempt in November 1940. In September 1941, Rudolf Haag attempted to escape from the camp, but the discovery of his two-metre long tunnel signalled another aborted attempt. Shortly thereafter the provosts discovered another tunnelling attempt in hut No. 34 A. However, this was the last recorded attempt at escape.[24]

The infrequency of escapes from Camp R and the failure of almost all is surprising in view of the camp's location on a trans-Canada railway line and its proximity to the border of the neutral United States of America, a mere 100 miles away. Equally surprising is the lack of any sophisticated scheme or any large-scale direct assault on the flimsy fences surrounding the enclosure, which many a military inspector had warned about. Did the prisoners in "the little Third Reich on Lake Superior" lack that creative, daredevil spirit which drove many officer POWs, Class I, in the camps at Calydor and Bowmanville to escape, as well as some of the "other ranks" at Angler? Certainly the terrain was favourable, the wire fences flimsy and even the power lines and floodlights not beyond disabling sabotage or diversion. Perhaps the enemy merchant seamen had more practical sense in risk-and-success calculations than the German officers, who like many military men subscribed to the questionable belief that "a soldier must escape."

In March 1941, the local military had been told by its "reliable" informer, internee Schmitt, that "a grandiose scheme for escape" was being hatched by the Nazis under the leadership of "Schmidt (South African), Guelcher (South African), Pilar, and Funk."[25] The informer proposed that two inmates, Possel and Haller, be recruited in an attempt to thwart this scheme. The escape plan envisaged the creation of a disturbance in the camp, while the escape of a dozen inmates was to occur elsewhere. The breakout was to coincide "with Hitler's birthday on April 25 [sic]." "Coach" Guelcher, the military recalled, had organized a similar (though aborted) caper previously in England in Camp Seaton, to commemorate the same event. At Red Rock nothing happened on the day set. Elsewhere, however, namely at Angler, a great escape was staged just a few days earlier—18–19 April 1941. The date was moved up because of rain that threatened to collapse the tunnels, so the escape did not occur on Hitler's birthday as planned.[26]

The reasons why civilian interned inmates wished to escape were as manifold as their personalities. On the basis of available evidence, it is impossible to report with any certainty about the prisoners' state of mental health in Camp R. Attested cases of mental illness were few; the number of undiagnosed, generally perturbed persons is unknown. While violence, harassment and juvenile pranksterism enhanced the monotonous existence of some inmates, others suffered unnecessary anguish and hardships. Sports, hobbies and education offered outlets for still others. Refugees faced most frightening worries about their families during the months of July, August and September of 1940. How could they help their families while sitting in Camp R? Based on recent experiences, they feared the worst. In this group, despair could drive them to seek escape. The mail service—that privilege of the Canadian-detained POW, Class II—was erratic, slow at best and unreliable. When advice was urgently needed, none was available. Rumours could bring hope or despair.

In his October Report, Kirkness offered three reasons why inmates sought to escape: First, the Nazis now feared a long war and a prolonged, intolerable period of incarceration; second, the anti-Nazis feared a German victory and consequently falling into Nazi hands; third, some wished to escape before the start of winter's snowfall which would make tracking fugitives easier. These were very pragmatic reasons. One wonders why some Nazis, like Guelcher, showed no desire to escape and seek to help the *Führer* win the war. Of course, with plenty of good food, very little work and an abundance of free time, life in Camp R might well be viewed as preferable to escape, which meant facing great physical hardships, unforeseeable emotional stress, mental tension and physical hardships, constant fear of discovery under conditions of a very dangerous pursuit, and lengthy solitary confinement or even death if caught. Regrettably, the evidence does not generally indicate the group affiliation of those trying to escape. Rarely, as in the case of Cohn, Fischer and Mueller, is it possible to identify the group identity: Nazi, anti-Nazi, Jew, or EMS. Prisoners, of course, had personal reasons for escaping. Foremost was the desire for personal freedom and for privacy, just getting away from everyone and out of the enclosure, out from behind the barbed wires, away from the monotonous routine, the stifling confinement of the camp and fellow inmates. Escape across the wire offered the ultimate solution to these problems. Some escapees may have hoped to join in the political struggle once in freedom; others may have hoped to escape from eventual capture by the Germans. They all failed in the end.

The complete failure of fifteen escape attempts, except Fischer's partial success, is an impressive achievement for Camp R's military. Colonel Alley's response to sensational Canadian press reports of escapes by German POWs did not apply at Red Rock. Here, evidently, did not exist what Alley termed a state of "staleness," which resulted in a lack of keenness and alertness among the Veterans Guard. As Alley argued, prolonged periods of continuous service in isolated areas, under severe conditions and without relief for the elderly soldiers, accounted for escapes elsewhere. Of course these failed escape attempts at Red Rock might be explained more simply: nearly all of them were individual efforts, so could be planned only using the limited resources of the individual and his personal talents or lack thereof. In the camps of POWs, Class I, where the "foolish concept of escape"[27] was elevated to a matter of honour, often the resources of the entire camp were organized and put at the disposal of the escapers.

With regard to the escapes, it is interesting to note that only in the case of escapee Fischer do the records refer to the use of photos as aids to identification. Can it be assumed that no photos for the other escapees were available? Or were photos available routinely so that therefore no mention was made? Was it only in the case of Schwaiger and Weisser that no suitable photo was ready? The regular process in Canadian internment camps was that shortly after their arrival all prisoners would be registered, fingerprinted (thumbs and all fingers) and photographed—one profile and one frontal view, each picture showing at the bottom the prisoner's number. It is possible that this process was not followed at Camp R; the War Diaries certainly did not note this event. Commissioner Paterson commented in his report that although the eastern camps kept records on each inmate, these records were of little use to him in assessing a prisoner's loyalty, his political views or his behaviour, since these camp records primarily registered canteen purchases, parcel deliveries and disciplinary infractions.

On Christmas Eve, December 24, 1940, Internment Operations circulated "Notes on Prevention of Escapes" to the DOCs of Military Districts 2, 3, 4, 7, 10 and 13. These four pages of "Notes" stressed that "constant alertness of each and every member of the staff and guard" was needed to prevent escapes. Reliance on mechanical equipment such as the array of electrical lights, fences, heavy trucks, or on deep frost or stony sub-soils would only lull the guards into a false sense of security and make them apathetic; "then escapes will occur." [28]

Guards were advised that their prisoners were not only watching them closely in order to detect weaknesses but were also imaginative in plotting escapes. Therefore vigilance was needed, ever altering patrols, surprise searches of prisoners and their quarters, observing prisoner habits such as sleeping during the day, having bulging pockets (filled with earth), undertaking strenuous exercises in preparation of escape, and many similar activities. Careful checking of working huts and regular workshops, keeping track of wood supplies and removing garbage and surplus materials were all part of the alert guard's duties. Guards were cautioned to observe civilian employees within the camp grounds; they were considered especially untrustworthy at that time. In order to discourage escapes the guards were also advised to warn prisoners, especially in isolated camps, of the dangers of the forest in the form of wild snakes, wolves, bears and exposures to frost, as well as the difficulty of rescue from the bush. The "Notes" also offered suggestions on how to read simple mail codes and how to handle the receipt and distribution of parcels. Following the twenty-six articles of the "Notes" would certainly have kept any soldier alert and busy.

In March 1941 another circular, after attempting to analyze the POWs' motivation for escape and conceding their "brilliant minds" and sole dedication to the implementation of their schemes, urged that the only effective device was "everlasting vigilance." For whatever reason, however, this extra warning was unnecessary to the soldiers of Camp R.

XI

Lighter and Darker Aspects of Camp Life

CAMP CANTEENS PLAYED A SIGNIFICANT ROLE in every internee's life and in the life of the camp community in general. Without a camp canteen, inmates felt deprived of the necessities of their daily existence such as cigarettes and tobacco, chocolates and sweets, and the lesser pleasures of hygiene such as soap, toothpaste, razors, combs and toilet paper. Somewhat ironically, lack of money only further aggravated the absence of a canteen. This was exactly the situation in Camp R during the early months. Especially vocal about this were the EMS; unable to find paid work around the camp, the sailors were without money since no funds were forthcoming from Germany for whatever reasons. Under the existing international arrangements, it was understood that the German employers were to continue to pay wages to their captured and interned employees. However, interned EMS maintained, both during and after internment, that they did not receive any wages in captivity.

After the war, in 1947, when they contacted their former employers, they were told that wages had been paid. Allegedly, these wages were transferred to agencies responsible for supplying gift parcels to the German prisoners held in enemy detention.[1] Moreover, since credits had not yet been transferred from Britain either, even wealthier inmates, like Spier, could not purchase any of the desired commodities. Having no canteen and therefore no canteen profits meant that the inmate community could not help itself. Missing canteen profits could not be used to help the impecunious experiencing real deprivation, or to purchase sports equipment and other materials for collective usage. Even after a canteen opened, a general poverty prevailed in Camp R caused by the non-existence of paid work. Inmates relied heavily first on money advanced by the Directorate and later on the charity of the War Prisoners' Aid Committee. The Directorate had made available one dollar per inmate at the opening of the camp, and by April 1941 the War Prisoners' Aid Committee of the YMCA had provided "$12,350.84 for destitute seamen" in Camp R for the acquisition of such necessities as soap, toothpaste and laundry powder.[2]

When a camp canteen finally opened in early 1941, its operation occurred under the auspices of Commandant Berry. He had the last word. The direct management of the canteen, however, was in the hands of the "Camp R Canteen Committee" whose members were "President, Capt. C.G. Bradshaw, No. 10 'A' Co[mpan]y, V.G. of C.; Members, Lieut. J.H. Murray, Lieut. F.F. Sewell" both of No. 10 'A' Company, V.G. of C., and the attached "Internee Committee, [of] Captain O. Scharf, C. von Pilar, Captain G. Beissel and Canteen Steward, W. Lueddeke."[3] The steward, appointed directly by the commandant, was not the manager; he operated only as an assistant to the Canteen Committee. He received the goods, supervised three assistants—whom Berry also appointed— and was responsible for the efficient and clean operation of the canteen. No loitering was permitted inside or outside. Daily hours of operation were from 0900 to 1130 hours and from 1430 to 1500 hours. Sunday was a day of consumers' rest. Although the internee committee initiated the purchase of goods, such requests had to be submitted in writing first to the "president" and next to the commandant for final approval. Colonel

Berry, moreover, approved the merchant, firm or agent, who eventually supplied the goods to the camp, but only after a designated officer issued a written and signed order for delivery. The two committees met on the fifteenth of every month to approve the previous month's accounts and arrange payments.

Any individual inmate was entitled to receive "no more than $5.00" in canteen money in coupons of twenty-five, five and one cent denominations. These coupons were issued twice monthly and were registered. No credit was extended. Beer, wine, and alcoholic liquor were not on sale and only "harmless medicine from reputable makers, previously approved by the medical officer," would be sold. No one under sixteen years of age could buy tobacco goods either. At the end of every business day, the steward had to deliver the day's takings to the Accountant Camp R, Orderly Room, at 1630 hours. Complaints concerning the canteen must be submitted to the commandant. "Profits," the standing order stated, "accruing from sales in internee canteen will be used for purposes which collectively benefit internees subject to the approval of the camp commandant."[4] In contrast to the operation of the two Veterans Guard canteens, one wet and the other dry, which required only six rules dealing primarily with discipline and default, the internees' canteen operated under twenty-six articles.[5]

One reason for such strict supervision may have been that fraternization between soldiers and inmates was strictly forbidden under existing military rules and orders. For this reason, exchanges of gifts such as money, cigarettes, tobacco, chocolate or sweets, chewing gum and souvenirs were forbidden and punishable under military law. Indeed, all types of communication were prohibited other than giving orders or instructions to the inmates. The concept of "fraternization" covered every form of social activity and discourse, including sexual intercourse. Nothing in the official records of Camp R points to the existence of same-sex sexual activity, either among the inmates or the Veterans Guard or between these two groups. However, one former internee, when interviewed, spoke of a pornographic artist and his partner who engaged in noisy sex.[6] The comments and various references by visiting military inspectors to the presence of the many boys and youth in the camp and these inspectors' repeated advice to transfer all the boys and youth to one place, in a separate "youth camp," preferably to Camp Q at Monteith (which had a farming complex attached), might imply concern about the possibility of sexual activity between the youth and older internees. Erich Koch states that same-sex sexual activity was common in the eastern internment camps among inmates and also between inmates and guards; he alleges that rape of inmates by soldiers occurred, and asserts that same-sex sexual activity became quite acceptable in an environment of prolonged incarceration and isolation from women.[7] One former internee in Camp Q commented that enforced, involuntary sexual abstinence was especially difficult to cope with for older, married men, some of whom sought sexual relief through the use of various mechanical contraptions provided by an ingenious entrepreneurial inmate. One witness claimed that some of the older men who resorted to such measures later felt so distraught that they committed suicide.[8] Same-sex sexual activity among internees, or former internees, significantly decreased once the men were free to associate with women.[9]

At Camp R, however, fraternization, sexual or otherwise, never became a major issue; violations of the prohibition against fraternization tended to involve the buying and selling of goods. The relationship between soldiers and internees changed over time, from extreme suspicion and fear to an effective and efficient professional military attitude; as contacts multiplied between guards and prisoners, so perceptions and attitudes changed. The new circumstances were then reflected in amendments to the standing orders. No reports exist which indicate that the Veterans Guard ever engaged in anti-Semitic or anti-German taunting of their prisoners. The most common type of contact between guards and internees centred instead around the illegal selling of German and Nazi military souvenirs, for which, as inmates soon discovered, a high demand existed among all ranks of the local military.

In the early weeks, the lack of money which every one of the inmates experienced, rich or poor, inspired the talented and the entrepreneur-ially-minded. Souvenir items were crafted in order to satisfy the local demand, first of the troops of the Fort Garry Horse and later of the Veterans Guard of Canada. Soon the manufacture of genuine hand-crafted German souvenir articles flourished, producing items such as phoney swastikas, fake parachutist badges, iron crosses of both classes, and model ships, in or out of bottles. As the market expanded outside, the shortage of money inside the enclosure eased considerably. This is how Spier recalled the situation in July: "[W]e arrived completely pen-niless such a short while ago, [but] a steady flow of dollars, cigarettes, tobacco, and chocolate was soon forthcoming."[10]

The camp craftsmen used only locally available raw materials; at hand were bottles and small pieces of wood and metal. Old socks and clothing supplied the coloured yarn for badges, and willing guards helped to acquire needles, bits of iron or other needed supplies. After the craftsmen built an embroidering frame, steady manufacture of sale-able Nazi trinkets began in earnest. Apparently, in this area of human activity, both Nazis and anti-Nazis were ready to cooperate temporarily to their mutual advantage. Jewish craftsmen borrowed badges and crosses from members of the EMS in order to copy these objects for reproduction. The eternal and universal lure of profit thus momentar-ily overcame the humbug of chauvinism, racial difference, ideological divergence and patriotism. The market expanded from Camp R to the bars, cafés and drugstore in Nipigon, then to the Lakehead cities and perhaps even to Winnipeg. Prices fluctuated; bottled model ships fetched as much as $1.25 in Charles M. Thompson's drugstore in Nipigon. At Christmas and New Year potential gifts might fetch prices as high as three to five dollars per item, according to conversations overheard between soldiers in Mr. Papas's Elisa Café in Nipigon. One dollar was paid to the producer; the guard conniving in the transaction received another dollar, and then onto the free market. Trade was brisk.

Eventually suspicions were aroused by an informer, well-known inmate Schmitt, who alleged that among the soldiers of Camp R a sales agency operated, both in and outside the camp, which facilitated trade between camp and town. The military called in the RCMP. An undercover agent visited the scene of the crime: Nipigon. He made discrete inquiries, questioned bar owners and waitresses, and hoped to catch the criminals in the act. Everyone with whom the agent spoke knew about transactions, had even observed the very act of exchange, but no one could identify the perpetrators, and no one ever again saw either seller or buyer. The investigation was a flop. The RCMP did not get its man; perhaps there were too many, or they had all moved back to their Winnipeg barracks before the agent appeared on the Nipigon–Red Rock crime front. Perhaps the RCMP officer investigating was right, when he surmised that in a town the size of Nipigon the saturation point for the sale of souvenir articles would soon be reached and that soldiers involved in the trade would then have some difficulty in disposing profitably of such items.[11] It can be assumed that this exchange trade granted mutual fiscal relief to all participants temporarily; however, it can also be asserted that none of them, in all fairness, is entitled to be labelled a war profiteer. By March 1941, the RCMP noted that trade in Nazi souvenirs had declined noticeably.

There is also some evidence for the existence of individual, small-scale and limited acts of fraternization which involved circumventing such legal restrictions as sending or receiving mail for inmates. According to correspondence between Camp R, the Headquarters of Military District No. 10 at Winnipeg, the Director of Internment Operations in Ottawa, and the RCMP, denunciations by experienced informant Schmitt led the military and the RCMP to conduct the initial investigations, which turned up only suspicions and rumours, but no substantive evidence. Also investigated was an allegation that soldiers could be bought for "twenty to thirty dollars." This rumour arose once wealthier inmates received their credit transfers from England and donations of money from relatives or friends in the United States began to arrive in the camp. It was alleged that the wealthy internees were able to extend small loans to the soldiers to help them pay off their gambling debts and other unexpected, current expenses. When the Officer Commanding Military District No. 10, Brigadier H.J. Riley, investigated these various allegations, he reached the conclusion that "there is no evidence to support this and I do not consider that there is any foundation whatever for making such a statement; nor do I believe that soldiers have borrowed any sum of money from the internees. I certainly have been able to get no information to support it."[12]

In January 1941, the RCMP initiated an investigation into illegal deliveries of prisoners' mail and again failed to produce any culprits. The police unearthed six suspects upon whom further aspersions were cast because these soldiers already had spotty military and personal records. They were known as heavy drinkers who lacked military bearing, had a poor or mediocre military record, were "of poor character, with records of previous misbehaviour" and had close, daily work contacts with a few inmates. The only other two discoveries the investigating constable made were, first, that the local postmistress, Mrs. Jane Marie Despins, managed simultaneously a hotel, a general store, and the post office. The constable found, not unexpectedly, that this very busy woman was "very slack in the operation of the mail room;" she left the post office unattended for long periods of time, with its door unlocked, and the post office room offered a scene of disorder. Second, he pointed out that there existed numerous ways in which any number of soldiers could dispose of internees' mail at any time during the day.

Yet, as in the case of the blind chicken in the proverb, the investigators too eventually found their kernel. The first case was Private J.P. O'Callaghan, serving as provost at Camp R. He was suspected of smuggling mail out of the enclosure. He aroused suspicion because he "was reported to be a likely person as he is of poor character" and had opportunity to contact prisoners daily since they worked with him in the kitchen. The RCMP found no evidence linking O'Callaghan directly to smuggling mail. He came to the attention of the RCMP when a law firm of Montreal inquired if a Rudolf Haller had been released from internment and if his new address was c/o O'Callaghan, 992 Talbot Avenue, Winnipeg. O'Callaghan was not charged; no mail had in fact been exchanged or received. He was, however, transferred to Camp Q at Monteith.[13]

The second, stronger and more convincing case was against Private W.C. Hill. In November 1941, Hill was arraigned in a Port Arthur court room and charged, as the local Crown Attorney, P.V. Ibbetson, phrased it, with "being in possession of National Registration Certificates not lawfully issued to him and secondly attempting to assist enemy aliens being prisoners of war to escape by offering to supply them with registration certificates." Hill had worked as a provost inside the enclosure with his pal and nemesis, Private James A. McIntosh, who observed Hill chatting "friendly like" with an internee. Afterwards he confided to McIntosh that he, Hill, had "made an easy forty dollars" by working inside the enclosure. Whether McIntosh's patriotism or jealous greed was kindled is not relevant here, but his suspicion was mobilized. He spoke to his corporal who advised him to report the incident to the commandant. But McIntosh decided his evidence was not sufficiently substantial and he needed more proof. He gained his comrade Hill's trust through pre-arranged heavy drinking at a local bootlegger's place, and when Hill was suspended from duty for drunkenness, McIntosh, the comradely instigator, stood in for him in the actual illegal transaction of the certificates to the prisoners. The certificates were traced back to Hill, who in the end confessed.

McIntosh received high praise from Crown Attorney Ibbetson, the RCMP, Lieutenant C. Chinn, the new Intelligence Officer at R, and sundry military commanders in Winnipeg, Red Rock, Hamilton and Windsor; however, poor Private McIntosh could not retrieve the thirty-one dollars which he had spent on taxi rides and booze in the service of King, Empire and Country. It took the combined effort of all these dedicated military leaders and six months of correspondence among several additional military bureaucrats, who requested further information and confirmation of the well-known facts of the case, and who demanded proper forms of declaration to resolve their doubts about entertainment expenses of thirty-one dollars for a mere Private, in order finally to restore poor McIntosh's investment in victory and honesty. As the financial military examiner of McIntosh's expenses noted, "thirteen dollars" (or did he mean thirty-one?) was a lot of money to spend on entertainment for a Private.[14]

One weapon the anti-fraternization advocates deployed was strict adherence to military discipline in the camps. On his inspection tours Col. Watson certainly recognized that "casualness" on the part of the military, in the daily operation of a camp, might lead to fraternization. Watson detected casualness in the loaded reference to inmates of Camp L as "refugees from Nazi Germany" when they should be referred to properly as "Prisoners of War, Class II." His sense of patriotism was sincerely confused when he witnessed, at Cove Field Barracks, these same "prisoners" sing "O Canada and God Save the King" at the end of one of their concerts. Nevertheless, they must not be referred to as "refugees." At Red Rock, neither Col. Watson nor any other inspector reported such casualness.

To help prevent fraternization between guards and internees, loitering around the canteen was forbidden; the inmates from the different hutments had, however, a chance to meet for congeniality and conversation by gathering in one of the camp's European-style cafés. It can be assumed that these cafés operated strictly along the existing lines of political and ideological divisions within the camp. It is interesting to note that Spier did not mention the existence of such cafés in Camp R, though he did relate an incident from Camp Lingfield in England in his memoirs. There, Spier's wife had received permission to visit him in camp on his birthday. In anticipation of her visit, Spier had arranged for a fellow inmate, who was both a pastry chef and a Nazi, to prepare her favourite chocolate cake. However, as it happened, Mrs. Spier preferred to eat the freshly prepared sandwiches instead of the cake, which was then generously donated to Nazi inmates who, after consuming this delicious gift, all became violently ill. Subsequent investigations revealed that Nazi helpers of the pastry chef, unbeknownst to him, had surreptitiously mixed soap flakes into the cake's batter.[15]

In any case, these cafés in the camp were not the only place where internees could enjoy political discourse, as this could also occur inside the hutments, as Spier reported. In the course of separating Nazis and anti-Nazis, he had moved in with members of the International Seamen's Union who were all German-born and called themselves Bolsheviks. With them, collectively and individually, Spier discussed not only "the benefits and happiness" that he derived from his religious views, but also the economic and political issues which beset the Bolsheviks in their struggle to overcome their implacable foe, the capitalists, of whom Spier was one. These exchanges failed to produce converts, though each participant learned much about the other's *Weltanschauung*; at the same time they raised the tone of discourse and made for a more pleasant atmosphere in this hut.[16]

From the perspective of their Canadian captors, the inmates of Camp R were all nothing more than "Prisoners of War, Class II" who were also all Category A—enemies of Great Britain. Nonetheless, as ordinary and homogeneous as this crowd of 1,142 men and boys appeared on first sight, among this aggregate of humanity, one finds interesting, even extraordinary, characters. The most noteworthy camp personalities were undoubtedly Captain Scharf; Eugen Spier, the Churchill lobbyist; Dr. Lachmann, the aerodynamic engineer; Dr. Hanfstaengl; Guelcher, Hitler's playboy sport-*führer*, and Baron Pilar. However, several perhaps lesser personalities should be mentioned briefly in order to offer a more complete, if still very limited, gallery of camp characters.

A notable, though much less influential, inmate was Freiherr Wilhelm von Richthofen, a cousin of the famous Manfred von Richthofen, German ace pilot of First World War fame, the "Red Baron." Cousin Wilhelm had lived for several years in England. He was an avowed anti-Nazi, belonged to the class of professional *literati*, with

Veterans Guard members ham it up. The man in the middle with hands behind his back appears to be the only prisoner. *[Courtesy of the Red Rock Historical Society]*

little talent but very high personal expectations. According to Kirkness, he was "heartily loathed by the Nazis, [and] he is held in almost the same low esteem by the other party. It is this general lack of popularity which, more than anything, includes him in the ranks of the notable personalities in camp."[17] He had few friends and existed as a loner. Why this Richthofen was interned is not quite clear; perhaps he was guilty by association and blood ties; perhaps he had been an officer in the Kaiser's army.

Count Albrecht von Montgelas was a figure of respect and importance in his own right. He was fifty-five years old, a devout Roman Catholic, and was the former well-known foreign correspondent of the *Vossische Zeitung*, a leading democratic and liberal, anti-Nazi German newspaper published in Berlin. Montgelas had worked for many years in the USA and Britain where he counted among his personal friends fellow journalists Dorothy Thompson and Sinclair Lewis. Although Spier did not regard Count Montgelas as a "strong convinced anti-Nazi,"[18] the Count was forced to flee from Germany for his outspoken anti-Nazi views; before the outbreak of war Montgelas earned his living in England as director of a Bavarian beer import agency. He was very likely listed in MI5's "updated" files as a possible saboteur, since he had attracted suspicion (unproven) while living in the USA during the First World War. To MI5, it would have seemed logical that the anti-Nazi and devout Catholic Count, prompted by national and patriotic blood ties, would resume his former sabotage, once for the Kaiser, now for the *Führer*. The Count, therefore, required arresting in September 1939. Montgelas acted briefly as camp spokesman at Clacton, but was dismissed.

Others in this gallery of less notorious personalities were Captain Beissel, Lueddeke (spelled Lueddecke in some records), Pastor Dr. K. Weber, Pastor Fritz Wehrhahn, Otto Slabke and young Muehlhausen. Kirkness characterized Captain Beissel in his Morale Report as "a hard bitten German seaman, a tough, honest, serious type, [who] claims to have been Germany's most successful blockade runner." In camp, Beissel served on the Internees Canteen Committee. Lueddeke, a young EMS from Hamburg, served as steward of the camp canteen and also worked as "secretary for the camp spokesman." Pastor Dr. K. Weber had served a parish in Seaton, England, before internment; he passively disapproved of the Nazis and their actions in the camp. Dr. Weber eventually served as pastor to the German Prisoners of War, Class I, in Camp 101 at Angler after its opening in January 1941. Why he was interned is not clear; perhaps he too was a former Imperial officer. In contrast, Fritz Wehrhahn, a sixty-six-year-old Lutheran pastor who formerly served as chaplain to the German consular community in London, was a notoriously "virulent, outspoken Nazi," who continued to preach his Nazi sermons unhindered in Camp R. Seventy-one-year-old

Otto Slabke, "the father of Camp R," was a tragic figure. He came to England in 1869 as the German-born baby of an English mother, grew up in the UK, never went back to Germany, married a Scottish wife and never learned to speak either English or German well, but was never naturalized; nonetheless he succeeded sufficiently well in the United Kingdom to be able to save and invest the sum of 8,000 pounds sterling in England as well as in Canada. He was interned in the First World War and was still considered a "dangerous enemy alien" in 1940, when he was again arrested and selected for deportation overseas. Sixteen-year-old Muehlhausen was the saddest and most tragic case among the camp's youth. He had worked as a cabin boy on a luxury liner and was diagnosed with tuberculosis and scheduled for treatment, but then went insane as well. There was also fifteen-year-old "Otto"—last name unknown—the youngest internee in camp, always smiling and happy, and "willing"—in Captain Kirkness's ambiguous phrase.

Unlike in England, where he proudly related his participation as canteen and accounts manager, Spier seemed to keep his activities in Camp R under wraps. Except for speaking to Commandant Berry and Captain Kirkness, Spier never elaborated on his participation in camp affairs. It is hard to believe that he stayed entirely out of all activities, and we may assume that he influenced the course of events indirectly from the sidelines through personal contacts. Having obtained sur-reptitiously, with the help of Dr. Lachmann, a copy of *Hansard*, Spier was able to lift up the spirits of the Jewish and anti-Nazi refugees in the camp by reading to them the report in *Hansard* of the debates in the Commons on 22 August 1940, concerning the massive internment and deportation process.[19]

XII

"The End Is Nigh"

The Closure of Camp R

SINCE BRIGADIER-GENERAL PANET'S first visit in July 1940, Camp R had been considered a temporary camp due to its "unsatisfactory" rating. From early on rumours circulated among the camp's military personnel about impending closure or replacement by two brand new camps nearby, but further east. By the end of July 1940—the very same month the camp opened—the Director of Internment Operations made the first request for the construction of two replacement camps: "W—to be located at the junction of the Little Pic River and Lake Superior" and "X—to be located at the Ontario Highway Construction Camp No. 12, near Angler."[1] In early August, when the needs for the coming winter preparations for the camp were first raised, the Military District Headquarters in Winnipeg requested a decision on the question of closure of Camp R from the Director of Internment Operations.

All the inspection reports submitted during the first five months of operation referred to the camp's unsuitability, citing its non-permanence and a variety of other deficiencies. While in July 1940 the order was given to start the construction of the new camps, each housing about 600 prisoners, in August the government informed Panet and Riley that plans to construct the new camps had been suspended, since the United Kingdom would be recalling many of the incorrectly deported interned refugees, and therefore no additional internment space was needed. Later in September, however, the temporary nature of Camp R and the need to find a substitute was again a matter of discussion at the Directorate. In November 1940, Col. Stethem suggested that Camp R be replaced by the new camps "W" and "X." Closure seemed almost certain now. At the same time, however, Stethem recommended that since "R" housed "Nazi" merchant seamen whom he expected to be troublesome, the camp required increased firepower in the form of Thompson machine guns. Red Rock was to get six Thompson guns, each with 1,000 rounds of ammunition.[2]

In view of numerous minor complaints and at least one major problem besetting the normal operation of the camp, the desire to close it and move prisoners was not surprising. Remarkably, the most important issue was the provision of a constant supply of potable water for the entire camp. It may seem incomprehensible that this was so, considering the camp's proximity to an incredibly large body of fresh water, namely Lake Superior. Nevertheless this problem, which had apparently existed when the camp was used by construction workers, had grown worse with time and with a growing, unceasing demand.

In February 1941, prisoners and Veterans Guards succumbed to an indiscriminate outbreak of gastroenteritis. The drinking water in the camp was declared dangerous for human consumption by the Director of the Department of Public Health of Fort William, who had been called in for consultation. On closer inspection, a consulting engineer found that the electric pump and the chlorination system had malfunctioned and further discovered that the intake pipe for the camp's drinking water supply was a few hundred yards downstream from an outlet for untreated sewage. He therefore urged that the intake pipe be extended into Nipigon Bay by 1,450 feet (just under 500 metres). In

Meeting the train, November 1940. *[Private collection]*

July 1941, it was confirmed that ice conditions in the Bay the previous winter had negatively influenced the water quality, yet the water situation had not much improved now that the ice had disappeared. The drinking water quality in the camp fluctuated between "satisfactory" and "not drinkable," depending, quite literally, on which way the wind was blowing. This is because the currents in Nipigon Bay controlled the flow of water passing by the intake pipe, and the winds, in turn, controlled the water currents. In order to solve this problem, the engineer proposed the construction of a sanitary sewage disposal system, which, however, was considered too expensive. Now tested twice weekly, the camp's chlorinated water remained satisfactory after the engineer's visit, with a grade A rating; nonetheless, the chlorination of all water was not a permanent solution. Raw water quality continued to fluctuate

Guardhouse, winter 1940–1941. *[Private collection]*

from grade B to D, unfit for human consumption, but Brigadier Riley from Winnipeg urged that all repairs be delayed until a decision on the camp's permanency had been reached. This challenging problem, and the expense required to solve it, thus contributed significantly to the decision to close Camp R.

Earlier inspections had produced what was primarily an engineering report concerned with the general problem of winterization of the camp. The camp needed one hundred and thirty additional pot-belly heating stoves in various camp buildings, including eighty stoves for the internees' twenty huts alone, to cope with the growing cold inside the non-winterized wooden buildings. A November 1940 report noted, furthermore, that the guards' outside pit latrine should be abandoned in favour of indoor plumbing, consisting of a simple two-metre long urine trough and five individual toilets with doors—unlike the door-less ones for the prisoners—all to be connected to a deep cesspool with a convenient overflow directly into pristine Nipigon Bay.[3] Although this proposed improvement would not raise the Veterans Guards' level of hygienic comfort to that of the officers comfortably lodged in the luxurious Red Rock Inn, it certainly represented a step forward. That the military engineer, and those of the Lake Sulphite Pulp and Paper Company, agreed to drain the raw sewage into Nipigon Bay, reflected the state of technology in civil and military engineering in the 1940s. The report's author was a true northerner of his day, who appreciated the over-abundance of pristine nature and its seemingly unlimited capacity for absorbing man-made pollution.

Another minor issue, which several inspection reports had mentioned, was the camp's need for more electrical power. Either an additional backup supply was required or an alternative source of power had to be found. This need was never presented as an urgent matter, but by April 1941 it was clear that the camp's generator, originally supplied by the Lake Sulphite Pulp and Paper Company, could no longer satisfy the camp's increased demands. This may have been due to the improved floodlight system, which had been installed following earlier inspectors' recommendations. In order to cope with new demands, the camp now needed a new low-voltage power supply line, the construction of which, from the Nipigon power station six kilometres distant, would cost $6,000. Due, it seems, to the rumours of the camp's expected closure, this project escaped implementation.

On 1 March 1941 Colonel Stethem personally conducted a most thorough and detailed inspection of Camp R. His report covered fourteen long, typewritten pages and was divided into thirty-four separate items, which ranged from Latrines, Fuel and Heating Systems, and Water Supply to Camp Transport, Staff and Guard, Education, and Work Programs. As this was the last major inspection performed by the Director, it deserves attention and discussion.[4] The minutiae collected in Stethem's report was astonishing. Much of his information appears to have been derived from interviews rather than by actual visual observations of the various facilities and agencies. Many of the problems mentioned in earlier reports reappear in this one, suggesting that little had changed. There existed continuing problems with sanitation, communication systems, housing, and food quality, and inmates faced health issues such as tuberculosis. Additionally mentioned was that the staffing had practically remained the same; the defects, the deficiencies and the problems were unchanged. The clamour for relief on such issues as care of the youngsters' education and recreation was yet louder and more insistent. The only significant difference was that Stethem ignored the issue of civilian workers on the campgrounds; these had greatly exercised previous inspectors, who saw civilians as a threat to camp security.

The report concluded by offering two pages of thoughtful solutions to the issues facing Camp R. Generally speaking, Stethem argued for the dissolution of the Red Rock camp and proposed to transfer the approximately eighty-two anti-Nazi seamen and civilians to Camp A at Farnham, Quebec, where they could become involved in war work. He also suggested the transfer "as soon as possible" of 100 inmates to Camp Q, which he considered "not only ideally located, but affords ample opportunity for farm and bush work." Camp Q at Montieth could house 1,500 inmates once additional accommodation was built. Included in this transfer, Stethem suggested, would also be "a few of the trouble makers of Camp R, who may be making plans for a break-out at that camp in the Spring." Stethem argued that the move to Monteith would be "economical."

In June 1941, the camp was once again visited by Major-General, The Honourable, Inspector General (Army) Western Canada W.A. Griesbach. He had visited Red Rock also in 1940, although on neither occasion was a report submitted. The last inspection of Camp R by the military occurred on 8 October 1941. This report echoed Col. Stethem's view and declared that the camp was in deplorable condition. The non-winterized huts had now developed leaky roofs; the non-potable water challenge was still unresolved, and future ice conditions could only worsen the situation; the shower facilities were insufficient; the lack of secure recreation space inside the enclosure persisted, and the absence of opportunities for paid work was still a reality. For the time being, however, no immediate remedial action was undertaken.

Of the several military inspection tours of Camp R, it can be said that they benefited the local camp administration. First, they pointed out deficiencies before these could become veritable disasters; second, they proposed improvements. The repeatedly amended standing orders bear witness to changes in procedures; for example, roll calls were improved, and the wearing of the mandatory prisoner's garb instead of civilian garments was instituted. Certainly, the inspectors agreed unanimously on the camp's many basic deficiencies, and their shared view helped bring about the decision to close Camp R.

On 6 March 1941, on behalf of the ICRC, Swiss Consul General Maag also submitted a summary report on his three visits of Camp R— in September, February and now March. He found that the food was excellent; the housing was, as before, a fire hazard and lacked sufficient space, and winter clothing was adequate. The Consul General pointed out that "paid work" existed only for twenty-six men, though from seventy-five to one hundred men were used daily to perform unpaid fatigue work. Maag observed that the single dentist in the camp could not cope with looking after inmates as well as guards; unfortunately the competent internee dentist was not allowed to practise under Canadian rules. Among the inmates were six cases that, in Maag's view, might qualify under Articles 68–70 for repatriation; the oldest of them was sixty-nine. Camp R had received a great deal of relief goods due to its peculiar circumstances, Maag informed his superiors, but continued to be in need. He concluded his report as follows:

Thanks to the splendid cooperation between the representatives of the Detaining Power and the Camp Leader the spirit at this Camp has been maintained at a high level in spite of the difficulties under which the camp has been operating. Tribute should be paid to the Camp Officers as well as the Camp Leaders for the high standard of moral[e] maintained.[5]

He noted that in the period from July 1940 to March 1941 eight attempts at escape had occurred and that all escapees were captured. It seems even the ICRC recognized that the camp's final days had come, for in October 1941, during another inspection visit, Consul General Maag noted the physical deterioration of the hutments, the inadequacy of the shower facility and the usual numerous complaints about mail deliveries and about delays in forwarding the prisoners' baggage from Britain. Once again, however, Maag commented on the relatively smooth operation of the local camp administration.[6]

The uncertain future of Camp R was affected indirectly by decisions taken elsewhere. One was of course the ongoing assessment of the need for more internment camps by the federal government and the Directorate in light of the new circumstances which saw most of the deported Jewish and anti-Nazi refugees, the former "dangerous enemy aliens," choose repatriation rather than stay securely incarcerated in a militarily controlled Canadian internment camp environment. The need for Camp R was greatly diminished, and Ottawa was engaged in the restructuring of its entire POW system. Second, the construction of the new camps at Angler and Neys was resumed some time during the fall of 1940. At conception these camps were regarded as replacements for Red Rock; they were, however, in fact utilized in January 1941 as regular POW, Class I camps; Angler was used for "other ranks" and Neys for officers and "other ranks." As Director Panet explained bluntly in an October memo: "Camp R (Red Rock) is to be abandoned." Its inmates were to be transferred to camps "X" and "W," which were "estimated to be ready October 15, 1940."[7]

By October 1941 Camp R had begun to experience the full impact of the reorganization process of the Canadian POW camp system. This process, it is true, had been started approximately a year ago and had gained in intensity after the arrival of Commissioner Paterson in

Hard cases leaving Camp R for Angler POW camp. *[Private collection]*

November 1940. Indeed, the very first group to be returned to England from Camp R were the four members of the German consular staff of Reykjavik, in August 1940. Then followed Dr. Meissner who, rumour had it, was returned for his urgently needed contributions to defence and research work. In November 1940, internees B. Zimmermann, K.H.E. Krueger, Dr. E. Granischstaedten and Rudolph von Detten were transferred to Camp B, Fredericton, New Brunswick, which then served temporarily as the base camp for repatriates leaving for the UK. They were the first group of interned refugees from Camp R scheduled to return to England. It is not clear whether or not Commissioner Paterson had any direct or indirect involvement in the repatriation of these four.

What started as a trickle gained force when Commandant Berry promised the beleaguered Jewish and anti Nazi minority that he would assist in arranging their transfer to separate camps. Subsequent events, of course, can be viewed as part of the ongoing process of sorting Britain's deportees in the eastern Canadian internment camps under the auspices of Paterson. Regardless, in January 1941, eighty-eight refugees were transferred out of Camp R. Thirteen of this group went to Camp A at Farnham, Quebec, designated an anti-Nazi camp, and seventy-five moved to Camp N at Newington, Quebec, among them Eugen Spier. At Camp N, the arrival of the "new comrades," most of whom were Jews, some Communists, all Category A, was expectantly awaited on Monday, 27 January 1941. Everyone in Camp N, apparently, had heard about the dreadful camp in the wilderness of northern Canada and its Nazi atmosphere in which the newcomers had much to endure. The popular and famous fugitive Manfred Fischer and the unpopular Freiherr Wilhelm von Richthofen both went to Camp A. In February 1941, a second, larger contingent of 188 inmates departed Camp R; of these eighty-eight refugees went on to Farnham, while one hundred prisoners, mostly young cabin boys and cooks' helpers, were sent to Camp Q at Monteith, Ontario. This camp was chosen because a farm formed part of its operation as a former juvenile jail. In May 1941, about 860 men were still left behind in Camp R.[8]

By the time Camp R finally closed down on 23 October 1941, only 847 inmates were left, and they had to be dispersed quickly. On 20 October, six CNR coaches for fifty men each and one coach for forty-seven were loaded in two hours and departed for Camp Q. On the following day, 21 October, at 1530 hours, the train for Camp 130 at Seebe, Alberta, departed from Red Rock station with seven coaches for fifty-one men each and three coaches for fifty. The camp spokesman, Ship Captain Scharf, was also transferred to Camp 130. On this day, four inmates decided to change their predetermined fate by switching places; Gustav Schroeder and Ernst Kloepper, destined for Camp Q, changed places with Karl Kircher and Lothar Baxdel, predestined for Camp 130. They were of course caught and received the customary punishment of twenty-eight days solitary confinement on arrival in the new camp.

By the end, the approximate financial cost for Camp R's fifteen months of operation, from July 1940 to October 1941, amounted to $181,125, or 35 cents per day per inmate.[9] Many months after the demise of Camp R, Canada's High Commissioner in London received a letter of complaint that offered this ambiguous assessment of the camp. Writing from inside a British internment camp at Fort Erin, on the Isle of Man, British-born Lilian Hasenberg, wife of an internee and herself an internee, wrote:

> ...conditions prevailing at Fort Henry, Kingston are still unbearable. Inmates have two hours of daily walking exercise outside these cruelly depressing high walls.... men are pestered by millions of mosquitoes and midges. Men are deprived of daylight in their dwellings and sleeping quarters and are compelled to herd together day and night, fourteen are sleeping in one room. [Some are] suffering from inflammation of eyes.... [they] have lost weight,...they are not criminals....There were no complaints from Camp R, all were sorry to leave.[10]

One internee who was not at all sorry to leave was Spier, who was finally, in January 1941, transferred with his fellow Jews from Camp R to Camp N, at Newington, a former railway engine repair shop and an "unmixed" camp. At first, he seemed no happier there, among fellow Jewish refugees, than in Red Rock. His memoirs record a pleasant train journey with ample food well-served, seemingly heralding a return to civilization, followed on arrival at the new camp by "a thundering voice of the traditional sergeant-major's pitch: 'Quick march, get out of here, ...quickly. Who the hell d'you think you are? Get out quickly.'" His first observation: "it was a dirty camp, entirely unsuitable for decent human habitation." Eventually, Spier met "Colonel Patterson [sic]" and was surprised to encounter not "a militant fierce Colonel in full battle-dress," but instead "a most kind looking middle aged gentleman in civilian clothes."[11] Overwhelmed by Paterson's kind reception and charm and the promise of a return to England, Spier experienced ecstatic joy and happiness. All his troubles would soon be over; he would leave behind abominable Canada and return home. Spier, perhaps in his exuberance, forgot that it was Great Britain that had incarcerated him and shipped him off to the colony. In any case, it took many more months of impatient waiting before Spier was able to return.

Once home he, his wife and young son were kept imprisoned on the Isle of Man until they were all released, late in November of 1941. It is remarkable that Spier, the former Churchill lobbyist and financier of Focus, was not among the very first consignment of returnees to Britain organized by Commissioner Paterson. Had Spier been forgotten by every one of his former influential and powerful friends and acquaintances in Focus? Years later, after the war, Spier once again met his old protégé Churchill, then in the declining years of his political career. According to Spier, Churchill acted at first awkward and uncomfortable when he saw Spier at the meeting, at which Duncan Sandys and H.A. Richards were also present, to discuss Churchill's role in the unification of the new postwar Europe. Spier took the initiative by saying to Churchill, "[W]hen the wheels of the war machine are set in motion these things do happen, and I have taken it all in a spirit of submission and feel no bitterness towards anyone." Obviously relieved—Spier continued his recollections—"Churchill patted my shoulder saying: 'very noble, very noble indeed.'"[12] Sir Winston, by this gesture, expiated his guilty conscience for his behaviour towards an ardent supporter in the gloomy days of his isolation in the political wilderness during the 1930s. Most unfortunate is that Spier never explained why neither Churchill nor any of the many other illustrious members of Focus failed to act to secure his or his family's release from the domestic detention camps in England or in Canada, or even an adjustment from Category A. It cannot be determined whether they tried, or refused to help, or forgot about his plight.

XIII

Epilogue

IT CAN BE ARGUED THAT in the troublesome summer of 1940, Camp R fulfilled an important and urgent function. It accommodated on short notice approximately half of the first shipload of deportees dispatched from Great Britain to Canada. Thereby Canada was able to respond supportively to Great Britain's urgent pleas for assistance. In a state of self-inflicted panic, the British government under Prime Minister Winston Churchill begged Canada to accept thousands of German POWs and thousands more of so-called "dangerous enemy aliens," who were depicted by the British military as potential fifth columnists threatening Britain's security. Actually, in their overwhelming major-ity, they were refugees from Nazi Germany. This deportation process was labelled by one observing participant a "story of muddle and malfeasance" and castigated by another as "a really criminal policy of internment and deportation."[1] At that crucial moment, however, Camp R provided much needed accommodation for 1,150 interned men and boys.

In July 1940, Camp R was the largest civilian internment camp among the fifteen then in operation throughout Canada. The site was chosen because its hutments were readily available to house large numbers of prisoners; it was isolated and yet enjoyed easy logistic access by rail; it had an ample water and electricity supply and required only a small investment of funds. Classified officially a "mixed" and Nazi camp on account of the British classification of its inmates as Category A— enemies of the British regime—the camp actually housed a large number of enemy merchant seamen and a dedicated troupe of radical Nazis, along with a minority of about two hundred Jewish and anti-Nazi refugees. It acquired a bad reputation in some quarters due to an initial high level of anti-Semitic harassment and violence perpetrated by the majority upon the minority, which is reflected in Koch's epithet, "the little Third Reich on Lake Superior."

Aside from the political violence of the early months, however, Camp R was one of the least troublesome among the early Canadian camps. At Camp R, the local military operated on the notion that these civilians, once interned, were just prisoners of war, Class II, who were more difficult to manage than regular disarmed enemy combatants because they lacked the military disposition and discipline of trained soldiers. Absent from the camp were constant disputes over kosher food and fatigue work on Sabbath or neglect of the infirm. The bulk of the camp's inmates, the seamen, were meek, hardly venturesome, and easily misled; even their escape attempts were unspectacular and unsuccessful. Those who were the instigators of the violent disturbances and harassment were not EMS. The EMS's misfortune was that in their docility and ignorance they encountered and fell victims to a small gang of unscrupulous Nazis who, for a while, succeeded in mobilizing their youthful patriotism and braggadocio for entirely nefarious anti-Semitic activities.

Camp R provided valuable lessons to the Canadian military. The camp, in terms of its construction, layout and location, like other unused factory sites, offered instant but only temporary

View of Camp R. *[Courtesy of the Red Rock Historical Society]*

accommodation for large numbers of prisoners. However, Camp R soon demonstrated the need for large, wide-open spaces inside the enclosure for roll calls, appeals and even sport activities. The closeness of its hutments created a constant fire hazard, and the absence of large halls for leisure activities such as hobbies, theatrical and musical performances, and educational work also became negative characteristics. Moreover, larger camps, the military discovered, could be operated more efficiently in both economic and military manpower terms. Isolation did not prevent escape, nor did it invite attempts at liberation by either home-grown or foreign fifth columnists. Camp R also demonstrated the importance of offering opportunities for paid work or for agricultural pursuits either nearby or on the property of the camp. The camp proved that the "mixed camp" concept did not work and, after months,

Prisoners and Veterans Guard leaving Red Rock, October 1941. *[Private collection]*

revealed the dysfunctional aspects of Great Britain's tribunal system of
categorizing German refugees from Nazism. These and perhaps many
other lessons were gleaned from the operation of Camp R.

The EMS were transferred to various internment camps after the
closure of Camp R, and lived apparently meekly and peacefully and
were never heard of again in the annals of the Directorate. The EMS and
the interned Nazis from Camp R remained in Canada for the duration
of the war and were repatriated in 1946–1947, first to England and then
home to a devastated Germany. Years later, many former EMS returned
as immigrants to Canada.

The Jews and anti-Nazis deeply resented their incarceration and
treatment, especially by the Canadian military, and often bitterly
blamed Canada rather than Great Britain for their sufferings in

internment. When offered a chance, many—some 1,537 individuals— returned to England, where they became His Majesty's "most loyal enemy aliens" and played important parts as soldiers or researchers or propagandists in the defeat of Nazism.[2] Many of those who were released and permitted to stay in Canada, eventually some 972 individuals, contributed to the war effort and the final defeat of Nazi Germany and then made valuable contributions in the professions, in arts and academia, in business and as workers in the building of this country. All inmates of Camp R were victims of fate and suffered the vicissitudes of war. They were tossed haphazardly together, first in internment camps in England and later in Canada, at Red Rock.

On the very last day of Camp R's official existence, 23 October, the Crown returned the camp, including the hutments and mill, the numerous smaller buildings, and the relatively luxurious Red Rock Inn, back to its previous owners. The ultimate physical demise of Camp R came finally in January 1942, when the Crown accepted a cheque, the "balance of thirty-seven dollars," from Mr. Uno J. Pajunen, as his final payment on a fifty-dollar tender for the removal of the frames of five watchtowers, one ice house, a Quartermaster store shed, seven window sashes and other miscellaneous items. The original total salvage value was $94. That was the peaceful and inglorious end of Camp R, which had served the Canadian government and the Directorate of Internment Operations very well in an urgent emergency in June 1940, despite its having earned the opprobrious title, "the little Third Reich on Lake Superior."

Notes

Preface

1. Eric Koch, *Deemed Suspect: A Wartime Blunder* (Toronto: Methuen, 1980), 110.

Introduction

1. Martin F. Auger, *Prisoners on the Home Front: German POWs and "Enemy Aliens" in Southern Quebec, 1940–46* (Vancouver: University of British Columbia Press, 2005), 4, 6; John Herd Thompson, *Ethnic Minorities during Two World Wars*, Canada's Ethnic Groups 19 (Ottawa: Canadian Historical Association, 1991), 7.
2. In the official history of the Canadian Army, prisoners of war and internees are both dealt with in the section on prisoners of war. Colonel C.P. Stacey, *Official History of the Canadian Army*, vol. 1, *Six Years of War: The Army in Canada, Britain and the Pacific* (Ottawa: Queen's Printer, 1957), 151.
3. For an example of the proposal for a national commemorative plaque, which treats the two essentially different categories, see Michelle Cinanni, *The Detention of Second World War Military Prisoners of War and of Enemy Aliens Sent to Canada from Great Britain*, Report No. 2009-1 (Ottawa: Historical Sites and Monuments Board of Canada, 2009).
4. On Canada's First World War internment operations see Joseph A. Boudreau, "Western Canada's 'Enemy Aliens' in World War One," *Alberta Historical Review* 12, no. 1 (Winter 1964): 1–9; Brenda Lee-Whiting, "'Enemy Aliens': German-Canadians on the Home Front," *The Beaver* 69, no. 5 (1989): 53–58; Georgia Green Fooks,

Prairie Prisoners: POWs in Lethbridge during Two World Conflicts (Lethbridge, AB: Lethbridge Historical Society, 2003); Bohdan S. Kordan, *Enemy Aliens, Prisoners of War: Internment in Canada during the Great War* (Montreal: McGill-Queen's University Press, 2002); Bohdan S. Kordan and Peter Melnycky, *In the Shadow of the Rockies: Diary of the Castle Mountain Internment Camp, 1915-1917* (Edmonton: Canadian Institute of Ukrainian Studies Press, 1991); Jean Laflamme, *Les Camps de Détention au Québec Durant la Première Guerre Mondiale* (Montreal: n.p., 1973); Lubomyr Y. Luciuk, *Internment Operations: The Role of Old Fort Henry in World War I* (Kingston, ON: Delta Educational Consultants, 1980); and William Buck, Lubomyr Y. Luciuk, and Borys Sydoruk, *In My Charge: The Canadian Internment Camp Photographs of Sergeant William Buck* (Kingston, ON: Kashtan Press, 1997); Bill Waiser, *Park Prisoners: The Untold Story of Western Canada's National Parks, 1915-1946* (Calgary: Fifth House, 1995). The local history of Kapuskasing also has a section on internment operations. See Margaret Paterson, *Carved From the Forest: A History of Kapuskasing; a Special Centennial Project of the Northern Times* (Kapuskasing, ON: Northern Times, 1967).

5. David Edward Smith, "Emergency Government in Canada," *Canadian Historical Review* 50, no. 4 (December 1969): 430-431; Jeffrey A. Keshen, *Propaganda and Censorship During Canada's Great War* (Edmonton: University of Alberta Press, 1996), 9-11; Desmond Morton, "Sir William Otter and Internment Operations in Canada during the First World War," *Canadian Historical Review* 55, no. 1 (March 1974): 35-38; and Lubomyr Y. Luciuk, *In Fear of the Barbed Wire Fence: Canada's First National Internment Operations and the Ukrainian Canadians, 1914-1920* (Kingston, ON: Kashtan Press, 2001), 3-4, 6.

6. Morton, "Sir William Otter and Internment," 36.

7. See Gerald G. Ross, "Fort William's Enemy Alien 'Problem' during the First World War," *Papers and Records* (Thunder Bay Historical Museum Society) 22 (1994): 3-22.

8. David J. Carter, *Behind Canadian Barbed Wire: Alien, Refugee and Prisoner of War Camps in Canada, 1914-1946* (Brooks, AB: Nesbitt, 1980), 20-21; Morton, "Sir William Otter and Internment," 25-27; John Herd Thompson, *Ethnic Minorities during Two World Wars*, 7-8; and Auger, *Prisoners on the Home Front*, 9-10. The statistics are largely based on William Otter, *Report on Internment Operations: Canada, 1914-1920* (Ottawa: King's Printer, 1921), 4-6.

9. See Bohdan S. Kordan and Craig Mahovsky, *A Bare and Impolitic Right: Internment and Ukrainian-Canadian Redress* (Montreal: McGill-Queen's University Press, 2004); Lubomyr Y. Luciuk, *Without Just Cause: Canada's First National Internment Operations and the Ukrainian Canadians, 1914-1920* (Kingston, ON: Kashtan Press, 2006); Lubomyr Y. Luciuk, ed., *Righting an Injustice: The Debate Over Redress for Canada's First National Internment Operations* (Toronto: Justinian Press, 1994); Lubomyr Y. Luciuk, ed., *Roll Call: Lest We Forget* (Kingston, ON: Kashtan Press, 1999); Frances Swyripa and John Herd Thompson, eds., *Loyalties in Conflict: Ukrainians in Canada during the Great War* (Edmonton: Canadian Institute of Ukrainian Studies Press, 1983); Lubomyr Y. Luciuk, *A Time for Atonement: Canada's First National Internment Operations and the Ukrainian Canadians, 1914-1920* (Kingston, ON: Limestone Press, 1988); and Orest T. Martynowych, *Ukrainians in Canada: The Formative Period, 1891-1924* (Edmonton: Canadian Institute of Ukrainian Studies Press, 1991), 323-334.

10. Auger, *Prisoners on the Home Front*, 11; Morton, "Sir William Otter and Internment," 57-58.
11. Carter, *Behind Canadian Barbed Wire*, 63.
12. Order in Council PC 2097, 20 August 1936, established the Canadian Defence Committee. Library and Archives Canada (hereafter LAC), RG 2, vol. 1592, file 1429G. Order in Council PC 531, 14 March 1938, created the Committee on the Treatment of Enemy Aliens on the Outbreak of Hostilities. LAC, RG 2, vol. 1653, file 1948G. See also Auger, *Prisoners on the Home Front*, 19-20, 165nn1-2; John Joseph Kelly, "The Prisoner of War Camps in Canada, 1939-1947," master's thesis, University of Windsor, 1976, 1-7; Daniel Robinson, "Planning for the 'Most Serious Contingency': Alien Internment, Arbitrary Detention, and the Canadian State, 1938-1939," *Journal of Canadian Studies* 28, no. 2 (Summer 1993): 6; John Stanton, "Government Internment Policy, 1939-1945," *Labour/Le Travail* 31 (Spring 1993): 22; J.L. Granatstein and Dean F. Oliver, "Internment," *Oxford Companion to Canadian Military History* (Don Mills, ON: Oxford University Press, 2011), 211.
13. Granatstein and Oliver, "Defence of Canada Regulations," "Internment," and "War Measures Act," *Oxford Companion to Canadian Military History*, 139, 211, 462; and Ramsay Cook, "Canadian Freedom in Wartime, 1939-1945," in *His Own Man: Essays in Honour of A.R.M. Lower*, ed. W.H. Heick and Roger Graham, (Montreal: McGill-Queen's University Press, 1974), 37-53.
14. Granatstein and Oliver state 763 were interned. "Internment," *Oxford Companion to Canadian Military History*, 211. See also John Herd Thompson, *Ethnic Minorities during Two World Wars*, 11-12; Auger, *Prisoners on the Home Front*, 20; Paul Jackson, "The Enemy Within: The Canadian Army and Internment Operations during the Second World War," *Left History* 9, no. 2 (2004): 45-83; Jonathan F. Wagner, *Brothers Beyond the Sea: National Socialism in Canada* (Waterloo, ON: Wilfrid Laurier University Press, 1981), 132-139; Lita-Rose Betcherman, *The Swastika and the Maple Leaf: Fascist Movements in Canada in the Thirties* (Toronto: Fitzhenry & Whiteside, 1975), 137-149; and Robert H. Keyserlingk, "Breaking the Nazi Plot: Canadian Government Attitudes Towards German Canadians, 1939-1945," in *On Guard for Thee: War, Ethnicity, and the Canadian State, 1939-1945*, ed. Norman Hillmer, Bohdan S. Kordan, and Lubomyr Y. Luciuk (Ottawa: Canadian Committee for the History of the Second World War, 1988), 53-69.
15. See Granatstein and Oliver, "Internment," *Oxford Companion to Canadian Military History*, 211; and John Herd Thompson, *Ethnic Minorities during Two World Wars*, 13-14. For a general discussion, see J.A. Ciccocelli, "The Innocuous Enemy Aliens: Italians in Canada during World War II," master's thesis, University of Western Ontario, 1977; Bruno Ramirez, "Ethnicity on Trial: The Italians of Montreal and the Second World War," in Hillmer, Kordan, and Luciuk, *On Guard for Thee*, 71-84; Franca Iacovetta, Roberto Perin, and Angelo Principe, eds., *Enemies Within: Italian and Other Internees in Canada and Abroad* (Toronto: University of Toronto Press, 2000); and Mario Duliani, *The City Without Women: A Chronicle of Internment Life in Canada during the Second World War*, trans. Antonino Mazza (Oakville, ON: Mosaic Press, 1994).
16. For a history of communism at the Lakehead before the Second World War, see Michel S. Beaulieu, *Labour at the Lakehead: Ethnicity, Socialism, and Politics, 1900-35* (Vancouver: University of British Columbia Press, 2011).

17. John Herd Thompson, *Ethnic Minorities during Two World Wars*, 14–15. See also William Repka and Kathleen M. Repka, *Dangerous Patriots: Canada's Unknown Prisoners of War* (Vancouver: New Star Books, 1982) and Reg Whitaker, "Official Repression of Communism during World War II," *Labour/Le Travail* 17 (Spring 1986): 135–166. Jehovah's Witnesses were also interned for anti-war attitudes. See William Kaplan, *State and Salvation: The Jehovah's Witnesses and Their Fight for Civil Rights* (Toronto: University of Toronto Press, 1989).

18. See Auger, *Prisoners on the Home Front*, 21.

19. See John Herd Thompson, *Ethnic Minorities during Two World Wars*, 15; and J.L. Granatstein and Gregory A. Johnson, "The Evacuation of the Japanese Canadians, 1942: A Realist Critique of the Received Version," in Hillmer, Kordan, and Luciuk, *On Guard for Thee*, 101–130.

20. John Herd Thompson, *Ethnic Minorities during Two World Wars*, 15–16.

21. John Herd Thompson, *Ethnic Minorities during Two World Wars*, 16. There is a substantial literature on the internment of Japanese Canadians. See, for example, Robert K. Okazaki, *The Nisei Mass Evacuation Group and POW Camp 101: The Japanese-Canadian Community's Struggle for Justice and Human Rights during World War II*, trans. Jean M. Okazaki and Curtis T. Okazaki (Scarborough, ON: Markham Litho, 1996); Takeo Ujo Nakano and Leatrice Nakano, *Within the Barbed Wire Fence: A Japanese Man's Account of His Internment in Canada* (Toronto: University of Toronto Press, 1980); Gabrielle Nishiguchi, "'Reducing the Numbers': The Transportation of the Japanese Canadians (1941–1947)," master's thesis, Carleton University, 1993; Tom Sando, *Wild Daisies in the Sand: Life in a Canadian Internment Camp* (Edmonton: NeWest Press, 2002); and Ken Adachi, *The Enemy That Never Was* (Toronto: McClelland & Stewart, 1976).

22. See Koch, *Deemed Suspect*, 36–68.

23. See Auger, *Prisoners on the Home Front*, 21–22; and Koch, *Deemed Suspect*, 27.

24. Sources vary on the number of prisoners held by Canada depending on whether the figures included those interned under Canadian regulations combined with those transferred from British custody. These figures would exclude the 21,000 Japanese Canadians evacuated. A total of 37,934 combatant prisoners is cited by Chris M.V. Madsen and R.J. Henderson, *German Prisoners of War in Canada and Their Artifacts, 1940–1948* (Regina: Hignell, 1993), 1, 5. Jeffrey A. Keshen states 40,000 Germans were imprisoned in Canada. Foreword to Auger, *Prisoners on the Home Front*, vii; John Melady gives the figure 35,046 prisoners of war and internees. *Escape From Canada! The Untold Story of German POWs in Canada 1939–1945* (Toronto: Macmillan, 1981), 34. The Canadian Army official historian gives the combined total as 34,193. Stacey, *Six Years of War*, 151.

25. "Other ranks" is the Canadian and British term used to described enlisted ranks. See Melady, *Escape From Canada*, 34; and Carter, *Behind Canadian Barbed Wire*, 309–312.

26. There is a considerable if disparate literature on prisoners of war in Canada. See Cecil Porter, *The Gilded Cage: Gravenhurst German Prisoner-of-War Camp 20, 1940–1946* (Gravenhurst, ON: Gravenhurst Book Committee, 1999); Tim Gallagher, *Espanola: POW Camp 21, 1940–1943* (Espanola, ON: privately printed, 1976); Sylvia Bjorkman, "Report on Camp 'W': Internment Camp '100' North of Lake Superior in World War II," *Ontario History* 89, no. 3 (September 1997): 237–243; Jeff Sumner, "World War II German POWs in Northwestern Ontario." *Papers and Records* (Thunder Bay

Historical Museum Society) 20 (1992): 2–13; Daniel Hoffman, *Camp 30 "Ehrenwort"*:
A German Prisoner Of War Camp in Bowmanville, 1941–1945 (Bowmanville, ON:
Bowmanville Museum, 1990); Ted Jones, *Both Sides of the Wire: The Fredericton
Internment Camp*, 2 vols. (Fredericton, NB: New Ireland Press, 1988–1989); Chris
M.V. Madsen, "German Prisoners of War in Canada during the Second World War,"
master's thesis, University of Western Ontario, 1992; Robert John Henderson,
An Introduction to Guarding Prisoners of War in Canada (Regina: privately printed,
2008); Robert John Henderson, *Ephemera of German Prisoners of War in Canada and
the Veteran's Guard of Canada* (Regina: privately printed, 2009); and Pamela Howe
Taylor, *The Germans We Trusted: Stories of Friendship Resulting From the Second
World War* (Cambridge: Lutterworth Press, 2003). In other cases local histories and
commemorative editions touch on the POW experience. See, for example, Sioux
Lookout Historical Society, *Tracks Beside the Water: Sioux Lookout* (Sioux Lookout,
ON: Sioux Lookout and District Historical Society, 1982); Dorothea Weigeldt
Belanger, "Prisoners of World War II on Lake of the Woods," in *Common Ground:
Stories of Lake of the Woods: Celebrating 5 Years of Storytelling; Common Ground,
2006–2010* (Kenora, ON: Common Ground Committee, Lake of the Woods Museum,
2010); and Marsha Scribner, *Transitions: Commemorating Camp Wainwright's 50th
Anniversary* (Winnipeg: Jostens, [1990]). The employment of POWs in Canada as
a source of labour is covered in Stephanie Cepuch, "The Public and the POWs:
Reaction to the Release of German Prisoners of War for Agricultural Labour," in
Canadian Papers in Rural History, vol. 9, ed. Donald H. Akenson (Gananoque, ON:
Langdale Press, 1994), 323–335. There are also a number of studies of the wider
POW experience. See, for example, Christopher R. Kilford, *On the Way! The Military
History of Lethbridge, Alberta (1914–1945) and the Untold Story of Ottawa's Plan to
De-Nazify and Democratise German Prisoners of War Held in Lethbridge and Canada
during the Second World War* (Victoria: Trafford, 2004); Don Page, "Tommy Stone
and Psychological Warfare in World War Two: Transforming a POW Liability into
an Asset," *Journal of Canadian Studies* 16, no. 3/4 (1981): 110–120; and John Joseph
Kelly, "Intelligence and Counter-Intelligence in German Prisoner of War Camps in
Canada during World War II," *Dalhousie Review* 58, no. 2 (1978): 285–294.

27. See Auger, *Prisoners of the Home Front*, 4, 147–152.

28. Madsen and Henderson, *German Prisoners of War in Canada*, 12.

29. Eugen Banauch, "'Home' as a Thought between Quotation Marks: The Fluid Exile
of Jewish Third Reich Refugee Writers in Canada 1940–2006," PHD diss., University
of Vienna, 2007; and Eugen Banauch, *Fluid Exile: Jewish Exile Writers in Canada
1940–2006, Anglistische Forschungen* 395 (Heidelberg: Winter, 2009).

30. Kelly, "Prisoner of War Camps in Canada, 1939–1947."

31. Carter, *Behind Canadian Barbed Wire*, reprinted as POW, *Behind Canadian Barbed
Wire: Alien, Refugee and Prisoner of War Camps in Canada, 1914–1946* (Elkwater, AB:
Eagle Butte Press, 1998), hereafter cited as Carter, POW.

32. See Yves Bernard and Caroline Bergeron, *Trop loin de Berlin: des prisonniers
allemands au Canada (1939–1946)* (Sillery, QC: Septentrion, 1995).

33. Pauline Dean, *Sagas of Superior: The Inland Sea and Its Canadian Shore*
(Manitouwadge, ON: Great Spirit Writers, 1992), 17–136.

34. Barbara Chisholm and Andrea Gutsche, *Superior: Under the Shadow of the Gods*
(Toronto: Lynx Images, 1998), 206–208.

35.   See Koch, *Deemed Suspect.*
36.   Paula J. Draper, "The Accidental Immigrants: Canada and the Interned Refugees," PHD diss., University of Toronto, 1983. Draper reiterates these critical commentaries in different publications such as "The Accidental Immigrants: Canada and the Interned Refugees: Part I," *Canadian Jewish Historical Society Journal* 2, no. 1 (Spring 1978): 1–38; and "The Politics of Refugee Immigration: The Pro-Refugee Lobby and the Interned Refugees 1940–1944," *Canadian Jewish Historical Society Journal* 7, no. 2 (Fall 1983): 74–88.
37.   Paula J. Draper, "The 'Camp Boys': Interned Refugees from Nazism," in Iacovetta, Perin, and Principe, *Enemies Within*, 171–193.
38.   Perhaps the best studies so far are the two theses by Kelly, "Prisoner of War Camps in Canada, 1939–1947"; and Madsen, "German Prisoners of War in Canada during the Second World War."
39.   See Erich Maschke, ed., *Zur Geschichte der deutschen Kriegsgefangenen des zweiten Weltkrieges*, 22 vols. (Munich: Gieseking Verlag, 1962–1974).

I   From Welcomed Refugees to "Dangerous Enemy Aliens"

1.   Norman Bentwich, "England and the Alien," *Political Quarterly* 12, no. 1–4 (1941): 81–93.
2.   Peter Gillman and Leni Gillman, *Collar the Lot! How Britain Interned and Expelled Its Wartime Refugees* (London: Quartet Books, 1980), 8, 91–92; Tony Kushner and Katherine Knox, *Refugees in an Age of Genocide: Global, National and Local Perspectives during the Twentieth Century* (London: Frank Cass, 1999), 173.
3.   Seyfert, "'His Majesty's Most Loyal Internees,'" 164–165. For a reliable biography of Anderson see Sir John Wheeler-Bennett, *John Anderson: Viscount Waverley* (London: Macmillan, 1962).
4.   By 9 September 1939, about 2,000 German nationals were repatriated in exchange for a similar number of British citizens. See Gillman and Gillman, *Collar the Lot*, 61, 63.
5.   Bernard Wasserstein, *Britain and the Jews of Europe, 1939–1945* (Oxford: Clarendon Press, 1979), 84.
6.   Gillman and Gillman, *Collar the Lot*, 37–38, 42–44; Ronald Stent, *A Bespattered Page? The Internment of His Majesty's "Most Loyal Enemy Aliens"* (London: Andre Deutsch, 1980), 35–37. Stent gives the number of tribunals as 106; Seyfert, "'His Majesty's Most Loyal Internees,'" gives 112; and Judex, *Anderson's Prisoners* (London: Victor Gollancz, 1940) gives 21.
7.   Stent, *Bespattered Page*, 39, 36n.
8.   Frederic W. Nielsen, *Emigrant für Deutschland in der Tschechoslovakei, in England und in Kanada: Tagebuchaufzeichnungen, Aufrufe und Berichte aus den Jahren 1933–1943* (Darmstadt: J.G. Blaeschke Verlag, 1977), 160. For additional examples of how the tribunal system operated, see Gillman and Gillman, *Collar the Lot*, 96–97; Eugen Spier, *The Protecting Power* (London: Skeffington & Son, 1951), 44; and Judex, *Anderson's Prisoners*, 22–28.
9.   For listings of well-known anti-Nazis interned as enemy aliens see Gillman and Gillman, *Collar the Lot*, 174–176; and Stent, *Bespattered Page*, 32–33.

10. For further details see Judex, *Anderson's Prisoners*, 22–28; Stent, *Bespattered Page*, 33–39; and Lafitte, *Internment of Aliens*.

11. Nielsen, *Emigrant für Deutschland*, 77.

12. Mark Lynton, *Accidental Journey: A Cambridge Internee's Memoir of World War II* (Woodstock, NY: Overlook Press, 1995), 14. First known as Max Otto Ludwig Loewenstein, when Lynton was finally allowed to join Britain's regular army in 1943, he dropped his old name for reasons of personal security in case of capture.

13. Henry Kreisel, *Another Country: Writings by and about Henry Kreisel*, ed. Shirley Neuman, NeWest Literary Documents Series, vol. 7 (Edmonton: NeWest Press, 1985), 13–17.

14. Tony Kushner, *Remembering Refugees: Then and Now* (Manchester: Manchester University Press, 2006), 119.

15. This section on Spier is based on Spier, *Protecting Power*, his autobiography; and Spier, *Footnote to the History of the Thirties* (London: Oswald Wolf, 1963), unless indicated otherwise.

16. John Charmley, *Chamberlain and the Lost Peace* (London: Hodder Stoughton, 1989), 55; David Irving, *Churchill's War*, Vol. 1, *The Struggle for Power* (Bullsbrook, Australia: Veritas, 1987), 54–55; and Graham Stewart, *Burying Caesar: The Churchill-Chamberlain Rivalry* (New York: Overlook Press, 2001), 260, 261, 324, 490; R.W. Thompson, *The Yankee Marlborough* (London: Allen & Unwin, 1963), 286. Irving's analysis is considered controversial. See also John Charmley, *A History of Conservative Politics, 1900–1996* (New York: St. Martin's Press, 1996).

17. Spier, *Protecting Power*, 9, 33–34. Some of the most prominent and influential members of Focus were Lady Churchill; H. Wickham Steed, a well-known anti-German and anti-Semitic journalist; Duncan Sandys, MP Churchill's son-in-law; Philip Noel-Baker, MP; Sir Arthur Salter, MP; Ronald Cartland, MP; Seymour Cocks, MP; Professor Philip and Mrs. Guedalla; Miss Eleanor Rathbone, MP; J. Arthur Rank; Sir Austen Chamberlain and Lady Chamberlain; the Duchess of Athol, MP; Professor Gilbert Murray; Kingsley Martin (of the *New Statesman*); Lady Violet Bonham Carter; Dingle Foot, MP; Arthur Henderson, MP; Sir Walter Citrine, leader of Trade Union Congress; Sir Robert Waley-Cohen, Chair of British Shell; the Bishop of Chichester; Capt. B.H. Liddell Hart; Harold Macmillan, MP; Emery Reeves, journalist; Wilson Harris (of *The Spectator*); James de Rothschild, MP; Rev. Benjamin Gregory (Wesleyan Methodist Connection); Rev. M. Johns (Assistant Secretary, Congregational Union); and Rev. S.M. Berry (Secretary, National Free Church Council). Spier, *Footnote to History*, 53–54, 59. Hart acted as military advisor to Focus. These outstanding representatives of Britain's establishment, collectively and individually, totally failed Eugen Spier in his hour of need. He stayed imprisoned in England in Category A and then later in Camp R, and even after his repatriation remained incarcerated with his family on the Isle of Man until November 1941.

18. Spier, *Protecting Power*, 15.

19. Spier, *Protecting Power*, 43–45, 73–74.

20. This personality sketch of Dr. Lachmann is based on Judex, *Anderson's Prisoners*, 35; and Stent, *Bespattered Page*, 89; as well as on the introductory and concluding remarks offered at the "Second Handley Page Memorial Lecture," presented by Dr. Gustav Viktor Lachmann and reprinted as "Sir Frederick Handley Page, the Man and His Work," *Journal of the Royal Aeronautical Society* 68, no. 143 (July

1964): 433–452. Also used was Library and Archives Canada (hereafter cited as LAC), Department of National Defence (hereafter DND), RG 24, vol. 11,249, file 10-2-2-R, Captain Kirkness, Morale Report No. 5, November 1940 (hereafter cited as Kirkness, Morale Report No. 5). Unless stated otherwise all references to Kirkness, Morale Reports are to LAC, DND, RG 24, vol. 11,249, file 10-2-2-R, which contains all Morale Reports, from No. 1 to No. 8, covering the period from August 1940 to March 1941.

21. As a resident of Cologne in May 1942 and thus as an eye-and ear-witness, I note—slightly ironically—that so-called "'Nazi'" Lachmann-designed planes played a very successful role in the first one-thousand-bomber raid on a German city.

22. Spier, *Protecting Power*, 99.

23. Koch claims that Lachmann participated in the development of the German fighter plane ME 109. See Koch, *Deemed Suspect*, 58. Stent claims that Lachmann participated in the development of the Vickers "Viscount" of which 400 were utilized by British European Airways, notwithstanding the denial of this by an anonymous reader of an earlier draft of this manuscript. See Stent, *Bespattered Page*, 89.

24. For more on these two men, see Kirkness, Morale Report No. 5; and Stent, *Bespattered Page*, 97–98.

25. Stent, *Bespattered Page*, 37. Wasserstein, *Britain and the Jews of Europe, 1939–1945*, 85, offers these numbers for January 1940: Category A 528; B 8,356; and C 60,000. The London-based *Sozialistische Mitteilungen: News for German Socialists in England*, a publication of the exiled *Sozialdemokratische Partei Deutschland* (SPD), gives 800 as the number of Category A internees for 1940. Special issue 30A (October 1941), 13–14.

26. Koch, *Deemed Suspect*, 10; and Spier, *Protecting Power*, 59.

27. Tony Kushner, *Persistence of Prejudice: Anti-Semitism in British Society during the Second World War* (Manchester: Manchester University Press, 1989), 143.

28. Reported by Leland Stowe for the *Chicago Daily News*, as quoted by Phillip Knightley, *The First Casualty: The War Correspondent as Hero and Myth-Maker from the Crimea to Kosovo*, introd. John Pilger, rev. ed. (London: Prion Books, 2000), 248. Even Churchill later admitted it was a "ramshackle campaign." Winston S. Churchill, *The Gathering Storm* (New York: Bantam Books, 1961), 542.

29. The concept of the fifth column originated during the Spanish Civil War from a comment attributed to Francisco Franco's General Emilio Mola. In September 1936, while preparing his attack on the Republican-held capital of Madrid, General Mola reportedly told a group of international journalists that the city would fall under the assault of four columns from outside and with the help of a fifth column already inside the city. See Gillman and Gillman, *Collar the Lot*, 73–74.

30. Gillman and Gillman, *Collar the Lot*, 71–72 and 82–87.

31. Gillman and Gillman, *Collar the Lot*, 5.

32. For an insightful exposition and stimulating discussion on the intriguing subject of alienisms in British society, see David Cesarani and Tony Kushner, eds., *The Internment of Aliens in Twentieth Century Britain* (London: Frank Cass, 1993), 26–34. See also Kushner's various books on this subject, some of which are listed in the bibliography.

33. Seyfert, "'His Majesty's Most Loyal Internees,'" 168. G. Ward Price, Hitler's most favoured British journalist, praised Hitler and Mussolini as the defenders of Western civilization against Bolshevism. *I Know These Dictators* (London: Harrap, 1937).

34. Lafitte, *Internment of Aliens*, 171.

35. Wasserstein, *Britain and the Jews of Europe*, 10–11; Stent, *Bespattered Page*, 41–44; Gillman and Gillman, *Collar the Lot*, 74–75; and Koch, *Deemed Suspect*, 11–12.

36. Lafitte, *Internment of Aliens*, 170.

37. Nielsen, *Emigrant für Deutschland*, 128; Francis L. Carsten, "German Refugees in Great Britain 1933–1945," in Gerhard Hirschfeld, ed., *Exile in Great Britain: Refugees from Hitler's Germany* (London: German History Institute, Berg, 1984), 21; Stent, *Bespattered Page*, 47, 51; and Lawrence Thompson, *1940: Year of Legend, Year of History* (New York: William Morrow, 1966), 142. For a more recent and very critical assessment of Britain's treatment of Jewish refugees during this period from 1933 to 1947, see Louise London, *Whitehall and the Jews, 1933–1948: British Immigration Policy, Jewish Refugees and the Holocaust* (Cambridge: Cambridge University Press, 2000).

38. Lafitte, *Internment of Aliens*, 174; and A.W. Brian Simpson, *In the Highest Degree Odious: Detention without Trial in Wartime Britain* (London: Clarendon Press, 1992), 140.

39. Stent, *Bespattered Page*, 19.

40. Clive Ponting, *1940* (London: Hamish Hamilton, 1990), 139. Tony Kushner states that at the end of April 1940 public anti-alienism and anti-Semitism existed mostly due to economic concerns. *The Persistence of Prejudice: Anti-Semitism in British Society during the Second World War* (Manchester: Manchester University Press, 1989), 144.

41. Stent, *Bespattered Page*, 56.

42. Seyfert, "'His Majesty's Most Loyal Internees,'" 165.

II From Mass Internment in Britain to Deportation to Canada

1. Ponting, 52–54; R.W. Thompson, *Yankee Marlborough*, 72. See also Cecil H. King, *With Malice Toward None: A War Diary*, ed. William Armstrong (London: Sidgwick & Jackson, 1970), 29.

2. Judex, *Anderson's Prisoners*, 6–7.

3. Gillman and Gillman, *Collar the Lot*, 28, 33; Koch, *Deemed Suspect*, 17–19; Stent, *Bespattered Page*, 33, 86; Nielsen, *Emigrant für Deutschland*, 151; and Spier, *Protecting Power*, 29.

4. Bland's report can be found in The National Archives of the United Kingdom (hereafter TNA), PRO, FO 371/25189/462, 14/5/1940. See also Gavin Schaffer, "Re-Thinking the History of Blame: Britain and Minorities during the Second World War," *National Identities* 8, no. 4 (December 2006): 405.

5. It is perhaps appropriate to remember in this context that some 21,000 Jewish and anti-Nazi German female refugees were working in English middle- and upper-class households as domestic servants. To hire out as domestics was, for most of these refugees, many of whom were women of German middle-class background, the only way of escaping from the terrors of Nazi Germany. See Judex, *Anderson's Prisoners*, 9; and Walter W. Igersheimer, *Blatant Injustice: The Story of a Jewish Refugee from Nazi Germany Imprisoned in Britain and Canada during World War II* (Montreal: McGill-Queen's University Press, 2005), 14. For Sir Neville's comments, see Gillman and Gillman, *Collar the Lot*, 101–103, 110–111.

6. Stent, *Bespattered Page*, 55; and Gillman and Gillman, *Collar the Lot*, 112.

7. Nielsen, *Emigrant für Deutschland*, 92–93 and 156.

8. Gillman and Gillman, *Collar the Lot*, 109–110. I thank Stephen Showers, Corporate Archivist at Otis Elevator Canada, for the information that, contrary to the Gillmans' claim, he found no evidence in 2004 that Sir Campbell Stuart had ever worked for the Otis Company in any capacity. E-mail to author, 20 February 2004. For a different and more positive assessment of Sir Campbell's work see Anthony Glees, *Exile Politics during the Second World War: The German Social Democrats in Britain* (Oxford: Clarendon Press, 1982), 56–57.

9. Gillman and Gillman, *Collar the Lot*, 81, 83, 85–86.

10. For a glowingly positive account see Michael Schapiro, "German Refugees in France," *Contemporary Jewish Record* 3, no. 2 (March–April, 1940): 134–140.

11. Geoffrey Hithersay Shakespeare, *Let Candles Be Brought in* (London: Macdonald, 1949), 261.

12. Gillman and Gillman, *Collar the Lot*, 85–86; and Stent, *Bespattered Page*, 56.

13. Gillman and Gillman, *Collar the Lot*, 33.

14. Seyfert, "'His Majesty's Most Loyal Internees,'" 168–169.

15. Stent, *Bespattered Page*, 70–71; and Gillman and Gillman, *Collar the Lot*, 113, 163–164.

16. Koch, *Deemed Suspect*, 27–28.

17. Gillman and Gillman, *Collar the Lot*, 162.

18. Simpson, *In the Highest Degree Odious*, 185.

19. Swinton, *I Remember* (London: Hutchison, [1948?]), 181.

20. Stent, *Bespattered Page*, 70; and Gillman and Gillman, *Collar the Lot*, 141.

21. Stent, *Bespattered Page*, 73. Emphasis original.

22. Stent, *Bespattered Page*, 75–76; Seyfert, "'His Majesty's Most Loyal Internees,'" 170, 188; and Kushner, *Persistence*, 145–146.

23. LAC, William Lyon Mackenzie King papers (hereafter MKP), MG 26, J 1, vol. 292, 247–101, Massey to King, 31 May 1940.

24. LAC, Department of External Affairs (hereafter DEA), RG 25, D 1, vol. 824, file 713, Massey to Secretary of State. The reference to refugees relates to civilians having fled from Poland, Norway and Holland.

25. LAC, DEA, RG 25, D 1, vol. 824, file 713, Massey to Secretary of State, 5 June 1940.

26. LAC, DND, RG 24, vol. 6585, file 4-2-1, letters, Stodart to Roger, 6 February 1940; and Coleman to Skelton, 28 February 1940.

27. Canada, Dominion Bureau of Statistics, *The Canada Yearbook 1939: The Official Statistical Annual of the Resources, History, Institutions, and Social and Economic Conditions of the Dominion* (Ottawa: King's Printer, 1940), xxv.

28. LAC, MKP, vol. 292, 247-128, letter, Massey to King, 7 June 1940; and Gillman and Gillman, *Collar the Lot*, 162–163.

29. LAC, MKP, vol. 292, 247-153, letter, King to Massey, 10 June 1940.
30. United Kingdom, TNA, Home Office (hereafter cited as HO) 10916/2580/ TNA 121108, Massey to Caldecote, 10 June 1940; and LAC, MKP, vol. 292, 247-132.
31. LAC, DEA, RG 25, D 1, vol. 824, file 713, Massey to Secretary of State, 10 June 1940.
32. Gillman and Gillman, *Collar the Lot*, 164.
33. TNA, Foreign Office (hereafter cited as FO) 916/2580/119965, memorandum, Ritchie to Stephenson, 14 June 1940.
34. Gillman and Gillman, *Collar the Lot*, 164, 166.
35. LAC, MKP, vol. 292, 247-175, letter, King to Massey, 19 June 1940.
36. Judex, *Anderson's Prisoners*, 85, 86.
37. Judex, *Anderson's Prisoners*, 10, 88.
38. Lafitte, *Internment of Aliens*, 95. The anxiety-inspiring clause of the Compiègne Armistice Agreement between France and Germany was Article 19, Clause 2, which reads: "The French Government to hand over all German subjects indicated by the German Government who are in France or French overseas territory."
39. Judex, *Anderson's Prisoners*, 58–59.
40. Judex, *Anderson's Prisoners*, 116.
41. Gillman and Gillman, *Collar the Lot*, 166.
42. Seyfert, "'His Majesty's Most Loyal Internees,'" 175.
43. TNA, FO 916/2580/TNA 12 11 08, Conference on move of Prisoners of War and Internees to Canada, held at the War Office, Room 08, at 5 p.m. on Monday, 17 June 1940.
44. Passenger shipping data are based on TNA, HO 205/265, 3, Prisoners of War and Civilian Internees sent to Canada. Memorandum for the Information of the Canadian Government. No signature, no date (hereafter cited as Memorandum). See also Alexander Paterson, TNA, HO 213/2391/11 95 65, 2-4, Report on Civilians Sent from the United Kingdom to Canada during the Unusual Fine Summer of 1940 (hereafter cited as Paterson Report); and Stent, *Bespattered Page*, 96. Alfred Draper claims that the *Duchess of York*, apparently in addition to her human freight, transferred 6.5 million pounds sterling of gold to Canada at the end of June 1940. *Operation Fish: The Race to Save Europe's Wealth, 1939–1945* (London: Cassell, 1979), 361.
45. Stent, *Bespattered Page*, 101–105; and Gillman and Gillman, *Collar the Lot*, 191–198.
46. United Kingdom, Home Office, *German and Austrian Civilian Internees: Categories of Persons Eligible for Release from Internment and Procedure to Be Followed in Applying for Release* (London: H.M. Stationery Office, 1940).
47. Koch, *Deemed Suspect*, 40, 46, 48; and Paterson Report, 2–3.
48. Michael J. Cohen, "Churchill and the Jews: The Holocaust," *Modern Judaism* 6, no. 1 (February 1986): 43.
49. Stent, *Bespattered Page*, 70–71; and Gillman and Gillman, *Collar the Lot*, 113, 163–164.
50. Winston S. Churchill, "We Shall Never Surrender," in *Charge! History's Greatest Military Speeches*, ed. Steve Israel (Annapolis, MD: Naval Institute Press, 2007), 140. Churchill gave this famous speech before the House of Commons, 4 June 1940.

III Onward to the New World and Its Old Problems

1. Spier, *Protecting Power*, 132–133.

2. For both quotations see Koch, *Deemed Suspect*, 56–57.
3. Gillman and Gillman, *Collar the Lot*, 170–171.
4. Spier, *Protecting Power*, 140.
5. Koch, *Deemed Suspect*, 58–59.
6. Johannes Lieberwerth describes an aborted attempt to seize the *Pasteur* on 10 March 1942 en route to Durban with 1,000 German POWs aboard. *Alter Mann und Corned Beef: Die andere Kriegsgefangenschaft in Afrika und Kanada* (Emmelshausen: Condo Verlag, 1999), 72–74.
7. Convention Relative to the Treatment of Prisoners of War, 1929, in *The Laws of Armed Conflicts: A Collection of Conventions, Resolutions, and Other Documents*, ed. Dietrich Schindler and Jiri Toman (Leiden, Netherlands: Brill), 1988, 339–366, hereafter cited as the Geneva Convention of 1929.
8. Carter, POW, 92.
9. Gillman and Gillman, *Collar the Lot*, 237.
10. Stent, *Bespattered Page*, 112; Koch, *Deemed Suspect*, 70–71; and Cesarani and Kushner, *Internment of Aliens*, 114–115.
11. Koch, *Deemed Suspect*, 72–73.
12. LAC, DND, RG 24, D 1, vol. 824, file 713, item Arnold #47.
13. Spier, *Protecting Power*, 147.
14. All quotations cited in this paragraph are from LAC, DND, Microfilm C-5378, HQS 7236-Org(a), Secret Memorandum, Instructions for Escort, 24 June 1940.
15. Spier, *Protecting Power*, 147.
16. Christopher Hill, *Cabinet Decisions on Foreign Policy: The British Experience October 1938–June 1941* (Cambridge: Cambridge University Press, 2002), 185.
17. William Lyon Mackenzie King, *The Mackenzie King Diaries, 1932–1949* (Toronto: University of Toronto, 1980), Microfiche edition, frame 150, entry for 24 June 1940.
18. J.L. Granatstein, *The Ottawa Men: The Civil Service Mandarins, 1935–1957*, 2nd ed. (Toronto: University of Toronto Press, 1998), 128.
19. LAC, MKP, MG 26, J 1, vol. 292, 247-340.
20. Canada, *House of Commons Debates* (11 June 1940), 664–666 (Mr. R.B. Hansen MP).
21. Canada, *Debates*, vol. 1, 107.
22. Canada, *Debates*, vol. 1, 442.
23. Canada, *Debates*, vol. 1, 442.
24. See Betcherman, *The Swastika and the Maple Leaf*.
25. Canada, *Debates*, vol. 1, 142–145, 670, 718.
26. Gregory S. Kealey and Reg Whitaker, eds., RCMP *Security Bulletins: The War Series*, vol. 1, *1939–1941* (St. John's, NL: Committee on Labour History, 1989–1993), 232, 238.
27. For a detailed discussion of the German-Canadian issue see Keyserlingk, "Breaking the Nazi Plot." For a different view see Iacovetta, Perin, and Principe, *Enemies Within*. D.M. McKale states that in Winnipeg and Montreal the German *Volksdeutsche* cultural clubs refused cooperation with Nazi representatives; for example, at meetings of the *Bund* the "Heil Hitler" salute was banned, as was the singing of Nazi songs. *The Swastika Outside Germany* (Kent, OH: Kent State University Press, 1977), 94.
28. Kealey and Whitaker, RCMP *Security Bulletins, 1939–1941*, 232, 238.
29. Canada, *Debates*, vol. 1, 911.
30. Gillman and Gillman, *Collar the Lot*, 178, 179, 180.

IV Getting Ready

1. Leslie Roberts, C.D.: *The Life and Times of Clarence Decatur Howe* (Toronto: Clarke, Irwin, 1957), 85.

2. This paragraph and the next three following are based on LAC, Department of the Secretary of State (hereafter cited as DSS), RG 6, A 1, vol. 207, file 2902, Pt. VIII-I includes letters and memoranda written by Panet to Secretary of State, P.F. Gasgrain, and several other government officials in June 1940. This correspondence concerns various problems encountered during the process of acquisition of Camp R. See file 2902, Pt. VII 1939 for Panet's Inspection Report of 27 July 1940, hereafter cited as Panet Inspection Report.

3. LAC, DSS, RG 6, A 1, vol. 207, file 2902, Pt. VIII-I, Paul Leduc to Panet, June 1940.

4. LAC, DSS, RG 6, A 1, vol. 207, file 2902, Panet to Secretary of State, 27 July 1940.

5. LAC, DSS, RG 6, A 1, vol. 207, file 2902, Pt. VIII-I, C.D. Howe to Panet, June 1940.

6. Details of the agreement can be found in LAC, DSS, RG 6, A 1, vol. 207, file 2902.

7. LAC, DSS, RG 6, A 1, vol. 207, file 2902, Panet to Secretary of State, 27 July 1940.

8. LAC, DSS, RG 6, A 1, vol. 207, file 2902, Pt. VIII-I, Panet to Secretary of State, 19 June 1940.

9. LAC, DND, RG 24, C 1, Microfilm C-5377, HQS 7236-12, copy of distress warrant.

10. See G.T. Service and J.K. Marteinson, eds., *The Gate: A History of The Fort Garry Horse* (Calgary: The Fort Garry Horse, 1971), 53, 54, 59; and Canada, Canadian Army, Historical Section, *The Regiments and Corps of the Canadian Army*, Canadian Army List 1 (Ottawa: Queen's Printer, 1964), 49–50. To my colleague, Captain David Ratz, I am indebted for guiding me to the above-mentioned sources and for acquainting me with the correct usage of military nomenclature.

11. LAC, DND, RG 24, C 1, Microfilm C-5420, HQS 7236-95-R, memorandum, Berry to Panet, 19 September 1940.

12. LAC, DND, RG 24, vol. 11,248, file 9-5-3-R, "Inspection Report and Confidential Comments on Camp Officers, August 1940," Lieutenant-Colonel H. de Norban Watson, hereafter cited as Watson Report.

13. LAC, DND, RG 24, C 1, Microfilm C-5378, HQS 7236-25, Secret Memorandum from Adjutant-General to Military Districts, 2, 3, 4, 5, 7, 10 and 13, 19 August 1940.

14. LAC, DND, RG 24, C 1, Microfilm C-5378, HQS 7236-25, Org 2 (c), 15 October 1940.

15. LAC, DSS, RG 6, A 1, vol. 207, file 2902, Pt. VII 1939.

16. Watson Report, 6.

17. Watson Report, 2.

18. Watson Report, 2–3.

19. LAC, DND, RG 24, C 1, Microfilm C-5378, HQS 7236-25-vol. 2, Memorandum, Oran to Adjutant-General, 28 August 1940.

20. LAC, DND, RG 24, C 1, Microfilm C-5378, HQS 7236-25-vol. 2, Memorandum, Re: Internment Camp Organization, Ralston to Adjutant-General, 28 August 1940.

21. This paragraph and the next are based on materials in the Robert J. Henderson collection of the Homefront Archives and Museum, Regina, Saskatchewan. File: Department of National Defence, *Orders and Instructions: Internment and Refugee Camps 1941*, 1–18, hereafter cited as Henderson collection, *Instructions*.

22. LAC, DND, RG 24, C 1, Microfilm C-5378, HQS 7236-25 Org 2 (c).

23. Paterson Report, 4. In their family history, Jacques Gouin and Lucien Brault provide details of Panet's early career and modestly describe his internment work thus: "For the first year he was responsible for the opening and operation of prison camps for enemy sailors and airmen transferred from English prisons camps to Canada...He was also in charge of camps for the internment of German and Italian nationals." Gouin and Brault, *Legacy of Honour: The Panets, Canada's Foremost Military Family* (Toronto: Methuen, 1985), 112–128, 135–136.

24. Paterson Report, 4.

25. Paterson Report, 4.

26. Paterson Report, 4–5.

27. Brereton Greenhous, *Dragoon: The Centennial History of the Royal Canadian Dragoons, 1883–1983* (Belleville, ON: The Guild of the Royal Canadian Dragoons, 1983), 168.

28. This event refers to the notorious "mass" outbreak of twenty-seven German POWs from Camp 101 at Angler, Ontario, 100 kilometres east of Red Rock, on 19 April 1940, in celebration of "The *Führer's*" (Hitler's) birthday on the next day. All prisoners were eventually recaptured. While escaping in pursuit of some mythical soldier's duty, one was shot and several were severely wounded. LAC, RG 24, C 3, vol. 15,414, vol. 10, War Diary, April 1941. On the myth of the duty to escape see Michael Walzer, "Prisoners of War: Does the Fight Continue after the Battle?" *American Political Science Review* 63, no. 3 (September 1969): 783–785.

29. Paterson Report, 8.

30. Paula J. Draper, "The Accidental Immigrants" (PHD diss.), 126.

31. Paterson Report, 8.

32. Paula J. Draper, "Accidental Immigrants" (PHD diss.), 125.

33. Spier, *Protecting Power*, 152.

34. See Watson Report.

35. Lloyd Roy, interview by the author, 14 May 2002.

36. University of Manitoba, Faculty of Medicine Archives, file 21.9 (Dr. A.A. Klass). Ms. Susan Bethune, Archivist of the Faculty of Medicine Archives, deserves special recognition and gratitude for her assistance in accessing the documents about Dr. A.A. Klass and for helpful advice enabling me to contact Dr. David J. Klass, College of Physicians and Surgeons, Toronto, son of Dr. A.A Klass. I thank Dr. David Chapman, Biologist, Lakehead University, for sharing with me his reminiscence of his father about the latter's friend and colleague, Dr. A.A. Klass.

37. LAC, DND, RG 24, vol. 11,249, file 10-2-2-R, Confidential to Director of Internment Operations Department of the Secretary of State, Ottawa from Brigadier H.J. Riley District Officer Commanding, Military District No. 10, Winnipeg. See also Kirkness, Morale Report No. 5.

38. LAC, DND, RG 24, C 3, vol. 15,414, War Diaries, vol. 7.

39. Regrettably, the official history of the Veterans Guard of Canada has not been written yet. Canada's three-volume *Official History of the Canadian Army in the Second World War*, by Col. C.P. Stacey, lists no entry in its index under Veterans Guard of Canada and offers only two paragraphs on vol. 1, page 151, with mostly statistical information. The information presented here has been gathered from many scattered sources. The main source, however, is a file in the Robert J. Henderson collection of the Homefront Archives and Museum, entitled *Report, Historical Section (G.S.) Army Headquarters: The Veterans Guard of Canada*, with

Appendices A to F (n.p., n.d.) DND Directorate of History and Heritage File 158.D13 (D 1), 50. Also LAC, RG 24, C 3, vol. 15,414, folder 1, vol. 1, War Diary, 120th Reserve Company, V.G. of C., June 1940. All references are to this script unless otherwise indicated. Another important source was both Carter, *Behind Canadian Barbed Wire* (1980) and the revised edition of Carter, POW (1998).

40. Stacey, *Official History*, 151.

41. LAC, DND, RG 24, C 1, Microfilm C-5378, HQS 7236-25-vol. 2, "Orders and Instructions to Commandants of Internment Camps," B.W. Browne to Camp Commandants, 23 August 1940.

42. The Vickers was a British version of the Maxim gun. It was adopted for frontline service before the First World War and remained so with the Canadian Army until the 1960's. The Lewis gun, in its air- or water-cooled and .303 or 30.06 caliber variants, was of American design and adopted by British Empire and Commonwealth forces in 1915. It was gradually phased out of frontline service by the more modern Bren light machine gun. Thereafter the Lewis was mostly found among rear area and reserve units. David Bercuson and J.L. Granatstein, *Dictionary of Canadian Military History* (Toronto: Oxford University Press, 1992), 23, 116, 218.

43. See LAC, DND, RG 24, C 3, vol. 15,414, War Diaries, vol. 7.

v Settling In and Sorting Out

1. LAC, DND, RG 24, C 1, Microfilm C-5378, HQS 7236-25, circular, Panet to DOC, Military District (hereafter cited as MD), 29 June 1940; and Microfilm C-5379, HQS 7236-30-vol. 2, Exhibits A2 and B2, same circular as above; and letter, Panet to DOC, MD No. 5, copy to CC Major C.W. Wiggs, Camp L, 28 June 1940.

2. Spier, *Protecting Power*, 148.

3. Spier, *Protecting Power*, 152–153.

4. In comparison and contrast to the comforts of Camp R, those internees, arriving at temporary Camp T, the Exhibition Grounds at Trois-Rivières, Quebec, found one outhouse and one urine collector ready to serve five hundred prisoners.

5. Spier, *Protecting Power*, 148.

6. Spier, *Protecting Power*, 148.

7. Henderson collection, *Instructions*, 3–4.

8. Lloyd Roy, interview by the author, 14 May 2002.

9. See Stent, *Bespattered Page*, 219; and Gillman and Gillman, *Collar the Lot*, 237.

10. See Spier, *Protecting Power*, 152–153.

11. Spier, *Protecting Power*, 149.

12. Apparently Spier missed an opportunity during disembarkation in Quebec City to contact home. According to High Commissioner Massey, it seems that several of Spier's fellow passengers of the *Duchess of York* sent telegrams to other countries informing families and friends about their new whereabouts. See LAC, DND, RG 24, D 1, vol. 824, ile 713-#47.

13. Spier, *Protecting Power*, 149.

14. All quotations in this paragraph from Spier, *Protecting Power*, 150.

15. All quotations in this paragraph from Spier, *Protecting Power*, 151.

16. All quotations in this paragraph from Spier, *Protecting Power*, 152.
17. Spier, *Protecting Power*, 150.
18. Spier, *Protecting Power*, 150.
19. All quotations in this paragraph from Spier, *Protecting Power*, 150.
20. LAC, DND, RG 24, C 3, vol. 15,414, War Diaries, vols. 2 and 3.
21. LAC, DEA, RG 25, A3b, vol. 2632, file 621-J-40, Consular Report, 21 September 1940.
22. Kirkness, "Types of Internees—Camp R." Percentage calculation based on Koch, *Deemed Suspect*, 36.
23. Kirkness, "Types of Internees—Camp R." See also LAC, DEA, RG 25, A3b, vol. 2632, file 621-J-40, Consular Report. N.d. 1940.
24. Kirkness, Morale Report No. 5.
25. No evidence confirms that the pro-Nazi crews of the *Pomona* and *Arcan* were in "R."
26. The term "Austrian-born" as used here simply means a person's place of birth was located in the territory of the old pre-1914 Austro-Hungarian Empire, which included parts of inter-war modern Poland, Czechoslovakia and the Province of Galicia, in what is now Ukraine.
27. Kirkness, "Types of Internees—Camp R." This report listed 174 interned refugees and noted a small group "of approximately 20 men, which is anti-Nazi. Most of the men in this group have lived in the United Kingdom for many year...However, the Anglophile tendencies increase and decline according to the development of the war." Numbers provided for the *Duchess of York* by the Paterson Report give the figure of 745 EMS for Camp R. Paterson Report, 2.
28. Stent, *Bespattered Page*, 219.
29. See Kirkness, Morale Reports No. 1 through No. 6. Further references to these Reports are in LAC, DEA, RG 25, vol. 2,632, file 621-J-40; DND, RG 24, vol. 11,253, file 11-2-14; RG 24, vol. 11,248, file 9-5-3-3; RG 24, vol. 11,253, files 11-2-2 and 11-2-14; and Microfilm C-5377, HQS 7236-12.
30. See LAC, RG 24, vol. 11,249, file 10-2-2-R.
31. The term "South Africans" may have included German nationals who were interned far away from South Africa such as the former Gold Coast or other territories still in the Great British imperial sphere of influence such as Egypt, Iran, Iraq and India. Gillman and Gillman, *Collar the Lot*, 62.
32. These sources of pride included the Vatican's signing of the infamous Concordat of 1933; the self-dissolution of the German conservative opposition parties in March 1933 in deference to the euphoric Nazis; the internationally acclaimed staging of the Olympic Games in 1936; the plebiscite and return of the Saarland to the Reich in 1935; the internationally accepted remilitarization of Germany and the return of the Rhineland in 1935 and in 1936 respectively; the Austrian *Anschluss* in 1938 and the "liberation" of the Sudetenland.
33. Letter from former internee. Original held in the Public Library of Marathon, Ontario; copy held by author. Unfortunately the letter's signature is illegible.
34. See Colin Holmes, *Anti-Semitism in British Society, 1876–1939* (London: Edward Arnold, 1979).
35. Spier, *Protecting Power*, 156, 157ff.
36. See Kirkness, "Types of Internees—Camp R."

VI Camp Life at R under Standing Orders

1. LAC, DND, RG 24, C 3, vol. 15,414, fold 1, vol. 8, Appendix 2, Sheet no. 1 and no. 2, February 1941; and Spier, *Protecting Power*, 148.
2. Kirkness, Morale Report No. 5.
3. This sketch of Captain O. Scharf is based on Spier, *Protecting Power*, 163, 156; and Kirkness, Morale Report No. 5.
4. Gillman and Gillman, *Collar the Lot*, 99.
5. Kirkness, Morale Report No. 5.
6. LAC, DND, RG 24, vol. 11,249, file 10-2-2-R, 14476 Chief Officer Moencke to A. Ahrenkiel, NY, from Kirkness, Morale Report No. 6, February 1941.
7. Spier, *Protecting Power*, 156.
8. Auswaertiges Amt. Politisches Archiv, Berlin, R 127557, Band 59, R XII Zv, letter, Kundt to Scharf, 3 June 1944.
9. Auswaertiges Amt. Politisches Archiv, Berlin, R 127557, Band 59, R XII Zv, letter, Kundt to Scharf, 3 June 1944.
10. Koch, *Deemed Suspect*, 112; and Stent, *Bespattered Page*, 99.
11. Stent, *Bespattered Page*, 99.
12. Interviews and conversations with former German POWs and civilian internees in Canadian detention camps.
13. LAC, DND, RG 24, C 3, vol. 15,414, War Diaries, vol. 9.
14. Kirkness, Morale Report No. 5.
15. Spier, *Protecting Power*, 55.
16. Kirkness, Morale Report No. 4, early November 1940.
17. This discussion of standing orders is based on LAC, DND, RG 24, C 3, vol. 15,414, War Diaries, vols. 1, 2, 8 and 9; various appendices; and RG 24, vol. 11,248, file 9-5-3.
18. LAC, DND, RG 24, C 3, vol. 15,414, War Diaries, vols. 1, 2, 8 and 9; various appendices; and RG 24, vol. 11,248, file 9-5-3.
19. LAC, DND, RG 24, C 3, vol. 15,414, vol. 2, Appendix 3, "Standing Order for Bridge Guard," signed Major V.P. Torrance.
20. LAC, DND, RG 24, C 3, vol. 15,414, War Diaries, vols. 1 and 9.
21. Paterson Report, 15.
22. LAC, DND, RG 24, C 3, vol. 15,414, War Diaries, vol. 1, Appendix 1.
23. Kirkness, Morale Report No. 5.
24. Spier, *Protecting Power*, 154–155.
25. Koch, *Deemed Suspect*, 19. See also Kirkness, Morale Report No. 2, September 1940.
26. These shower calculations were made on the basis of data provided by a Swiss diplomat and found in Swiss Federal Archives (SFA), Toronto, Band 2, E 2200-164(-)-/2. Red Rock Folder. See also LAC, DND, RG 24, C 3, vol. 15414, War Diaries, vols. 1 and 8, Appendix 1.
27. This account of Edwin Guelcher is based on Kirkness, Morale Report No. 5; and also documents of the University of Cape Town Library Archive, BC 640, E 3. 266. p. 16, par. 13.
28. Extensive research in relevant published sources has unfortunately not produced any confirmation of Guelcher's direct or prominent involvement in any of these events. He may have been a bystander. Consulted were Ernst von Salomon, *Der Fragebogen* (Hamburg: Rowohlt Verlag, 1951) and the English edition *The Answers of Ernst von Salomon to the 131 Questions in the Allied Military Government Fragebogen,*

trans. Constantine Fitzgibbon (London: Putnam, 1954); von Salomon, ed., *Das Buch vom deutschen Freikorpskaempfer* (1938; Strukum, Ger.: Verlag für ganzheitliche Forschung und Kultur, 1988); Friedrich Felgen, ed., *Femgericht*, 4th ed. (1932; Strukum, Ger.: Verlag für ganzheitliche Forschung und Kultur, 1988); E.J. Gumbel, *Verräter verfallen der Feme* (Berlin: Malik Verlag, 1929); Gumbel, *Vier Jahre politischer Mord* (Berlin-Fichtenau: Verlag der Neuen Gesellschaft, 1922); and David B. Southern, "Anti-Democratic Terror in the Weimar Republic: The Black Reichswehr and the Feme-Murders," in Wolfgang J. Mommsen and Gerhard Hirschfeld, eds., *Social Protest, Violence, and Terror in Nineteenth and Twentieth Century Europe* (London: German Historical Institute, 1982), 330–341.

29. Benjamin Bennett, *Hitler over Africa* (London: T. Werner Laurie, 1939), 100–106.
30. Albrecht Hagemann, *Südafrika und das "Dritte Reich": Rassenpolitische Affinität und machtpolitische Rivalität* (Frankfurt: Campus Verlag, 1989), 122–123.
31. Kirkness, Morale Report No. 5.
32. Heinz Blobelt of Hamburg, Germany, former internee in Canada, conversation and interview with the author, summer 2000.
33. Spier, *Protecting Power*, 88, 210.
34. LAC, DSS, RG 6, A 1, vol. 207, file 2902, Pt. VII 1939, Panet to Secretary of State, ca. July 1940.
35. LAC, DSS, RG 6, A 1, vol. 207, file 2902, Pt. VII 1939, Panet to Secretary of State, ca. July 1940.
36. LAC, RG 24, C 1, Microfilm C-5379, HQS 7236-33-vol. 2, Panet to Berry, ca. July 1940.
37. LAC, DSS, RG 6, A 1, vol. 207, file 2902, Pt. VII 1939, Panet to Secretary of State, ca. July 1940.
38. LAC, DND, RG 24, C 1, Microfilm C-5420, HQS 7236-95-06.

VII Issues in Camp Life

1. LAC, DND, RG 24, C 1, Microfilm C-5379, HQS 7236-33-vol. 2, Memorandum, Panet to Berry, August 1940. See also LAC, RG 25, A3b, vol. 2,777, file 621-DN-40, and vol. 2,623, file 621-A-40, correspondence, Maag to External Affairs, July 1940.
2. LAC, DND, RG 24, C 1, Microfilm C-5379, HQS 7236-33-vol. 2, Memorandum, Panet to Berry, August 1940.
3. LAC, DND, RG 24, C 3, vol. 15,414, Internment Camp R, folder 1, vol. 8, Appendix 2, Sheet no. 1, items 25 and 26, 1–28 February 1941.
4. In the Convention Relative to the Treatment of Prisoners of War, signed at Geneva, 27 July 1929, Article 34 states:
   "Prisoners of war shall not receive pay for work in connection with the administration, internal arrangement and maintenance of camps. Prisoners employed on other work shall be entitled to a rate of pay, to be fixed by agreement between the belligerents. These agreements shall also specify the portions which may be retained by the camp administration, the amount which shall belong to the prisoner of war and the manner in which this amount shall be placed at his disposal during the period of his captivity. Pending the conclusion of the said agreements, remuneration of the work of prisoners shall be fixed according to the following standards: (a) Work done for the State shall be paid for according to the rates in force for soldiers of the national forces doing the work, or, if no such rates

exist, according to a tariff corresponding to the work executed. (b) When the work is done for other public administration or for private individuals, the conditions shall be settled in agreement with the military authorities. The pay which remains to the credit of prisoner shall be remitted to him on the termination of his captivity. In case of death, it shall be remitted through the diplomatic channel to the heirs of the deceased." Geneva Convention of 1929, 349.

5.   Paterson Report, 16.

6.   LAC, DND, RG 24, vol. 11,249, file 10-2-2-R, Kirkness, Morale Report No. 8, 7 March 1941.

7.   LAC, DND, RG 24, vol. 11,246, file 9-1-3-R, Stethem to Berry, March 1941. Unfortunately the circular, which incorporated the Swiss explanation, could not be located.

8.   LAC, DND, RG 24, vol. 11,246, file 9-1-3-R, Stethem to Berry, March 1941.

9.   Paterson Report, 8.

10. LAC, DND, RG 24, vol. 11,246, file 9-1, Memorandum, Judge Advocate General, 15 July 1940. See also RG 24, C 1, Microfilm C-5379, HQS 7236-33-vol. 2.

11. University of Toronto Archives (hereafter UTA), Boeschenstein fonds, B 84-0014/001(08), Report No. 2, by Dr. Jerome Davis, 28 December 1940.

12. UTA, Boeschenstein fonds, B 84-0014/001(08), Report No. 2, by Davis, 28 December 1940.

13. Kirkness, Morale Report No. 5.

14. Stent, Bespattered Page, 221.

15. Seyfert, "'His Majesty's Most Loyal Internees,'" 182–184.

16. Interview with Lloyd Roy, Red Rock, 14 May 2002.

17. This composite sketch of Dr. Hanfstaengl is based primarily on Ernst Franz Sedgwick Hanfstaengl, Zwischen Weissem und Braunem Haus: Memoiren eines Politischen Aussenseiters, 2nd ed. (Munich: R. Piper Verlag, 1970), translated as Unheard Witness, introd. Brian Connell (New York: Lippincott, 1957) and as Hitler: The Missing Years, introd. John Toland, afterword Egon Hanfstaengl (New York: Arcade, 1994); and Kirkness, Morale Report No. 5. See also Jay Franklin, The Catoctin Conversation, introd. Sumner Welles (New York: Scribner's, 1947), an imaginative reconstruction of alleged talks between Roosevelt, Churchill and Hanfstaengl. These standard works were consulted: Joachim C. Fest, Hitler (New York: Harcourt Brace Jovanovich, 1974); John Toland, Adolf Hitler: The Definitive Biography (New York: Anchor Books, 1976); Werner Maser, Hitler: Legend, Myth and Reality (New York: Harper & Row, 1973). Also consulted was Charles B. Flood, who claims to have had access to the unpublished memoirs of Hanfstaengl's wife. Hitler: The Path to Power (Boston: Houghton Mifflin, 1989).

18. Hitler's Table Talk 1941–1944: His Private Conversations, 3rd ed., ed. H. Trevor-Roper, trans. Norman Cameron and R.H. Stevens (New York: Enigma Books, 2000), 564.

19. Koch, Deemed Suspect, 51.

20. LAC, DND, RG 24, Microfilm C-5778, HQS 7236-12, correspondence, Stethem to Berry and Robertson, July 1941.

21. Ernst Hanfstaengl, Hitler: The Memoirs of a Nazi Insider Who Turned Against the Führer (New York: Arcade, 2011), 292–299.

22. See Manfred Jenke, Verschwörung von Rechts? Ein Bericht über den Rechtsradikalismus in Deutschland nach 1945 (Berlin: Colloquium Verlag, 1961).

23. LAC, DND, RG 24, C 3, vol. 15,414, War Diaries, Internment Camp R, folder 1, vol. 8, Appendix 2, Sheet no. 1, item 26, 1–28 February 1941.

24. All excerpts quoted in the next couple of paragraphs are from Kirkness, Morale Report No. 5.

VIII A Canadian Conundrum

1. Paula J. Draper, "Accidental Immigrants" (PHD diss.), 35.

2. In July 1940, these camps were Cove Field Barracks, Trois-Rivières Exhibition Grounds, Île aux Noix Fortress and St. Helen's Island, all in the Province of Quebec; in Ontario, camps were located at Fort Henry (Kingston), Mimico/New Toronto, Calydor Sanatorium, Gravenhurst, Espanola and Monteith.

3. The National Archives of the United Kingdom (hereafter TNA), Home Office (hereafter HO), 215/265, Memorandum for the Canadian Government, unsigned and undated.

4. Gillman and Gillman, *Collar the Lot*, 239; and Paula J. Draper, "Accidental Immigrants" (PHD diss.), 36.

5. Charles Ritchie, *The Siren Years: Undiplomatic Diaries, 1937–1945* (Toronto: Macmillan, 1974), 61.

6. TNA, HO 215/265, Massey to Caldecote, 22 July 1940. All quotations in this paragraph are from this source.

7. For details see Irving Abella and Harold Troper, *None Is Too Many: Canada and the Jews of Europe, 1933–1948*, 3rd ed. (Toronto: Lester, 1991). Quotation from Major E.H.J. Barber in TNA, HO 215/265, Voyage of SS *Ettrick*: conditions in Canadian camps on arrival.

8. TNA, HO 215/265, Memorandum for the Canadian Government, unsigned and undated, 3.

9. Library and Archives Canada (hereafter LAC), Department of National Defence (hereafter DND), RG 24, C 5, vol. 6585, 4-2-1.

10. TNA, Foreign Office (hereafter FO) 371/ 25210/ TNA 121108, War Cabinet. *Arandora Star* Inquiry. Report by Lord Snell, October 1940 (hereafter cited as Lord Snell Inquiry).

11. Lord Snell Inquiry, Lord Snell's amicable phrase.

12. See Ian Darragh's foreword in Igersheimer, *Blatant Injustice*, xii; and Koch, *Deemed Suspect*, 31.

13. Gillman and Gillman, *Collar the Lot*, 240.

14. Gillman and Gillman, *Collar the Lot*, 182 and 196.

15. United Kingdom, HO, *German and Austrian Civilian Internees*.

16. TNA, FO 916/ 2580 /TNA 121108, Minutes of the Conference of 17 June 1940.

17. Gillman and Gillman, *Collar the Lot*, 267.

18. Paterson Report, 38.

19. Lynton, *Accidental Journey*, 17, 26, 52–53.

20. Paterson Report, 23.

21. Harry Seidler, *Internment: The Diaries of Harry Seidler, May 1940–October 1941*, ed. Janis Wilton, trans. Judith Winternitz (Sydney: Allen & Unwin, 1986), 105, 132.
22. Paterson Report, 15.
23. Lynton, *Accidental Journey*, 17, 26, 52–53.
24. Paterson Report, 16, 17; and Koch, *Deemed Suspect*, 212.
25. Igersheimer, *Blatant Injustice*, 50, 59.
26. Paterson Report, 7.
27. Paterson Report, 14.
28. Paterson Report, 12.
29. For details and differing versions of this affair see Paterson Report, 33; Chaim Raphael, *Memoirs of a Special Case* (Toronto: Little, Brown, 1962), 203–204; and Paula J. Draper, "Accidental Immigrants" (PHD diss.), 178.
30. Paula J. Draper, "Fragmented Loyalties: Canadian Jewry, the King Government and the Refugee Dilemma," in Hillmer, Kordan, and Luciuk, *On Guard for Thee*, 151–177.
31. David Stafford, *Churchill and the Secret Service* (London: John Murray, 1998), 181; and Paula J. Draper, "Fragmented Loyalties," 155n30.
32. These comprehensive comments on Canadian anti-Semitism are based on articles by Paula J. Draper, "Fragmented Loyalties," 151–177; Paula J. Draper, "The Politics of Refugee Immigration: The Pro-Refugee Lobby and the Interned Refugees 1940–1944," *Canadian Jewish Historical Society Journal* 7, no. 2 (Fall 1983): 74–88; and Irving Abella and Harold Troper, "'The line must be drawn somewhere:' Canada and Jewish Refugees, 1933–9," *Canadian Historical Review*, 60 (June 1979): 78–209.
33. Koch, *Deemed Suspect*, x–xii.
34. Paula J. Draper, "The Politics of Refugee Immigration," 74–88.
35. Pierre Anctil, "Interlude of Hostility: Judeo-Christian Relations in Quebec in the Interwar Period, 1919–39," Alan Davies, ed., *Antisemitism in Canada: History and Interpretation* (Waterloo, ON: Wilfrid Laurier University Press, 1992), 135–165; Robert Bothwell, *Canada and Quebec: One Country, Two Histories* (Vancouver: University of British Columbia Press, 1998), 69–70; Abella and Troper, *None Is Too Many*.
36. Paula J. Draper, "The Politics of Refugee Immigration," 74–88.
37. Paula J. Draper, "The Politics of Refugee Immigration," 74–88.
38. Paula J. Draper, "Fragmented Loyalties," 158–160.
39. Canadian Jewish Congress Archives, Montreal (hereafter cited as CJC), Series CA, box 17, file 125E, memorandum, Hayes to Rosenberg, 14 February 1941.
40. See Koch, *Deemed Suspect*, 110.
41. Spier, *Protecting Power*, 149.
42. Nielsen, *Emigrant für Deutschland*, 192.
43. Koch, *Deemed Suspect*, 80.
44. Seidler, *Internment*, 67. The 10 August 1940 issue of the *New Statesman* reported that the Swiss consular staff mistakenly assumed that the label POW meant exactly that and therefore had passed internee information to Nazi Germany.
45. Darragh, Foreword to Igersheimer, *Blatant Injustice*, vii; Koch, *Deemed Suspect*, xiv; and Spier, *Protecting Power*, 161–162.
46. LAC, DEA, RG 25, A3b, vol. 2,768, file 621-MB-40, Consular Report.
47. Gillman and Gillman, *Collar the Lot*, 225.
48. Paula J. Draper, "Fragmented Loyalties," 151–177.
49. Paula J. Draper, "The Politics of Refugee Immigration," 74–88.

50. Seidler, *Internment*, 108.
51. Spier, *Protecting Power*, 161.
52. Koch, *Deemed Suspect*, 92–93.
53. This observation is based on a number of conversations and correspondence the author had with a number of former Red Rock POWs over the years.
54. Paula J. Draper, "Accidental Immigrants" (1978), 11, 32–33. Additionally, this observation is based on a number of conversations and correspondence the author had with a number of former Red Rock POWs over the years. See also Paula J. Draper, "The Politics of Refugee Immigration," 77.
55. This observation is based on a number of conversations and correspondence the author had with a number of former Red Rock POWs over the years.
56. Stent, *Bespattered Page*, 218.
57. Stent, *Bespattered Page*, 96.
58. Stent, *Bespattered Page*, 71 and 96.
59. Koch, *Deemed Suspect*, 27–35.
60. Koch, *Deemed Suspect*, 30.
61. Gillman and Gillman, *Collar the Lot*, 161–162.
62. Stent, *Bespattered Page*, 72.
63. Gillman and Gillman, *Collar the Lot*, 203.

IX Other Aspects of Camp Life

1. Watson Report. All references in the following paragraphs are to this report, unless indicated otherwise.
2. "Berry rode around the camp with his motorbicycle and the funny side-car." Lloyd Roy, interview by author, 14 May 2002. For information on transport detachment, see LAC, DND, RG 24, vol. 11,253, file 11-2-14, Col. H. Stethem, Inspection Report, 1 March 1941.
3. The *Kyffhaeuser Bund* and its affiliated *Kriegshilfswerk*, founded in Philadelphia in 1938, were the American branch of the German *Kyffhaeuser Bund*, a World War I veterans and soldiers association controlled by the Nazi Party after 1933. See Birte Pfleger, "Hitler's Shadow in Philadelphia: The GSP from the 1930s through the 1960s," in *Ethnicity Matters: A History of the German Society of Pennsylvania* (Washington, DC: German Historical Institute, 2006), 78–95. Rudolph Schwedler, a US citizen, was named as the sponsor by Canadian authorities.
4. LAC, DND, RG 24, vol. 11,253, file 11-2-2, Military Inspection Report on Camp R, Colonel P.A. Puize, Provost Corps, Colonel T. Daun, Deputy Commissioner of RCMP, and Major G.T. Goad, Warden of Dorchester Prison, New Brunswick, 21 September 1940.
5. LAC, DEA, RG 25, vol. 2777, file 621-DN-40, and Microfilm C-5377, HQS 7236-12-9-Org-2c, Report, unsigned, 20 August 1940.
6. LAC, DND, RG 24, vol. 11,253, file 11-2-2, Military Inspection Report on Camp R, 21 September 1940.
7. LAC, RG 24, vol. 11,248, file 9-5-3-R, Report by Swiss Consul E. Maag, 14 September 1940.
8. LAC, DND, RG 24, vol. 11,253, file 11-2-2, Military Inspection Report on Camp R, 21 September 1940.

9. Swiss Federal Archives (SFA), Toronto, Band 2, E 2200-164(-)-/2, Consular Report. See also Consular Reports in LAC, DEA, RG 25, A3b, vol. 2,768, file 621-BV-40; RG 25, 3Ab, vol. 2,632, file 621-J-40; and DND, RG 24, vol. 11,248, file 9-5-3.
10. SFA, Toronto, Band 2, E 2200-164(-)-/2, Consular Report.
11. *Dictionary of Jesuit Biography: Ministry to English Canada, 1842–1987*, Vol. I (Toronto: Canadian Institute of Jesuit Studies, 1991). I thank Roy Piovesana, Archivist, Roman Catholic Diocese of Thunder Bay, for information on Jesuit contacts with Camp R.
12. On the question of the service of a Rabbi see Paula J. Draper, "The 'Camp Boys': Interned Refugees from Nazism," in Iacovetta, Perin, and Principe, *Enemies Within*, 171–193; and CJC, Series CA, box 17, file 125E, relevant letters.
13. CJC, Series CA, box 17, file 125E, letter, B. Rappoport to Rabbi Dr. Eisendraht, July 1941.
14. CJC, Series CA, box 17, file 125E, memorandum, Hayes to Rosenberg, 14 February 1941.
15. CJC, Series CA, box 17, file 125E, Glaser to Kirkness, n.d.
16. LAC, DND, RG 24, vol. 11,253, file 11-2-14, Col. H. Stethem, Inspection Report, 1 March 1941.
17. UTA, Boeschenstein fonds, B 84-0014/001(08), Serving Prisoners of War in Canada, Dr. J. Davis; and Spier, 217–218.
18. Kirkness, Morale Report No. 7, 3.
19. Koch, *Deemed Suspect*, 51.
20. Paula J. Draper, "Accidental Immigrants" (PHD diss.), 54. See also Spier, *Protecting Power*, 155–156.
21. Seidler, *Internment*, 118; and Nielsen, *Emigrant für Deutschland*, 234.
22. Nielsen, *Emigrant für Deutschland*, 195–196.
23. Spier, *Protecting Power*, 158–164.

x "The Little Third Reich on Lake Superior"

1. See Koch, *Deemed Suspect*, 110.
2. Captain Kirkness, Morale Report No. 5.
3. Spier, *Protecting Power*, 204.
4. Spier, *Protecting Power*, 204.
5. Spier, *Protecting Power*, 205.
6. Spier, *Protecting Power*, 168.
7. Koch, *Deemed Suspect*, 111.
8. Based on interviews with various former POWs, Class I and Class II in Canadian detention.
9. LAC, DND, RG 24, C 1, Microfilm C-5377, HQS 7236-12-(R-1-1-5) and C-5378, HQS 7236-25-vol. 2, Report: Riot, 4 October 1940; and Berry to Headquarters, MD, 10 October 1940.
10. Koch, *Deemed Suspect*, 114.
11. See LAC, Microfilm C-5378, HQS 7236-12-(R-1-1-5), for copy of translation of Capt. Scharf's speech to the interned German nationals.
12. In 1943 Capt. Scharf served as spokesman in Camp 130, Kananaskis/Seebe. See Koch, *Deemed Suspect*, 115.

13. LAC, DND, RG 24, C 1, Microfilm C-5378, HQS 7236-12-(R-1-1-5), copy of translated petition.
14. Kirkness, Morale Report No. 5.
15. Koch, *Deemed Suspect*, 114; and LAC, DND, RG 24, vol. 11,246, file 9-1-3-R.
16. LAC, DND, RG 24, C 1, Microfilm C-5378, HQS 7236-25-vol. 2, Streight to Judge Advocate General, 6 November 1940 and Judge Advocate General to Assistant Judge Advocate General, Winnipeg, 14 November 1940.
17. Kirkness, Morale Report No. 5.
18. Kirkness, Morale Report No. 5.
19. Kirkness, Morale Report No. 5.
20. LAC, DND, RG 24, C 1, Microfilm C-5378, HQS 7236-25-vol. 2, Browne to all DOCS, 18 September 1940.
21. Affidavit by Lloyd Roy, in author's possession. For details on escapes, see LAC, DND, RG 24, C 3, vol. 15,414, War Diary, vols. 1, 2, 3.
22. Letter to Mr. Monk, n.d. deposited in the Marathon Public Library.
23. LAC, DND, RG 24, C 3, vol. 15,414, War Diary, vol. 3.
24. LAC, DND, RG 24, C 3, vol. 15,414, War Diary, vols. 13 and 15 and RG 24, C 1, Microfilm C-5377, HQS 7236-12, Report, 20 January 1941 and Berry to MD, 10 January 1941. Reference Desk, Chancellor Paterson Library, Lakehead University provided information on price of railway ticket in 1940 from newspapers at the time.
25. Koch, *Deemed Suspect*, 117.
26. Melady, 119.
27. G. Rudi John, former EMS interned at Monteith, Neys, and local farm work camps, interview by author, May 2003.
28. LAC, DND, RG 24, C 1, Microfilm C-5377, HQS 7236-14, Circular. Notes, 24 December 1940.

XI Lighter and Darker Aspects of Camp Life

1. Anonymous former interned EMS, interview by author, n.d. See also Archives of Manitoba, Colonel H.N. Streight collection, "Geneva Convention," Lecture by Col. H.N. Streight, Director of Internment Operations, 19 April 1943.
2. LAC, DND, RG 24, vol. 11,246, file 12-14-13, Donations to Camp R, Davis to Directorate, April 1941.
3. LAC, DND, RG 24, C 3, vol. 15,414, Internment Camp R, War Diary, vols. 1, 2, 8 and 9.
4. Kirkness, Morale Report No. 5.
5. LAC, DND, RG 24, C 3, vol. 15,414, Internment Camp R, War Diary, vols. 1 and 2.
6. Anonymous former internee, interview by author, n.d.
7. Koch, *Deemed Suspect*, 157–158.
8. John, interview.
9. Koch, *Deemed Suspect*, 159; and John, interview.
10. Spier, *Protecting Power*, 156–157.
11. LAC, DND, RG 24, C 1, Microfilm C-5378, HQS 7236-25-vol. 2.
12. LAC, DND, RG 24, C 1, Microfilm C-5378, HQS 7236-25-vol. 2, Riley to Directorate.
13. LAC, DND, RG 24, C 1, Microfilm C-5378, HQS 7236-25-vol. 2, and file R-1-1-5, Report on O'Callaghan, Stethem to Adjutant-General, 8 April 1941.
14. LAC, DND, RG 24, C 1, Microfilm C-5378, HQS 7236-25, vol. 12, file on Hill.

15. Spier, *Protecting Power*, 57–59.
16. Spier, *Protecting Power*, 156–161.
17. Koch, *Deemed Suspect*, 80; and Kirkness, Morale Report No. 5.
18. Spier, *Protecting Power*, 18, 55.
19. For more on this series of events, see Spier, *Protecting Power*, 74–99.

XII "The End Is Nigh"

1. LAC, DND, RG 24, C 1, Microfilm C-5378, HQS 7236-25 Memorandum, Quartermaster-General to DOC, No. 10, 21 July 1940.
2. LAC, DND, RG 24, C 1, Microfilm C-5377, HQS 7236-95-06, and Microfilm C-5379, HQS 7236-33, correspondence, Panet and Stethem to Department of National Defence.
3. For commentary on the November 1940 report, see LAC, DND, RG 24, vol. 11,253, file 11-2-14, Stethem Report, 1 March 1941.
4. LAC, DND, RG 24, vol. 11,253, file 11-2-14, Stethem Report, 1 March 1941. This visit by Col. Stethem of Camp R invalidates Commissioner Paterson's criticism of the Director and his staff that they never visited the camps. All references in the following paragraphs are to this Report.
5. LAC, DND, RG 24, vol. 11,248, file 9-5-3-R, ICRC Report Camp R, 1941.
6. LAC, DND, RG 24, vol. 11,248, file 9-5-3-R, ICRC Report Camp R, 1941.
7. LAC, DND, RG 24, C 1, Microfilm C-5377, HQS 7236, file 5-2-5, Memorandum, Panet to Adjutant-General, 3 October 1940.
8. Nielsen, *Emigrant für Deutschland*, 204.
9. LAC, DND, RG 24, C 3, vol. 15,414, War Diary, vol. 15; Canada, *House of Commons Debates* (2 July 1940), p. 1262 (Mrs. Nielson, MP). The monthly cost per inmate was $10.50 or for the camp some $12,075 per month.
10. LAC, DEA, RG 25, A3b, vol. 2,768, file 621-BV-49, Hasenberg to Massey, 3 July 1942. See also Hanfstaengl, *Zwischen Weissem*.
11. Spier, *Protecting Power*, 224–225, 232.
12. See Spier, *Protecting Power*, 232.

XIII Epilogue

1. Stent, *Bespattered Page*, 14; and Nielsen, *Emigrant für Deutschland*, 175.
2. See Lynton, *Accidental Journey*.

Bibliography

Archival Sources

Archives of Manitoba (Winnipeg)
    Colonel H.N. Streight collection.
Auswaertiges Amt. Politisches Archiv (Berlin)
    R 127557, Band 59, R xii Zv.
Canadian Jewish Congress Archives (Montreal)
    Central Files series, Series CA.
Homefront Archives and Museum (Regina)
    Robert J. Henderson collection.
Library and Archives Canada (Ottawa)
    Department of the Secretary of State fonds, RG 6.
    Department of National Defence fonds, RG 24.
    Department of External Affairs fonds, RG 25.
    William Lyon Mackenzie King collection, MG 26.
The National Archives (Kew, Richmond, United Kingdom)
    Foreign Office fonds.
    Home Office fonds.
Swiss Federal Archives (Bern, Switzerland)
    Schweizerische Vertretung, Toronto: Zentrale Ablage (1906–1958), E2200.164-02.
University of Cape Town, Manuscript and Archives Department (Cape Town, South Africa)
    H.G. Lawrence papers.

University of Manitoba, Faculty of Medicine Archives (Winnipeg)
    File 21.9 (Dr. A.A. Klass).
University of Toronto Archives and Records Management Services (Toronto)
    Hermann Boeschenstein fonds.

Interviews

Anonymous former interned EMS, n.d.
Heinz Blobelt, Summer 2000.
Lloyd Roy, May 2002.
G. Rudi John, May 2003.
Various anonymous interviews, 1999–2008.

Books and Articles

Abella, Irving, and Harold Troper. "'The line must be drawn somewhere': Canada and Jewish Refugees, 1933–9." *Canadian Historical Review* 60 (June 1979): 78–209.
————. *None Is Too Many: Canada and the Jews of Europe, 1933–1948.* 3rd ed. Toronto: Lester, 1983.
Adachi, Ken. *The Enemy That Never Was: A History of the Japanese Canadians.* Toronto: McClelland & Stewart, 1976.
Anctil, Pierre. "Interlude of Hostility: Judeo-Christian Relations in Quebec in the Interwar Period, 1919–39." In *Antisemitism in Canada: History and Interpretation,* edited by Alan Davies, 135–165. Waterloo, ON: Wilfrid Laurier University Press, 1992.
Auger, Martin F. *Prisoners on the Home Front: German POWs and "Enemy Aliens" in Southern Quebec, 1940–46.* Vancouver: University of British Columbia Press, 2005.
Banauch, Eugen. "'Home' as a Thought between Quotation Marks: The Fluid Exile of Jewish Third Reich Refugee Writers in Canada 1940–2006." PHD diss., University of Vienna, 2007.
————. *Fluid Exile: Jewish Exile Writers in Canada 1940–2006.* Anglistische Forschungen 395. Heidelberg: Winter, 2009.
Beaulieu, Michel S. *Labour at the Lakehead: Ethnicity, Socialism, and Politics, 1900–35.* Vancouver: University of British Columbia Press, 2011.
Belanger, Dorothea Weigeldt. "Prisoners of World War II on Lake of the Woods." In *Common Ground: Stories of Lake of the Woods; Celebrating 5 years of Storytelling, Common Ground, 2006–2010,* 21–31. Kenora, ON: Common Ground Committee, Lake of the Woods Museum, 2010.
Bennett, Benjamin. *Hitler over Africa.* London: T. Werner Laurie, 1939.
Bentwich, Norman. "England and the Alien." *Political Quarterly* 12, no. 1 (1941): 81–93.
Bercuson, David, and J.L. Granatstein. *Dictionary of Canadian Military History.* Toronto: Oxford University Press, 1992.
Bernard, Yves, and Caroline Bergeron. *Trop loin de Berlin: des prisonniers allemands au Canada (1939–1946).* Sillery, QC: Septentrion, 1995.
Betcherman, Lita-Rose. *The Swastika and the Maple Leaf: Fascist Movements in Canada in the Thirties.* Toronto: Fitzhenry & Whiteside, 1975.

Bjorkman, Sylvia. "Report on Camp 'W': Internment Camp '100' North of Lake Superior in World War II." *Ontario History* 89, no. 3 (September 1997): 237–243.

Bothwell, Robert. *Canada and Quebec: One Country, Two Histories.* Vancouver: University of British Columbia Press, 1998.

Boudreau, Joseph A. "Western Canada's 'Enemy Aliens' in World War One." *Alberta Historical Review* 12, no. 1 (Winter 1964): 1–9.

Buck, William, Lubomyr Y. Luciuk, and Borys Sydoruk. *In My Charge: The Canadian Internment Camp Photographs of Sergeant William Buck.* Kingston, ON: Kashtan Press, 1997.

Canada. Canadian Army. Historical Section. *The Regiments and Corps of the Canadian Army.* Canadian Army List 1. Ottawa: Queen's Printer, 1964.

———. Dominion Bureau of Statistics. *The Canada Yearbook 1939: The Official Statistical Annual of the Resources, History, Institutions, and Social and Economic Conditions of the Dominion.* Ottawa: King's Printer, 1940.

———. *House of Commons Debates,* 11 June 1940.

———. *House of Commons Debates,* 2 July 1940.

Carsten, Francis L. "German Refugees in Great Britain 1933–1945." In *Exile in Great Britain: Refugees from Hitler's Germany,* edited by Gerhard Hirschfeld, 11–28. Leamington Spa, UK: Berg, 1984.

Carter, David J. *Behind Canadian Barbed Wire: Alien, Refugee and Prisoner of War Camps in Canada, 1914–1946.* Calgary: Tumbleweed Press, 1980.

———. *POW, Behind Canadian Barbed Wire: Alien, Refugee and Prisoner of War Camps in Canada, 1914–1946.* Elkwater, AB: Eagle Butte Press, 1998.

Cepuch, Stefanie. "The Public and the POWs: Reaction to the Release of German Prisoners of War for Agricultural Labour." In *Canadian Papers in Rural History,* edited by Donald H. Akenson, 9, 323–355. Gananoque, ON: Langdale Press, 1994.

Cesarani, David, and Tony Kushner, eds. *The Internment of Aliens in Twentieth Century Britain.* London: Frank Cass, 1993.

Charmley, John. *Chamberlain and the Lost Peace.* London: Hodder & Stoughton, 1989.

———. *A History of Conservative Politics, 1900–1996.* New York: St. Martin's Press, 1996.

Chisholm, Barbara, and Andrea Gutsche. *Superior: Under the Shadow of the Gods.* Toronto: Lynx Images, 1998.

Churchill, Winston S. *The Gathering Storm.* New York: Bantam Books, 1961.

———. "We Shall Never Surrender." In *Charge! History's Greatest Military Speeches,* edited by Steve Israel, 134–141. Annapolis, MD: Naval Institute Press, 2007.

Ciccocelli, J.A. "The Innocuous Enemy Aliens: Italians in Canada during World War II." Master's thesis, University of Western Ontario, 1977.

Cinanni, Michelle. *The Detention of Second World War Military Prisoners of War and of Enemy Aliens Sent to Canada from Great Britain.* Submission Report No. 2009-91. Ottawa: Historic Sites and Monuments Board of Canada, 2009.

Cohen, Michael J. "Churchill and the Jews: The Holocaust." *Modern Judaism* 6, no. 1 (February 1986): 27–48.

Connell, Brian. Introduction to *Unheard Witness* by Egon Hanfstaengl. New York: Lippincott, 1957.

Convention Relative to the Treatment of Prisoners of War. 1929. In *The Laws of Armed Conflicts: A Collection of Conventions, Resolutions, and Other Documents,* edited by Dietrich Schindler and Jiri Toman, 339–366. Leiden, Netherlands: Brill, 1988.

Cook, Ramsay. "Canadian Freedom in Wartime, 1939–1945." In *His Own Man: Essays in Honour of Arthur Reginald Marsden Lower*, edited by W.H. Heick and Roger Graham, 37–54. Montreal: McGill-Queen's University Press, 1974.

Dean, Pauline. *Sagas of Superior: The Inland Sea...and Its Canadian Shore*. Manitouwadge, ON: Great Spirit Writers, 1992.

Dictionary of Jesuit Biography: Ministry to English Canada, 1842–1987. Toronto: Canadian Institute of Jesuit Studies, 1991.

Draper, Alfred. *Operation Fish: The Race to Save Europe's Wealth, 1939–1945*. London: Cassell, 1979.

Draper, Paula J. "The Accidental Immigrants: Canada and the Interned Refugees: Part I." *Canadian Jewish Historical Society Journal* 2, no. 1 (Spring 1978): 1–38.

———. "The Accidental Immigrants: Canada and the Interned Refugees." PHD diss., University of Toronto, 1983.

———. "The 'Camp Boys': Interned Refugees from Nazism." In Iacovetta, Perin, and Principe, *Enemies Within*, 171–193.

———. "Fragmented Loyalties: Canadian Jewry, the King Government and the Refugee Dilemma." In Hillmer, Kordan, and Luciuk, *On Guard for Thee*, 151–177.

———. "The Politics of Refugee Immigration: The Pro-Refugee Lobby and the Interned Refugees 1940–1944." *Canadian Jewish Historical Society Journal* 7, no. 2 (Fall 1983): 74–88.

Duliani, Mario. *The City Without Women: A Chronicle of Internment Life in Canada during the Second World War*. Translated by Antonino Mazza. Oakville, ON: Mosaic Press, 1994.

Felgen, Friedrich, ed. *Femgericht*. 1932. 4th ed. Strukum, Ger.: Verlag für ganzheitliche Forschung und Kultur, 1988.

Fest, Joachim C. *Hitler*. New York: Harcourt Brace Jovanovich, 1974.

Flood, Charles B. *Hitler: The Path to Power*. Boston: Houghton Mifflin, 1989.

Fooks, Georgia Green. *Prairie Prisoners: POWS in Lethbridge during Two World Conflicts*. Lethbridge, AB: Lethbridge Historical Society, 2003.

Franklin, Jay. *The Catoctin Conversation*. Introduction by Sumner Welles. New York: Scribner's, 1947.

Gallagher, Tim. *Espanola: POW Camp 21, 1940–1943*. Espanola, ON: privately printed, 1976.

Gillman, Lena, and Peter Gillman. *Collar the Lot! How Britain Interned and Expelled Its Wartime Refugees*. London: Quartet Books, 1980.

Glees, Anthony. *Exile Politics during the Second World War: The German Social Democrats in Britain*. Oxford: Clarendon Press, 1982.

Gouin, Jacques, and Lucien Brault. *Legacy of Honour: The Panets, Canada's Foremost Military Family*. Toronto: Methuen, 1985.

Granatstein, J.L. *The Ottawa Men: The Civil Service Mandarins, 1935–1957*. 2nd ed. Toronto: University of Toronto Press, 1998.

Granatstein, J.L., and Dean F. Oliver. *Oxford Companion to Canadian Military History*. Don Mills, ON: Oxford University Press, 2011.

Granatstein, J.L., and Gregory A. Johnson. "The Evacuation of the Japanese Canadians, 1942: A Realist Critique of the Received Version." In Hillmer, Kordan, and Luciuk, *On Guard for Thee*, 101–129.

Greenhous, Brereton. *Dragoon: The Centennial History of the Royal Canadian Dragoons, 1883–1983*. Belleville, ON: The Guild of the Royal Canadian Dragoons, 1983.

Gumbel, E.J. *Verräter verfallen der Feme*. Berlin: Malik Verlag, 1929.

————. *Vier Jahre politischer Mord*. Berlin-Fichtenau: Verlag der Neuen Gesellschaft, 1922.

Hagemann, Albrecht. *Südafrika und das "Dritte Reich": Rassenpolitische Affinität und machtpolitische Rivalität*. Frankfurt: Campus Verlag, 1989.

Hanfstaengl, Ernst Franz Sedgwick. *Zwischen Weissem und Braunem Haus: Memoiren eines Politischen Aussenseiters*. 2nd ed. Munich: R. Piper Verlag, 1970. Translated as *Unheard Witness* (introd. Brian Connell, New York: Lippincott, 1957) and as *Hitler: The Missing Years* (introd. John Toland, afterword Egon Hanfstaengl, New York: Arcade, 1994).

————. *Hitler: The Memoirs of a Nazi Insider Who Turned Against the Führer*. New York: Arcade, 2011.

Henderson, Robert J. *An Introduction to Guarding Prisoners of War in Canada*. Regina: privately printed, 2008.

————. *Ephemera of German Prisoners of War in Canada and the Veterans' Guard of Canada*. Regina: privately printed, 2009.

Hill, Christopher. *Cabinet Decisions on Foreign Policy: The British Experience October 1938–June 1941*. Cambridge: Cambridge University Press, 2002.

Hillmer, Norman, Bohdan Kordan, and Lubomyr Y. Luciuk, eds. *On Guard for Thee: War, Ethnicity and the Canadian State, 1939–1945*. Ottawa: Canadian Committee for the History of the Second World War, 1988.

Hitler, Adolf. *Hitler's Table Talk, 1941–1944: His Private Conversations*. 3rd ed. Edited by Hugh Trevor-Roper. Translated by Norman Cameron and R.H. Stevens. New York: Enigma Books, 2000.

Hoffman, Daniel. *Camp 30 "Ehrenwort": A German Prisoner-of-War Camp in Bowmanville, 1941–1945*. Bowmanville, ON: Bowmanville Museum, 1990.

Holmes, Colin. *Anti-Semitism in British Society, 1876–1939*. London: Edward Arnold, 1979.

Iacovetta, Franca, Roberto Perin, and Angelo Principe, eds. *Enemies Within: Italian and Other Internees in Canada and Abroad*. Toronto: University of Toronto Press, 2000.

Igersheimer, Walter W. *Blatant Injustice: The Story of a Jewish Refugee from Nazi Germany Imprisoned in Britain and Canada during World War II*. Edited with foreword by Ian Darragh. Montreal: McGill-Queen's University Press, 2005.

Irving, David. *Churchill's War*. Vol. 1, *The Struggle for Power*. Bullsbrook, Australia: Veritas, 1987.

Jackson, Paul. "The Enemy Within: The Canadian Army and Internment Operations during the Second World War." *Left History* 9, no. 2 (2004): 45–83.

Jenke, Manfred. *Verschwörung von Rechts? Ein Bericht über den Rechtsradikalismus in Deutschland nach 1945*. Berlin: Colloquium Verlag, 1961.

Jones, Ted. *Both Sides of the Wire: The Fredericton Internment Camp*. 2 vols. Fredericton, NB: New Ireland Press, 1988–1989.

Judex [Herbert Delauney Hughes]. *Anderson's Prisoners*. London: Gollancz, 1940.

Kaplan, William. *State and Salvation: The Jehovah's Witnesses and Their Fight for Civil Rights*. Toronto: University of Toronto Press, 1989.

Kealey, Gregory S., and Reg Whitaker, eds. RCMP *Security Bulletins: The Depression Years*. Vol. 1, *1933–1934*. St. John's, NL: Committee on Labour History, 1993–1997.

————. RCMP *Security Bulletins: The War Series*. Vol. 1, *1939–1941*. St. John's, NL: Committee on Labour History, 1989–1993.

Kelly, John Joseph. "Intelligence and Counter-Intelligence in German Prisoner of War Camps in Canada during World War II." *Dalhousie Review* 58, no. 2 (Summer 1978): 285–294.

———. "The Prisoner of War Camps in Canada, 1939–1947." Master's thesis, University of Windsor, 1976.

Keshen, Jeffrey A. Foreword to *Prisoners of the Home Front: German POWs and "Enemy Aliens" in Southern Quebec, 1940–46* by Martin Auger. Vancouver: University of British Columbia Press, 2005.

———. *Propaganda and Censorship During Canada's Great War.* Edmonton: University of Alberta Press, 1996.

Keyserlingk, Robert H. "Breaking the Nazi Plot: Canadian Government Attitudes towards German Canadians, 1939–1945." In Hillmer, Kordan, and Luciuk, *On Guard for Thee*, 53–70.

Kilford, Christopher R. *On the Way! The Military History of Lethbridge, Alberta (1914–1945) and the Untold Story of Ottawa's Plan to De-Nazify and Democratise German Prisoners of War Held in Lethbridge and Canada during the Second World War.* Victoria: Trafford, 2004.

King, Cecil H. *With Malice Toward None: A War Diary.* Edited by William Armstrong. London: Sidgwick & Jackson, 1970.

King, William Lyon Mackenzie. *The Mackenzie King Diaries, 1893–1950.* Toronto: University of Toronto Press, 1973–1980. Microfiche.

Kirkness, Captain Kenneth. Morale Reports Nos. 1–8 (August 1940–March 1941). RG 24, vol. 11,249, file 10-2-2-R. Department of National Defence. Library and Archives Canada.

———. "Types of Internees—Camp R, Headquarters, Camp R, Red Rock, Ontario prepared for Commandant by Capt. K. Kirkness, R.A., British Liaison Officer." RG 24, vol. 11,253, file 11-2-14, 12 August 1940. Department of National Defence. Library and Archives Canada.

Knightley, Phillip. *The First Casualty: The War Correspondent as Hero and Myth-Maker from the Crimea to Kosovo.* Rev. ed. London: Prion Books, 2000.

Koch, Eric. *Deemed Suspect: A Wartime Blunder.* Toronto: Methuen, 1980.

Kordan, Bohdan S. *Enemy Aliens, Prisoners of War: Internment in Canada during the Great War.* Montreal: McGill-Queen's University Press, 2002.

Kordan, Bohdan S., and Craig Mahovsky. *A Bare and Impolitic Right: Internment and Ukrainian-Canadian Redress.* Montreal: McGill-Queen's University Press, 2004.

Kordan, Bohdan S., and Peter Melnycky, eds. *In the Shadow of the Rockies: Diary of the Castle Mountain Internment Camp, 1915–1917.* Edmonton: Canadian Institute of Ukrainian Studies Press, 1991.

Kreisel, Henry. *Another Country: Writings by and about Henry Kreisel.* Edited by Shirley Neuman. Edmonton: NeWest Press, 1985.

Kushner, Tony. *The Persistence of Prejudice: Anti-Semitism in British Society during the Second World War.* Manchester: Manchester University Press, 1989.

———. *Remembering Refugees: Then and Now.* Manchester: Manchester University Press, 2006.

Kushner, Tony, and Katherine Knox. *Refugees in an Age of Genocide: Global, National, and Local Perspectives during the Twentieth Century.* London: Frank Cass, 1999.

Lachmann, Gustav Viktor. "Sir Frederick Handley Page, the Man and His Work." *Journal of the Royal Aeronautical Society* 68 (July 1964): 433–452.

Lafitte, François. *The Internment of Aliens.* 1940. Reprinted with new introduction by Lafitte. London: Libris, 1988.

Laflamme, Jean. *Les Camps de Détention au Québec Durant la Première Guerre Mondiale.* Montreal: n.p., 1973.

Lee-Whiting, Brenda. "'Enemy Aliens': German-Canadians on the Home Front." *The Beaver* 69, no. 5 (1989), 53–58.

Lieberwirth, Johannes. *Alter Mann und Corned Beef: Kriegsgefangenschaft in Afrika und Kanada.* Emmelshausen: Condo Verlag, 1999.

London, Louise. *Whitehall and the Jews, 1933–1948: British Immigration Policy, Jewish Refugees, and the Holocaust.* Cambridge: Cambridge University Press, 2000.

Luciuk, Lubomyr Y. *In Fear of the Barbed Wire Fence: Canada's First National Internment Operations and the Ukrainian Canadians, 1914–1920* (Kingston, ON: Kashtan Press, 2001).

Luciuk, Lubomyr Y. *Internment Operations: The Role of Old Fort Henry in World War I.* Kingston, ON: Delta Educational Consultants, 1980.

Luciuk, Lubomyr Y., ed. *Righting an Injustice: The Debate over Redress for Canada's First National Internment Operations.* Toronto: Justinian Press, 1994.

Luciuk, Lubomyr Y., ed. *Roll Call: Lest We Forget.* Kingston, ON: Kashtan Press, 1999.

Luciuk, Lubomyr Y. *A Time for Atonement: Canada's First National Internment Operations and the Ukrainian Canadians, 1914–1920.* Kingston, ON: Limestone Press, 1988.

Luciuk, Lubomyr Y. *Without Just Cause: Canada's First National Internment Operations and the Ukrainian Canadians, 1914–1920.* Kingston, ON: Kashtan Press, 2006.

Lynton, Mark. *Accidental Journey: A Cambridge Internee's Memoir of World War II.* Woodstock, NY: Overlook Press, 1995.

Madsen, Chris M.V. "German Prisoners of War in Canada during the Second World War." Master's thesis, University of Western Ontario, 1992.

Madsen, Chris M.V., and R.J. Henderson. *German Prisoners of War in Canada and Their Artifacts, 1940–1948.* Regina: Hignell, 1993.

Martynowych, Orest T. *Ukrainians in Canada: The Formative Period, 1891–1924.* Edmonton: Canadian Institute of Ukrainian Studies Press, 1991.

Maschke, Erich, ed. *Zur Geschichte der deutschen Kriegsgefangenen des zweiten Weltkrieges.* 22 vols. Munich: Gieseking Verlag, 1962–1974.

Maser, Werner. *Hitler: Legend, Myth and Reality.* New York: Harper & Row, 1973.

McKale, Donald M. *The Swastika Outside Germany.* Kent, OH: Kent State University Press, 1977.

Melady, John. *Escape from Canada! The Untold Story of German POWs in Canada, 1939–1945.* Toronto: Macmillan, 1981.

Morton, Desmond. "Sir William Otter and Internment Operations in Canada during the First World War." *Canadian Historical Review* 55, no. 1 (March 1974): 32–58.

Nakano, Takeo Ujo, and Leatrice Nakano. *Within the Barbed Wire Fence: A Japanese Man's Account of His Internment in Canada.* Toronto: University of Toronto Press, 1980.

Nielsen, Frederic W. *Emigrant für Deutschland in der Tschechoslowakei, in England und in Kanada: Tagebuchaufzeichnungen aus den Jahren 1933–1943.* Darmstadt: J.G. Blaeschke Verlag, 1977.

Nishiguchi, Gabrielle. "'Reducing the Numbers': The Transportation of the Japanese Canadians (1941–1947)." Master's thesis, Carleton University, 1993.

Okazaki, Robert K. *The Nisei Mass Evacuation Group and POW Camp 101: The Japanese-Canadian Community's Struggle for Justice and Human Rights during World War II.* Translated by Jean M. Okazaki and Curtis T. Okazaki. Scarborough, ON: Markham Litho, 1996.

Otter, William. *Report on Internment Operations: Canada, 1914–1920*. Ottawa: King's Printer, 1921.

Page, Don. "Tommy Stone and Psychological Warfare in World War Two: Transforming a POW Liability into an Asset." *Journal of Canadian Studies* 16, no. 3/4 (Fall 1981): 110–120.

Panet, Brigadier-General Edward Bellefeuille. Inspection Report. File 2902, Pt. VII 1939, 27 July 1940. Department of the Secretary of State, Library and Archives Canada.

Paterson, Alexander. Report on Civilians Sent from the United Kingdom to Canada during the Unusual Fine Summer of 1940. HO 213/2391/11 95 65, 2–4. The National Archives.

Paterson, Margaret. *Carved from the Forest: A History of Kapuskasing; A Special Centennial Project of the Northern Times*. Kapuskasing, ON: Northern Times, 1967.

Pfleger, Birte. *Ethnicity Matters: A History of the German Society of Pennsylvania*. Washington, DC: German Historical Institute, 2006.

Ponting, Clive. *1940: Myth and Reality*. London: Hamish Hamilton, 1990.

Porter, Cecil. *The Gilded Cage: Gravenhurst German Prisoner-of-War Camp 20, 1940–1946*. Gravenhurst, ON: Gravenhurst Book Committee, 1999.

Price, G. Ward. *I Know These Dictators*. London: Harrap, 1937.

Ramirez, Bruno. "Ethnicity on Trial: The Italians of Montreal and the Second World War." In Hillmer, Kordan, and Luciuk, *On Guard for Thee*, 71–84.

Raphael, Chaim. *Memoirs of a Special Case*. Boston: Little, Brown, 1962.

Repka, William, and Kathleen M. Repka. *Dangerous Patriots: Canada's Unknown Prisoners of War*. Vancouver: New Star Books, 1982.

Ritchie, Charles. *The Siren Years: Undiplomatic Diaries, 1937–1945*. Toronto: Macmillan, 1974.

Roberts, Leslie. *C.D.: The Life and Times of Clarence Decatur Howe*. Toronto: Clarke, Irwin, 1957.

Robinson, Daniel. "Planning for the 'Most Serious Contingency': Alien Internment, Arbitrary Detention, and the Canadian State, 1938–1939." *Journal of Canadian Studies* 28, no. 2 (Summer 1993): 5–22.

Ross, Gerald G. "Fort William's Enemy Alien 'Problem' during the First World War." *Papers and Records* (Thunder Bay Historical Museum Society) 22 (1994), 3–22.

Sando, Tom. *Wild Daisies in the Sand: Life in a Canadian Internment Camp*. Edmonton: NeWest Press, 2002.

Schaffer, Gavin. "Re-Thinking the History of Blame: Britain and Minorities during the Second World War." *National Identities* 8, no. 4 (December 2006): 401–419.

Schapiro, Michael. "German Refugees in France." *Contemporary Jewish Record* 3, no. 2 (March–April 1940): 134–140.

Scribner, Marsha. *Transitions: Commemorating Camp Wainwright's 50th Anniversary*. Winnipeg: Jostens, [1990].

Seidler, Harry. *Internment: The Diaries of Harry Seidler, May 1940–October 1941*. Edited by Janis Wilton. Translated by Judith Winternitz. Sydney: Allen & Unwin, 1986.

Service, G.T., and J.K. Marteinson, eds. *The Gate: A History of The Fort Garry Horse*. Calgary: The Fort Garry Horse, 1971.

Seyfert, Michael. "'His Majesty's Most Loyal Internees': The Internment and Deportation of German and Austrian Refugees as 'Enemy Aliens': Historical, Cultural, and Literary Aspects." In *Exile in Great Britain: Refugees from Hitler's Germany*, edited by Gerhard Hirschfeld, 163–193. London: German History Institute, 1984.

Shakespeare, Geoffrey Hithersay. *Let Candles Be Brought in*. London: Macdonald, 1949.

Simpson, A.W. Brian. *In the Highest Degree Odious: Detention without Trial in Wartime Britain*. London: Clarendon Press, 1992.

Sioux Lookout Historical Society. *Tracks Beside the Water: Sioux Lookout*. Sioux Lookout, ON: Sioux Lookout and District Historical Society, 1982.

Smith, David Edward. "Emergency Government in Canada." *Canadian Historical Review* 50, no. 4 (December 1969): 429–448.

Snell, Henry, 1st Baron. *Arandora Star* Inquiry. FO 371/ 25210/ TNA 121108, War Cabinet. The National Archives.

Sozialistische Mitteilungen: News for German Socialists in England (London), special issue 30A (October 1941).

Southern, David B. "Anti-democratic Terror in the Weimar Republic: The Black *Reichswehr* and the Feme-Murders." In *Social Protest, Violence, and Terror in Nineteenth and Twentieth Century Europe*, edited by Wolfgang J. Mommsen and Gerhard Hirschfeld, 381–393. London: German Historical Institute, 1982.

Spier, Eugen. *Focus: A Footnote to the History of the Thirties*. London: Oswald Wolff, 1963.

——. *The Protecting Power*. London: Skeffington & Son, 1951.

Stacey, C.P. *Official History of the Canadian Army in the Second World War*. Vol. 1, *Six Years of War: The Army in Canada, Britain and the Pacific*. Ottawa: Queen's Printer, 1956–1957.

Stafford, David. *Churchill and the Secret Service*. London: John Murray, 1998.

Stanton, John. "Government Internment Policy, 1939–1945," *Labour/Le Travail* 31 (Spring 1993): 203–241.

Stent, Ronald. *A Bespattered Page? The Internment of His Majesty's "Most Loyal Enemy Aliens."* London: Andre Deutsch, 1980.

Stewart, Graham. *Burying Caesar: The Churchill-Chamberlain Rivalry*. New York: Overlook Press, 2001.

Sumner, Jeff. "World War II German POWs in Northwestern Ontario." *Papers and Records* (Thunder Bay Historical Museum Society) 20 (1992), 2–13.

Swinton, Philip Cunliffe-Lister, 1st Viscount. *I Remember*. London: Hutchison, [1948?].

Swyripa, Frances, and John Herd Thompson, eds. *Loyalties in Conflict: Ukrainians in Canada during the Great War*. Edmonton: Canadian Institute of Ukrainian Studies Press, 1983.

Taylor, Pamela Howe. *The Germans We Trusted: Stories of Friendship Resulting from the Second World War*. Cambridge: Lutterworth Press, 2003.

Thompson, John Herd. *Ethnic Minorities during Two World Wars*. Canada's Ethnic Groups 19. Ottawa: Canadian Historical Association, 1991.

Thompson, Laurence. *1940*. New York: William Morrow, 1966.

Thompson, R.W. *The Yankee Marlborough*. London: Allen & Unwin, 1963.

Toland, John. *Adolf Hitler: The Definitive Biography* New York: Anchor Books, 1976.

United Kingdom. Home Office. *German and Austrian Civilian Internees: Categories of Persons Eligible for Release from Internment and Procedure to Be Followed in Applying for Release*. London: H.M. Stationery Office, 1940.

von Salomon, Ernst. *The Answers of Ernst von Salomon to the 131 Questions in the Allied Military Government Fragebogen*. Translated by Constantine Fitzgibbon. London: Putnam, 1954. Originally published as *Der Fragebogen* (Hamburg: Rowohlt Verlag, 1951).

———, ed. *Das Buch vom deutschen Freikorpskämpfer*. 1938. Strukum, Ger.: Verlag für ganzheitliche Forschung und Kultur, 1988.

Wagner, Jonathan F. *Brothers beyond the Sea: National Socialism in Canada*. Waterloo, ON: Wilfrid Laurier University Press, 1981.

Waiser, Bill. *Park Prisoners: The Untold Story of Western Canada's National Parks, 1915–1946*. Saskatoon, SK: Fifth House, 1995.

Walzer, Michael. "Prisoners of War: Does the Fight Continue after the Battle?" *American Political Science Review* 63, no. 3 (September 1969): 777–786.

Wasserstein, Bernard. *Britain and the Jews of Europe, 1939–1945*. Oxford: Clarendon Press, 1979.

Watson, Lieutenant-Colonel H. de Norban. "Inspection Report and Confidential Comments on Camp Officers, August 1940." RG 24, vol. 11,248, file 9-5-3-4. Department of National Defence. Library and Archives Canada.

Wheeler-Bennett, John. *John Anderson: Viscount Waverley*. London: Macmillan, 1962.

Whitaker, Reg. "Official Repression of Communism during World War II." *Labour/Le Travail* 17 (Spring 1986): 135–166.

Index

terminology, 180–81
See also Jewish internees
Arandora Star (ship), 41–42, 184–85, 189, 203
armaments and weapons
about, 93–94
ammunition, 93, 134, 151, 272
guns (revolvers), 105, 217
hand grenades, 93–94
Lewis machine guns, 93, 94, 151, 217, 303n42
rifles and bayonets, 93, 134, 217
shooting practices, 151
standing orders, 134
sticks and whistles, 105, 210, 216
tear gas grenades, 93–94, 151
Thompson machine guns, 272
training, 93–94, 218
Vickers machine guns, 93, 151, 217, 303n42
army unit, Camp R. *See* Fort Garry Horse (CASF)
Articles of the Geneva Convention. *See* Geneva Convention
assaults. *See* violence
Auger, Martin, xx, xxvi
Austrian-born internees
category status revisions, 183
statistics on, 110–11, 180
terminology, 304n26
tribunal categories, 6, 7
Austro-Hungarian Canadians, xxii, 60, 62–63

Banauch, Eugen, xxvii
barbed wire fences, 100, *103*, 150–51, 209, 211, 217, 252
Baron Pilar von Pilchau. *See* Pilchau, Konstantin, Baron Pilar von
Bavarian-born internees. *See* Guelcher, Edwin
Baxdel, Lothar, 280–81
Beissel, G., 258, 268
Bergeron, Caroline, xxvii
Bernard, Yves, xxvii
Berry, Raymond Barrat, *82*
about, 76–77, 83–84

camp commandant duties, 70–71, 73, 76
camp inspections by special appointees, 149–50, 212, 213, 219, 234
chain of command, 76–78, 132
command of Veterans Guard, 92
dual control issue, 73–74, 212–13
mixed camps, 83
personal traits, 71, 128–29, 212
response to violence, 238–39, 243
segregation of political groups, 237
solitary confinement use by, 84, 86, 238–39, 243, 254
Spier's interview with, 105–06
standing orders, 76, 77, 132
vehicles, 207
Blair, F.C., 195
Bland, Sir Neville, 26–28, 30
Bolshevik internees. *See* communist and Bolshevik internees
books, 176, 177, 229
boxing, 144, 146, 148–49
Bradshaw, C.G., 258
Braun, Max, 5–6
bridge guards, *101*
Britain
declaration of war, xxiii
invasion fears, 32–33, 36, 234–35, 245
invasion fears reduced, 186, 244
See also Chamberlain, Neville, government; Churchill, Winston, government; World War II
Britain, anti-Nazis
domestic servants, 298n5
internment camps, 25–26, 30, 294n9
MI5 lists, 30, 268
organizations, 8–10, 282, 295n17
See also Spier, Eugen
Britain, anti-Semitism
associations and clubs, 19–20
fifth column fears, 18–19
internment camps, 30
MI5 lists, 30
in mixed camps, 25–26
newspapers, 16–18
public opinion on, 18–19
terminology, 180–81

British Union of Fascists (BUF), 19–20
Bruenn, Max, 242–43
Buenos Aires International Postal
    Convention, 163
Bulgarian Canadians, xxii

cafés for internees, 229, 265–66
Caldecote, Viscount, 35–37, 182, 184, 202
Calydor Sanatorium. *See* Camp C (#20)
    (Gravenhurst, Ontario)
Camp 20. *See* Camp C (#20) (Gravenhurst,
    Ontario)
Camp 21 (E) (Espanola, Ontario), 66, 69
Camp 22. *See* Camp M (#22) (Mimico,
    Ontario)
Camp 23. *See* Camp Q (#23) (Monteith,
    Ontario)
Camp 31. *See* Camp F (#31) (Fort Henry,
    Kingston, Ontario)
Camp 33 (P) (Petawawa, Ontario), 69
Camp 40. *See* Camp A (#40) (Farnham,
    Quebec)
Camp 41. *See* Camp I (#41) (Fort Lennox,
    Île aux Noix, Quebec)
Camp 42. *See* Camp N (#42) (Newington,
    Quebec)
Camp 43. *See* Camp S (#43) (St. Helen's
    Island, Montreal, Quebec)
Camp 70. *See* Camp B (#70) (Little River,
    New Brunswick)
Camp 100. *See* Camp W (#100) (Neys)
Camp 101. *See* Camp X (#101) (Angler)
Camp 130 (Kananaskis/Seebe, Alberta)
    Canadian civilian internees, 69
    facilities, 69
    repatriation of internees, 126
    Scharf as camp spokesman, 124–25,
        280, 311n12
    transfers from Camp R, 280
Camp A (#40) (Farnham, Quebec)
    anti-Nazi camp, 280
    camp newspaper, 168
    communist internees, 119
    Jewish and anti-Nazi internees, 188
    new camp, 69, 188
    transfers from Camp R, 276, 280
Camp B (#70) (Little River, New
    Brunswick)

camp newspaper, 168
communist internees, 119
facilities, 69
Jewish and anti-Nazi internees, 188
Nazi internees, 130
new camp, 188
repatriations, 279
transfers from Camp R, 279
Camp C (#20) (Gravenhurst, Ontario)
    Calydor Sanatorium, 50, 69–70
    dual control issue, 74
    escapes, 74, 252
    German POW officers, 50, 69
    letter and numerical identification, 70
    other ranks of internees, 69, 292n25
Camp E (#21) (Espanola, Ontario), 66, 69
Camp F (#31) (Fort Henry, Kingston,
    Ontario)
    about, 69–70
    facilities and conditions, 69
    internees, 53, 69, 174, 281
    letter and numerical identification, 70
    living conditions, 281
    transfers to Camp N, 198
Camp I (#41) (Fort Lennox, Île aux Noix,
    Quebec), 69, 188
Camp L (Cove Fields, Quebec)
    communist internees, 119
    facilities, 69
    food, 139–40
    internees, 69, 189, 308n2
    military discipline, 265
    treatment of internees, 189, 197
Camp M (#22) (Mimico, Ontario), 66, 68,
    70
Camp N (#42) (Newington, Quebec)
    communist internees, 119
    Jewish and anti-Nazi internees, 188–
        89, 190, 198, 224, 280–82
    living conditions, 281
    new camp, 69, 188
    transfers from Camp F, 198
    transfers from Camp R, 190, 224,
        280–82
Camp P (#33) (Petawawa, Ontario), 69
Camp Q (#23) (Monteith, Ontario)
    administration, 200
    capacity for internees, 276

handicraft sales, 151, 160, 168, 229, 261–62

international transfers, 41, 105–06, 160, 257, 262–63

investigations of, 262–63

morale, 160

prisoner start-up fund, 151, 160, 209, 258

relief societies' donations, 258

seamen's wages, 257–58

See also canteen; work, paid

Monteith, Ontario. *See* Camp Q

Montgelas, Albrecht, Count von, 13, 123, 131, 267–68

Muehlhausen (German youth), 269

Mueller, Ernst, 236, 248–50, 254

Mueller, Louis, 213

Murray, J.H., 258

Namibia (South West Africa), 113, 144–45

See also South African internees

National Unity Party, 59

Nazi and pro-Nazi internees

about, 112–14

camp assistants, 128

display of Nazi paraphernalia, 156–57, 219, 234, 244

escape plan, 252–53

flags, pictures, and songs, 114–15, 157, 237

guards' treatment of, 199–200

harassment of minorities by, 220–21, 235–38, 243–44, 247

Hitler's memorial service, 146

influence on seamen, 113–15

morale shifts, 113–14, 176, 235–36, 243–44, 253

repatriation of, 286

segregation from anti-Nazis, 112, 124, 188, 237

statistics on, 108–09, 111, 115, 119, 184

threats of homefront retaliation on, 117

violent hospital incident, 238–42

wartime background, 113–14, 225–26, 234–36, 243–44

winter solstice celebrations at Lingfield, 173, 224

See also enemy merchant seamen; Guelcher, Edwin; mixed camps; Pilchau, Konstantin, Baron Pilar von; South African internees; Wehrhahn, Fritz

New Brunswick camp. *See* Camp B (#70) (Little River, New Brunswick)

Newington, Quebec. *See* Camp N

newspapers

anti-alienism, 60–61

fifth column reports, 17–18, 56, 59–60, 194

by internees, 168

for internees, 168, 176, 220, 225, 229, 232, 235

support for repatriation, 191–92

See also Britain, newspapers

New Toronto camp. *See* Camp M

Neys, Ontario. *See* Camp W

Nichols, Beverley, 16–17

Nielsen, Frederic W., 4–5, 27–28

Nipigon, Ontario

about, 95

handicraft sales, 261–62

map and location, xviii, 95

power station, 275

Nipigon Bay, Ontario

map and location, xviii

sewage disposal, 272–75

swim parades, 148, 210–11

Nixon, H.C., 66

Noffke, G., 235

Norway, in WWII, 14–15, 23–24, 28–29

Norwegian internees, 108–09, 166

Novotny, Hans, 238

O'Callaghan, J.P., 263–64

Oertly, John, 220

older internees

Category A reputation *vs.* reality, 104–05, 179–80

oldest internee, 268–69

transportation of, 39

Olympia Hall, London, England, camp, 9, 10, 30, 129, 131, 173

Ontario, internment camps

about, 68–69

available facilities, 65–66

Espanola (*See* Camp 21)

cleanliness, 127–28, 136–37, 190–91, 210

daily routine, 92–93, 131–32, 134–37

delays in implementation, 212

display of national paraphernalia, 157, 244

escapes, 132–33

escort of prisoners, 132–33

fires, 132, 134, 150

fraternization, 133, 136, 260

hut elders, 127–28

mail, 226–27

medical emergencies, 122

pass system, 133

political songs, 157

prohibited items, 135–36

roll calls, 135, 215–16

sentries, 132, 134

shootings, 101–02, 121–22, 134

sick parades, 138

smoking, 135

social and recreational activities, 136, 138

theatre and variety performances, 175

uniforms, 133–34, 135–36, 244

Veterans Guard's knowledge of, 92–93

Stent, Ronald, 111, 127, 296n25

Stethem, Hubert

about, 80–83

chain of command, 190

inspection before closure, 275–78, 313n4

paid/unpaid work policies, 162–65

personal traits, 80–81, 162–64

POW terminology, 162–64

on unsolicited mail from Zionists, 223

Stodart, Tom W., 35–36

Stovel, E.F., 70–71, 72, 212

Streight, Hubert, 83, 243

Stuart, Sir Campbell, 28

students as internees. *See* university student internees; young internees

Sudeten internees. *See* Czechoslovakian internees

Swedish language, 166

swimming, 148, 210–11

Swinton, Philip Cunliffe-Lister, 32

Swinton Committee, 32–34, 38–39, 43, 181, 183, 202

Switzerland as Protecting Power, 49–50, 64, 78–79, 156, 211

See also Geneva Convention

table tennis, 167

Taylor, J.M., 91

Tebrich, Kurt, 46–47

Teddern, Clive, 46–47

telephone lines, 208–09, 248, 251–52

terminology

anti-Jewish and anti-Semitism, 180–81

anti-refugee, 180–81

camp, 162, 164

civilian internees, xx, 161–64

concentration camp, xx

enemy aliens, xxi

fifth column, 296n25

habeas corpus, 164

other ranks, terminology, 292n25

paid/unpaid work, 163–64

POW Class I and II, xx, 161–64

See also categories of internees

Thelen, Heinz, 242–43

toilets. *See* water and sanitation

Toronto, Ontario, 60

See also Camp M (#22) (Mimico, Ontario)

Torrance, V.P., 76, 87

tribunals. *See* Britain, tribunals

Trois-Rivières, Quebec. *See* Camp T

Trout Creek, 100

Turkish Canadians, xxii

Ukrainian Canadians, xxii, 60–61

uniforms and clothing, 137

about, 135–36

escape prevention, 211, 215

resentment about, 136, 242, 244

standing orders, 135–36

Union of South Africa. *See* South African internees

United Jewish Refugee and War Relief Agencies, 81, 195–96, 222–23

United Kingdom. *See entries beginning with* Britain

United States
   border location, xviii, 103, 252
   Hanfstaengl's contacts, 169, 174,
      307n17
   Lend-Lease arrangements, 186
   objections to Canadian internment
      camps, 64
   as Protecting Power, 64
   refusal to re-unify Jewish families,
      192–93
   return of escapees, 215
university student internees
   Category A reputation *vs.* reality,
      104–05
   deportations, 39
   Loewenstein's status, 6–7, 189, 295n12
   repatriation and release, 189, 191–92
   See also young internees
unpaid work. *See* work, unpaid (fatigue)

variety shows, 175
Veterans Guard
   about, 87–91
   commander of (Berry), 92
   history of, 88–91
   removal of unsuitable guards, 248
   research on, 302n39
   rotation of units, 96
   statistics on, 91
   training of, 248
Veterans Guard (Camp R), 72, 77, 85, 88, 93,
      101, 208, 219, 267, 273
   about, 91–94
   arrival of, 87
   chain of command, 77, 92
   daily routine, 92–93, 96
   difficulties faced by, 96, 254
   dual control issue, 73, 76, 87, 213
   duties, 91–94
   facilities, 95–96
   fraternization, 94–95
   inspection reports on, 206, 217–18
   medical care, 84, 206–07
   provosts, 92, 210, 216–17, 237–38
   recreation and entertainment, 95–96
   sentries in watchtowers, 94
   statistics on, 217
   training of, 92–94, 218

treatment of internees, 138, 197–98,
   237–38, 246, 260–61
See also armaments and weapons;
   Berry, Raymond Barrat;
   fraternization; standing orders
violence
   about, 284
   assaults, 85–86, 242–43
   causes, 112, 237–38, 243–44
   hospital incident, 238–42
   mixed camp factors, 112, 119, 239
von Pilchau, Konstantin Pilar. *See*
   Pilchau, Konstantin, Baron
   Pilar von

Warkentine, S.A., 71, 87, 206
War Measures Act, xxi, xxiii, 61
   See also *Defence of Canada Regulations*
War Prisoners' Aid Committee (YMCA)
   about, 221
   education, 165–66
   funds for internees, 258
   inspection reports by, 221–22
   sports and recreation donations, 142,
      168
   Stethem's views on, 81
watchtowers and sentries, 94, *116, 216*
   about, 100–01
   construction, 217
   lights and heat, 134, 209, 217, 275
   machine guns, 92, 217
   sentries, 92, 134, 217
water and sanitation
   about, 140–41, 272–75
   drinking water, 140, 272–74
   inspection reports on, 211, 276–77
   sanitary facilities, 100, 220
   sewage disposal, 272–75
   showers, 140–41, 211
Watson, Hugh de Norban
   on Berry, 84
   inspection reports, 74, 196–97, 205–13,
      234, 265
weaponry. *See* armaments and weapons
Weber, K., 268
Wehrhahn, Fritz, 113, 221, 236, 268
Weiss, A. (ship captain), 176
Weisser, Erich, 250–51, 255

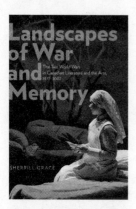

Landscapes of War and Memory
The Two World Wars in Canadian Literature
and the Arts, 1977–2007
Sherrill Grace
636 pages | 30 B&W photographs, notes, bibliography, index
978-1-77212-000-4 | $49.95 (T) paper
War and Cultural Memory/Literature, Visual Arts & Film

Great Canadian War Stories
Muriel Whitake, Editor
Peter Stursberg, Foreword
296 pages
978-0-88864-383-4 | $19.95 (T) paper
Literature/Short Stories

The Unwanted
Great War Letters from the Field
John McKendrick Hughes
John R. Hughes, Editor
416 pages | B&W photographs, maps, notes, bibliography, index
978-0-88864-436-7 | $32.95 (T) paper
History/War/Agriculture History/Canada History/
War/Propaganda